FROMMER'S FOOD LOVER'S COMPANION TO
FRANCE

FROMMER'S FOOD LOVER'S COMPANION TO

FRANCE

BY
MARC AND KIM MILLON

Macmillan • USA

*To our dear friends Joan and Gal for their love of France
and to Polly, for being part of our family*

Macmillan Travel
A Simon & Schuster
Macmillan Company
1633 Broadway
New York, NY 10019

ISBN 0-02-860925-5
Library of Congress Catalog Card No.:
95-81807

Manufactured in Italy by
Rotolito Lombarda
Color separations by Global Colour

Conceived, edited, and designed by
Websters International Publishers
Axe and Bottle Court
70 Newcomen Street
London SE1 1YT

10 9 8 7 6 5 4 3 2 1

First Edition

Please be advised that travel information
is subject to change at any time — and
this is especially true of prices. We
therefore suggest that you write or call
ahead for confirmation when making
your travel plans. The authors, editors,
and publisher cannot be held responsible
for the experiences of readers while
traveling. Your safety is important to us,
however, so we encourage you to stay
alert and be aware of your surroundings.
Keep a close eye on cameras, purses, and
wallets, all favorite targets of thieves and
pickpockets.

Project Editor Shirin Patel • *Art Editor* Joanna Pocock
Designer Adelle Morris • *Editors* Julia Colbourne, Hugh Morgan, Pauline Savage
Design Manager Jason Vrakas • *Production* Charles James
Illustrations James G. Robins • *Index* Naomi Good

CONTENTS

The food lovers' companions

Introduction

A NATION OF GOURMETS

O F THE MANY MOTIVES that compel us all to visit France, arguably one of the most popular is to discover and enjoy at source all the riches that the greatest gastronomic nation on earth has to offer.

The pleasures of eating and drinking in France are ever present, and range from the simplest — sinfully rich *chocolat chaud* (hot chocolate) and buttery *croissants* for breakfast, a *crêpe* bought at a roadside stand — to the most exalted — a meal in one of the handful of truly great three-star restaurants whose chefs are national and international superstars. Food and wine are, quite simply, of great daily importance to the French and, at whatever level, are taken very seriously indeed. If a nation is what it eats, then the French are nothing if not discerning, critical, appreciative of the genuine and authentic, and full of the sensual pleasure and *joie de vivre* with which both good eating and good living go hand in hand.

From waking in the morning to the smells of *pâtisseries* and freshly baked bread, to retiring at night after one last post-prandial Cognac, Armagnac, or Calvados, no matter what your interests or activities in between, it is a fair bet that some of your finest and most lasting memories will be of foods eaten, wines tasted, markets visited, picnics or restaurants enjoyed. It is not going too far to say that the enjoyment of food and wine is at the very heart of daily life in France.

We assume that many of you, like us, may prefer to mix stays in hotels with time in rented accommodation, an option that allows you to buy fresh foods to prepare yourself as well as to eat out in restaurants. Whether you are shopping in markets, at small specialty shops, or at the *hypermarché* (one of the great superstores of France), putting together a picnic to take out to the wine country, making friends at the local bar or bistro, or planning a visit to any of France's great and famous restaurants, this guide will help you on your way.

We take you on a gastronomic journey through France, outlining the wealth of local produce and specialties on offer, showing you how and where to eat with the locals, directing you to little-known but excellent country wines and local cheeses, and guiding you to the best and most colorful markets, the finest *pâtisseries* and sources of local candies, our favorite oyster bars by the sea, and into vineyards, or up a mountain in search of cheeses made by alpine herdsmen in summer chalets.

It has been a hugely enjoyable task traveling throughout France to put this book together, and we are certain that you too will enjoy using it to discover the finest foods and wines of France and to make many good friends along the way.

Bon voyage and *bon appétit!*
Marc and Kim Millon

Regional France

In this book, we have divided France into five main regions.
The North includes Nord-Pas de Calais, Picardy,
Champagne-Ardennes, and Alsace-Lorraine.
The Northwest includes Brittany, Normandy,
the Loire Valley, and Poitou-Charentes.
The Southwest includes Bordeaux and the
Landes, the Dordogne and Lot,
Gascony, and the
Basque Country.
The East &
Center is made up
of Burgundy, Lyon
and hinterland,
Franche-Comté,
Savoie and Dauphiné, and Central
France. And The South is
comprised of Languedoc-
Roussillon, Provence and the Côte d'Azur,
and, off shore, the island of Corsica.

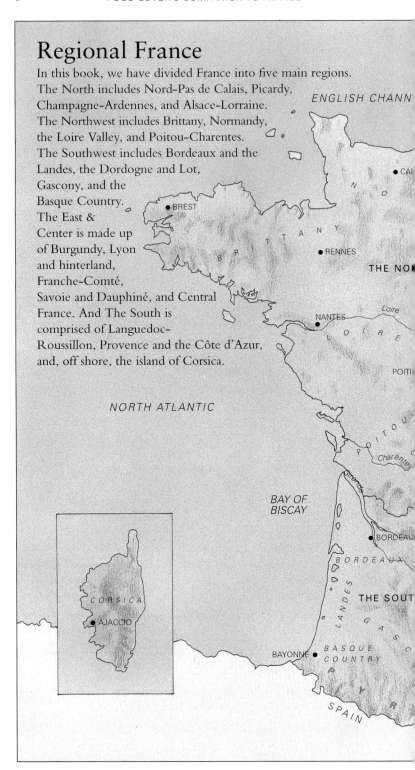

ENGLISH CHANN

● CAI

N

O

● BREST

B R I T T A N Y

B R

● RENNES

THE NO

NANTES

Loire

L O I R E

NORTH ATLANTIC

POITI

P O I T O U

Charente

Gironde

BAY OF
BISCAY

● BORDEA

B O R D E A U X

L A N D E S

THE SOUT

G A S

BAYONNE ●

B A S Q U E
C O U N T R Y

P Y R

SPAIN

CORSICA

● AJACCIO

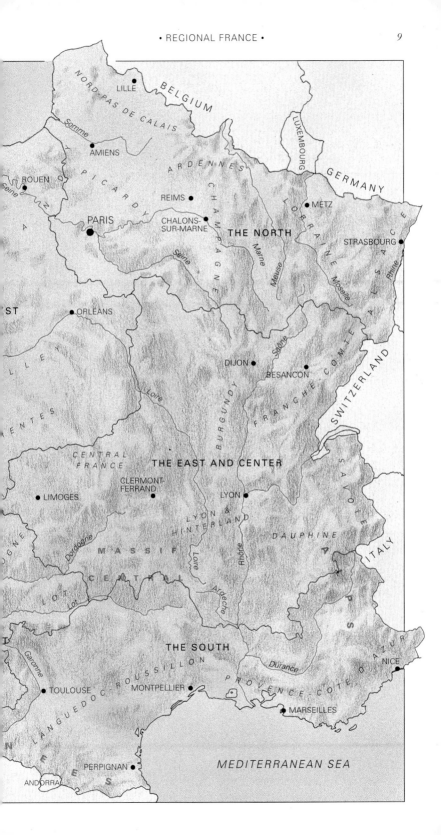

A National Treasure

THE GASTRONOMY OF FRANCE

O F ALL THE GIFTS that the nations of the world have contributed to civilization, arguably, one of the most significant is the great culinary heritage of France: not simply because French *haute cuisine* is rightly regarded among the greatest in the world, nor merely because of the wealth, ingenuity, and sophistication of regional, local, and seasonal specialties, but primarily because in France the simple act of everyday eating has been taken beyond the realms of daily necessity and elevated instead to something approaching an art form.

Witness fruit *tartes* in a *pâtisserie* window in any town or village in the land; the care with which fruits and vegetables are arranged on market stalls; wooden boxes of glistening *fruits glacés;* the unadorned sensuousness of a green-tinged oyster on the half shell; and the carefully composed, artistically arranged plates presented in many restaurants — truly, food pictures as beautiful to look at as to eat. All these bear testimony to a national passion bordering on obsession with the pleasures of gastronomy.

In homes or on farms; in city center brasseries and famous starred restaurants; whether shopping in markets, specialist artisan shops, or great sprawling *hypermarchés;* enjoying a *crêpe* standing up, or a slice of piping hot *socca* (chickpea pancake) in the market, the everyday acts of buying, preparing, and enjoying food are here carried out with great care, seriousness, and, above all, inimitable Gallic style: so that eating and drinking in France, no matter how or when, remains one of the principal and most memorable attractions for the visitor.

Enjoying food, one of the great pleasures of France

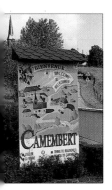

Camembert, world-famous for its cheese

FOOD AND WINE TOURISM

Gastronomy in France is an important and essential element of the nation's economy. Shrewd marketeers and self-publicists as always, the French have long known the way to tourists' hearts: towns proclaim their particular gastronomic specialties alongside listings of monuments and other amenities, and great regional dishes, local sweets, wines, and other *produits du terroir* (regional products) are considered valid tourist attractions in their own right as places to visit, so that we arrive anticipating what we are going to eat, which wines we want to sample, and which local *spécialités* we have to hunt out at source.

A REPUTATION STILL VALID?

And yet, it can be easy for a nation to dine out too long on a reputation that may not any longer be wholly accurate or up-to-date. We have, we confess, eaten many plates of indifferent *cassoulet* (bean stew) and over-priced *bouillabaisse,* tough *steak-frites* (steak and French fries), and meals without a fresh vegetable in sight, so we cannot guarantee that every meal or food experience that you will have in France will be wonderful. Contrary to popular conception, not every French man or woman claims or even aspires to be a gourmet or wine connoisseur. Even the French, especially the young, have rushed to embrace *"le fast food"*....

And yet, and yet: when all is said and done, this still is a nation where, more so than virtually anywhere else (except perhaps Italy), the daily activities of eating and drinking well are so engrained, such a part of the national consciousness, as to be part and parcel of life and good living itself.

Preparing that special omelet at Mère Poulard on Mont-St.-Michel, Normandy

THE BEST OF FRANCE

The aim of this book, then, is not simply to eulogize French foods and wines, to heap praise on obscure dishes that no longer exist or can never be found by the visitor, or to propagate food myths that may never have been valid in the first place. Rather, our task has been to look at France afresh, taking off our wine-tinted spectacles to examine critically as well

Hervé Liegent, chef of authentic Champenois food in his restaurant Le Vigneron, Reims

as appreciatively those elements, enduring or newly emerging which, yes, still make France, in our opinion, the greatest gastronomic nation on earth, and, at the same time, to catalog, delineate, define, and highlight the local, regional, and classic foods and wines of contemporary France.

There is much that is enduring, that is classic, foods and wines that remain benchmarks of the highest order. At the same time, we found that there is a new, exciting, and dynamic energy on the French food scene today. *Nouvelle cuisine* may now be considered old hat, but the principles that it engendered have been taken on board by a new generation of (mainly) young chefs who, in many cases, are applying them to their own regional traditions, creating personal and creative variations using fine local produce and products.

Moreover, having traveled extensively throughout the nation and interviewed people across many different fields and disciplines, we have discovered no shortage of committed and enthusiastic growers, producers, fishermen, cheesemakers, winemakers, bakers — young and old — who, far from resting on national laurels, have such intense pride in their own activities that they are determined to create their own personal stamp, to add something new and individual to the great, collective, and ever-evolving *opus* that is the gastronomy of France. Searching out such individuals is part of the rewards of a gastronomic *tour de France*.

Roland Gauthier picking fresh herbs to use in his kitchen at the Auberge de la Grenouillère, Montreuil

A PORTRAIT OF FRANCE FOR TODAY

This book is an accurate, up-to-date, and appetizing portrait of food and drink in France today. There are portraits of people we have met — all passionate about their subjects, landscapes in all seasons, markets, wine and cheese cellars, as well as photographs of foods in shops and restaurants, showing them as you, the curious, the hungry visitor, will actually encounter them.

The gastronomy of France is a vast and voluminous subject. Like the myriad and beautiful lanes of France, it meanders and weaves its way across an intricate and finely interconnected network on its journey from source to consumer. From farm or sea, woods, lakes, rivers, or vineyards; from market stalls, artisan workshops, and remote mountain chalets; from dairies and distilleries, orchards and olive groves; it makes its way across regions and seasons to arrive, through the skill of trained chefs, eventually at our table.

It may not be essential for the visitor in search of fine food and drink to be always aware of this interconnection, of the links between land, people, and tradition: but for the curious food and wine traveler, an appreciation of French gastronomy begins, as always, at its source.

RECOMMENDED ESTABLISHMENTS

This book does not aim to be a comprehensive restaurant or shopping guide, but, throughout, we do include the addresses of places that we consider to be essential points of reference for the finest or most typical and authentic French foods and drink, at whatever level. Such establishments may range from the greatest (and most expensive) temples of gastronomy in France to humble but genuine bistros, *crêperies*, brasseries, and bars; from some of

Traveling the tree-lined country lanes of France in search of good food and wine

the world's most famous wine estates and châteaux to simple walnut oil mills and alpine cheese dairies. Visit them when you can, but don't confine your gastronomic wanderings to our personal selections, for France has countless wonderful places to discover for yourself.

We also suggest that you consult the guides we recommend (see pp.45–46) for more detailed listings for eating out. As a rough indication only, we have included the following price coding:

$ = Inexpensive
$$ = Moderate
$$$ = Expensive
$$$$ = Very expensive

The Concept of Terroir
THE WEALTH OF FRANCE

FRANCE IS THE SOURCE of, literally, an overwhelming abundance of exceptional produce and products, and these primary materials are, of course, the cornerstones of French gastronomy. In this most important agricultural nation in Western Europe, with an estimated seven per cent of its workforce employed in agriculture and fishing (compared to three

Melons from Provence

per cent in the United States), national policy since the war has been toward rationalizing and consolidating fewer farms into large, highly modernized, and mechanized units.

Today, France is Western Europe's leading producer of beef, veal, poultry, and cheese; a leading producer of wheat, milk, and eggs; and probably the most important wine-producing country in the world in terms of both quality and quantity. Though, in comparison with farming, fishing is undertaken on a more modest scale in world terms, both the Atlantic and Mediterranean seaboards yield an impressive catch of fish and shellfish, and there is an efficient nation-wide transportation network which ensures that fresh fish is usually available even far inland.

In great *hypermarchés* as well as in weekly markets in even the smallest town, there is always plenty.

An assortment of fresh fruits from Picardy, showing the great variety available in the region

TERROIR
What is perhaps more significant, from our point of view, than sheer abundance is that, while creating an agricultural system that is essentially rational and productive, the French have not lost sight of the need to maintain tradition and quality.

In France, there remains an inherent and deep-seated, almost unquestioning, belief that tradition is the arbiter of quality. This has dictated that regions, provinces, and even localities and individual communities have always concentrated on their particular areas of expertise, whether that is the production of world-famous wines, or growing the tastiest carrots, the sweetest, juiciest melons. Inherent in this is the French concept of *terroir* — an all-encompassing term embracing the land, its climate, and microclimate, as well as prevailing local traditions and culture. An awareness of *terroir* is central to the understanding and appreciation of French gastronomy for the visitor.

APPELLATION D'ORIGINE CONTROLEE
To pinpoint such excellence, based, above all, on *terroir*, the French have developed the most complex and precise system in the world — *appellation d'origine contrôlée* — a system that aims to link quality foods and wines with the precise region, locality, or even individual plot of land from which they originate. This may apply to foods as diverse as green lentils from Puy, chickens from Bresse, oysters from the Belon River, honey from Lorraine, and, of course, to any number of excellent cheeses and wines, and much else. Searching out such products, and discovering the validity of the French concept of *terroir* for yourself is one of the most enduring pleasures of being a peripatetic food lover in France.

APPELLATIONS AND LABELS — AN OBSESSION

Do carrots from Créances, olives from Nyons, chickens from Bresse, or butter and cream from Isigny really taste superior to produce or products from elsewhere? I believe so: in a blind comparative tasting, they would stand out in quality even if only experts could identify their exact provenance.

Only those products conforming to rigorous standards of production are entitled to *appellation d'origine contrôlée* status. At the time of writing, apart from *appellations* for wines, spirits, and cheeses, there are *appellations d'origine* for:

Beurre Charentes-Poitou, beurre des Charentes, beurre des Deux-Sèvres Butter from Poitou-Charentes (The Northwest).

Carottes de Créances Carrots from Créances (The Northwest).

Chasselas de Moissac Table grapes from Moissac (The South).

Crème fraîche, crème d'Isigny, beurre d'Isigny Butter and tangy, slightly soured cream from Isigny (The Northwest).

Huîtres de Belon Native oysters from the Belon River (The Northwest).

Lentilles vertes du Puy Green lentils from Puy (The East & Center).

Miel de Lorraine, miel des Vosges Honey from Lorraine and the Vosges Mountains (The North).

Noix de Grenoble Walnuts from Grenoble (The East & Center).

Olives de Nyons, olives noires de Nyons, huile d'olive de Nyons Olives, black olives, and olive oil from Nyons (The South).

Pintadeau de la Drôme Guinea hen from Drôme (The East & Center).

A famously tasty chicken

Volaille de Bresse, dinde fermière de Bresse Bresse chicken, Bresse free-range turkey (The East & Center).

LABELS ROUGES AND LABELS REGIONAUX

There are also a number of other schemes that confer superior status on produce or products. In particular, it is worth looking out for the *Labels Rouges* and the *Labels Régionaux*. The *Label Rouge* or "red label" may be used for approved regional or national products which are produced to rigorous standards and which have been passed by an independent and impartial commission. It can be taken as an indication of superior quality (and a justification for slightly higher prices) for a range of produce or products, such as potatoes, beef, poultry, *pâtés*, hams, and even sea salt.

Labels Régionaux, on the other hand, may apply to a range of produce and products typical of particular regions. Look out for such labels for genuine regional producers.

At the time of writing, *Labels Régionaux* apply to approved products from the following areas:

Ardennes de France (The North)
Centre-Val de Loire-Berry (The Northwest)
Corse (The South)
Franche-Comté (The East & Center)
Limousin (The East & Center)
Lorraine (The North)
Midi-Pyrénées (The South and The Southwest)
Nord-Pas de Calais (The North)
Savoie (The East & Center)

Regional France

A GASTRONOMIC TOUR DE FRANCE

IN FRANCE, more than anywhere else on earth, you may anticipate surely and precisely what you will eat by where you are.

If you are in Alsace, the postcard-pretty region along the banks of the Rhine, then it has to be fattened goose liver followed by immense platters of *choucroute (sauerkraut)* garnished with sausages and cured meats. In the Languedoc, you will find *cassoulet,* a great bean stew garnished with conserved duck and sausages. If you visit Bordeaux, then there is little better than an *entrecôte bordelaise,* a rare rib steak in a red wine sauce, the perfect accompaniment to a fine red from the Médoc. In Burgundy, by contrast, *coq au vin* or *boeuf bourguignon* provide the perfect foil for rich, silky red wines from Pommard or Nuits St.-Georges.

In Brittany, you will feast on the freshest and finest shellfish anywhere in the world, and in the French Alps of Savoie, you will enjoy communal meals originally devised for mountain herdsmen, such as the traditional cheese *fondue savoyarde.* If you are in Provence, the garlic-laden foods of the sun — *bouillabaisse,* that magnificent festival of the sea, or, if it's Friday, *le grand aïoli,* the pungently hot garlic mayonnaise spread in quantity onto boiled fish, snails,

Rustic elegance in Champagne

potatoes, and salt cod — await you. In the Southwest, especially in the Dordogne and Gascony, a rich diet based on duck, duck, and more duck *(foie gras, confit de canard, magret de canard,* or *pâtés)* is yours to enjoy. Further south still, in the Basque Country, the cuisine is distinctive and unlike that found anywhere else in France, with its red-pepper-tinged dishes that have hard to pronounce names.

And if you happen to find yourself in Vichy, having been to or sampled all or some of the above, then it is quite probable that you have suffered the proverbial French *crise de foie* (a "liver crisis" brought on from overindulgence) and so retired to that elegant spa town in the Auvergne for a curative dose of its famous mineral waters.

France is made up of a wealth of diverse and varied regions, all of which have their own traditions, culture, and distinctive local foods and wines.

While it would have been possible to divide the second part of this book into individual regional chapters or even smaller areas based on French *département* groupings, we have chosen, instead, to look at France in larger geographical segments, and to discuss regional specialties and local produce and products within the broader framework of the overall context of national French gastronomy.

Our approach, we feel, is more relevant to the way people actually travel, and it has also allowed us to avoid the trap, in the name of comprehensiveness and authenticity, of writing and cataloging items that are so local and obscure as to be virtually non-existent and thus of little interest to any save the regional or local food historian.

Restaurant in the Basque Country serving colorful, local foods

Traditional France

FOOD AND WINE AS CULTURE

FRENCH GASTRONOMY is firmly based on tradition: the artisan *savoir-faire* of generations of committed producers, cheesemakers, farmers, fishermen, bakers, wine-makers, pastry chefs, *charcutiers,* and butchers, not to mention chefs. With the wealth of excellent available material, and, in many cases, following methods of production little changed for decades or centuries, they elevate and transform the merely excellent into the wondrous.

A maître affineur testing a roquefort *cheese*

methods is necessarily adept at them — if the best bread undoubtedly comes from wood-fired ovens, at the same time, so can the worst. Further-more, the French are crafty marketeers, and some are not averse to capitalizing on the premium that tradition brings by packaging indifferent or industrially produced products with false nostalgia.

Indeed, in France, there is a deep-seated belief, an almost unquestioned acceptance, that the way things were done in the past was and remains undoubtedly better than methods today. Or, to put it another way: the artisan-made, the hand-made, is almost always considered superior to the mass-produced, the industrial, or those products manufactured with the stainless steel technology of today.

Fromages fermiers — farmhouse cheeses hand-made from unpasteurized milk — are preferred to cheeses made in large-scale dairies. Bread cooked in a *four à bois* (wood-fired oven) emerges (albeit sometimes a little burnt) with a flavor and crust that is inimitable. *Pâtés,* sausages and other *charcuterie,* hand-made chocolates, beautiful *tartes* and *pâtisseries:* all are best when made by committed individual producers following traditional methods handed down the generations.

CAVEAT VIATOR

So richly seductive are the gastronomic traditions of France, that it can be easy to get carried away. Let the traveler beware: not everything labeled *"à l'ancienne"* is necessarily marvelous. For a start, not everyone following old precepts or

Ultimately, it is reassur-ing to know that France is not a nation of Luddites. For the French know more than most that for "tradition" to continue to have any real meaning, it is essential to maintain an ongoing process of testing, discarding, refining, learning from the present as well as the past in order to pass onto the future. In this sense, traditional France protects its gastronomic culture and its heritage jealously, while being aware, always, that that which is new and excellent today may become traditional tomorrow.

Pain au levain, *a rustic, sourdough loaf baked in a wood-fired oven*

Cereals and Grains

BREAD, THE STAFF OF FRENCH LIFE

THE BASIC SIGNIFICANCE of *pain* (bread) in the French diet cannot be overestimated. When the Bastille was stormed, starting the French Revolution, it was, in part, due to the high price of bread. ("Let them eat *brioche*," Marie Antoinette is reputed to have said.) But the Revolutionaries thought otherwise: poor Marie Antoinette lost her head, France became a republic, and, today, by law, every village in the land must have at least one shop making or selling bread daily. Moreover, since the favorite white *pain* or smaller *baguette*, made from no more than soft wheat flour, yeast, salt, and water, becomes stale after only a few hours, most *boulangeries* bake twice, even thrice, daily, and many are open on Sundays.

Freshly baked baguettes, *the national favorite*

Wheat is grown extensively, particularly in the Paris basin, and France ranks fifth in world production. Other grains

Wheatfields planted on former battlefields in Champagne

cultivated include corn, oats, barley, rye, and buckwheat, and rice is grown in the Rhône Delta, particularly in the Camargue.

But bread, primarily white made with wheat flour, has been and remains indispensable at every meal. For visitors, bread is a good start to a gastronomic tour of France, for it is ever present, and one of the most immediate and accessible of pleasures. Even bad French bread — airy, light, tasteless — is a good vehicle for slabs of garlicky *pâté* or wedges of *camembert* or *brie* cheeses. Good bread, however, can be sublime, particularly when made with a sourdough starter and baked in a wood-fired oven.

Regional breads are covered in the second part of this book, but the main types of bread found throughout the nation are listed below, together with other products of the *boulangerie* (bakery).

Baguette The classic, long, thin loaf.

Bâtarde or **pain bâtarde** Traditional white loaf, slightly larger than a *baguette*.

Boule A round loaf.

Campagne Rustic country loaf, often, though not always, round, and usually made with a mixture of white, whole-wheat, and rye flours.

Couronne Circular, crown-shaped loaf, often densely textured and with a hard, chewy crust.

Ficelle Literally "string"; a very thin, narrow *baguette*.

Fougasse Flat loaf with slits, to allow more crust to form; sometimes filled with olives, cheese, or bits of meat.

Natte Shaped into a braid.

Pain Roughly twice the size of a *baguette*, a large family loaf weighing usually about 500 g. (about 1 lb.).

Pain au levain Classic bread made with a sourdough starter and allowed to benefit from a long, slow rising, which contributes to both flavor and texture. Such traditional bread is sometimes labeled *"pain à l'ancienne."*

Pain aux algues Bread made with seaweed.

Pain aux cinq céreales Bread made with five different grains; varieties depend on the baker.

Pain aux fines herbes Herb bread.

Pain aux noix Bread made with walnuts.

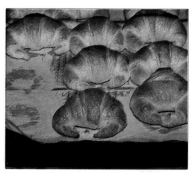

Croissants, *hot from the oven*

Pain aux olives Bread made with olives and olive oil.

Pain aux raisins Raisin bread.

Pain biologique Bread from organic wholewheat flour.

Pain complet Wholewheat bread, usually soft in texture.

Pain de mie Rectangular, white sandwich loaf.

Fougasse, *with characteristic slits*

Pain de seigle Rye bread, usually made from a mixture of rye and soft wheat flours, and bearing little resemblance to the dark, chewy rye breads we are more familiar with.

Pain de son Bread made with extra added bran.

Pain paillasse Immense country loaf, usually made with wholewheat flour and a sourdough starter.

Petit pain Small roll, sometimes made with *brioche* dough.

PATISSERIES — BREADS, CAKES, AND PASTRIES

Brioche Sweet, yeasty breakfast bread.

Croissant The best are extremely flaky, feather light in texture, and made with fresh, not concentrated, butter.

Eclair au chocolat Cream-filled *choux* pastry, topped with chocolate-flavored icing.

Madeleines Lemon tea-cakes baked in scallop-shaped molds.

Pain au chocolat Buttery flaky pastry, with a stick of chocolate inside.

Pithiviers Large cake or small individual cream- and almond-filled pastries.

Tarte au citron Lemon tart.

Tarte aux mirabelles, aux quetsches, aux reines-claudes Fruit tarts made with *mirabelle, quetsch,* or greengage plums, depending on the season.

Tarte aux pommes Classic individual or large apple tart; **tarte normande** variation made with shortcrust pastry and flavored with Calvados; **tarte Tatin** French upside-down apple tart.

Fruits et Légumes
FRUITS AND VEGETABLES

A VISIT TO ANY MARKET in France demonstrates the wealth of excellent fresh fruits and vegetables available throughout the year. Though, in some cases and at certain times, such produce can be imported from other regions and even other nations, the French overwhelmingly prefer local fruits and vegetables, on the assumption that the nearer the produce to the source, the fresher and better it is.

Strawberries from Carpentras

As a result, and at virtually any time of the year, during their short season, there is a veritable glut of particular fruits or vegetables on market stalls, and at prices which seem almost give-away. At such times, old-style methods of conservation come into play, as *tomates* (tomatoes), *haricots verts* (green beans), and *petits-pois* (small fresh peas) are bottled and sterilized; fruits such as *fraises* (strawberries), *framboises* (raspberries), *cerises* (cherries), and *groseilles* (redcurrants) are steeped in alcohol; and *reines-claudes* (green-gages), *mirabelle,* and *quetsche* (yellow and blue plums) as well as much else are transformed into delectable *confitures* (jams and preserves). In Provence, the traditional method of conserving the rich abundance of seasonal fruits is to candy them in sugar syrup, a process still carried out by hand on an artisanal scale (see p.226).

Modern transportation from across the world, of course, means that it is possible to find fruits and vegetables outside their traditional seasons, as there is no shortage of exotic or foreign produce from far-off climes. But still, much of the pleasure of shopping in France (or even just browsing) lies in marking the seasons and the regions by the local produce.

Regional produce is discussed in the respective chapters in the second part of this book, but the following is a brief glossary of principal fruits and vegetables found throughout France, along with their approximate seasons.

Fresh, local seasonal fruits and vegetables at a market

LES FRUITS — FRUITS

Abricot Apricot (end of Jun–Aug).
Brugnon/nectarine Nectarine (Jun–Sep).
Cassis Blackcurrant (Jun–Jul).
Cerise Cherry (May–Jul).
Clémentine Clementine, a type of tangerine (end Nov–end Mar).
Datte Date (Nov–Dec).
Fraise Strawberry (mid Apr–Jul).
Fraise de bois Tiny, wild strawberry (summer).

White asparagus, a great seasonal delicacy

Framboise Raspberry (Jun–Sep).
Groseille Redcurrant (Jun–Aug).
Kiwi Kiwi fruit (Nov–Mar).
Melon Melon (end May–mid Sep).
Pêche Peach (mid Jun–Sep).
Poire Pear (mid Jul–end Nov).
Pomme Apple (mid Aug–Dec).
Prune Plum; including *reine-claude, mirabelle, quetsche* (Jun–end Sep).
Pruneau Prune (fall).
Raisin Table grape (mid Aug–Nov).

LES LEGUMES — VEGETABLES

Ail Garlic (Jun–Aug).
Artichaut Globe artichoke (mid May–end Oct).
Asperge Asparagus (Apr–Jun).
Aubergine Eggplant (Jun–Sep).
Basilic Basil (summer).
Betterave Beet (Sep–Mar).
Cardon Cardoon (late summer–fall).
Carotte Carrot (Jul–May).
Céleri Celery (end Apr–Nov).
Céleri-rave Celeriac (Aug–Oct).
Cèpe *Boletus edulis* or cepe mushroom (end Aug–mid Oct).
Champignon de Paris White button mushroom (cultivated year round).
Chanterelle or girolle Orange, trumpet-shaped wild mushroom *Cantharellus cibarius* (Jun–Aug).
Chou Cabbage (Jun–Apr).
Chou-fleur Cauliflower (Jul–May).
Concombre Cucumber (Apr–Oct).
Courgette Zucchini (Jun–Sep).
Echalote Shallot (Apr–Nov).
Endive Endive (Dec–Mar).

Epinard Spinach (Jul–Oct).
Fenouil Bulb fennel (Jun–Sep).
Haricot vert Green bean (Jun–Aug).
Laitue Lettuce (many types available throughout the year).
Marron/châtaigne Chestnut (Oct–Nov).
Morille Morel mushroom (late Apr–May).
Navet Turnip (Nov–May).
Noisette Hazelnut (Sep–Nov).
Noix Walnut (Sep–Nov).
Oignon Onion (throughout the year).
Olive Olive (Nov–Dec).
Persil Parsley (throughout the year).
Petit-pois Fresh peas (May–Jul).
Poireau Leek (Sep–Apr).
Poivron Bell pepper (May–Oct).
Poivron rouge Red bell pepper (May–Oct).
Pomme de terre Potato (throughout the year but new potatoes mid May–Jul).
Radis Radish (May–Sep).
Tomate Tomato (Apr–Nov).
Truffe Truffle (Dec–Feb).

LES PRIMEURS

Nouvelle cuisine has brought a vogue for tiny, almost miniature, *primeur* vegetables, as beautiful to look at carefully arranged on a plate as they are delicate and tasty to eat. Look for the first, youngest, new season carrots, turnips, potatoes, zucchini, sugar snap peas, and baby corn.

Meat and Poultry
A NATION OF MEAT EATERS

FEW MEALS IN FRANCE are complete without meat or poultry in some form, whether cured *charcuterie* or fresh beef, lamb, pork, or chicken or other fowl. Consequently, rearing livestock for home consumption as well as for export is an important part of the economy.

Both the type of animal and where it is reared are paramount determinants of quality. Thus, for *boeuf* (beef), there are some four breeds of cattle that are considered superior enough to warrant named status: Charolais, Limousin, Maine-Anjou, and Blond d'Aquitaine. Indeed, the names of such breeds can be seen on meats displayed in *boucheries* that take pride in the quality of their meat, as well as on the menus of restaurants.

Veau (veal) is another meat highly popular in France. The best comes from milk-fed animals that are no more than three months in age *(veau sous la mère)*. Some of the finest, from Limousin, benefits from *Labels Régionaux*. Veal cuts, like all meats, differ significantly from North American equivalents, and while such premium cuts as *côte de veau* (veal chop) and *escalopes* are much enjoyed, cheaper cuts such as *poitrine* (breast), *jarret* (knuckle), and *blanquette* (stewing cubes cut from the shoulder) are widely served.

The French are avid lovers of *agneau* (lamb), especially, says the vociferous farm lobby, French lamb. Lamb, more than beef, is a meat that gains its flavor through where and what the animals have grazed upon. The most distinctive

Charolais cattle from Burgundy, source of some of the finest meat

---

---

invariably comes from *pré-salé* salt marshes in Picardy, the Normandy coast around Mont-St.-Michel, or on the alluvial, sometimes flooded banks of the Gironde, near the famous wine town of Pauillac. Excellent lamb with a distinctive flavor of herbs comes from the Alpilles in Provence, where tough, scraggy beasts roam the *garrigues* (scrubby uplands), supplementing their diet with tufts of wild rosemary and oregano.

Much *agneau* so labeled and sold in France comes from near mature animals and is, in fact, much closer to *mouton* (mutton). *Chevreau* (kid) is also raised, primarily in mountain areas, and is prepared in similar ways.

Porc (pork) is reared for eating fresh, as well as for curing. In general, leaner breeds are raised for the former, while fatter pigs yield the higher proportion of fat to lean required by the *charcutier*. Brittany is the foremost region for raising pigs. The best may be labeled *"élevés en plein air,"* raised outdoors.

The finest poultry, too, usually comes from farms where the birds are *"élevés en plein air,"* often sold still alive and kicking in markets. Superb *poulet fermier* (free-range chicken) and other poultry such as *chapon* (capon) and *dinde* (turkey) come not only from Bresse, but from other named areas including Licques in Nord-

Pas de Calais, the Bourbonnais in the Auvergne, Mayenne, Challan, and Aubrières-les-Vallées.

Canard (duck) and *oie* (goose) are reared extensively in Southwest France, particularly in the Gers and Landes for *foie gras* (fattened liver). In addition to its liver, duck yields, inevitably, a ready supply of fresh *magret* (duck breast), *aiguillettes* (strips of meat cut out from the back of the carcass), and other cuts, and both goose and duck are preserved as *confits* (salted, then slowly cooked in their own fat, see p.149). *Pintadeau* guinea hen or fowl, rather like a lean but more flavorsome chicken, is an extremely popular bird, while *pigeon* (pigeon) and *caille* (quail) are also reared domestically.

For all the good meat available, we still find it difficult to comprehend the taste for horsemeat in the French diet. Once, it

Sheep grazing near Mont-St.-Michel, Normandy

was exceedingly inexpensive compared to beef, but this is no longer the case, yet many French still love the sweet, rather rich, dark flavor of *cheval*.

FAIR GAME

Fall in France and hardly a wood or open field escapes the attention of the *chasseurs* — camouflaged hunters, armed with rifles or shotguns, who appear ready to take a pot shot at anything that moves. Even tiny song birds are considered fair game, to be roasted undrawn and eaten whole, bones and all. Pheasant, quail, and pigeon, on the other hand, are often raised domestically like guinea hen, though the former may be released for a brief period to satisfy the egos of the *chasseurs*. Large game still freely roam throughout the woods and forests of much of France: deer and wild boar provide sport as well as good eating. Game in season may include:

Alouette Lark.
Bec-figue Fig pecker, a tiny bird.
Bécasse Woodcock.
Bécassine Snipe.
Biche Doe.
Caille Quail.

Cerf Stag or red deer.
Chevreuil Roebuck or roe deer; general name for venison.
Coq de bruyère Wood grouse.
Faisan Pheasant.
Lièvre Hare.
Marcassin Baby boar.
Ortolan Bunting.
Palombe Wood pigeon.
Perdreau Young partridge.
Perdrix Partridge.
Pigeon Pigeon.
Sanglier Wild boar.

Roast pigeon with wild mushrooms

Charcuterie

CURED PORK AND OTHER MEAT PRODUCTS

Cured and preserved meats, usually made from pork, are termed *charcuterie,* from *chair cuite* or cooked meat. Every town, every village in France, has at least one noteworthy *charcuterie,* and it is here, as much as anywhere else, that the sheer wealth, inventiveness, and essential character of French gastronomy is revealed.

It is here, too, that hungry visitors are likely to make their way, for the town or village *charcuterie* is the source of a wealth of delicious ready-to-eat meals as well as the makings of memorable picnics.

The pig, of course, was for long the mainstay of rural economies throughout Europe, and, in the not-so-distant past, most farms and rural households kept at least one beast, to be slaughtered annually by an itinerant *charcutier,* and salted into hams, sausages, and conserved meats to last throughout the winter. If E.U. hygiene laws and the advent of the home deep freezer has, to a great extent, put an end to such private rural practices (although, we last witnessed such a home slaughter on a smallholding near Calais as recently as 1993), the craft of the *charcutier* still lives gloriously on.

The artisan *charcutier,* basically, transforms on the premises fresh pork into *jambon* (ham), *saucisses* and *saucissons* (sausages and dried sausages), *pâtés,*

A charcuterie stall in Les Halles market, Lyon, a city renowned for its cured pork products

galantines, and blood sausages. Using traditional methods of salting (both dry and in brine), drying, smoking, or cooking, the range of products prepared from the pig can be quite astounding, and varies from *charcutier* to *charcutier* and from region to region, ranging from the rustic and, literally, "gutsy" in flavor to the exceedingly fine and sophisticated.

Though many regional *charcuterie* products are covered in the second part of this book, listed below are some of the standard items generally found in good *charcuteries* throughout France. Some items require cooking (*saucisses, andouillettes, boudins,* etc.), but many are ready to eat.

Andouille Large, knobbly sausage made usually with chitterlings or tripe; usually smoked; to be eaten cold.

Andouillette Much smaller sausage, made with pork or veal chitterlings, tripe, or *fraise* (mesentery, a frilly membrane surrounding the intestines). Already cooked, but must be broiled and eaten hot.

Boudin blanc Expensive, finely textured, creamy white sausage-like product containing, usually, finely ground pork, sometimes chicken, sometimes rabbit, cream, milk or eggs, and seasonings. To be warmed up gently in a skillet.

Boudin noir Blood sausage made in as many versions as there are *charcutiers,* and with a huge variety of ingredients, including fresh pig's blood, fat, apples, chestnuts, cream, onions, spices. To be broiled or fried.

Cervelas Meaty, boiling sausage, usually flavored with garlic.

Confit de porc, de canard, d'oie Conserved meats — pork, duck, or goose — first salted, then slow cooked in their own fat; usually sold in jars, to be heated up in a skillet.

Crépinette Meat patty encased in lacy caul fat; to be heated up in a skillet.

Epaule cuite Cured and cooked shoulder of pork, a tasty but fattier alternative to cooked *jambon* (ham), though also usually less expensive. Good for picnics.

Foie gras Fattened liver of duck or goose, a great national delicacy (see p.151).

Fromage de tête Head cheese or brawn; made from the cooked meat from a pig's head and set in a thick, tasty gelatin.

Galantine Boned poultry or game, usually stuffed, cooked, then pressed and set in gelatin; to eat cold.

Hure Brawn; set usually in a tasty, thick layer of gelatin.

Jambon Ham.

Jambon d'Ardennes Should be dry cured and smoked: the genuine can be outstanding.

Jambon de Bayonne The term is applied indiscrimately to raw, salted, and air-dried ham in the style of Parma; artisan hams from the Southwest can be superb (see p.150).

Jambon d'York or **de Paris** Cooked ham usually cured in brine, unsmoked, and ready to eat.

Jambon fumé Smoked ham.

Jambon persillé Chunks of ham set in a parsley, wine, and garlic gelatin.

Jambonneau Small, breaded hock of cooked pork knuckle.

Jésus Smoked pork sausage; usually served hot.

Museau de boeuf en vinaigrette Cooked ox muzzle, sliced and marinated in *vinaigrette*.

Pâté Meat spread or paste; usually made from pig's liver, ground lean and fat of pork or other meats and variety meats, together with any number of ingredients and flavorings.

Rosette de Lyon, one of the finest French sausages

A selection of charcuterie

Pâté de campagne *Pâté* made from coarsely chopped or ground meat.

Pâté de lapin *Pâté* made with pork and rabbit.

Pâté en croûte *Pâté* cooked in a pastry crust.

Petit salé Salted pork belly; usually used for cooking.

Pied de porc pané Breaded, cooked pig's trotter; to be broiled.

Porc rôti Most *charcuteries* sell fresh roast pork, ready to eat, cut in slices.

Rillettes Potted meat paste of shreds of slow cooked pork, pork fat, or sometimes goose or duck.

Rillons Little pieces of pork belly, slow cooked until almost candied. Delicious picnic fare; or serve warm over salad.

Rosette Fine air-dried sausage made from ground pork and fat, flavored with garlic and wine.

Saucisse Fresh pork sausage.

Saucisse à cuire Boiling sausage, usually made with fatty meat such as *poitrine* (pork belly); needs to be cooked for upward of 45 minutes.

Saucisse de Francfort Pure pork frankfurter-type boiling sausage.

Saucisse de Strasbourg or **knack** Pork and beef frankfurter-type sausage.

Saucisse de Toulouse Meaty, coarse-ground sausage sold in an unlinked coil.

Saucisson sec Salami-like salted and air-dried sausage; to be eaten cold in slices; flavorings vary widely.

Terrine de campagne These days, the terms *terrine* and *pâté* are used interchangeably. *Terrine de campagne* usually indicates a homemade, rough, garlicky country *pâté* served from an earthenware *terrine* or crock.

Entre Deux Mers

FROM SEA TO SHINING SEA

FRANCE IS BOUNDED by water on three sides, on the west by the Atlantic Ocean and the Bay of Biscay, on the northwest by the English Channel, and on the southeast by the Mediterranean Sea.

This lengthy mainland coastline, which extends for some 2,800 km. (about 1,750 miles), naturally, has numerous *ports de pêche* (fishing ports), out of which large and small fleets of boats embark to fish in inland coastal waters as well as in the much deeper waters of seas further out.

On the quayside of the Basque port of St.-Jean-de-Luz

LES CRIEES — WHOLESALE FISH MARKETS

Fish is landed and sold at *criées,* great wholesale fish auctions where buyers load their purchases onto waiting refrigerated trucks that speed them away to cities and towns to be further distributed to smaller retail *poissonneries* (fishmongers') or supermarkets. Fish auctions usually take place very early in the morning. Although they are not open to the public, you may be able to watch the spectacle if you seek permission from the *directeur.* The most important *criées* (by tonnage) are:

Boulogne-sur-Mer (Nord-Pas de Calais)

Lorient, Concarneau, Douarnenez, Guilvinec (Brittany)

Port-en-Bessin, Dieppe (Normandy)

Les Sables-d'Olonne, La Rochelle (Poitou-Charentes)

Hendaye, St.-Jean-de-Luz (the Basque Country)

Sète (Languedoc)

Port-de-Bouc (Provence)

Though in international terms, France is not a world leader in fishing, the local industry remains an important and vociferous one (witness the recent and sometimes violent disputes between French fishermen and their Spanish or English counterparts).

Ports de pêche range from the enormous, such as Boulogne-sur-Mer and Concarneau, where immense trawlers land huge quantities of fish on an industrial scale, to smaller fishing towns and villages, where traditional boats still land a catch mainly destined for local markets and the surrounding region.

In a nation where once almost everyone ate fish at least on Fridays (no longer true today), there is a well-established network of transportation that ensures that even far inland, there is always fresh fish available. (Curiously, the penchant for *morue,* dried salt cod, remains strongest along the Mediterranean seaboard and throughout the Midi.)

The colder waters of the English Channel and the North Atlantic yield a catch that is quite different to that landed in fishing ports along the Mediterranean seaboard. In the first place, fishing fleets from the former may roam far beyond the traditional inland fishing grounds of France, casting their nets deep and wide, as far away as offshore Africa and the waters of Iceland and Newfoundland.

By its nature, fishing is a specialized occupation, as fleets must not only make use of different methods in search of specific varieties of fish, but also follow the movements of fish to different waters at different times of the year. The Concarneau fleet in Brittany, for example, has a tradition of going out in search of *thon blanc* (albacore tuna). Fishermen from St.-Jean-de-Luz in the

Basque Country, by contrast, seek out *thon rouge* (bluefin tuna) during summer months and anchovies and sardines through the winter. And, at Collioure and Port Vendres, in Roussillon near the Spanish Catalan frontier, the fishermen specialize in hunting for succulent fresh anchovies.

Fish typical of various regions is dealt with in the respective chapters in the second part of the book, but below are some of the more common types found throughout France in markets as well as in restaurants.

Alose Shad.

Anchois Anchovy.

Anguille Eel.

Bar or **loup de mer** Sea bass.

Barbue Brill.

Cabillaud Cod.

Cernier Stone bass or wreckfish.

Chinchard or **saurel** Horse mackerel.

Congre Conger eel.

Daurade Gilt-head porgy or sea bream.

Dorade commune Red porgy or sea bream.

Eglefin Haddock.

Espadon Swordfish.

Esturgeon Sturgeon.

Flétan Halibut.

Grondin gris Gray gurnard, sea robin.

Grondin rouge Red gurnard.

Hareng Herring.

Lieu Pollack.

Limande Dab.

Lotte or **baudroie** Monkfish.

Maquereau Mackerel.

Merlan Silver hake, whiting.

Merlu Hake.

Mulet Striped or gray mullet.

Pageot Pandora, a type of porgy or sea bream.

Plie Plaice.

Raie Skate.

Rascasse Scorpion fish.

Rouget Red mullet, goatfish.

Roussette Dogfish.

Sardine Sardine.

Sar Striped porgy or sea bream.

Saumon Salmon.

Sole Sole.

Sole limande Lemon sole.

St.-Pierre John Dory.

Thon blanc or **germon** Albacore tuna.

Thon rouge Bluefin tuna.

Truite Trout.

Truite de mer Salmon or sea trout.

Turbot Turbot.

The harbor in Dieppe, an important fishing port in Normandy

Fruits de Mer

SHELLFISH AND MORE SHELLFISH

NOTHING CAN MAKE an outsider feel more so than the sight of a French family getting on with the serious business of eating shellfish. Not only are the types of shellfish on offer often bafflingly unfamiliar, the skills needed to

Moules à la marinière, *a classic*

your hands, crack, slurp, and generally make as much noise as required: the French will at least appreciate your chutzpah.

Araignée de mer Spider crab.

Bigorneau Winkle, sea snail.

Cigale de mer Flat

tackle them effectively and with some semblance of dignity are, one feels, probably only inherited. Our advice? Leave vanity aside, take courage, roll up your sleeves, and enjoy. Like eating Maine lobster or Dungeness crab, much of the pleasure lies in the sheer challenge of getting every last morsel out of the stubborn shell.

The French eat enormous quantities of shellfish, including seemingly weird varieties elsewhere disregarded or even shunned. Much of what is enjoyed is eaten raw, or else simply boiled and served with the minimum of fuss. Look around and see what others are eating. If you are unsure about how to attack something, ask either fellow diners or the waiter for instruction. If in doubt, use

lobster, slipper lobster.

Coquille St.-Jacques Scallop.

Crevette Shrimp; **crevette grise** shrimp, brown shrimp.

Etrille Swimming crab.

Homard Lobster.

Huître Oyster; **huître plate** native oyster.

Langouste Spiny lobster, crawfish.

Langoustine Dublin Bay prawn, Norway lobster.

Moule Mussel.

Oursin Sea urchin.

Palourde Carpet-shell clam.

Pouce-pied Goose-necked barnacle.

Poulpe Octopus.

Praire Warty Venus clam.

Telline Small, smooth-shelled clam.

Tourteau Crab.

A bank of oysters at Cancale, Brittany

Cheese and Other Dairy Products

AN INGENUITY BEYOND IMAGINATION

GENERAL DE GAULLE, defining his country, mused, "Nobody can bring together a nation that has 265 types of cheese." In fact, for once, the great man's hyperbole was understated: France boasts certainly well in excess of 350 different named cheeses, as well as many more individual variations and types that exist only locally.

French cheese is, quite simply, one of the great glories of Western gastronomy. It has been produced for thousands of years by coagulating milk solids with rennet in order to transform perishable fresh milk into a more durable solid. Yet, what variation exists within this basic equation: no other nation on earth transforms the milk, from cow, ewe, or goat, with such ingenuity and into a greater variety of types and styles of cheeses than France.

Huge rounds of hard, aged mountain cheese like *cantal* and *salers* made by shepherds in the high hills of the Auvergne; pungent, orange cheeses rind-washed in beer or *eau-de-vie;* pale, runny white *camembert* in its characteristic wooden box; blue, ewe's milk cheeses wrapped in tin and left to develop in the airy *caves* of Roquefort, gaining, in the process, rich flavor and distinctive blue-green veins; or fresh or hard disks of goat's milk cheese, flavored with ash, herbs, peppercorns, or wrapped in walnut or chestnut leaves: these and many, many more are the cheeses of France.

LAIT CRU — UNPASTEURIZED MILK
French cheeses are made industrially in modern dairies as well as by hand on farms in the old, time-tested artisan fashion. The finest, most individual cheeses undoubtedly are produced in this way, invariably using *lait cru* (unpasteurized milk) which comes from the cheesemaker's own herd or from neighboring herds. Cheeses made from unpasteurized milk have deeper, rounder flavors and more individual character; moreover, they continue to develop and mature more fully and completely.

However, that said, in recent years, there have been health concerns related to eating soft cheeses made from unpasteurized milk, and current health guidelines suggest that those who are concerned, especially high risk groups including pregnant women and the

---

BUTTER AND *CREME FRAICHE*

Where would French cuisine be without butter and cream? True, dietitians have been advising us all to cut down on saturated fats, but, thankfully, the French approach such important matters with something less of the "nanny knows best" attitude that we are bombarded with. Butter, sweet and unsalted from Normandy or Poitou-Charentes, as well as semi-salted from Brittany, and *crème fraîche* — a sort of thick, slightly fermented

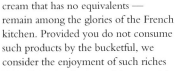

cream that has no equivalents — remain among the glories of the French kitchen. Provided you do not consume such products by the bucketful, we consider the enjoyment of such riches to be part of the essential experience of visiting France. The best butter is bought cut from huge slabs, while *crème fraîche,* unpasteurized and straight from the dairy, is often scooped out direct into jars in markets or *fromageries-crémeries* (cheese shops). Enjoy!

Tomme de Savoie, *one of the great mountain cheeses of Savoie*

Maroilles AC, *one of the mildest of the pungent rind-washed varieties*

Langres AC, *a soft rind-washed cheese from Champagne*

Fougeu, *a* pâte fleurie *cheese like brie, from the North of France*

infirm or elderly, should seek advice from their physician.

FAMILIES OF FRENCH CHEESES

It is hardly possible to describe every named French cheese, though, of course, scores of both classic (especially cheeses entitled to select *appellation d'origine contrôlée* status) as well as important regional and local varieties are highlighted in the second part of this book. It may be more helpful here to understand the basic types of French cheeses, so that when you come across unknown varieties, you will at least have points of reference. In restaurants, unfamiliar cheeses may be described with the following terms relating to their methods of production.

Pâte fleurie Family of cheeses with a white, edible rind. Such rind-ripened cheeses develop a surface bloom or mold that forms the characteristic, white, edible crust. As the cheeses age, the interior usually is transformed from a rather chalky texture to a runny one.

Classic examples of *pâte fleurie* cheeses include *camembert, brie de Meaux, chaource,* and *coulommiers*.

Pâte lavée Rind-washed cheeses. These are unpressed cheeses whose crusts, once formed, are washed in salt water and/or mixtures of local *eau-de-vie* or beer. Bacteria forms on the surface and turns it a striking orange color and also ripens the cheese in the process. They are always pungent in aroma, and their flavors can range from the surprisingly mild and mellow to intensely rich.

Examples of *pâte lavée* cheeses include *livarot, maroilles, munster,* and *epoisses*.

Pâte cuite Family of mountain cheeses made by heating curds before pressing; this gives a rubbery texture to the cheeses when young, but allows them to be conserved for lengthy periods.

French *beaufort, comté,* and *gruyère* are classic examples of *pâte cuite* cheeses.

Pâte pressée Hard, pressed cheeses made from the milk of cows and ewes: mild in flavor and texture when young, such cheeses develop a hard crust and a tasty, pronounced character with age.

Classic *pâte pressée* cheeses include *cantal, salers, tomme de Savoie,* and the ewe's milk *ossau-iraty-brebis-pyrénées.*

Pâte persillée Blue cheeses made from cow's or ewe's milk, lightly pressed then aged in moist *caves* so that a mold (*Penicillium roquefortii,* in the case of *roquefort*) grows inside the cheese, giving them their striking blue-green veins and sharp, spicy, rich flavor and aroma.

The best-known French blue cheeses include *roquefort* (made from ewe's milk), *bleu de Gex, bleu d'Auvergne,* and *bleu des Causses* (all from cow's milk).

Fromages de chèvre A vast variety of cheeses made from goat's milk are produced in France, ranging from exceedingly mild and fresh, to hard, pressed, aged, and pungent.

Choosing cheese

Cheese is a live product, and choosing one is something of an art and an acquired instinct. Your selection will depend on a number of factors, including, primarily, personal taste (the French often prefer *camembert* when it is still quite chalky and firm), as well as knowing when you will eat the cheese, for one purchased in perfect condition today may be well over the top tomorrow.

The best way to tell how ripe a cheese is is to handle it if possible: press a *camembert* firmly with your thumbs (it should be soft but not overly so, with a yellow tinge visible through the wrapper). Cheeses should never smell of ammonia. Though you may be able to feel a cheese in a supermarket, it will be difficult to do so at a specialist *fromagerie* (cheese shop). However, cheese specialists, especially that select group entitled to call themselves *maîtres fromagers* (master cheese specialists) will always be more than happy to advise you, as well as to let you taste various cheeses before you decide which to buy.

In restaurants, when the cheese trolley or platter is presented, always ask for advice on local cheeses and choose those that look in the best condition. Also, try to vary your selection with examples from the different cheese families.

Cows grazing in Normandy, a region famous for its fine cheeses

Confectionery, Chocolates, and Other Sweets

A NATIONAL SWEET TOOTH

FRANCE IS NOTHING SHORT of heaven for children and all lovers of sweets: something akin to hell, we imagine, for those on a diet or who have given up candy and sweets for Lent, for the temptations in any town or village are immense. Quite apart from such buttery luxuries as *croissants* and *pain au chocolat* for breakfast, not even counting the outrageously irresistible displays of *pâtisseries* which constantly assault you, forgetting for a moment too, the gorgeous desserts, and the trays of *petits fours* offered after meals with the coffee, there are still scores of regional and local sweets and candies begging to be sampled.

It is quite possible to mark a voyage through France by the local and regional sweets encountered, beginning in Nord-Pas de Calais with *berlingots* from Berck and *bêtises de Cambrai,* continuing to Champagne, pausing to sample chocolate corks filled with *marc,* and onward. Visitors heading to the South inevitably pass through Montélimar and few can resist stopping to buy bars of almond and

A selection of pâtisseries, *as on offer in most towns throughout France*

honey *nougat.* In Toulouse, on the other hand, tiny candied violet flowers mark a journey to the Languedoc or Roussillon, and in St.-Emilion it is as obligatory to sample *macarons* as it is wine. In the Dordogne, new season walnuts are covered in chocolate and dusted with cocoa *(arlequins de Carlux)* and in Central France, fresh chestnuts are candied in vanilla sugar to emerge as luxury *marrons glacés.* Vichy's mint *pastilles,* meanwhile, help mask the taste of minerally Vichy water for those taking a cure in that fashionable spa town in the Auvergne, while *fruits confits* — glistening fruits candied in sugar — from Provence are among the most beautiful and delicious edible gifts that you can enjoy or take home with you. Discovering and savoring such local candies for yourself is one of the most pleasurable aspects of visiting France.

FRENCH CHOCOLATE

Though we are not ourselves great "chocoholics," we consider hand-made French chocolate to be the best we have sampled, surpassing even that from Belgium. The French taste is primarily for intensely dark, bitter chocolates made with quality ingredients and a very high percentage of cocoa solids. Fresh hand-made chocolate, it should be stressed, is completely different from manufactured, packaged chocolate: it is marked foremost by an intensity of flavor, and a sensuous texture that could be seriously addictive.

A tempting display of confectionery to invite the browser

Produits du Terroir

REGIONAL AND LOCAL SPECIALTIES

VIRTUALLY EVERY TOWN or village in France has its own *spécialités* (specialties), and, in great measure, the purpose of this book is to describe and highlight them, whether they be a local or regional dish, particular produce, cheeses, or local meats, fish, or shellfish.

In many cases, however, there are *produits du terroir* — local or regional specialties — that do not neatly fit into such categories but which are, none-theless, important elements of local, regional, and traditional gastronomy. These include such specialties as vinegars,

Macarons *and* tuiles d'Amiens, *almond macaroons and chocolates from that town*

Mustard, the specialty of Dijon

mustards, and oils; farm-produced honey made from local flowers or from specific, named areas; home-made *confitures* (jams and conserves) made by housewives and farmer's wives using the bounty of local and seasonal fruits; jars or cans of prepared foods or conserved meats, in-cluding *foie gras, confits, cassoulet, pâtés,* and other *plats cuisinés* (prepared, ready-to-eat foods); local cakes, cookies, or sweets; and homemade liqueurs, cordials, juices, and ciders.

No matter where you find yourself in France, there will be opportunities to purchase such *produits du terroir,* for they are almost universally considered a part of each town or region's cultural heritage, and locals are always keen that visitors try them, better still, purchase their town specialties to take back home with them (on such edible items sometimes are entire local economies seemingly based).

Montélimar is a town that lives, breathes, and survives on its famous, chewy *nougat.* It is virtually obligatory to visit the Grey-Poupon shop in Dijon, if not to buy mustard, then to purchase reproductions of antique mustard jars. In

Amiens, meanwhile, few visitors to Picardy's capital would, we imagine, leave without first sampling a delectable *macaron d'Amiens.* And throughout Southwest France, in almost every town or village, there are scores of oppor-tunities to purchase home-conserved *foie gras, confits de canard,* and other farm-produced duck and goose derivatives. Markets are one of the best sources for such *produits du terroir,* and you can often come across them also in highway service areas and shops as well as in specialty boutiques.

THE MONASTIC TRADITION

During the Middle Ages and later, monasteries and abbeys safeguarded French gastronomic traditions and winemaking. Today, a number of monasteries continue to cultivate produce and make products which they sell direct to the public: cheeses from the Trappist Abbaye de Belval and Mont des Cats (Nord-Pas de Calais), *crème de mûres* liqueur from the Abbey d'Aiguebelle (Savoie), *le pâté périgourdin* from the Abbaye d'Echourgnac (Périgord), *le gâteau breton* from the Abbaye de Campénéac (Brittany), and honey gathered by the monks of Lévignac (Haut Langue-doc) are just a few examples. Visit such institutions when you come across them to sample their products.

Le Shopping
WHERE AND WHAT TO BUY

SHOPPING FOR FOOD in France can be both an exciting and challenging experience: exciting because of the range of new and different produce and products that confront us, challenging because it provides an opportunity to meet and socialize with the French. If catering for daily meals at

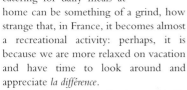

The bread "depot," for bread supplied fresh at least twice daily

home can be something of a grind, how strange that, in France, it becomes almost a recreational activity: perhaps, it is because we are more relaxed on vacation and have time to look around and appreciate *la différence*.

Though the French have wholly embraced American concepts of huge superstores, complete with shopping malls, every city, town, or village still has its small shops which cater to the local population. While French *hypermarchés* have to be seen to be believed, we still consider that the most worthwhile and enjoyable experiences come through visits to individual and committed

specialists. Therefore, shop as the French still do, heading first to the *boulangerie,* then across the road to the *charcuterie* or the *fromagerie* before, perhaps, heading for wine country to buy a bottle or two direct at source. Not only will you find better, fresher, more carefully prepared produce and products than in the *hypermarché,* you will also, I am certain, have more enjoyable, personal encounters.

When we visit France, we shop for food for different reasons: because, as always, we are hungry and need to pick up provisions for a picnic at those times when we are not eating out; if we are staying in a rented *gîte* or campsite, then we may enjoy shopping locally so that we can cook with whatever ingredients and local produce are at hand; or else, we may be looking for food gifts to take back home; at other times, we enjoy visiting specialist shops or markets for the sheer spectacle and fun of it.

Food shop selling a host of good things to eat and drink, from foie gras *to local cheeses*

SPECIALIST FOOD SHOPS

La boucherie Butcher's shop selling fresh *boeuf* (beef), *veau* (veal), *agneau* (lamb), *mouton* (mutton), *porc* (pork), as well as poultry, including *poularde* or *poulet* (chicken), *dinde* (turkey), *canard* (duck), and *pintadeau* (guinea hen).

Some *boucheries* may be *boucherie-charcuteries* and offer a limited range of cured pork products (see **la charcuterie** below). A **boucherie chevaline** sells horsemeat butchered similarly to beef, and is always identifiable by a gilt horse-head on the shop front.

La boulangerie Bakery selling *pain* (bread, see pp.18–19) and *croissants, brioches,* and other sweet or savory pastries. Some but not all *boulangeries* are also *pâtisseries* (see below).

La charcuterie Pork butcher's and delicatessen selling a range of prepared pork products (see pp.24–25), and often a selection of canned or bottled food products, hot or cold prepared, ready-to-eat foods (see **le traiteur** below), and wine.

La fromagerie–crémerie Specialist cheese shop; the best offer a range of both local and national varieties along with farm fresh cream, butter, and eggs. A *fromager-affineur* not only sells cheese but buys young cheeses and cares for and raises them in his/her own *caves.* There are some 60 *maîtres fromagers,* master cheese *affineurs* and retailers, who are considered the most serious cheese specialists in the nation.

La pâtisserie–confiserie–chocolaterie Pastry and sweets or candy specialist offering a range of baked goods, *tartes,* cakes, biscuits, and hand-made candies and chocolates. This is the place to come to buy a gift if you are asked to a French friend's house for lunch or dinner.

La poissonnerie Fish shop or stall offering a range of fresh fish and shellfish and sometimes prepared fish dishes, bottles of *soupe de poisson* (fish soup), and/or cooked shellfish. Come to the

poissonnerie to buy oysters for a seaside picnic: if you don't feel like shucking them yourself, ask the fishmonger to open them for you. Some *poissonneries* will prepare full-blown *plateaux de fruits de mer,* the selection of shellfish cracked and ready to eat to take out to the beach, your *gîte,* or campsite.

High-quality copper cookware, worth buying from Villedieu-les-Poêles, Normandy

SHOPPING HOURS

Remember, when you are thinking about shopping for a picnic, French food shops close at lunchtime!

The approximate opening hours for shops are 7:30 a.m.–12:30 p.m. and 3:30–7 p.m., though this can vary considerably. In the Midi, for example, especially in the heat of summer, many shops may not re-open in the afternoon until 5 p.m. or even later.

Shops usually close one day a week (often Mondays), though many may be open Sunday mornings. *Hypermarchés* may sometimes remain open at midday, and often stay open until late in the evening, at least Fridays and Saturdays.

Le supermarché; l'hyper-marché Though we exhort you to visit the various French specialist shops, French supermarkets and *hypermarchés* (super-stores) can be fun too, if only to see how the French themselves shop and live. *Hypermarchés* as well as many large supermarkets sell far more than just foods, including clothing and electrical appliances. Apart from foods, good buys

Farmhouse cheeses on offer

include Le Creuset enamelled cast-iron ware as well as other cookware, kitchen utensils and knives, tableware, French breakfast coffee cups or bowls, inexpen-sive crystal glasses, and colorful tablecloths.

   Hypermarchés and *supermarchés* are able to charge lower prices for their goods than for similar items in smaller shops. The trade-off is usually in quality and freshness, but not always. *Hypermarchés* have an enormous turnover, and the large chains have an influential collective buying power, reflected not only in price, but also in freshness of regular supplies of local and regional products.

Le traiteur-cuisinier Ultimate take-out shop: sometimes found alongside *charcuterie* counters or a specialist shop in its own right, usually selling an impressive range of ready-to-eat hot and cold foods to take out. These may include hot *plats du jour* (specials that vary daily), salmon in aspic, cold roast beef or pork, *pâté en croûte*, *quiches* and other savory tarts and pies, and an ex-tensive range of freshly prepared cold salads. Often, such places also supply disposable tableware, and may have a limited selection of chilled drinks.

A selection of ready-to-eat foods from a traiteur-cuisinier *to take out*

BUYING FOOD — SOME USEFUL PHRASES AND CONVERSIONS

Je voudrais … I would like …
Une tranche A slice (specify *des tranches fines* thin slices; *extra fines* extra thin; or *épaisses* thick.
Un morceau A piece; the usual way of purchasing cheese — specify how large by indicating when the shop assistant places the knife on the cheese.
La pièce The whole piece; can apply, for example, to a whole pie or *tarte* or to a *charcuterie* product such as *jambonneau* or *saucisson*.
Une douzaine de … A dozen …
Cent grammes 100 g. (3½ oz.)

Qu'est-ce que c'est, ça? What is that?
Combien? How much (does it all come to)?

APPROXIMATE CONVERSIONS
200 g. = 7 oz.
500 g. = 1 lb.
1 kg. = 2¼ lbs.
1 liter = 1 (U.S.) quart or
        1¾ Imperial pints
1 (U.S.) pint = 0.5 liter
1 (Imperial) pint > 0.5 liter

A la Ferme

DOWN ON THE FARM

FRANCE HAS a long farmhouse tradition of selling directly to the public, and along any country lane there are *"vente directe"* signs urging visitors to stop to taste and buy.

In season, fruits and vegetables are sold direct, usually in large quantities or crates, as many French come to buy such seasonal produce in bulk, then conserve it at home themselves. Sometimes you can pick your own, a particularly congenial activity, especially in the case of soft fruits such as *fraises* (strawberries) and *framboises* (raspberries) when you invariably end up eating as much as you gather.

There are also scores of opportunities to buy direct other farm products, including farmhouse cheeses, cream, butter, and eggs; conserves and bottled prepared foods such as *foie gras, cassoulet,* and *pâtés;* jars of *confitures* and honey; specialties such as *escargots* (snails) or farmed *truite* (trout); smoked foods, including *ail fumé* (smoked garlic) and smoked *salaisons* (salted, smoked meats such as *jambon fumé*). You can also buy wines and spirits such as farm-distilled Calvados, Cognac, and Armagnac direct from growers or distillers.

Some farms let you sample home-grown produce by serving either *table d'hôte* (homecooked meals, usually taken with the family), *goûter à la ferme* (a farm visit followed by an afternoon snack or light meal), or more elaborate and ample meals in welcoming *fermes auberges* (farmhouse restaurants) which must, by law, serve foods based predominantly on the farms' own produce.

Visiting farms in France to taste and buy at source provides an outstanding opportunity not only to discover genuine and delicious farmhouse produce and products: it takes you into the heart of rural life in France. For the farmers themselves, selling direct is a welcome means of additional income, as there is no recourse to a middleman (nor, we imagine, the tax man). But more than

Advertising farm products in Normandy

this, it provides country folk living in rural *milieus* with the welcome opportunity to meet people from other walks of life or from different nations, and we have almost always encountered a particularly warm welcome, whenever we've taken pot luck, and stopped to taste and purchase. So take our advice, and be adventurous: and whenever you see a roadside sign, follow it to source to track down fresh, genuine produce and traditional products, sniff out what is on offer, and stop to talk, to taste, and to buy. You won't be disappointed.

Savoie herdsman and wife offering hand-made tommes made in their mountain chalet

Au Marché

MARKETS, MARKETS, AND MORE MARKETS

MARKETS *EN PLEIN AIR* (outdoors), as well as inside pavilions made up of permanent or semi-permanent stalls, are one of the most enduring features in France, from the great wholesale and neighborhood *marchés* of Paris (see p.71), to anonymous, local country markets made up of no more than a half-dozen traders who move daily from isolated village to small rural town.

How we love them! Nothing transports us more immediately into the region than a visit to a market: from the cold, chilly markets of Northern France, where, even in summer, produce may be laid out under inclement rainy skies, to the glorious street festivals of Provence, where huge, striped umbrellas line the streets to block out the ever present sun; and from the large, regionally important daily gatherings, to the minor and unexceptional, once-a-week local.

Markets provide a focus and rhythm to daily or weekly life in France, and whole towns (or so it seems) turn out to browse and shop on the day that the market comes to town.

Many stallholders are professionals, moving their special trucks from town to town, depending on the day of the week, loaded with anything from fruits and vegetables, fresh meat and *charcuterie,* cheeses, olives, wine *en vrac* (sold on tap to be bottled at home), tablecloths, and

The bustle of a Saturday market in Carcassonne, Languedoc

kitchenware. Indeed, should you be fixated on markets like us, then you may well find that you are following the same group of traders around a region, so much so, that, by the end of a week, you may feel you have come to know them personally!

In addition to such professional stall-holders, markets provide an outlet for small producers, often elderly farmers who come to town clutching baskets containing no more than a couple of their cabbages, a few dozen freshly laid eggs, some scallions, a lettuce or two, still moist from the last night's dew, or some wild berries gathered along the way. This is produce at its freshest, most genuine, and truly local.

You can find virtually everything that you want in markets, and, of course, regional and traditional produce and products take pride of place. In Normandy, stalls boast impressive selections of local farmhouse cheeses, *crème fraîche* (tangy, slightly sour cream), and mountains of deep yellow, farm-churned butter. In Provence, on the other hand, the choice of local and seasonal fruits and vegetables is quite astounding, and huge stalls sell as many as 20 different types of olives, as well as mountains of dried *fines herbes* and exotic spices from North Africa. The markets of the Dordogne may offer a *marché au gras* (literally, a "fat

Sunday market in Annecy, Savoie

market") as a fascinating sideshow, where fresh *magret de canard* (duck breast) and *foie gras* (fattened liver) are sold direct by the duck or goose farmers, together with conserved products such as *confits de canard* or *d'oie* (conserved duck or goose), *gésiers confits* (jars of conserved duck or goose gizzards), and goose or duck fat (see p.144).

The market in the small square of Ribeauvillé, Alsace

Markets are one of the principal ways of marking the changing seasons: spring heralds the new crop of *asperges* (asparagus); high summer sees a glut of *tomates* (tomatoes), *aubergines* (eggplant), and *courgettes* (zucchini); fall brings baskets of wild mushrooms, especially the prized *cèpes* (cepes or *Boletus edulis*); and, in winter, mountains of cabbages, potatoes, and other root vegetables appear.

For visitors without access to cooking facilities, markets are good places to come to purchase the makings of good picnics.

There are always bread stalls, as well as stalls offering local cheeses and *charcuterie,* while we can rarely resist the banks of revolving, spit-roasted *poulets rôtis* (roast chickens) or stalls selling Vietnamese fritters and other oriental savories (which are, today, a truly ubiquitous and genuine taste of France).

Other good buys to look out for include tableware, glasses, kitchenware such as ceramic and wooden utensils, and knives as well as attractive tablecloths and other household linen.

The principal market days of each region are listed in their respective chapters, but wherever you find yourself, make sure you ask in the *syndicat d'initiative* (tourist office) where and when local markets take place. Make your way there and join in, selecting, sniffing, rejecting — shopping for local specialties as the locals themselves do.

Tarte aux pommes, *apple tart*

Apricots

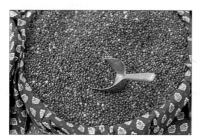

Red peppercorns

Chives

One of Life's Great Pleasures

EATING AND DRINKING IN FRANCE

In his classic, *Physiologie du Goût,* an elegant compendium on the art of dining and living well, published in 1825, the great gastronome Brillat-Savarin stated unequivocally, "Tell me what you eat and I will tell you who you are." Many of us may not care for such introspection, fearful of what the mirror of our diets might reveal. Today, even the French, dare I say, might feel uneasy if their shopping carts from the Mammouth or Carrefour *hypermarchés* were to be scrutinized too closely by the brilliantly witty mayor of Belley, in Eastern France, who was forced to take refuge in the United States during the Reign of Terror.

Yet, if we are what we eat, then the first rule, when in France, is to accept and appreciate how and what the French themselves eat and drink. For France remains secure in its preeminent position among the great gastronomic nations of the world, and few concessions are made to visitors or foreigners. If you cannot bear a meal without a glass of ice water as you sit down, bread without butter, or weak coffee without artificial cream, then you are likely to be disappointed. But if, on the other hand, you come to France with an open mind and are prepared to be adaptable, then French food will be an exciting adventure and a memorable and worthwhile experience in itself.

FRENCH MEALS

The day begins with *le petit déjeuner* (breakfast), which usually consists of *café au lait* (milky coffee) served in a large cup or, at home, often in a bowl. *Thé* (tea) may be available, but it is usually lukewarm and may be

Taking time over a long leisurely lunch in Lyon

served *au citron* (with lemon). *Chocolat chaud* (hot chocolate), on the other hand, can be truly superb, freshly made with real drinking chocolate and frothy milk, and definitely not just for the kids. Fresh bread, *croissants,* and *pain au chocolat* are the usual breakfast stand-bys and how delicious they can be when fetched still warm from the local *boulangerie,*

Coffee with croissants, *the perfect breakfast*

or, better still, when baked in-house as in most of the best *hôtels-restaurants*. A really good French breakfast should include fresh, unsalted butter (about the only time of day that the French plaster butter on their bread), homemade *confitures* (thick jams and fruit conserves), *miel* (honey), and sometimes *yaourt* (yogurt) and/or *fromage blanc* (fresh, creamy white curd cheese).

Dejeuner (lunch) traditionally has been, and to a large extent remains, the main meal of the day, usually taken between 12:30 and 2 p.m. (though restaurants may stop serving as early as 1:30 p.m.). Make no mistake: this is almost always a substantial, sit-down affair of at least three courses and wine. It is, of course, usually possible in restaurants to eat only a light single-course meal, say, a plate of *charcuterie,* a salad, or an omelet, but it is as well to know that this is not usually done by the French themselves.

Goûter is an afternoon snack, not taken by all, but eaten with great gusto by ravenous schoolchildren filling in the lengthy gap between lunch and dinner. *Le goûter* provides an opportunity to indulge at *salons de thé* or *pâtisseries* in a range of cakes, *tartes,* and desserts, as well as savory snacks accompanied by tea, *tisane* (herbal infusion), or coffee. *Goûters à la ferme* (farmhouse afternoon teas) can be ample and superb.

Le dîner (supper or dinner) is usually eaten between 7 and 9:30 p.m. Dining habits in France have evolved in recent years, particularly now that in so many households both partners go out to work. Thus, even if in theory, dinner may be still considered a somewhat lighter meal than lunch, in practice, both can still be pretty hefty. In fact, in many restaurants, there is no difference between the *menus* offered at midday and in the evening. Even a light, simple dinner is always made up of at least three courses, and a more considered *repas gastronomique* (gourmet meal) may consist of as many as seven or eight separate courses, starting with an *amuse-gueule* (a little tidbit or appetizer served with the *apéritif* "to amuse your palate") and ending with *petits fours* (miniature pastries) served with the coffee.

The Cuisines of France
TYPES AND STYLES

FRENCH CUISINE is probably the finest in the world. Certainly, at its highest level, it can be incredibly complex, refined, and sophisticated, based on classic precepts honed over some 300 years and codified earlier this century by the great chef, Auguste Escoffier. Yet, even at its most basic, French cuisine never fails to surprise and satisfy — a plate of grilled duck breast, thinly sliced and arranged in a fan, a salad of hot, goat's milk cheese, or, to finish, a beautifully glazed *tarte aux pommes*. In all its varied forms, good French cuisine has a Gallic *je ne sais quoi* which remains indescribably beguiling and delicious.

Of course, there is more than one style of French cooking, and it is useful to be aware of different styles and schools, as each may appeal to different tastes and on different occasions.

HAUTE CUISINE — *LA CREME DE LA CREME*

Classic French cuisine is what many of us consider great French cooking to be all

Michel Guérard, master chef, at his restaurant at Eugénie-Les-Bains, Landes

about: richly extravagant, expensive, and making ample use of such luxuries as *foie gras* (fattened duck or goose liver), truffles, lobsters and shellfish, plenty of cream, butter, alcohol, and rich and time-consuming sauces. Not only are the ingredients luxurious, the culinary repertoire and skills needed to produce true *haute cuisine* are considerable and, traditionally, have only been acquired through years of apprenticeship in top restaurants under the guidance of master chefs.

At its best, French *haute cuisine* truly is the epitome of fine western dining, especially in those few elite temples of gastronomy that have earned the profession's highest accolade, three rosettes from Michelin. Some of the finest chefs today have moved on from the rigid precepts of Escoffier to create their own personal styles of "new classic cuisine," and meals in such establishments really are dining at its best. Admittedly, there may be much more at stake than merely the cooking. Rather, the setting, the plates and silver and crystal, the formal service, and the complicated, classic, and rich cuisine combine to create an aura of extreme luxury and exclusivity. Perhaps it has always been so: for *haute cuisine* is also theater, its refined, sophisticated, richly extravagant luxury foods make you feel special, raised above the workaday world of *poulet au pot* (boiled chicken). For those really special occasions, classic and new classic French cuisine can be an experience of a lifetime.

NOUVELLE CUISINE — OLD HAT?

Nouvelle cuisine is no longer new. It developed in the early 70s in reaction to many of the excesses associated with traditional *haute cuisine* and in response to the public taste for essentially lighter, less rich foods. In place of immense quantities of butter, fats, and flour, sauces were made through intense reductions, and with vegetable purees and lighter ingredients such as *fromage blanc* or smaller

In the presence of famous chefs at the Restaurant Paul Bocuse, near Lyon

amounts of *crème fraîche*. Portions, too, were reduced considerably, and in place of full plates, came food pictures, beautiful to look at, if sometimes less than substantial or filling.

Nouvelle cuisine was propelled by a desire to be free from the restraints and strictures of classical cuisine. Thus, a whole range of new, sometimes exciting tastes, flavors, and combinations were tried, many of which were successful, others less so. Undoubtedly, *nouvelle cuisine* freed chefs from old ways of thinking. Even if, today, some of the extremes of the *nouvelle* movement have been abandoned, its precepts have en-couraged and developed a new and exciting philosophy of *cuisine improvisée* — spontaneous, creative cooking using fresh ingredients from the day's market in original and inventive ways. Such creative cooking, at its best, can be thrilling, even exhilarating.

CUISINE MINCEUR — GOURMET SLIMMING CUISINE
It is highly ironic that one of France's greatest three-rosette chefs, Michel Gué-rard, famous for his brilliantly creative *cuisine gourmande,* is located in Eugénie-les-Bains, a minor spa town where French *curistes* come to treat problems of obesity. Because many dieters staying in Eugénie were perforce having to eat a low calorie slimming diet, Monsieur

Guérard saw the opportunity to create *cuisine minceur,* gourmet slimming cuisine, a new style that stealthily addressed health requirements without sacrificing flavor or gastronomic satisfaction.

Michel Guérard achieved this by using almost scientific precepts to replace the fattening ingredients upon which classic cuisine is based with flavorful alternatives as well as by adapting different techniques. Fresh herbs are used extensively, sauces are made by intense reduction, classic ingredients are replaced with often unusual alternatives, and healthy methods of cooking such as steaming and char-broiling are employed.

"Imaginative classic cuisine can be magnificent because classic ingredients give food flavor and sensuality," says Guérard. "The challenge with *cuisine minceur* is to create dishes that have *taste* using ingredients that are not fattening. Food, above all, must taste, it must be sensual, it must give pleasure."

Cuisine minceur, as practiced by Michel Guérard, does just that. Moreover, the influence of Guérard, one of the giants of modern French cooking, is such that many of his principles and precepts have been adopted by chefs throughout France, even though they may not necessarily advertise their cuisine as "*minceur.*"

CUISINE BOURGEOISE
Cuisine bourgeoise, the so-called cooking of the middle classes, is the sort of simple, French home cooking that you will often find in restaurants throughout France, especially those offering a range of inexpensive fixed price *menus.* The foods may be predictable, rarely exciting, but they can be satisfying all the same, and often represent good value for money. Meals often start with simple stand-bys, such as *pâté, museau en vinaigrette* (ox muzzle marinated in *vinaigrette*), or *crudités* (a selection of raw vegetables and salads), and main courses might include *entrecôte* (rib steak), *gigot d'agneau* (roast leg

of lamb), *blanquette de veau* (veal in white sauce), or *truite meunière* (rainbow trout floured and pan-fried), often served with *pommes frites* (French fries) but no other vegetable. A selection of cheeses may follow, and dessert often includes predictable classics like *mousse au chocolat* (chocolate mousse), *tarte aux pommes* (apple tart), or *île flottante* (light egg white soufflés in a lake of custard).

CUISINE REGIONALE

France, of course, is a great country for regional specialties and *produits du terroir,* and many regions boast great and famous dishes which no visitor should miss. Getting a taste of a region through its local dishes is one of the most enjoyable aspects of traveling in France, and one of the principal aims of this book. Moreover, inventive regional cooking should do more than merely recreate classic and famous favorites that have become almost culinary clichés. Rather, regional foods become most exciting when, in the hands of talented chefs, local produce and products are used to create new or personal versions of regional classics, often using *nouvelle* or creative cuisine methods.

The celebrated omelette *at Mère Poulard, Mont-St.-Michel, Normandy*

Bistro foods and wine in a simple but attractively appointed Lyonnais bouchon

SOME FAVORITE NATIONAL STAND-BYS

Boeuf au gros sel Boiled rib of beef, served with coarse sea salt on the side.

Coq au vin Chicken (usually a cockerel) stewed in wine.

Cuisses de grenouille Frog's legs; classically, sautéed in butter, with shallots, and parsley.

Escargots Snails; most usually baked in the shell with parsley and garlic butter.

Langue de boeuf, sauce piquant Boiled beef tongue, served with a sharp, caper sauce.

Lapin à la moutarde Rabbit in a mustard sauce.

Onglet à l'échalote Broiled flank steak served with chopped shallots.

Pot au feu Boiled one-pot meal, usually consisting of beef, chicken, or veal, cooked with vegetables.

Sole meunière Sole or flounder dredged in flour and fried in butter.

Soupe à l'oignon Onion soup, served with a slice of bread or *croûtons* and melted *gruyère* cheese.

Steak-frites Thin slice of beef, usually pan fried rare, and served with French fries.

Tête de veau, sauce gribiche Boiled calf's head, served with sharp mayonnaise made with pickles.

Au Restaurant

EATING OUT IN FRANCE

WHEREVER YOU ARE in France, there is never a shortage of restaurants to choose from, and it is unlikely that you will go far wrong and highly probable that you will be pleasantly surprised, sometimes even astonished.

CHOOSING A RESTAURANT

The number one rule in France, or anywhere else for that matter, is to find a restaurant that is crowded with locals, or at least with French tourists (restaurants that cater for international tourists, even when crowded, may be perfectly acceptable at best, but they inevitably lack genuine, local atmosphere).

By law, all restaurants in France must display a sample *menu* outside. If there is no *menu* outside, or if the one displayed is incomplete or imprecise, ask to have a look at one before you take a table. There is nothing more embarrassing than sitting down at a table, actually starting on the bread, then deciding that, for whatever reason, you have made a dreadful mistake and wish to leave. But should this occur (and it has happened a number of times to us!) don't suffer in silence or let your evening be ruined: explain the situation, offer to pay for anything consumed, and take your leave with as much salvaged style as possible under the circumstances.

To find or locate good restaurants, we usually rely on local knowledge and expertise. That is to say, we always seek advice, from the hotel desk (not always reliable), tourist offices, people in shops or markets, virtually anyone we happen to meet. Most French people have an opinion on such important matters.

A GUIDE TO THE GUIDES

There is no shortage of restaurant guidebooks advising you where to eat. Here is a list of those we consider essential and reliable (publishing details in the bibliography p.248):

Michelin Red Guide First published in 1900, this is still, for many, the grand-daddy of all annual hotel-restaurant guides. Certainly, a rosette or two or the ultimate three is the most coveted accolade that a restaurant can aspire to, and chefs go to great lengths to come close to or to achieve this pinnacle.

Michelin defines a three-rosette restaurant as, "Exceptional cuisine, worth a special journey. Superb food,

Perusing the menu displayed outside a restaurant

fine wines, faultless service, elegant surroundings. One will pay accordingly!" For a three-rosette restaurant provides more than merely food: it approaches a total luxury experience, the sort that most of us reserve for special occasions. Better value, in terms of food alone, can sometimes be enjoyed in restaurants with only one or two rosettes (still remarkable and noteworthy achievements), and *"repas"* printed in red before the price of the *menus* indicates restaurants offering "good food at moderate prices."

Michelin is still something of the standard against which all other guides are judged, but we do find its shorthand format of merely listing establishments, with no text describing what to expect, to be rather dry and dated.

Gault Millau G-M is the only serious competition to Michelin. This idiosyncratic and personal guide manages to cover comprehensively a range of types and styles of restaurants at all levels.

G-M has been credited (and by some, blamed) for proselytizing the gospel of *nouvelle cuisine,* and, indeed, this opinionated guide distinguishes excellence not only by the number of *toques* (chef's hats) granted (up to a maximum four), but also by their color: red, to indicate creative cuisine; black, traditional. Regional cooking is also singled out by the *"laurier du terroir"* symbol for restaurants that give particular pride of place to traditional (or revived) regional recipes.

G-M states unequivocally that it grants its accolades to restaurants based only on the quality of the cooking, not on the depth of the cushions in the lounge, or any of the other considerable trappings usually associated with three-rosette Michelin luxury.

Logis de France This guide lists small and medium-sized, independent, usually family run hotels, and we consider them to be some of the most congenial places to stay in France. Many *logis* have quite adequate restaurants which are certainly worth eating in if you are staying in the hotel. Moreover, the Fédération Logis encourages and gives annual awards to restaurants serving *cuisine du terroir* (regional cooking), and those establishments that have won such accolades (listed separately in the front of the guide), are certainly worth a visit.

Relais Routiers The French truck driver's bible, this is the guide to roadside restaurants usually serving wholesome, inexpensive, copious, set-price meals to a discerning (and hungry) clientele. Such establishments are marked by the Relais Routier sign outside the door, but they are usually most easily found by the number of immense semis and European juggernauts lined along the roads outside at lunchtime.

Bienvenue à la Ferme Useful guide to all aspects of farmhouse tourism, and an essential source for hard-to-find details of *fermes auberges* (farmhouse restaurants), as well as farms offering *chambres d'hôtes* (bed and breakfast) and *table d'hôte* (home-cooked meals, often taken with the host).

One of the finest and most famous restaurants in France, near Lyon

TYPES OF EATING ESTABLISHMENTS

There are scores of different types of places to go out to eat. The following are those most frequently encountered:

Auberge This signifies an inn, and may offer rooms as well as meals. As in hotel-restaurants, an *auberge* may offer *demi-pension* or *pension* rates per person which include the room, breakfast, and full lunch and/or dinner. *Auberges* can range from rustic inns to the most stylish and expensive country hotel-restaurants.

Bar à vins Wine bars, usually found in city centers, provide a good range of wines by the glass or bottle, served usually with either simple drinking snacks, or the daily specials, *plats du jour*.

Bistro A bistro usually signifies a small, intimate, and fairly informal place to eat, in theory, inexpensive, although *chic* and fashionable bistros can be as expensive as good restaurants. More often than not, a bistro will offer a range of *plats du jour* (dishes of the day) as well as foods chosen from the *carte* rather than a selection of fixed-price *menus*.

Brasserie Strictly speaking, this is a city center phenomenon, usually, a large, bright, busy beerhouse (hence the name), serving shellfish, *plats du jour,* draft beer, and wines by the bottle, carafe, or glass. It is always acceptable to order simply one course, if you wish.

Café or **café-bar** The café or bar (see p.65), though mainly providing drinks, can also do quick snack foods and sandwiches, useful when you do not have the time or inclination for a full meal.

Crêperie Informal restaurant serving *galettes* (savory buckwheat pancakes) as well as sweet French *crêpes* (wheat pancakes), traditionally accompanied by dry, naturally sparkling, alcoholic farm cider (see pp.132–133).

Ferme-auberge Farmhouse restaurants must, if authentic, mainly use their own produce or that from neighboring farms and prepare local home-cooked dishes that respect regional traditions. Most

Dining for two at Le Vigneron, Reims

fermes-auberges pride themselves on ensuring country satisfaction by serving foods in enormous quantity, cooked usually by the mother (or grandmother), with father and children helping out with the service. Often, meals are eaten informally at communal trestle tables. *Fermes-auberges* can provide outstanding opportunities not only to taste authentic and always fresh produce of the land, but also to meet local country people. Many *fermes-auberges* also offer accommodation (see pp.156–157).

Libre-service Self-service restaurants *"Le self"* are French cafeterias in roadside service areas, shopping malls, and city centers and can provide quick, wholesome meals at reasonable prices.

Restaurant Restaurants range from the extremely simple and unpretentious to the famous and luxurious, from typical family-run places to grand *châteaux-hôtels*. Full, three-course meals are usually eaten at restaurants, either from fixed-price *menus* or chosen from the *carte* (the menu).

Saladerie Salad restaurants have cropped up increasingly in recent years, usually providing a range of main-course salads to cater both for vegetarians as well as for those who may prefer a lighter meal, especially at midday.

Salon de thé A tea room may not sound very French, but we have come across a growing number of such establishments, usually serving English tea (with milk or lemon), *tisanes* (herbal infusions), and light snacks and desserts.

Wistub or **winstub** Mainly an Alsatian type of wine bar, the sort of informal place that serves good wines by the glass, carafe, or bottle, together with both informal drinking foods (such as *tarte flambée,* a sort of "pizza" topped with cream cheese, onions, and bacon), as well as more elaborate regional classics.

LE MENU OR *A LA CARTE*?

From the most basic hostelry to the grandest château, restaurants in France invariably offer a choice of both fixed-price *menus* consisting of several courses and meals chosen separately from *la carte* (the menu). In inexpensive restaurants, there may be, for example, a choice of *menus* at, say, 75 F., 110 F., and 150 F.,

Setting a table for lunch outdoors — with Gallic precision and style

each, in theory, offering more enticing, more appetizing, or more luxurious foods. Each will consist of at least a first course, main course, and cheese or dessert (the more expensive *menus* include cheese and dessert). If you choose from the *carte,* on the other hand, then it is up to you to select each course separately, from appetizer or first course, entrée or main course, cheese and/or dessert.

Menus, it must be said, usually offer irresistible *rapport qualité-prix* (value for money): if you were to add up the cost of the items as individually priced on the *carte,* the all-inclusive *menu* is always considerably cheaper. Even at top restaurants, a *menu* proposed by the chef is often outstanding value. On the other hand, though there is often a choice of items from each course, it is not usually possible to deviate from *menus,* so they are only worth considering if what is on offer is really what you would like to eat.

The *carte* can be more interesting and exciting and where the skill of the chef most fully revealed. However, beware a restaurant with an overly long *carte,* for it would clearly not be possible to keep all such ingredients fresh on hand daily: some chefs, even in well-reputed restaurants resort to using dishes prepared and packaged *sous vide* (chilled and vacuum-packed) to be reheated.

Generally speaking, therefore, our advice is: first, peruse the fixed-price *menus* and choose one if *all* the courses offered really are what you want to eat. If not, choose from the *carte,* but ask the waiter's advice for what is really good and fresh that day.

TYPES OF MENUS

Menu de la mer Seafood menu, with appetizer and main course of fish or shellfish.

Menu d'affaires To be avoided: a menu devised to accommodate the *homme d'affaires* (businessman), to whom time, of course, is money. At such places, you are likely to be irritated by the constant disturbance of mobile phones ringing as businessmen discuss, as the Little Prince would say, "matters of consequence."

Menu d'enfant In theory, a good idea, but children's menus often consist of little more than *jambon frites* (a slice of cold ham and French fries), or the ubiquitous *steak hâché* (a fancy name for a hamburger), followed by a pre-packaged dessert and a fizzy drink. Better, often, we feel, to choose something off the *carte,* such as an omelet, grilled sausages, or a bowl of steamed mussels.

Menu dégustation "Tasting menu" consisting of as many as five to eight tiny courses (no more than a bite or two each) which allow chefs to show off their expertise and diners to experience a range of exciting and contrasting tastes. Sometimes accompanied by suggested wines with each course.

Menu du terroir Regional menu.

Menu du marché Menu based on whatever the chef has found fresh and good at market that morning. Changes daily or weekly.

Menu gastronomique or **menu gourmand** Menu with extravagant or richly luxurious specialties.

CASSE-CROUTE — SNACKING

There are times when you may have neither the inclination nor the opportunity to plan either a full meal in a restaurant or even get together the wherewithal for a picnic, times when you simply need a quick bite, French style. Bars and cafés can fill this need most ably, and are usually open all day and late into the night serving the likes of:

Croque madame The same as *croque monsieur,* but with a fried egg.

Croque monsieur Sort of open-faced toasted cheese and ham sandwich.

Frites French fries.

Huîtres Oysters; a dozen or so together with a glass or two of Muscadet.

The casual and homey setting of a farmhouse restaurant

Mâchon A Lyonnais term for a mid-morning snack: usually comprises a plate of *charcuterie* served with sharp, vinegary pickles, and a *pot* (46-cl. bottle or under a pint) of Beaujolais to wash it down.

Moules-frites Favorite snack in the North, a steaming bowl of mussels accompanied by French fries served with mayonnaise.

Omelette Omelet; **aux fines herbes** with fresh or dried mixed herbs; **au fromage** with cheese; **au jambon** with ham.

Quiche lorraine Try a slice of the classic *quiche,* made with cream, eggs, and bacon, or other variations on offer throughout the country.

Sandwich Usually a split buttered *baguette* filled **au fromage** with cheese; **au jambon** with ham; **au pâté** with *pâté;* **au saucisson** with salami.

Steak-frites Thin, broiled or pan-fried steak served with French fries.

Tarte aux pommes A slice of glazed apple tart together with a *grand café crème* (large double espresso with steamed milk) will help stave off hunger pangs between meals.

Tartines Open-faced sandwiches spread with any number of ingredients, including warm goat's milk cheese, *rillettes* (pork, duck, or goose spread), *foie* *gras* (fattened duck or goose liver), coarse, country *pâté,* or much else — a couple make a good snack together with a glass or two of *vin rouge*.

LE FAST FOOD AND GOING ETHNIC

France has embraced American-style fast food with a vengeance, a fact bemoaned by traditionalists and French gourmands alike, not to mention the Académie Française (the organization charged with preserving French culture and language). There is now a McDonald's on the Champs Elysées as well as other similar chain outlets in almost every city or town.

But before popping in for *le hamburger,* consider both fast food French style, including *crêpes* and buckwheat *galettes,* as well as such tempting ethnic fare as *merguez* (spicy mutton sausage), *couscous* (North African medley of steamed semolina topped with spicy lamb, vegetables, or fish), Vietnamese fried savories, often available from market stalls, or, near the Spanish and Italian borders respectively, *paella* and pasta and pizza.

A menu de la mer at a seaside restaurant

L'ADDITION — PAYING AND TIPPING

At the end of any meal — good, bad, or indifferent — comes *l'addition,* the check. The good news is that in France, the bottom line is what you pay, for restaurant prices almost always include both IVA (sales tax) as well as tip *(service compris)* in the prices stated on the *menu* or *carte*. Strictly speaking, you are not expected to leave any additional remuneration and you should certainly never feel pressured into doing so. But as always, if you have received extra special attention or would like to reward good service, then an additional five to ten per cent added to the check will be all the more appreciated since it will not have been wholly expected.

Credit cards are now widely accepted in France, notably, Visa and MasterCard, and to a lesser extent, American Express and Diners. But in rural areas, in particular, first check whether credit cards are accepted if you have no other means of payment.

RESTAURANT-SPEAK — SOME USEFUL PHRASES

S'il vous plaît (s.v.p.) Please

**Je voudrais réserver une table ...,
s.v.p.** I would like to reserve a table ..., please.

Nous sommes deux/quatre There are two/four of us.

Pourriez-vous me recommander des spécialités de la maison? Can you recommend the house specialties?

Je voudrais voir la carte des vins, s.v.p. I would like to see the wine list, please.

Puis-j'avoir ... Can I have ...

Une autre ..., s.v.p. I would like another ..., please.

Où sont les toilettes? Where are the restrooms?

L'addition, s.v.p. The check, please.

C'est compris, le service? Is service included?

Merci bien Thank you very much.

Nous avons très bien mangé, merci We really enjoyed our meal, thank you.

Le Pique-Nique
IMPROMPTU MEALS OUTDOORS

UNDOUBTEDLY, SOME of the finest meals you can have in France will be enjoyed outside, *en plein air.* For, if *le pique-nique* is yet another example of *"le franglais,"* English words adopted by the French and so hated by the purist Académie Française, picnicking itself is quintessentially and indubitably French.

With its wide open country and airy parks and central squares in every city, town, or village, France easily lends itself to relaxed eating outdoors. Wooden picnic tables, set up by roadside rest areas, parks, and woods, inevitably begin to fill up by midday in fine weather: red and white checked tablecloths are spread out, plates, knives, and forks laid, and bottles of wine and water brought out.

Picnics provide excellent opportunities to taste and enjoy regional breads, *charcuterie,* and cheeses. Rather than simply buying a *baguette* and a *camembert* or some *pâté* (as delicious as that simple repast can be), take the opportunity to seek out local produce and products as well as fresh

A loaf of bread, a glass of wine, some local reblochon *cheese, by the banks of Lake Annecy, Savoie*

seasonal fruits and vegetables, at specialist shops or in markets, to be washed down with local or regional wines.

Another picnic idea that we find hard to resist is a hot chicken, bought from a market stall that spit-roasts a bank of birds, enticingly timed to be always just ready when you are at your hungriest — at about midday.

When we are by the sea, we love to buy oysters, to be shucked sitting by the water, then sucked off the shimmering half-shell with no more than a squeeze of lemon, a gulp of chilled white wine, a hunk of bread.

Picnics also provide the opportunity to sample luxury foods — the money saved from not eating in restaurants means that you can splurge on a jar of *foie gras mi-cuit,* a half-bottle of really good Sauternes (the classic combination), and still come out with change from what would have been spent on a mediocre meal in a restaurant. Or else, visit a good *traiteur* for ready-to-take-out foods. The only thing left is to find that perfect, secluded spot ...

GOOD PICNIC FOODS

In addition to the *charcuterie,* a good *traiteur* is the place to come for the ingredients of a really special picnic. Try some of the following:

Carottes rapées Grated carrot in a *vinaigrette* dressing.

Céleri-rémoulade Shredded celeriac dressed in mayonnaise.

Champignons à la grecque Marinated mushrooms.

Foie gras Purchase a jar of *foie gras mi-cuit* for a luxury picnic.

Museau en vinaigrette Cold meat salad of pressed ox muzzle served in slices in a *vinaigrette* dressing.

Pâté en croûte *Pâté* encased in a baked pastry crust.

Rosbif Rare roast beef, sliced.

Salade de tomates Tomato salad.

Saumon en gelée Salmon steak, poached then glazed in a wine gelatin.

Tabbouleh Middle Eastern salad, made from cracked bulgar wheat, chopped parsley, and fresh mint.

A Noble Tradition

THE WINES OF FRANCE

FOR CENTURIES, FRANCE HAS BASKED in its reputation for producing the greatest wines in the world. That position essentially remains unchallenged, in spite of intense competition from both traditional as well as newly emerging wine countries. The reason is quite simple: France has produced and continues to produce virtually all the world's classics, wines that everyone else is trying to approach or imitate.

Cabernet Sauvignon and Chardonnay, for example, may be the world's runaway favorite wine grapes, but the generic varietals produced from each have as their role models red Bordeaux and white Burgundy, unarguably, at best, still among the very greatest wines in the world. Most sparkling wines seek to emulate the fresh, racy, sometimes deep and biscuity flavors of Champagne. Light, fruity reds, vinified to be drunk immediately, have as their archetype Beaujolais, and zesty, herbaceous wines produced from the distinctive Sauvignon Blanc, whether in other parts of France or as far away as New Zealand or California, can, at their very best, rival if rarely surpass the great wines of Sancerre and Pouilly Fumé. Pinot Noir, of course, is the great grape of Burgundy: if today it has been transplanted to Spain, Oregon, California, Australia, or New Zealand, the benchmark for this silky, hauntingly scented, and most seductive of wines still is and always will remain the fabled slopes of the Côte d'Or.

If, for us, the world of wine is a big and exciting place which we can roam and eclectically explore through a wineglass, for the French, it begins and ends, quite simply, in their own country, even sometimes,

Vines stretching endlessly in Languedoc

their own region or locality. "Why drink wines from anywhere else," they say with that inimitable and self-assured Gallic shrug, "when our own are the standards against which all others are measured." Why indeed? For the wine lover weaned on wines from throughout the world, a visit to France can become something of a wine pilgrimage, an opportunity to visit the shrine, and to taste at source the benchmark classics of the world.

Yet, the pleasures of drinking wine in France are by no means confined to the great, expensive, and sometimes unapproachable. France offers nearly every type and style of wine under the sun: the classic, the archetypal, the unattainably expensive, certainly, as well as the strictly local and forgettable, the *vin de table* in five-star returnable bottles that is about as exciting as the *carafe* of tap water offered alongside. And there is every shade in between, from exquisitely light, delicate wines from cool northern vineyards to pungent fortified wines made from grapes that bake in the Midi sun; wines ranging from the faintest pale green in color through the vinous spectrum of pinks, ruby, and precious garnet to brick red and almost black. French wine is nothing if not vivid, varied, and complex.

Our advice, as always, is: be adventurous, enquiring about all matters of taste, not least of all wine. By all means enjoy and compare the great classics at source, but don't shun the less well-known yet still characterful country wines of France either. And above all, put aside any prejudices and preconceived tastes in order to sample the full gamut of French wine in all its glory. *A votre santé!*

THE FRENCH PARADOX

In spite of their high fat diets and other contradictory lifestyle habits, the French have a considerably lower incidence of coronary disease — less than half the rate, in fact, than of the Americans. This is the so-called French paradox. Over the last two decades, there have been extensive studies carried out internationally in an attempt to understand this, and, though not yet entirely conclusive, research suggests that key factors include moderate consumption of wine (particularly red wine) with meals, combined with a healthy Mediterranean diet based on using olive oil in place of butter, and regular consumption of plenty of fresh fruits and vegetables.

Before you reach for the cork-screw, however, remember, France has one of the highest rates of cirrhosis of the liver. But enough evidence has been collected to suggest that, if we enjoy wine in moderation, then, when in France, we should continue to do so. It certainly makes life more pleasurable, and, who knows, it may even help us to live longer.

Les Grands Vins

THE GREAT CLASSICS

FRANCE IS THE ONLY COUNTRY in the world that has so meticulously studied, classified, and cataloged its wines and vineyards over the course of not merely decades but centuries.

Elsewhere in Europe, in Italy or Spain for example, the concept of fine wine as a precious commodity rather than a daily, unremarkable one is a relatively recent phenomenon. In France, on the other hand, vineyards producing wines praised by popes, kings, or emperors centuries ago have been cultivated uninterrupted down the ages and their wines still rank unchallenged as the greatest in the world.

Through stringent observation carried out in part by the Church (once probably the most important landowner in the country), and through tradition based on excellent results, the French defined and delineated long ago those regions, communities, even individual plots of land that have historically produced the finest wines. This contrasts with New World wine producing countries with little or no tradition or historical antecedents; they, on the other hand, are freer to experiment with huge ranges of new grape varieties and selected clones of grape varieties and methods of training, and to plant vineyards on lands never before cultivated with *Vitis vinifera*.

In France, centuries of trial and error have demonstrated that certain grape varieties have definite affinities to particular regions, and that particular methods of wine-making gave and still give the best results in different areas. Thus, the Gamay grape was banned from Burgundy's Côte d'Or, retiring instead to splendid isolation in the granite hills of the Beaujolais to the south. The blind cellarmaster Dom Pérignon proved that

The cellars of Château Mouton-Rothschild, Bordeaux

Champagne was best produced with a *cuvée* of wines made from Chardonnay, Pinot Noir, and Pinot Meunier, the generally accepted *assemblage* that is still used today. And accordingly, while Cabernet Sauvignon has been planted in virtually every wine region of the world, one place it would most certainly never appear would be Burgundy, any more than Pinot Noir would ever be tried in the Médoc.

Iconoclasts and those of us raised in a less certain world might well ask why not. The fact is that, just as the Académie Française is charged with the protection of the French language and culture and carries out this task with a zeal that seems to border, at times, on the fanatical, so is the concept of French fine wine, above all else, based on the sacred and unshakable principles of *typicité* and *terroir*.

Typicité charges that a wine must demonstrate the character of its region or locality, not that borrowed from somewhere else; it must be typical of its *terroir,* that all embracing term which means not only the land but also its precise geographical location and microclimate.

Great wine in France historically has been synonymous with wine that could be kept for lengthy periods, even improving in the process. This arose from the fact that, before the basic principles of fermentation were discovered by Louis Pasteur, wines were essentially perishable, save those concentrated enough in extract, tannin, and alcohol to protect them from the effects of acetification and premature spoilage.

Today, great French wines are still those that are the longest lived (with the exception of Champagne, though there is also a taste, and market, for aged vintages). The Bordelais, almost alone in the world, are able to create an *en primeur* market each year, getting connoisseurs and wine merchants to stump up for wines that are not even yet in the bottle, and which, once bottled, may need to be left for a decade or longer before they are ready to drink.

The following are what we consider to be the classic wines of France. Remember, all of them can be enjoyed in all their forms, from the most prestigious and expensive to affordable, generic examples.

Vineyards of St.-Emilion, Bordeaux

Red Bordeaux Cabernet Sauvignon based examples from classified châteaux in the Médoc and Graves, and Merlot/ Cabernet Franc based wines from Pomerol and St.-Emilion. Remember, the French themselves often enjoy red Bordeaux when young and not fully mature or developed. Such youthful wines can be hard and tannic.

Red Burgundy Pinot Noir wines from the individual named communes and vineyards in the Côte de Nuits and Côte de Beaune of the Côte d'Or. Silky, powerful, with the haunting character typical of Pinot Noir.

White Burgundy Great white wines produced from Chardonnay grapes grown in Chablis, Côte de Beaune, Côte Chalonnaise, and the Mâconnais. Many top examples are vinified and aged in new oak barrels.

Sauternes and **Barsac** Sweet dessert classics produced in the best years from Sémillon and Sauvignon grapes, affected by *pourriture noble* (noble rot), a natural process that concentrates grape sugar and glycerin. The wines are luscious, unctuous, dessert marvels. Try such wines by the glass or half-bottle.

Champagne Sparkling wine produced from *cuvées* of Chardonnay, Pinot Noir, and Pinot Meunier, by an elaborate process of secondary fermentation in the bottle (see p.93) followed by strict aging discipline. Excellent examples come from both famous *grandes maisons* as well as from *récoltants-manipulants*.

Northern Rhône Red Syrah wines from Côte Rôtie, St.-Joseph, Cornas, and Hermitage, and white wine from Condrieu, produced from the exciting and relatively rare Viognier grape.

Southern Rhône Classic red Rhône wine produced from a cocktail of Mediterranean grape varieties, especially from named communities such as Châteauneuf-du-Pape, Gigondas, and Vacqueyras.

Varietal wines from Alsace Single grape, aromatic wines from Alsace are made from grapes such as Riesling, Gewürztraminer, Pinot Gris, and Muscat, vinified in the classic French style as dry, characterful wines to enjoy with food. In certain years, small amounts of outstanding late-harvested sweet wines are also produced.

Sauvignon wines from the Loire and the Central Vineyards Pungent yet elegant white wines from the distinctive Sauvignon grape come from around the towns of Sancerre and Pouilly-sur-Loire (Pouilly Fumé).

Sweet wines from the Loire Great but undervalued and little-known sweet wines, produced from the Chenin Blanc grape affected in best years by noble rot, notably at Vouvray, Montlouis, Quarts de Chaume, and Bonnezeaux.

Appellation d'Origine Contrôlée
CLASSIFICATIONS OF QUALITY

THE SYSTEM of classification for French wines, *appellation d'origine contrôlée* (AC), is the most precise and highly developed system in the world for guaranteeing authenticity and origin of wines as well as for controlling and safeguarding place names. Indeed, it is the model upon which most other countries have based their own systems.

A story in every bottle

This rational, empirical system, derived from close observation and tradition over centuries, and securely anchored to the French concept of *terroir,* classifies and defines wines by their exact geographical locations, and, at the same time, lays down rigid strictures relating to permitted grape varieties, yields per hectare (2½ acres), and methods of cultivation and production.

The essential rationale behind the system is that the physical environment — *terroir* — is the determinant of quality as well as individual grape character: the greater the wine, the more precisely can its *terroir* be pinpointed.

Thus, within a broad and large defined wine region, AC is granted first broadly (Bourgogne AC or Bordeaux AC), then, gradually more precisely, by sub-region (Côte de Beaune AC, Entre-Deux-Mers AC), individual community (Margaux AC, Gevrey-Chambertin AC), or, even, in exceptional cases, individual parcel or vineyard (La Tâche AC, Le Montrachet AC). The rationale is that, at any level, the character of the defined *terroir* should be evident in the wine itself. Thus, the more precise the *appellation,* in theory, the greater the wine, for only exceptional wines are able to make particular statements about their precise *terroir.*

THE CLASSIFICATION OF 1855
Unlike Burgundy, Bordeaux classified its greatest wines not by individual *appellations* relating to actual vineyards, but by a ranking undertaken in 1855 based largely on the historical prices that the wines of the Médoc (and one Graves) and Sauternes had fetched.

Here, the rationale was equally logical: wines that had historically commanded the highest prices should be the greatest (see p.158).

SAVOIR LIRE — READING THE LABEL

Mis en bouteille au château/ domaine Estate bottled.

Négociant Wine merchant.

Négociant–éleveur A wine merchant who purchases wines for blending and aging.

Propriétaire–récoltant Grower: indicates wine made with own grapes.

Récolte Vintage.

Alcoholic strength Expressed in percentage per volume.

Grand cru, Grand cru classé Classified wine.

Grand Vin Term loosely applied with no legal significance.

Elevé en fûts de chêne Wine that has spent some time in oak barrels.

Cuvée prestige, tête de cuvée, réserve, grande réserve Arbitrary terms that indicate wines that have undergone a more rigorous selection process.

Médaille d'or/d'argent Gold- or silver-medal winning wines from national or regional wine fairs; can be helpful when choosing wines.

Lesser Appellations and Vins de Pays
REGIONAL AND COUNTRY WINES

FRANCE IS BY NO MEANS a country simply for wine connoisseurs or the very rich wine drinker. Many of the most enjoyable bottles you will come across are often local country wines with names you may never have heard before, made by local growers or in cooperative wineries, at best capable of demonstrating the character and provenance of their origin at affordable prices.

French country wines, whether minor AC, VDQS, or *vins de pays,* can do this, and for the wine drinker, there is an almost embarrassing wealth of them to discover nearly everywhere in France. Indeed, there are very few regions that do not boast their own local country wines (even virtually vineless Brittany manages to claim Gros Plant de Pays Nantais and Muscadet as its own). So, wherever you happen to be, it is worth asking for advice and sampling local wines.

What makes a country wine? There is really no precise definition; in fact, the term is rather vague, imprecise but suggestive. I consider a country wine primarily one that, while it may or may not ever be encountered outside of its zone of production, nonetheless demonstrates regional or local character at an affordable price. Many unknown as well as little encountered AC wines fall into this category, which also includes, almost by definition, wines produced under the VDQS and *vins de pays* classifications.

VDQS — *VIN DELIMITE DE QUALITE SUPERIEURE*

This classification stands somewhere between select *appellation d'origine* status and the more lowly *vins de pays.* It also stands as a guarantee of quality for the consumer, for VDQS wines, like AC, must adhere to strictures (usually less rigid) relating to permitted grape varieties, yields, minimum alcohol levels, and methods of production.

VINS DE PAYS

Literally "country wines," this classification covers an immense number and quantity of minor but often extremely satisfying and still very inexpensive wines which are made the length and breadth of the country. The *vin de pays* classification can cover wines made in broad geographical regions (*vins de pays régionaux,* such as Vin de Pays du Jardin de la France from the Loire Valley), from specific *départements* (*vins de pays départementaux,* such as Vin de Pays du Gard), or from individual specified zones (*vins de pays de zone,* such as Vin de Pays Charentais).

Vineyards on hills overlooking Port Grimaud, the Côte d'Azur

A Full and Varied Spectrum
TYPES AND STYLES OF WINES

Wine is no more than the fermented juice of grapes, but what a fascinating variety exists within this simple definition! Undoubtedly, the plethora of types and styles, confusing names and *appellations* can be baffling for the less than single-minded visitor. The following are the broad types of wine available, together with some suggestions for each.

LIGHT, DRY WHITE WINES
Though the French drink far more red wine than white, there is no shortage of enjoyable, well-made simple dry white wines for everyday drinking. Ask for a *vin blanc sec* or specify wines such as Muscadet, Saumur, Pineau de la Loire, Entre-Deux-Mers, Bordeaux Blanc, Bourgogne Blanc, Bourgogne Aligoté, Petit Chablis, or *vins de pays,* such as Côtes de Gascogne or Jardin de la France.

MEDIUM-DRY WHITES
Medium-dry white wines in France may be known as *vin blanc demi-sec* or *moelleux,* and can range from the just off-dry to the fairly sweet. Good examples come from Vouvray, Montlouis, and Coteaux du Layon, all in the Loire Valley.

MEDIUM- TO FULL-BODIED WHITES
This category includes an immense range of white wines made from numerous grape varieties, some vinified and/or aged in oak barrels. Medium- and full-bodied white wines are often best enjoyed with food. Excellent examples are Chablis, Sancerre, Pouilly Fuissé, Pouilly Fumé, Savennières, Mâcon, Montagny, and white Châteauneuf-du-Pape.

AROMATIC WHITES
White wines made from aromatic grape varieties include the range of varietals from Alsace: Riesling, Gewürztraminer, Pinot Gris, Sylvaner, Pinot Blanc, and Muscat. Characterful Muscat wines, with the intense, grapy fragrance of that odoriferous variety, are also produced elsewhere, notably in the Midi, where they are usually fortified.

ROSE WINES
Pink wines, for some reason, are shunned by wine connoisseurs as not being serious or worthy of consideration. The best, from Tavel, Lirac, Coteaux d'Aix-en-Provence, or Côtes de Provence, combine fruity freshness with full body. Good *rosés* also include Bourgogne

Vineyards of Coteaux d'Aix-en-Provence

Marsannay, Sancerre, and Bordeaux *clairet,* but those from the Loire, especially Rosé d'Anjou, are often too sweet for our tastes.

LIGHT, FRUITY REDS

Wines produced in whole or part by a method of whole grape vinification known as *macération carbonique* (carbonic maceration) can be delightful, to be enjoyed young, within a year or two at most of their production. Wines pro-

The steeply terraced vineyards at Banyuls, Roussillon

duced by this method gain intense fruity aromas, plenty of color, but only a minimum of tannin. Good examples include Beaujolais, Mâcon, many young wines from Côtes du Rhône, Côtes de Provence, Minervois, Corbières. Good, light, fruity red wines also come from the Loire, notably, Chinon, Bourgueil, St.-Nicolas-de-Bourgueil, and Saumur-Champigny.

MEDIUM- AND FULL-BODIED REDS

There is no shortage in France of good, medium- to full-bodied red wines that pack in plenty of flavor, tannin, and alcohol. These can range from classics such as red Bordeaux, Burgundy, and Côtes du Rhône, to less well-known but eminently satisfying country wines, including Madiran, Cahors, Bergerac, Fitou, Collioure, Côtes de Buzet, and many more.

RED WINES FOR LAYING DOWN — *VINS DE GARDE*

Wines for laying down need to be vinified with sufficient alcohol and tannin so that they can be kept for lengthy periods. Conversely, this means that they are often too hard and unforgiving when consumed young. Classic *grands crus classés* from individual communes and châteaux in Bordeaux, *premiers* and *grands crus* from

Burgundy, and full-bodied wines from the Rhône Valley are the traditional wines to lay down. These are the wines to purchase for special occasions in the future — so always ask for advice on individual properties and vintages (see pp.244–245).

SWEET WINES AND FORTIFIED SWEET WINES

Great sweet white wines, produced in the best years from grapes affected by *pourriture noble* (noble rot) come from Sauternes, Barsac, Monbazillac, and the Loire communities of Quarts de Chaume, Bonnezeaux, Vouvray, and Montlouis. Excellent *Sélection de Grains Nobles* dessert wines are also made in Alsace in the best years only.

Fortified sweet wines are the specialty of the Midi, and outstanding examples are produced from Muscat grapes at Beaumes-de-Venise, Rivesaltes, Lunel, and Frontignan. Red fortified wines, port-like in character, come from Banyuls and Rasteau.

SPARKLING WINES

Sparkling wines are produced by either the classic method of secondary fermentation in the bottle (see p.93); the *charmat* or *cuve close* method, whereby secondary fermentation takes place in an autoclave (a sealed tank) before the wines are bottled; or, the cheapest but least successful method, simply by pumping carbon dioxide into still wines.

Champagne, of course, is unique, but other successful sparkling wines made by the classic method come from Saumur and Vouvray (Crémant de Loire), Limoux (Blanquette or Crémant de Limoux), Die (Crémant de Die), Burgundy (Crémant de Bourgogne), and Alsace (Crémant d'Alsace).

No Hard and Fast Rules

WINE WITH FOOD

ONE OF LIFE'S great mysteries, some would have us believe, is matching the "correct" wine with food. Taste, in all things, is very much a matter of personal preference, and, frankly, we believe you should drink what you like with whatever you want.

Even general dictates such as white wine being obligatory with fish may not sometimes be apt: salmon is often best partnered with a light red wine, while *morue* (salt cod) can stand up to a full-bodied red.

That said, we believe firmly that regional foods in France are best partnered by local wines. Lamb that has grazed on the *garrigues* (herb-scented scrubby uplands) of the Alpilles is best partnered by a red Les Baux-de-Provence, the warm, herbal tones of the wine accentuating the rather assertive, herby flavor of the meat. *Fines de claires* (oysters from the Marennes) are most delicious with an inexpensive, lemony Vin de Pays

Roquefort *and Barsac, a* perfect combination

Charentais. *Coq au vin* in Burgundy positively cries out for a comforting red from the Côte de Beaune, and a steaming platter of *choucroute garnie* in Alsace is partnered by nothing so well as a full-bodied Pinot Gris.

Just as there are regional combinations of wine and food that are inseparable, so there are classic combinations that can be fascinating to try. *Foie gras,* that most unctuous and luxurious food, is partnered best with a similarly unctuous and rich, sweet classic, such as Sauternes or Barsac. *Roquefort,* unusually, also goes well with a similar sweet wine, the rich, salty flavor of the cheese complemented by the weight, depth of flavor, and sweetness of the wine.

Consult our food and wine suggestions in the back of the book (pp.246–247) by all means, but don't worry overly about matching foods and wines. The French themselves are much more relaxed about this than we often are. Above all, use, common sense.

LA CARTE DES VINS — CHOOSING WINE IN RESTAURANTS

In French restaurants, the choice is generally whether to opt for the *vin de la maison* (house wine) or to choose something better from the *carte des vins* (wine list). Generally speaking, even in inexpensive restaurants, red house wines are often quite drinkable, especially if you specify that you would like the *réserve de la maison* (house reserve), which usually costs only a few francs more. House white wines, on the other hand, are more variable and less consistently reliable.

In France, as often elsewhere, restaurants, unfortunately, mark up wine prices considerably. Normally, the better the restaurant, the more heavily weighted is its list toward Bordeaux (unless you are in Burgundy).

Most French wine lists are arranged both by region and color. Begin, always, by looking at the local wines and, if in doubt, ask the *sommelier* (wine waiter) for a recommendation.

When tasting wine, look out for the off, musty smell and flavor that indicates a corked bottle (unfortunately, an increasingly common occurrence). If you are unsure, ask the *sommelier* to sample the wine.

Visitez les Caves
S T O P   T O   T A S T E ;   S T O P   T O   B U Y

O NE OF the most enjoyable aspects of touring the French country for the wine lover is the chance to taste and buy wines direct at source, *chez le viticulteur.*

Indeed, such "wine tourism" is more highly developed in France than in any other wine producing country we have visited, and producers — even world-famous ones — are well used to visitors knocking on their doors in order to taste wines and perhaps buy a few bottles or more.

In all of the classic wine regions of France, as well as throughout many minor ones too, there are sign-posted *routes du vin,* quiet roads that meander through the vineyards and wine country, passing along the way scores of individual wine producers, *négociants* (wine merchants), and *caves coopératives* (wine cooperatives), where you can taste and buy their wines.

In those regions where international prestige and image are most at stake, large, well-known firms may keep "open house" and offer free tours of cellars and aging *chais,* with multilingual guides on hand to take you through the cellars and offer you a drink at the end of it all.

Elsewhere, small individual growers

A selection of wines on sale from a négociant

welcome visitors for the not insignificant direct sales that may result. Tasting and buying wine direct not only allows you to view the vineyards from where a wine is produced, and to taste before you buy, it also provides the opportunity to meet the winegrowers themselves.

In the second part of the book, we have included the names and addresses of wine properties of all types that receive visitors. It is important, however, to telephone (or have your hotel do so) in advance, simply to make sure that someone is on hand to receive you. If there are particular wine estates that you are especially keen to see, prior to your visit, ask the wine importer or agent in your country to write a letter of introduction for you.

BUYING WINE *EN VRAC*

One of the most economical ways of buying wine in France is *en vrac,* i.e., unbottled, either decanted into your own container, or else decanted into the winery's own five-, ten-, or even 25-liter containers (about 1¼ to 6¼ gallons). Even reasonable quality AC wines can often be bought *en vrac* when you visit a winery or *cave coopérative.* Once home, the wines should be bottled and corked, or else drunk as quickly as possible. Buying wine *en vrac* is fun, but be warned: having large quantities on tap can soon lead to promiscuous consumption!

Selling wine en vrac

Apéritifs and Liqueurs
PRE-AND POST-PRANDIAL TIPPLES

FRANCE HAS NO shortage of local as well as internationally known pre- and after-dinner drinks. In theory, an *apéritif* is meant to stimulate the appetite by encouraging the gastric juices, while a *digestif* helps digestion after a meal. Traditionally, therefore, many such drinks have been made using mixtures of plant and herb extracts.

Pastis, *the* apéritif *of the South*

brands include Pernod and Ricard.

Pineau des Charentes Unfermented grape juice muted by adding Cognac, then aged in wood. Fruity, sweet, and powerful.

Pommeau Unfermented apple juice, blended with Calvados, and aged in wood.

Vermouth Fortified wine infused with a mixture of herb and spice extracts. Popular vermouths include Noilly Prat from the Languedoc, and Chambéry from Savoie.

VOULEZ-VOUS PRENDRE UN APERITIF?

In all but the most basic French res-taurants, you may be asked, as you sit down, whether you would like to *"prendre un apéritif."* It is by no means obligatory, and if you don't feel like a pre-dinner drink simply reply, *"Non, merci"* (no, thanks). Indeed, serving an *apéritif* is one way by which restaurants can bump up the check, so if you are on a budget, it may be worth avoiding. On the other hand, in good restaurants, the *apéritif* is often served with an enticing tidbit or appetizer known as an *amuse-gueule,* so it may well be worth having at least a glass of wine or mineral water so as not to miss out. Favorite French *apéritifs* include:

Floc de Gasgogne Unfermented grape juice and Armagnac, aged in wood.

Kir One of the favorite French pre-dinner drinks, named after Félix Kir, once, mayor of Dijon. Strictly speaking, *kir* should be made from white Bourgogne Aligoté added to a finger or so of *crème de cassis* (blackcurrant liqueur).

Kir Royal The same as *kir* but made, more luxuriously, with Champagne or some other sparkling wine.

Pastis The archetypal French *apéritif,* especially in the Midi: anise-flavored, to be diluted with ice and water to taste, a delicious long, cooling drink. Favorite

UN DIGESTIF?

The days when a Cognac or Armagnac were *de rigueur* after a meal along with a cigar may be long gone for most of us, but, undoubtedly, there are times when the pleasure of a good meal is prolonged by an after-dinner drink. French favorites include:

Armagnac Gascony's riposte to Cognac: brandy distilled and aged in oak (see p.167).

Calvados Apple brandy; the finest comes from Normandy's Pays d'Auge (see p.132).

Cognac The quintessential distillation of the grape, usually blended. Old reserves (XO, Vieille Reserve) can be heavenly (see pp.134–135).

Eaux-de-vie The finest *eaux-de-vie* are produced by distilling fruits, including cherries, mirabelle, greengage and quetsch plums, raspberries, and pears (see p.103).

Fine Brandy made by distilling the lees left over after the wines have been racked (transferred to clean barrels).

Marc Spirit made by distilling the *marc* or grape residue left over after the wine-making process.

La Bière et Le Cidre
BEER AND CIDER

BEER DOES NOT immediately come to mind as a traditional drink of France, but the nation is more than exceedingly fond of its amber nectar, increasingly so the young; in fact, some wine producers are more than a little worried about their future home market.

The most interesting French beers come from small, regional, or "boutique" breweries, mainly near the Belgian border in Nord-Pas de Calais. Here, artisan Flemish brewing traditions remain intact, and some distinctive, strong ales are brewed that can be outstanding. The best are unpasteurized and continue to condition and improve in the bottle. Try Jenlain, Bière des Trois Monts, Au Baron, or Pelforth.

Good, blond, lager-style beers are brewed on an immense scale, primarily in

Cidre fermier *from Normandy, the best cider in France*

Alsace and Lorraine, regions that have long enjoyed a beer drinking tradition. Kronenbourg, Mutzig, Kanterbräu, and Fischer are all reliable brands. Remember, in a bar, a draft beer is *"un demi"* (25 cl. or ½ pint.)

Cider is the most common alcoholic drink in Normandy and, to a lesser extent, Brittany. Farm ciders can be excellent, or they may be undrinkable. The best come from Normandy's Pays d'Auge.

The term *cidre bouché* indicates cider which is bottled before fermentation is complete. This results in a natural sparkle which comes from a secondary fermentation in the bottle. A sediment always remains, so take care when pouring. Good cider also comes from the French Alps, made from apples from Savoie.

DRINK AND THE DRIVER

In spite of an apparently cavalier attitude to drinking and driving which includes selling alcoholic beverages in highway service areas, France has severe laws against drinking and driving. Obviously, it is advisable never to drink and drive. Many French people, however, continue to do so, as drinking wine (rarely anything stronger) with meals is still considered a sacrosanct custom.

Therefore, take particular care when driving on French roads, either after the lunch hour or in evenings, when other vehicles may be driven by drivers who, if not wholly under the influence, may be less than fully alert.

For drivers not partaking of alcoholic beverages, France offers some interesting and delicious alternatives:

Citron pressé Freshly squeezed lemon juice, topped up with water and sweetened with sugar to taste.

Jus de raisin Unfermented juice from wine grapes; can be outstanding, though always quite sweet.

Orange pressée Freshly squeezed orange juice.

Orangina A popular French brand of orange soda.

Pétillant de raisin A sparkling grape juice which has a very low alcoholic content (usually, no more than one to three per cent, but check the label); drier than *jus de raisin* and more acceptable as an accompaniment to food.

Sirops Most bars and cafés offer a range of fruit syrups which are topped up with mineral water, seltzer, or lemon soda.

Les Eaux Minérales
FOUNTAINS OF LIFE

JUST AS A GOOD BOTTLE of wine is a natural accompaniment to a meal in France, so a bottle of *eau minerale* equally is essential. France is number one in the world in terms of both producing and consuming bottled mineral water.

The French view mineral water not just as a pure beverage, but as something bestowing positive therapeutic benefits. A source, after careful testing, may be *déclarée d'intérêt public,* of declared public interest, indicating that the water is beneficial to health. Certain waters are considered helpful for whole ranges of different ailments and maladies, and a *cure* at a spa town is still something that the French take regularly, a mainstream health treatment even paid for by the State.

The Ministry of Health vigorously controls the bottling of mineral waters to ensure purity. Naturally carbonated waters emerge from the ground fully sparkling, though the carbon dioxide may be captured separately then put back into the water at the bottling line.

In addition to French mineral waters, there are also spring waters, *eaux de source,* which make no claim to beneficial properties. French bottled waters can be either *eau gazeuse* (sparkling) or *eau plate* (still). Favorites include:

> **"UNE CARAFE D'EAU, S.V.P."**
> French tap water is perfectly fine to drink, and it usually tastes O.K., too. So if you don't want to pay for bottled mineral water, simply ask for *"une carafe d'eau, s'il vous plaît."* All restaurants should gladly bring you one and refill it as many times as necessary. Getting them to bring you *les glaçons* (ice cubes) — now that's another matter.

Badoit One of the most popular sparkling waters to accompany food in restaurants: soft in flavor, due to its light sodium bicarbonate content, and only gently sparkling.

Contrexéville Still water from the Vosges Mountains, with high mineralization. Popular with dieters.

Evian The French favorite still water, considered so pure that it is widely used in mixing baby formulas.

Perrier One of the world's most popular waters, with a high carbonation and a fresh, lemony zip which makes it ideal as an *apéritif* or a drink on its own.

Vichy Saint-Yorre A powerfully flavored sparkling water, high in minerals, from a variety of sources around and near to Vichy.

Vichy Source des Célestins Long considered the preeminent French mineral water and beloved by French expatriates, sparkling Vichy, with its high bicarbonate of sodium and other mineral content and its distinctive, rather salty taste is considered an aid to digestion, though, for many, it may be something of an acquired taste.

Vittel Grande Source Another highly popular and nationally available still mineral water with a low sodium content, noted for its purity.

Volvic This still, lightly mineralized water percolates down from the volcanic granite terrain of the Auvergne.

One of the best-known sparkling mineral waters, from Languedoc

Au Bar

A HOME FROM HOME

BARS IN FRANCE, unlike their counterparts in many other nations, are rarely simply places exclusively for alcohol. In fact, there is little distinction between a bar and a café and both serve, in city and village, as something of a community or neighborhood focal point, frequented by people of all ages.

The bar or café, moreover, is usually a place that is open all day and also most of the night. It is where you come in the morning for a *grand crème* (see below) and buttery *croissant* (it is often advisable to skip breakfasts in hotels if there is a good bar nearby); it is where you repair to when tired of sightseeing and need to sit down and freshen up with a cool *citron pressé*. Bars and cafés can provide simple snacks and lunches when you just need a quick bite; and they are where you head to both for a drink before going out to eat, as well as on your way home again, for a final nightcap.

It is essential to be aware that there are two tariffs in most bars and cafés, one for food or drink taken standing at the bar itself, the second, more expensive, for sitting down, either inside or out. In fashionable locations, the difference between the two can be considerable.

Meeting at a café — an ideal informal rendezvouz

However, once seated, it is perfectly acceptable to nurse that cup of coffee or glass of wine for as long as you care to, while reading or simply watching the world go by.

Wherever you are in France, in Paris or in the provinces, find your own bar where you can hang out: after only a visit or two, you will already be regarded as a regular, your favorite drink brought to your table almost before you have ordered it.

BAR TALK — WHAT TO ORDER

Café/café noir/café express *Demi-tasse* (small cup) of strong black *espresso* coffee.

Café crème Small cup of coffee with steamed milk.

Café calva Black coffee with a dash of Calvados.

Déca/café décaféiné Decaffeinated coffee; often, a freshly brewed *espresso*.

Grand crème Same as *café crème*, but in a large breakfast cup.

Café au lait Hot milk with coffee.

Chocolat chaud Hot chocolate.

Thé nature, thé citron, or **thé au lait** Plain tea, with lemon, or with milk.

Tisane/infusion Usually means a caffeine-free herbal infusion.

Bière Beer.

Bière en bouteille Bottled beer.

Demi Glass of draft beer: 25 cl. (½ pint).

Panaché Refreshing mixture of lemon soda and draft beer.

Vin blanc White wine.

Vin rouge Red wine.

Sirop Fruit syrup topped up with lemon soda or mineral water.

Pastis Anise-flavored *apéritif*, served with water to dilute to taste, which turns it characteristically cloudy.

Food Capital of the World

PARIS

PARIS IS THE UNDISPUTED gastronomic capital of the Western world. Here, the freshest and the finest produce from all over France makes its way daily: fish dispatched in the earliest hours of the morning from Nord-Pas de Calais' Boulogne-sur-Mer; the best oysters, mussels, and lobsters from Brittany; enticing seasonal fruits and vegetables from Provence and Languedoc; poultry from Bourg-en-Bresse and the Landes; beef and lamb from the Limousin; *foie gras* and duck *confits* from the Dordogne and Gascony; cheeses from the cows, goats, and sheep that

Aux Deux Magots, the famous literary café on the Left Bank, Paris

graze on the lush pastures of Normandy and the high alpine meadows of Savoie and Dauphiné; and not forgetting the finest (and best value) wines from both the classic as well as the still little-known wine regions.

HAUTE CUISINE

The best of these ingredients are transformed in some of the city's most elegant and historical restaurants into masterpieces by chefs whose names read like a gastronomic roll of honor, for Paris' reputation is, indeed, based on an esteemed pedigree. After the Revolution, chefs who had worked in the kitchens of the aristocracy, catering to their refined and extra-vagant tastes, soon found themselves out of a job as their employers fled the nation for safer climes. Many of these chefs set up what were to become known as "restaurants." In some instances, they furbished their establishments to recreate the palatial splendors they had left behind. These were the forerunners of today's temples to food, which offer not just the pinnacle of gastronomic pleasure but a whole ambience to match the experience.

From the 19th-century chef Georges Auguste Escoffier to contemporary figures such as Joël Robuchon and Alain Senderens, *haute cuisine* has been shaped by innovators often prepared to break with tradition and forge new culinary paths, for *haute cuisine* is still celebrated with fervor in Paris.

REGIONAL AND ETHNIC CUISINE

Since all the finest produce and products come to the capital, you can enjoy a wide-ranging epicurean *tour de France* without ever leaving Paris. You can sample the sea-fresh, salt tang of Brittany from the banks of iced oysters and other shellfish on display in brasseries throughout the capital, while Lyon's inimitable, mainly *charcuterie* based foods are on offer in bistros, along with fruity Beaujolais served in the 46-cl. (almost a pint) Lyonnais *pot*. The restaurant Altitude 95, located on the first level of the Eiffel Tower, serves complete menus from four different regions of France, which change regularly throughout the year.

With so many tempting choices on offer, it would be easy to overlook France's extensive colonial heritage. Whether Algerian couscous or Vietnamese noodles, the capital's ethnic cuisine, like that of its bistros and brasseries, can also be an affordable way to experience some of its best food.

But don't run away with the impression that Paris is all about an ostentatious display of style and wealth. Except for the top restaurants, you are not expected to dress formally for dinner, and children are almost always welcomed, not merely tolerated. There may not be special facilities on hand, so make sure you bring what you need: restaurants are always willing to heat up baby foods or puree vegetables, if necessary.

BUYING FOOD AND DRINK

Shopping for food and drink in Paris can be either an active pursuit or a spectator sport. Don't miss the bewildering yet fascinating experience of the capital's street markets, where you can follow the local tradition of buying fresh produce every day. There is no better place than a Parisian delicatessen to stock up on your favorite treats. Some, such as Fauchon (see p.73), have even gained worldwide reputations for the excellence of their fare.

Quality is all: Parisians will tolerate nothing short of the best, willing to stand in long lines for a still warm-from-the-oven loaf of *pain Poilâne* (see p.72) or the first of the season's *abricots* (apricots) from Roussillon.

Produce and products that have been granted select *appellation d'origine contrôlée* status or *Labels Rouges* or *Régionaux* are proudly advertised on menus or in shops, from *lentilles vertes du Puy* (green lentils from the Auvergne, see p.182) to *poulet de Bresse* (Bresse chicken, see p.174). For Parisians are nothing if not the most knowledgeable, most discerning and discriminating consumers of food and drink in the world.

Parisians making their selection from the best of fresh produce from all over France at their local street market

The Top of the Top

RESTAURANTS, BISTROS, AND BRASSERIES

PARIS IS HOME to world-renowned chefs, many of whom are pioneers in their field; and, not surprisingly, their restaurants are very much in demand and prices soar accordingly.

We list here those that have achieved the ultimate accolade, the Michelin three rosettes, as well as a personal selection; for a fuller account consult specialist guides (see p.45). Remember, the desire to ex-perience — and to be *seen* to experience (this is Paris, after all) — such culinary excellence often leads to waiting lists that are several months long.

A cheaper and less formal way to sample the capital's good foods is in bistros and brasseries: here, you can order just a single dish if you don't care for a full three-course meal. But, even for bistros, it is always worth booking.

TOP RESTAURANTS IN PARIS

MICHELIN'S THREE ROSETTES

Joël Robuchon
59, Avenue Raymond Poincaré, 16°
tel: 47 27 12 27
fax: 47 27 31 22
The cult status of this Parisian institution explains the long waiting lists — but so does the food.
$$$$+

L'Ambroisie
9, Place des Vosges, 4°
tel: 42 78 51 45
Sumptuous and romantic decor in this former jewelry shop, surpassed only by faultless cuisine.
$$$$+

La Tour d'Argent
15–17 Quai de la Tournelle, 5°
tel: 43 54 23 31
fax: 44 07 12 04
Overlooking the Seine, this restaurant is the height of elegance and the cuisine is strictly classic. The wine list is just as magnificent as you would expect.
$$$$+

Lucas-Carton
9, Place Madeleine, 8°
tel: 42 65 22 90
fax: 42 65 06 23
Art nouveau meets nouvelle cuisine in Alain Senderens' dramatic restaurant. Constantly innovative cuisine is com-plemented by a suggested wine for each dish.
$$$$+

Taillevent
15, Rue Lamennais, 8°
tel: 44 95 15 01
fax: 42 25 95 18
Considered by many the best restaurant in Paris, not just for Jean-Claude Vrinat's neoclassic haute cuisine but also for its discreet ambience, and its sensational wine list.
$$$$+

"SUPER SECONDS"

Guy Savoy
18, Rue Troyon, 17°
tel: 43 80 40 61
fax: 46 22 43 09
The constantly changing carte is always based on fresh, seasonal foods. A feast for the eyes as well as the taste buds; don't miss the calorie-rich, regime-busting desserts.
$$$$

Jacques Cagna
14, Rue des Grands Augustins, 6°
tel: 43 26 49 39
fax: 43 54 54 48
Stunning mix of classic and modern, with a hint of the Orient; cheaper fare at his La Rotisserie d'en face (see opposite).
$$$$

Le Divellec
107, Rue de l'Université, 7°
tel: 45 51 91 96
fax: 45 51 31 75
Considered by many to be the capital's best fish restaurant.
$$$$

Le Grand Véfour
17, Rue de Beaujolais, 1°
tel: 42 96 56 27
fax: 42 86 80 71
Celebrate in the grand style in this restaurant, once frequented by Napoleon. The cuisine is as flamboyant as the directoire-style decor.
$$$$

Michel Rostang
20, Rue Rennequin, 17°
tel: 47 63 40 77
fax: 47 63 82 75
Intimate restaurant with an ambitious style blending traditional cuisine with improvised ideas; exquisite duck and an interesting wine list.
$$$$

Vivarois
192, Avenue Victor Hugo, 16°
tel: 45 04 04 31
fax: 45 03 09 84
Claude Peyrot is another great chef, serving wonderful food in sharp, modern surroundings.
$$$$

PARISIAN BISTROS AND BRASSERIES

Au Pied de Cochon
6, Rue Coquillière, 1°
tel: 42 36 11 75
fax: 45 08 48 90
Come to this brasserie for its classic soup à l'oignon, pig's trotters, or impeccable shellfish. Open 24 hours a day.
$$

Aux Charpentiers
10, Rue Mabillon, 6°
tel: 43 26 30 05
fax: 46 33 07 98
Typical bistro with wide-ranging and reasonably priced fare.
$–$$

Aux Crus de Bourgogne
3, Rue Bachaumont, 2°
tel: 42 33 48 24
fax: 40 26 66 41
True Lyonnais bouchon serving simple, tasty fare — coq au vin, boeuf gros sel — washed down with house Beaujolais.
$$–$$$

Benoît
20, Rue St-Martin, 4°
tel: 42 72 25 76
fax: 42 72 45 68
Superb bistro with traditional decor and cuisine.
$$$

Bofinger
5–7, Rue de la Bastille, 4°
tel: 42 72 87 82
fax: 42 72 97 68
One of the oldest brasseries in Paris; specialties include shellfish and choucroute.
$$

Brasserie Lipp
151, Blvd. St.-Germain, 6°
tel: 45 48 53 91
fax: 45 44 33 20
Favorite with politicians, this Left Bank brasserie specializes in andouillettes

Le Petit Zinc

endorsed by the A.A.A.A.A. (see p.87) and pretty good choucroute.
$$–$$$

Chez Georges
273, Blvd. Pereire, 17°
tel: 45 74 31 00
fax: 45 74 02 56
Classic à la carte menu in authentic bistro surroundings.
$$

La Coupole
102, Blvd. du Montparnasse, 14°
tel: 43 20 14 20
fax: 43 35 46 14
Paris' largest brasserie; don't miss the seafood.
$$

La Fermette Marbeuf 1900
5, Rue Marbeuf, 8°
tel: 53 23 08 00
fax: 53 23 08 09
Serves fresh, seasonal, brasserie-style foods. Entire menus can be based on appellation d'origine contrôlée products.
$$–$$$

La Rôtisserie d'en face
2, Rue Christine, 6°
tel: 43 26 40 98
fax: 43 54 54 48

Stylish yet informal: the cuisine of Jacques Cagna at brasserie prices.
$–$$

Le Petit Zinc
11, Rue St.-Benoît, 6°
tel: 42 61 20 60
fax: 49 27 09 33
Classic Left Bank bistro serving good, fresh seafood in a belle époque atmosphere.
$$

Le Train Bleu
20, Blvd. Diderot, 12°
tel: 43 43 09 06
fax: 43 43 97 96
Stunning belle époque interior, situated in the Gare de Lyon, serving upmarket brasserie food.
$$$

Le Vieux Bistro
14, Rue du Cloître Notre-Dame, 4°
tel: 43 54 18 95
fax: 44 07 35 63
Despite its proximity to Notre Dame, this has a healthy mix of locals sampling the Lyonnais specialties.
$$

Pharamond
24, Rue de la Grande Truanderie, 1°
tel: 42 33 06 72
fax: 40 28 01 81
19th-century bistro serving Normandy specialties; best tripes in Paris.
$$–$$$

Terminus Nord
23, Rue de Dunkerque, 10°
tel: 42 85 05 15
fax: 40 16 13 98
Fabulous big city brasserie. The shellfish is always fresh, while there are the usual daily specials, choucroute, and grilled meats.
$$–$$$

Discovering the Diversity of Paris
OTHER OPTIONS FOR EATING OUT

AMONG THE WEALTH of choices for eating out in Paris are a host of less formal options. Simple meals are served through the day in cafés, and wine bars can also be lively places to sample good foods. As former hang-outs of the famous, many bars and cafés have retained turn-of-the-century decor, and are still important meeting places for locals.

Paris also provides an excellent opportunity to sample some of France's ethnic foods (especially Vietnamese and North African), as well as the best of its regional cuisine.

Some of Paris' best-loved sights have decent restaurants, and are ideal for taking the weight off your feet. But if all you want is to contemplate the world over a *demi* glass of beer then a sidewalk café table provides the perfect opportunity — although bear in mind that you are charged almost double for the privilege.

OTHER OPTIONS

CAFES AND WINE BARS

Aux Deux Magots
170, Blvd. St.-Germain, 6°
tel: 45 48 55 25
fax: 40 50 16 37
Famous Left Bank café littéraire *popular with writers from Hemingway to Sartre.*

Café de Flore
172, Blvd. St.-Germain, 6°
tel: 45 48 55 26
fax: 45 44 33 39
Great rival to the above and, in its heyday, equally popular with literary giants.

Fouquet's
99, Avenue des Champs-Elysées, 8°
tel: 47 23 70 60
fax: 47 20 08 69
The place to sit out nursing a café or a demi at one of the sidewalk tables while watching the world go by.

La Tartine
24, Rue de Rivoli, 4°
tel: 42 72 76 85
Classic Parisian wine bar of the 1900s with a good range of wines and snacks.

L'Ecluse Les Halles
5, Rue Mondétour, 1°
tel: 40 41 08 73
Good-quality wine bar chain specializing in Bordeaux. Branches throughout Paris.

Le Rubis
10, Rue du Marché-St.-Honoré, 1°
tel: 42 61 03 34
Crowded wine bar with an excellent wine list and an appetizing selection of meals and snacks.

Willi's Wine Bar
13, Rue des Petits Champs, 1°
tel: 42 61 05 09
fax: 47 03 36 93
English-run wine bar with a range of homegrown and foreign wines — but the menu is resolutely French.

ETHNIC AND REGIONAL RESTAURANTS

Altitude 95
1st Floor, The Eiffel Tower
Parc du Champ de Mars, 7°
tel: 45 55 20 04
fax: 45 05 94 40
Ultra-modern decor with a regional carte *that changes weekly.*
$$-$$$

Ambassade d'Auvergne
22, Rue du Grenier-St.-Lazare, 3°
tel: 42 72 31 22
fax: 42 78 85 47
Top Auvergnat restaurant with a traditional, rustic atmosphere; specialties include cabbage and Roquefort soup.
$$

Moissonnier
28, Rue des Fossés St.-Bernard, 5°
tel: 43 29 87 65
Family-run bistro serving mainly Lyonnais specialties.

Tan Dinh
60, Rue de Verneuil, 7°
tel: 45 44 04 84
fax: 45 44 36 93
Extensive Vietnamese menu with huge wine list.
$$-$$$

Wally Le Saharien
36, Rue Rodier, 9°
tel: 42 85 51 90
fax: 42 81 22 77
Popular North African restaurant.
$-$$

AT THE SIGHTS

Le Grand Louvre
at the entrance to the Louvre, 1°
tel: 40 20 53 41
fax: 42 86 04 33
A good value find underneath the glass pyramid.
$$-$$$

Restaurant Jules Verne
2nd Floor, The Eiffel Tower
Parc du Champ de Mars, 7°
tel: 45 55 61 44
fax: 47 05 29 41
Only the sumptuous nouvelle cuisine *beats the stunning views.*
$$$$

Markets

STREET LIFE AT ITS BEST

ONE OF THE MOST ENDEARING features of this glamorous city is that lively markets still take place in almost every Parisian neighborhood, bringing an air of the provinces not just with the fresh produce but the attendant communal atmosphere.

Invariably, markets are held in streets which have other local food shops, concentrating all one's food shopping in a convenient area. Wandering among the bustling stalls can be the best way to witness France's diverse cultures at work and experience French food shopping habits first hand.

Here, you will see Parisians in time honored tradition buying the freshest produce daily, selecting the best from a vast array rushed in from all the corners of France. Most of the markets set up for business by 7 or 8 a.m. and close by mid-afternoon, so get there early.

POPULAR PARIS MARKETS

Marché Enfants Rouges,
3° *(Tue–Sun) Spread both indoors and outdoors along the Rue de Bretagne, this characterful market is one of the city's oldest, dating from 1620.*

Marché Président Wilson, 16° *(Wed, Sat) Upmarket, in the chic part of Paris between Place d'Iéna and Rue Debrousse.*

Marché Raspail, 6°
(Tue, Fri, Sun) Sunday is the best day to come here for an outstanding range of organically grown produce; between Rue du Cherche-Midi and Rue de Rennes.

Marché St.-Germain, 5°
(Tue–Sun) Clean and quiet, this is one of the few remaining covered markets in Paris. The family-run stalls specialize in ethnic and organic produce.

Rue Cler, 7°
(Tue–Sat) Rub shoulders with some of the city's elite in this spacious pedestrianized precinct south of Rue de Grenelle. The pâtisseries and cheeses from the surrounding shops are just about as well-presented as the clientele.

The market at Rue Mouffetard

Rue de Seine and Rue de Buci, 6°
(Tue–Sun) In the St.-Germain quartier, this is one of Paris' best and most popular — not to mention most expensive — street markets. Check out Barthélémy's fresh curd cheese.

Rue de Lévis, 17°
(Tue–Sun) Busy market near the Parc Monceau with several excellent fromageries and charcuteries.

Rue et Place d'Aligre, 12°
(daily) One of the cheapest and busiest in the city, this market has an African flavor; located near the Bastille.

Rue Lepic, 18°
(Tue–Sun) Conveniently situated for Montmartre. The market begins at Place Blanche.

Rue Montorgueil, 1°
(Tue–Sun) Not so much a street market as a street devoted to fine food and drink shops; this is all that now remains of the former Les Halles wholesale market.

Rue Mouffetard, 5°
(Tue–Sun) Located in the heart of medieval Paris, this is one of the best street markets for good fruits and vegetables, permanent specialist food shops, and typical Parisian atmosphere.

Rue Poncelet, 17°
(Tue–Sun) Away from the tourist-orientated areas of Paris, this market, specializing in a variety of products from the Auvergne, has a more authentic feel than some.

Tang Frères, 13°
(Tue–Sun) An enormous Oriental bazaar, reflecting Paris' cosmopolitan population; stocked with exotic produce and products, including a Far Eastern flower shop.

Buying the Best
FOOD SHOPS IN THE CAPITAL

FOR THE VISITOR to Paris, one of the perennial joys, wherever you are, is the chance to take in the enticing sights and smells of fine foods displayed carefully and beautifully in food shops throughout the capital.

Whether you are simply peckish after breakfast, and just cannot resist popping into the neighborhood *pâtisserie* for a chocolate *éclair* or a glazed *tarte aux fraises* (strawberry tart), or

Ice cream from Maison Bertillon

whether you wish to put together an elaborate picnic, from *pâtisseries* and *boulangeries, charcuteries* and *fromageries,* there is no shortage of fine food shops to tempt you.

Of course, food gifts, especially canned, bottled, or packaged goods that are easy to pack, can be the best souvenirs to take back home with you. A visit to

such gourmet shops as Fauchon and Hédiard, both on the Place de la Madeleine, is a must for a special taste of Paris — even if you can only afford to look. Luxury *foie gras,* fresh and conserved truffles, and caviar are the specialty here, but luckily for the majority of us, the range also extends to more mundane (but affordable) mustards, vinegars, and salad and cooking oils.

As one would expect, there is no shortage of shops selling fine wines, and the connoisseur in search of a special or rare bottle will probably find it in Paris. Once again, even if you don't buy, a look around the merchants' *caves* is something not to be missed. Don't overlook, either, the chance to buy fine tableware and professional quality cookware and utensils.

PAIN POILANE

In Paris, as throughout France, bread is the cornerstone of the daily diet. It is perhaps not surprising, therefore, that one of the most famous and most sought out specialty shops sells this basic commodity. So delicious is the hard-crust, sourdough bread of Lionel Poilâne, that a veritable cult has arisen around it: some of the best restaurants in the capital (and even all over France) are proud to use it, and a sandwich made with *pain Poilâne* is elevated immediately to another plane. It is reassuring to find that the shop, located in the St.-Germain quarter, has still retained its charming

and old-fashioned style, even in the face of such celebrity. Here the famous bread, made with a high proportion of wholewheat flour, salted with *sel de Guérande* from Brittany, emerges hot every two hours from the wood-fired oven in the basement, with its characteristic slashed square design.

Buy it by the loaf (or, if that is too much, by the slice) together with other delicious goods baked on the premises.

Lionel Poilâne
8, Rue du Cherche-Midi
Paris 6°
tel: 45 48 42 59

FOOD SHOPS IN PARIS

Androuët
41, Rue d'Amsterdam, 8°
tel: 48 74 26 93
One of the most famous — and best — cheese shops in Paris; established since 1909.

Aux Vrais Produits d'Auvergne
98, Rue Montorgueil, 11°
tel: 42 36 28 99
Specialist stockist of Auvergnat favorites.

Boulangerie Poujauran
20, Rue Jean Nicot, 7°
tel: 47 05 80 88
Some of the most interesting breads in Paris.

Boursault
71, Avenue du Général Leclerc, 14°
tel: 43 27 93 30
One of the best cheese shops in Paris.

Caves Taillevent
199, Rue du Faubourg St.-Honoré, 8°
tel: 45 61 14 09
One of the finest caves in the capital. For that rare or really special bottle, start your search here.

Charles
10, Rue Dauphine, 6°
tel: 43 54 25 19
Charcuterie *well known for its* boudin blanc *and* jambon.

Culinarion
99, Rue de Rennes, 6°
tel: 45 48 94 76
Extensive collection of fine French cookware.

Fauchon
26-28-30, Pl. de la Madeleine, 8°
tel: 47 42 60 11
One of the greatest gastronomic emporia in France.

Fresh fruit from Hédiard, one of the great food shops of Paris

Flo Prestige
42, Place du Marché St.-Honoré, 1°
tel: 42 61 45 46
High quality bread, cheese, charcuterie, *prepared foods, and wine.*

Hédiard
21, Pl. de la Madeleine, 8°
tel: 43 12 88 88
Exquisite foie gras, *excellent jams, conserves, and mustards, good wines, or just a perfect apple.*

Kraemer
60, Rue Monge, 5°
tel: 47 07 84 23
Top selection of cheeses.

La Grande Epicerie de Paris (du Bon Marché)
38, Rue de Sèvres, 7°
tel: 44 39 81 00
The best food hall on the Left Bank.

La Maison de la Truffe
19, Pl. de la Madeleine, 8°
tel: 42 65 53 22
Come here for black truffles (Nov–mid Mar), white truffles from Italy's Piemonte, and conserved truffles, truffle pastes, and truffle oils.

La Maison du Chocolat
225, Rue du Faubourg St.-Honoré, 8°
tel: 42 27 39 44;
fax: 47 64 03 75
Best chocolates in town.

Maison Bertillon
31, Rue St.-Louis-en-l'Ile, 4°
tel: 43 54 31 61
One of the simplest treats is a scoop — or more — of Bertillon ice cream.

Marie-Anne Cantin
12, Rue du Champ-de-Mars, 7°
tel: 45 50 43 94
Cheeses made by a campaigner for preservation of traditional methods.

Nicolas
31, Pl. de la Madeleine, 8°
tel: 42 68 00 16
The closest to a chain of wine shops in France; the range is always reliable. Branches everywhere.

Pâtisserie Boulangerie Alsacienne
4, Rue du Cardinal Lemoine, 5°
tel: 43 26 15 80
Full range of Alsatian pastries, one of the richest and most distinctive styles in France.

Pâtisserie Lenôtre
44, Rue d'Auteuil, 16°
tel: 45 24 52 52
The original of Monsieur Lenôtre's empire of pastry shops, turning out an irresistible range of pastries, cakes, and breads.

Pou
16, Ave des Ternes, 17°
tel: 43 80 19 24
A Parisian favorite, selling pâté en croûte, *Lyonnais sausages, and* foie gras.

Ryst-Dupeyron
79, Rue du Bac, 7°
tel: 45 48 80 93
Attractive setting for wine, port, and whisky; will personalize bottles for special occasions.

The North

NORD-
PAS DE CALAIS

PICARDY

CHAMPAGNE-
ARDENNES

ALSACE-LORRAINE

TUCKED AGAINST THE FRONTIERS OF Germany, Luxembourg, and Belgium, the North reflects more its industrious, beer-drinking neighbors than the popular stereotype of wine-flushed Mediterranean France. Relentless wars waged on its soil over centuries — the inheritance of borderland — has left a sadness in its soul. But in times of peace, as in times of strife, the inhabitants simply get on with the quiet business of living. Though unemployment in recent years has laid waste to much of the industrial heartland of the region, Northern France remains a hardworking section of the nation. This is reflected in the local foods, which tend to be hearty, filling, warming, substantial, the sort that have traditionally satisfied the cavernous appetites of miners, steel-workers, fisherfolk, and farmers.

Yet the myth of the North as a uniform, gray industrial land, punctuated only by the bone-white headstones of the military cemeteries that are found throughout, is no longer wholly valid. Perhaps, in part, because it has always been an area that visitors to France pass through not stop in, the North remains, today, delightfully unspoiled, truly lovely rural France *par excellence*.

A rank of trees on guard near the former battlefield of Agincourt

NORD-PAS DE CALAIS

The two *départements* of this region encompass the ancient regions of Flanders and Artois. Their names may sound dull, compounded by images of the soulless town that is, for millions of Britons at least, the first port of entry to France, one that for most remains simply a place to get through and away from as quickly as possible. Yet the region is quiet and surprisingly charming, and well worth dipping into for a short break. Many come to Northern France to tour its battlefields and war cemeteries (from centuries-famed Agincourt to the trenches of the Somme), but there are happier reasons for coming here too. Boulogne-sur-Mer, the number-one fishing port in the nation, is one of the pleasantest of all Channel ports, and the gateway to fine, rural places, such as the lovely Vallée de la Canche that leads to Montreuil, one of our favorite walled northern towns. French visitors have been making their way to fashionable Le Touquet for so long that the town has been dubbed "Paris-Plage" — "Paris-by-the-Sea." Inland, the country is truly pretty. The pasturelands of the Avesnois-Thiérache in the far east of the region are the source of one of the great cheeses of the North, *maroilles*. Flemish brewing

Ramparts of Montreuil, Nord-Pas de Calais

traditions have remained intact here, making this the finest region in France for outstanding beers.

PICARDY

Picardy is another little-known region. Amiens, with its magnificent, immense Gothic cathedral rising above the Somme, is a city that deserves to be visited, not least for the chance to idle along the canals of its *hortillonages,* a complex system of waterways amid the rich marshlands. Here, in the recent past, scores of small market gardeners cultivated fruits and vegetables to supply the city, which they punted down to the evocatively named *Marché d'eau* (water market) in traditional flat-bottomed barges, an event still commemorated once a year in the *Fête des hortillonages*. Fine lamb comes from the salt marshes of the Baie de Somme around St.-Valery-sur-Somme and Le Crotoy, while the Somme itself is the source of plentiful freshwater fish. Noyon is famous for soft red fruits, best enjoyed fresh, perhaps topped with whipped genuine *crème crue* (unpasteurized cream) from Chantilly.

CHAMPAGNE-ARDENNES

Champagne is, of course, world-renowned for — Champagne. But the region itself, essentially a vast agricultural land, only partly cultivated with vines, remains at great odds with the cosmopolitan image of Champagne, the wine. Reims, with its magnificent cathedral, where the kings of France traditionally came to be crowned, and Epernay, much smaller, but the true capital of the wine region, are two cities that no lover of wine, art, and history will wish to miss. To the north of Champagne lies an even more rustic and wild region, the Ardennes, whose dense, thick forests are popular with French — and Belgian and German — hunters, who come here to shoot wild boar and deer. The Ardennes is also the source of superlative artisan *charcuterie,* especially smoked hams and *pâtés*.

ALSACE-LORRAINE

Any region politically buffeted about as continuously as Alsace-Lorraine has been might, you imagine, suffer something of an identity crisis: yet in gastronomic matters at least, adversity has forged a unique identity that is nothing less than formidable.

Wines produced from Germanic sounding single grape varieties — Sylvaner, Riesling, Tokay (Pinot Gris), Klevner (Pinot Blanc), Gewürztraminer — are vinified in the French manner and emerge as steely yet aromatic classics. Even *sauerkraut,* in Alsace, translates into *choucroute,* immediately more appetizing and infinitely finer than its German counterpart. *Quiche lorraine* originates in this region: made with no more than cream, eggs, and some smoked *lardons* (bacon cubes), and baked in shortcrust or flaky pastry, these simple, savory tarts are something to write home about. There are wonderful traditions of yeast cakes such as the decidedly un-French-sounding *kugelhopf,* marvelous fruit tarts, and the finest fruit *eaux-de-vie,* produced from Williams pears, *mirabelle* and *quetsche* plums, cherries, wild strawberries, and other soft fruits.

NORTHERN FRANCE — THE CENTER OF A NEW EUROPE

If, in the past, the North was a stern, hardworking, and rather humorless outpost, one senses today the beginnings of a regeneration as European realignments place this region at the heart of a new and exciting continent. The Channel Tunnel, and with it high-speed rail links, has considerably improved the infrastructure of the North. Strasbourg is the seat of the European Parliament and Lille remains one of the most vibrant (if least known) cities in France, with a Flemish character that is utterly charming and unique, especially when this usually sober city explodes into celebration during its annual *Braderie* festival, when mountains of *moule* (mussel) shells litter the cobbled streets of its Vieille Ville.

From Dunkerque, a seaside port nearly on the frontier with Belgium, forever associated with deeds of heroism and the spirit of the "little ships," across Flanders' fields and the broad, flat plain of Champagne; from the forests of the Ardennes, past the smokestacks of industrial Lorraine to the picture-postcard villages of Alsace: the North remains a part of France that is often passed through with hardly a bat of an eyelid, yet one which well repays detailed exploration.

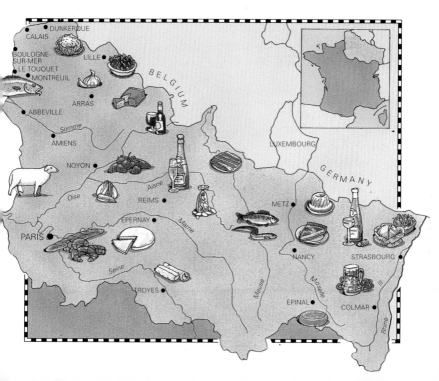

Produits Régionaux
REGIONAL PRODUCE

THE NORTH has a wetter, chillier climate than the rest of the country, and does not benefit from the prolonged sunshine of the South. Yet, this is a fertile land even if it principally yields produce that can by no stretch of the imagination be considered exotic or exciting: *chou* (cabbage), *betterave* (beet), *navet* (turnip), *chou-fleur* (cauliflower), *carotte* (carrot), *choux de Bruxelles* (sprouts), *oignon* (onion), *céleri-rave* (celeriac), *poireau* (leek), and *pomme de terre* (potato). Such mainstays have traditionally nourished the people of the North through hard times: simple, hearty, potato-thickened *potages de légumes* (vegetable soups) are still regularly enjoyed at homes and in restaurants, and every region, locality, or household has its own version of the ever

Cauliflowers from Nord-Pas de Calais

present *potée,* a soupy and substantial one-pot stew containing seasonal root vegetables cooked with fresh or salt pork.

In Nord-Pas de Calais, especially on the rich cultivated marshlands of the Clairmarais near St.-Omer, farmers work the land traditionally, harvesting a superlative and much-prized crop of *choux-fleurs* in summer and *endives* (Belgian endive) in winter. The vegetables are still in some cases transported from the fields to market by boat. A system of floating gardens used to exist in Amiens, capital of Picardy, where the extensive network of *hortillonages* market gardens lie virtually within the city center, laced by a network of canals that link up to the city's *Marché de l'eau.*

Nearby, in the the lush country of the Somme, especially around the Gothic town of Noyon, a fine array of soft fruits is harvested in summer, and, indeed, there is an annual market festival here each year, when people from the surrounding country stock up with enough fruits to make preserves and jams to last the year.

Alsace-Lorraine is the source of exceptional fruits. Both *pommes* (apples) and *poires* (pears) grown in these cooler

SMOKED GARLIC

Arleux, a small town on the dull, flat Flemish plain between Arras and Douai, comes as something of a surprise, for the whole place is redolent of the scent of garlic. *Ail* (garlic), *oignons* (onions), and *échalotes* (shallots) are sold from stands that line the streets of the town.

Arleux's great specialty is *ail fumé d'Arleux* (smoked garlic). Long braided strings of Arleux garlic are hung on

tenterhooks over a smoldering fire of sawdust, reeds, and wheat chaff for a week or longer. This process allows the garlic to be preserved for a year or more, and it also adds a delicate, not overly strong flavor and aroma that are outstanding.

Come to the Petite Ferme to see the smoke-houses and buy.

La Petite Ferme
9, Rue Rily
59151 Arleux
tel: 27 89 50 77

northern climes manage to combine sweetness with refreshing fruity acidity. An enormous range of *prunes* (plums) is also cultivated, especially *mirabelle, quetsche,* and *reine-claude,* grown both for eating and to be made into jams. These and other fruits, including *poires Williams* (Williams pears), *cerises* (cherries), and *mûres* (mulberries) are also distilled into fiery, aromatic, and smooth *eaux-de-vie* liqueurs that are the finest in the land.

Amiens' hortillonages, *market gardens among the canals*

IN SEASON

Asperge blanche White asparagus, a specialty of Alsace (early Apr–end May).
Chou-fleur Enormous, snowy-white cauliflower; delicious raw in salads or baked in a white sauce (Jun–Sep).
Endive Belgian endive, a bitter winter vegetable, is a specialty of Nord-Pas de Calais (Dec–Mar).
Fruits rouges Soft red fruits; especially *fraises* (strawberries), *framboises* (raspberries), *groseilles* (redcurrants) from Picardy (May–Jun).
Haricots de mer Samphire; a tasty wild sea plant that grows on the salt marshes of Nord-Pas de Calais and Picardy (eaten fresh in summer; pickled, all year).

Jets d'houblon The North is brewing country and hops are widely cultivated. In Flanders and Alsace, young shoots from the male plant are steamed and eaten with butter (spring, early summer).
Navet Turnip; the humble root vegetable adds its delicate flavor to stews and can be delicious as *navet confit,* shredded and salted like *choucroute* (winter).
Pissenlit Young, tender dandelion leaves are a Champagne winegrower's favorite, gathered to make *salade aux lardons,* with the slightly bitter leaves dressed in hot bacon fat and wine vinegar (spring, summer).

THE KINGDOM OF THE CABBAGE

Chou (cabbage) is the most typical vegetable of Alsace. Enormous, hard as cannon balls, white cabbages are cultivated in the plains around Strasbourg. The cabbages are harvested in mid June and immediately shredded and salted to produce the year's first *"choucroute nouvelle"* in time for the 14 July celebrations. (Connoisseurs scorn such early offerings, preferring the deeper flavor of more mature *choucroute* from September onward.) Fresh *choucroute* (as opposed to conserved and cooked canned *sauerkraut*) is crisp and delicious, and the basis for *choucroute garnie* — *choucroute* cooked in Riesling wine and garnished with cured and smoked meats, a typical dish that has come to be enjoyed not just in Alsace, but in brasseries throughout France.

Au Marché
M A R K E T S

NORD-PAS DE CALAIS

Ardres	Mon, Thu
Arras	Wed, Sat
Avesnes-sur-Helpe	Fri
Boulogne-sur-Mer	Wed, Sat
Calais	Wed, Thu, Sat
Cambrai	Tue–Sat
Desvres	Tue
Dunkerque	Wed, Sat
Etaples	Tue, Fri
Fruges	Sat
Hazebrouck	Tue
Hesdin	Thu
Le Touquet	Thu, Sat (Mon in season)
Licques	Mon
Lille	Thu, Sun
Maroilles	Tue
Montreuil	Sat
St.-Omer	Wed, Sat

PICARDY

Abbeville	Thu
Amiens	Thu, Sat
Compiègne	Wed, Sat
Laon	Tue, Thu, Sat
Le Crotoy	Fri
Noyon	Wed, Sat
Péronne	Sat
St.-Quentin	Wed, Sat
Soissons	Wed, Sat

CHAMPAGNE-ARDENNES

Châlons-sur-Marne	Wed, Sat
Charleville-Mézières	Tue, Thu, Sat
Châtillon-sur-Marne	Wed
Coulommiers	Wed, Sun
Epernay	Sat, Sun
Jouy-les-Reims	Wed
Reims	Wed, Fri, Sat
Troyes	Sat

The market in the picturesque town of Ribeauvillé, Alsace

ALSACE-LORRAINE

Andlau	Wed
Colmar	Thu, Sat
Commercy	Mon, Fri
Kaysersberg	Mon
Metz	Tue–Sat
Mulhouse	Tue, Thu, Sat
Munster	Tue, Sat
Nancy	Tue–Sat
Obernai	Thu
Ribeauvillé	Tue, Sat
Riquewihr	Fri
Strasbourg	Tue, Wed, Fri, Sat

FETES ET FOIRES FESTIVALS AND FAIRS

NORD-PAS DE CALAIS

Arleux *Foire à l'ail (garlic)* early Sep

Beussent *Fête du chocolat (chocolate)* mid Aug

Licques *Fête de la dinde (turkey)* weekend before Christmas

Lille *La Braderie (flea market and mussels festival)* early Sep

Maroilles *Fête de la flamiche (cheese tart)* mid Aug

Wimereux *Fête de la moule (mussels)* early Aug

PICARDY

Amiens *Fête des hortillonages (market gardens)* 3rd Sun Jun

Noyon *Marché aux fruits rouges (soft fruits)* 2nd Sun Jul

CHAMPAGNE-ARDENNES

Bar-sur-Aube *Foire des vins de Champagne (Champagne)* mid Sep

Chaource *Foire aux fromages (cheese)* mid Oct

Various villages in Champagne *Fête de St.-Vincent (winegrowers' festival)* Jan 22

ALSACE-LORRAINE

Colmar *Foire aux vins (wine)* mid Aug

Geipolsheim (near Strasbourg) *Fête de la choucroute (sauerkraut)* early Sep

Mirecourt *Fête de la quiche (quiche lorraine)* May

Ribeauvillé *Fête du kugelhopf (yeast cake)* early Jul

Foire aux vins (wine) end Jul

In Search of Real Quiche
SAVORY PIES OF THE NORTH

O F ALL FRANCE'S varied foods, surely the most abused is the simple *quiche* of Lorraine. The sorry versions found throughout France (let alone the rest of the world) are often so insipid, soggy, and tasteless that you may well wonder what all the fuss is about. However, real *quiche* as well as other savory pies from the North truly are fine regional foods worth seeking and sampling.

The word *quiche* is evidence of the German influence that extends over Northeast France, for it is derived from the word *Kuchen* (cake). In the course of its linguistic transition from cake to *quiche,* it became miraculously lighter and now signifies a pie pastry filled with any number of ingredients (shellfish along the coast, zucchini and peppers in Provence). But classic *quiche lorraine* still remains the favorite, made with flaky pastry and a filling of beaten eggs and cream, studded with fried *lardons* (cubes of smoked bacon). Individual *quiches* are ideal picnic fare and along with other savory pies are usually sold in markets.

TRY TO SAMPLE

Flamiche aux poireaux (Picardy) Deliciously creamy savory pie filled with leeks sautéed in butter.

Tarte au maroilles (Nord-Pas de Calais) Savory cheese tart made with pungent, rind-washed *maroilles,* one of the great cheeses of the North (see p.90).

Tarte à l'oignon or **zewelwaï** (Alsace) Onion tart; should be creamy and sweet, the fried onions ever so slightly burned and caramelized. Best eaten hot straight from the oven, accompanied by Riesling.

A slice of quiche *and salad, the makings of a good, simple lunch*

FLAMMEKUECHE OR TARTE FLAMBEE

Alsace's *flammekueche* or *tarte flambée* is served in simple *winstubs* along the Route du Vin d'Alsace. This simplest of foods originated on farms in the Bas-Rhin, made whenever bread was being baked. While the wood-fired oven was heating up, farmers' wives used to roll out unleavened bread dough until very thin, top it with a mixture of *fromage blanc* (cream cheese) and rich *crème fraîche* (soured cream), together with finely sliced onions and cubes of smoked bacon. This was popped into the oven for just a few moments,

and thanks to the ferocious heat of the wood fire, the edges of the *tarte* caught fire, hence the name.

To eat, slice, then roll up, and enjoy piping hot, accompanied by chilled Alsace Sylvaner, Edelzwicker, or Vin du Pistolet, a wine made by Jean-Paul Seilly, who bakes *flammekueche* on weekends in his restaurant.

Caveau du Vigneron
18, Rue du Général
Gouraud
67210 Obernai
tel: 88 95 53 10;
88 95 55 80
fax: 88 95 54 00
$

Les Spécialités
REGIONAL SPECIALTIES

ON FIRST IMPRESSION, Northern France does not appear to be one of the nation's great areas for regional foods. Few visit the North with sampling food and wine as the primary motive (with the exception of Alsace, one of the great gastronomic meccas of France). However, throughout, there are distinct styles of regional *cuisine* that deserve to be better known, sampled, and enjoyed.

Flemish influence extends across Nord-Pas de Calais, evident in local architecture, accent, and language, and not least in attitudes to food and drink. This is one of few bastions in France of beer-drinkers, for Flanders has a great artisan brewing tradition. And beer, rather than wine, finds its way into the cooking pot in such classics as *carbonnade à la flamande,* a gooey, rich, beef-in-beer stew, and *coq à la bière*, chicken (preferably from Licques) braised in dark ale.

Picardy does not boast a strongly defined *cuisine,* but its superlative produce and products — from both sea and land — are used generally to excellent effect in restaurants serving both solid *cuisine bourgeoise* and more creative and innovative dishes.

There could hardly be a greater contrast between the select and prestigious image of Le Champagne, the wine, and the rustic heartiness of the true foods of La Champagne, the region. However, in this most select wine land, not surprisingly, an equally select *haute cuisine champenoise* has evolved that is a fitting partner to the most elegant sparkling

wine in the world. In many cases, Champagne is used in variations of classic dishes, a practice that appears almost as wasteful as the Grand Prix driver's insistence on spraying rather than drinking the contents of bottles generously supplied by the sport's sponsors.

But in simple country *auberges,* the true foods of the Champagne region remain hearty and forthright: northern dishes that satisfy the appetites of hardworking people. The Ardennes, to the north, has a great reputation for its *cuisine* based on game from its forests, as well as for its superlative range of *charcuterie.*

If adversity is a forge in which great character is melded, then the turmoil in which Alsace has found itself over the centuries has certainly fired one of the greatest and most distinctive *cuisines* of France. The constant tug-of-war between France and Germany for this fertile and strategic strip of land bounded by the Vosges Mountains and the Rhine River means that Alsace cuisine today fuses both Germanic and French traditions into a glorious whole that is far greater than the sum of its parts.

APPETIZERS AND FIRST COURSES
Canard en croûte au foie gras (Amiens) Great regional specialty: layers of duck breast, pork, and *foie gras de canard* baked in a savory pie with a hand-raised crust.
Cassolette de petits gris (Champagne) Snails, a vineyard pest, are now being farmed in Champagne and may be offered simmered in a creamy Champagne sauce.
Caudière (Nord-Pas de Calais) Chowder made with fish caught in the cold waters of the Channel and North Atlantic, including cod, hake, whiting, and mackerel; always cooked with potatoes.
Craquelot (Nord-Pas de Calais) Grilled smoked herring.
Escargots à l'alsacienne (Alsace) Plump snails from the vineyard

Soupe de poissons

simmered in Riesling wine, then baked with a garlic and parsley butter stuffing.

Escavèche (Nord-Pas de Calais) Cold concoction of fish (usually freshwater, such as trout) marinated in vinegar, onions, and spices, then cooked and allowed to set in a tasty, sharp gelatin.

Ficelle picarde (Picardy) Pancake or *crêpe* filled with ham, mushrooms, and a creamy sauce, covered with cheese, and baked.

Flamiche aux poireaux (Nord, Pas-de-Calais, and Picardy) Flemish leek and cream tart.

Flammekueche or **tarte flambée** (Alsace) Flattened bread dough baked with *fromage blanc,* cream, *lardons,* and sliced onions in an extremely hot wood-fired oven (see p.81).

Foie gras (Alsace) Some of the finest, most unctuous *foie gras d'oie* (fattened goose liver) traditionally comes from Alsace. *Pâté de foie gras* is not pure *foie gras* (see p.151), but makes a rich starter all the same. *Foie gras en croûte* is a whole goose or duck liver baked in a pastry crust. Good *foie gras de canard* (duck liver) is now being produced on farms in Nord-Pas de Calais and Picardy.

Jambon d'Ardennes (the Ardennes) Real, dry-salted and air-cured Ardennes ham, sometimes smoked, is one of the greatest hams in the world.

Harengs marinés (Nord-Pas de Calais) Pickled herring marinated usually in white wine or vinegar with onions, black peppercorns, salt, and seasoning. Eaten cold as a first course.

Lewerknepfles or **quenelles de foie** (Alsace) Liver dumplings made with finely ground pork or calf's liver, bread crumbs, onions, parsley, and seasoning, gently poached, then fried in butter.

Moules-frites (Nord-Pas de Calais) The favorite snack in the North, a steaming bowl of mussels cooked in wine, cider, or beer, served with a mountain of French fries on the side. The fries are eaten with mayonnaise.

Choucroute garni

Pieds de porc à la Ste.-Menehould (Champagne) Pig's trotters poached until tender, boned, rolled in bread crumbs, and sizzled under a hot broiler.

Presskopf (Alsace) Head cheese or brawn; a popular first course in Alsatian *winstubs.*

Quiche lorraine (Lorraine and all France) Strictly speaking, a real *quiche* should be made only with flaky pastry and a filling of eggs, cream, and bacon (see p.81).

Salade de pissenlits aux lardons or **salade aux lardons** (Champagne) Salad classically made with *pissenlits* (young dandelion leaves) dressed with cubes or strips of hot fried bacon and wine vinegar. If dandelion leaves are not available, a robust, bitter lettuce such as *frisée* (chicory) may be used.

Salade tiède de St.-Jacques (Nord-Pas de Calais) Warm salad of lettuce with gently poached scallops on top.

Soupe de poissons (Nord-Pas de Calais and Picardy seaboards) Fish soup; made with a mixture of the local catch, both fish and shellfish, served usually in the style of the Midi, i.e., with *croûtons* and fiery *rouille* (a chili-spiked mayonnaise) on the side.

Tarte à l'oignon or **zewelwaï** (Alsace) Savory onion tart (see p.81) served warm as a first course in *winstubs.*

Tarte au maroilles (Nord-Pas de Calais) Classic savory tart made with pungent and flavorful *maroilles* cheese (see p.90).

Terrine de lapereau
(Picardy) Coarse *terrine*
made with hare and pork.

MAIN COURSES

**Agneau pré-salé de la
Baie de Somme**
(Picardy and all North)
Excellent lamb from the
salt marshes that border
the Somme Bay finds its
way to the best restau-
rants in the North.

Andouillette grillée
(Nord-Pas de Calais and
Champagne) This
"gutsy" favorite, a cooked sausage made
with chitterlings, tripe, or *fraise de veau*
(veal mesentery) is enjoyed throughout
the North, but the finest examples come
from Troyes in Champagne, and from
Arras and Cambrai in Nord-Pas de
Calais. Best grilled and enjoyed with
mustard and beer.

Anguille au vert or **paling in t'groen**
(Nord) Eel stewed in wine with plenty
of parsley and other herbs: a Flemish
classic. Can be hot or cold.

Baeckenoffe or **baekhoffa** (Alsace)
Hearty one-pot stew made with several
kinds of meat — beef, pork, lamb, and
mutton — generously soaked in wine,
layered in an earthenware casserole with
potatoes and other vegetables, then
slowly baked. Traditionally, these meat-
filled crocks were taken to the local
baker's to be cooked for hours in the
slowly cooling ovens.

Blanc de volaille à la crème de
maroilles

**Blanc de volaille à la
crème de maroilles**
(Champagne) Poached
chicken breast in a cheese
sauce made with pungent
maroilles cheese.

Canard au Bouzy
(Champagne) Duck
braised in red Bouzy
wine, one of the finest
still wines of the Cham-
pagne region. A classic.

**Carbonnade à la
flamande** (Nord-Pas de
Calais) Beef slowly
braised in local beer.

Choucroute garnie (Alsace) The great
dish of Alsace: lightly pickled cabbage
simmered in Riesling or other wine,
then garnished with a variety of outstanding Alsace *charcuterie,* including
Strasbourg sausages, smoked ham,
knuckles of pork, bacon, and much else,
served with boiled potatoes and carrots.
Choucroute royale is simmered in sparkling
Crémant d'Alsace.

Civet de chevreuil (the Ardennes and
Alsace) Rich venison stew cooked in
wine and usually thickened with blood.

Coq à la bière (Nord-Pas de Calais)
Chicken, ideally, flavorful free-range
from the renowned poultry center of
Licques, stewed in local beer.

Coq au Riesling (Alsace) Alsace's
version of chicken in wine; in this case,
first flambéd in *eau-de-vie,* then simmered
in Riesling with onions and mushrooms,
finished with cream, and served always
with homemade egg noodles.

**Coquilles St.-Jacques au sabayon de
Champagne** (Champagne) Scallops
pan-fried in butter and served in a light
sabayon — a frothy egg-yolk and cream
sauce — made with Champagne.

Gainée boulonnaise (Boulogne-sur-
Mer and all Pas de Calais) Substantial
one-pot seafood medley made with a
variety of North Atlantic fish, poached
and finished in cream.

Coquilles St.-Jacques au sabayon de Champagne

Hochepot (Nord-Pas de Calais) Northern variation of *pot-au-feu,* a thick casserole of beef, pork, veal, or mutton, together with pig's foot or oxtail to add richness, cooked slowly in an earthenware crock with root vegetables.

Jarret de porc (Alsace-Lorraine) Knuckle of pork simmered in wine.

Marcassin ardennais (the Ardennes) Wild boar from the Ardennes, marinated in wine, juniper berries, and other seasonings, then slowly roasted in an oven.

Matelote champenoise (Champagne) Freshwater fish, including pike, trout, carp, river crayfish, and eel simmered in still white wine and finished with cream.

Potée lorraine (Lorraine) Substantial stew made with a large piece of salt pork cooked together with white beans and vegetables such as potatoes, turnips, rutabaga, carrots, and onions.

Potjevleesch (Nord) Cold terrine made with chunks of rabbit, chicken, pork, and veal, cooked and set in a tasty gelatin. Usually eaten as a main meal accompanied by *pommes frites*.

Truite au bleu (Alsace) Extremely fresh trout (taken from the *vivier* — the pool where live fish are kept), poached in a vinegar- or wine-dominated *court bouillon* which turns the fish a striking and vivid shade of blue.

Waterzooï (Nord) Flemish classic of either chicken or fish poached in wine with vegetables. The cooking liquid is then finished in cream and served with the chicken or fish.

VEGETARIAN AND VEGETABLE DISHES

Chou-rouge (Nord-Pas de Calais and Alsace-Lorraine) Red cabbage, cooked in vinegar with raisins.

Jets d'houblon (Nord and Alsace) Young tender hop shoots, usually poached, then served with melted butter.

Nouilles à l'alsacienne (Alsace) Fresh, homemade egg noodles; usually served with butter and cream.

Salade de betterave (Nord-Pas de Calais) Beet, a popular Northern vegetable, boiled, then served in a creamy dressing.

Spaetzli or **spätzle** (Alsace) Small, noodle-like dumplings, poached, then pan-fried in butter.

Witloof or **endive** (Nord-Pas de Calais) Belgian endive; usually braised, sometimes served *au gratin,* topped with white sauce and cheese, then baked.

DESSERTS

Gaufres à la flamande (Nord) Belgian waffles, usually topped with whipped cream or powdered sugar.

Sorbet au marc de Champagne (Champagne) A bracing finish to a meal: sorbet made with *marc de Champagne,* usually garnished with raisins plumped up in the same potent alcohol.

Sorbet de fruits rouges (Picardy) The wonderful soft summer fruits of Picardy are widely used to make delicious fruit ices.

Tarte au fromage (all North) Light cheesecake made with *fromage blanc* (cottage cheese) and eggs.

Tarte au gros bord (Nord-Pas de Calais) Custard and sugar tart with a thick pastry border, hence the name.

Tarte aux mirabelles, aux framboises, aux quetsches, aux reines-claudes (Alsace-Lorraine) A delectable range of fruit tarts made with whichever soft fruits are in season, including yellow plums, raspberries, blue plums, and greengages.

Tarte au gros bord

Charcuterie

CURED PORK AND OTHER MEAT PRODUCTS

NORTHERN FRANCE OFFERS an outstanding range of cured pork products made by artisan *charcutiers*. Traditionally, Alsace wins on choice; indeed, it is claimed that there are no fewer than 200 local *charcuterie* specialties, drawing on both French and German traditions, but, as always, fusing them into a delicious style that remains uniquely *"alsacienne."*

The wooded and still rustic Ardennes that extends up to the frontier with Belgium also boasts an important *charcuterie* tradition, its *jambon d'Ardennes,* in particular, one of the great cured hams of the world. But much of the *charcuterie* products labeled as such, including the ubiquitous *pâtés d'Ardennes,* are industrially manufactured mush: it is worth exploring until you find the real thing in this delightful region.

Huge quantities of *charcuterie* products are consumed throughout the North of France, forming an enjoyable part of a meal. For visitors, especially, the range on offer means that there are plenty of good regional and local specialties to choose from wherever you are when putting together a picnic.

TRY TO SAMPLE

Andouillette (Troyes, Cambrai, Arras) The finest *andouillettes* — chitterling sausages — come from the North (see opposite).

Boudin blanc (the Ardennes) The most delicate (and one of the most expensive) of all *charcuterie* products,

Terrine de pieds de porc à la Ste.-Menehould

usually made with finely ground lean pork mixed with bread crumbs, eggs, milk, and seasoning.

Cervelas (Strasbourg and all Alsace) Large, smooth sausage of finely ground pork, sometimes lightly smoked, to be boiled and eaten hot or cold.

Foie gras (Alsace) Alsace is one of the great centers in France for fattened liver from specially reared ducks and geese, and most restaurants serve this great delicacy. You can also buy it from *charcuteries,* both fresh and in jars or cans. It is worth remembering that the finest *foie gras* is *entier,* i.e., where the liver is in a whole piece. *Pâté de foie gras* is *foie gras* together with a mixture of pork, pork liver, and seasoning (the percentage of *foie gras* should be stated).

Francfort (Alsace) Finely ground, pure pork frankfurter-type boiling sausage.

Jambon d'Ardennes (the Ardennes) Outstanding dry-cured ham, usually smoked, eaten raw in thin slices. Best of all is *noix de jambon d'Ardennes,* a boneless center-cut from the ham that can be easily sliced.

Jambon de marcassin (the Ardennes) Salted and cured wild boar ham.

Jambonneau de Reims (Champagne) Small, individual, cured, and cooked pork hock, usually covered with bread crumbs and ready to eat; excellent picnic fare.

Kassler (Alsace) Smoked and cured tenderloin of pork.

Langue fumée (Lille and all Nord) Smoked lamb's tongue.

Pâté de gibier (the Ardennes) Game *pâté* made from whatever is plentiful and in season, including hare, thrush, deer, and wild boar.

Pâtés en croûte (all North) There is a great predilection in this part of the country for *pâtés* wrapped in a pastry crust, baked, and served either hot or cold in slices. In Amiens, delicious duck *pâté* is so prepared and, in Alsace, smooth liver *pâtés* (especially *pâté de foie gras*) can be found *en croûte.*

Jars of conserved potjevleisch

Pieds de porc à la Ste.-Menehould

(Champagne) Pig's trotters, boiled, boned, pressed in bread crumbs, and sold ready to broil. The cooked meat is also used to make a tasty, cold *terrine de pied de porc à la Ste.-Menehould*.

Potjevleisch

(Nord) Pork, chicken, rabbit, and veal, slowly cooked in large chunks, then allowed to go cold in a sharp, vinegary aspic sometimes flavored with *genièvre de Houlle* (local Dutch-style gin). Available from *charcuteries* freshly prepared or conserved in jars, *potjevleisch* makes a tasty and substantial instant meal.

Presskopf (Alsace) Local variation of *hure* (head cheese); made from meat from pig's or calf's head, set in a Riesling-enriched gelatin: classic cold fare served with potato salad in *winstubs* along the Route du Vin d'Alsace.

Saucisse de Strasbourg or **knack-wurst** or **knack** (Alsace) Pork and beef frankfurter-type boiling sausage.

Saucisson de bière or **bierwurst** (Alsace) Pork and garlic sausage, not made with beer but to accompany it; cut into thick slices and eaten with bread.

Saucisson de foie or **leberwurst** (Alsace) Liver sausage; used as a spread.

Saucisson de jambon or **schinkenwurst** (Alsace) Finely ground pork sausage with pieces of lean ham embedded in it.

Saucisson de pistache (Alsace) Cold sausage made from finely ground pork with pieces of tongue and pistachio nuts.

Schieffala or **schiffela** (Alsace) Smoked shoulder of pork; usually served hot with pickled turnips.

ANDOUILLETTES

Andouillettes (chitterling sausages) are one of the most ubiquitous of all *charcuterie* products, encountered on the menus of brasseries and bistros throughout France. But this, literally, gutsy favorite is authentically a product of Northern France— loved and celebrated by its proponents to such a degree that there is even a gastronomic society known as the *Association Amicale d'Amateurs d'Authentiques Andouillettes* or A.A.A.A.A.

Like many of the most delicious *charcuterie* products, *andouillettes* are made from those less desirable parts of the pig. Chitterlings are the usual main ingredients, sliced and layered with pork, veal, or beef tripe, herbs, spices, and seasoning, and stuffed into a natural skin casing. Always sold ready cooked, *andouillettes* need only to be reheated gently, so that the skin does not burst, and are served with Dijon mustard.

Three towns are preeminent for their *andouillettes:* Troyes in the Champagne region, renowned for its moist, pure pork sausages, and Cambrai and Arras in Nord and Pas de Calais, both of which make their *andouillettes* with pure *fraise de veau* or veal mesentery, resulting in particularly delicate sausages.

Poissons et Fruits de Mer

FISH AND SHELLFISH

Boulogne-sur-Mer, a fairly unremarkable Channel port that looks across the English Channel to the English coast of Kent (Napoleon came to Boulogne, gazed across the waters, and dreamed of invasion and conquest), is far and away the most important fishing port in France, accounting for a full third of all the fish landed in the country. Boulogne is home to a fleet of long-ranging trawlers that land an immense tonnage daily. The fish is packed in trays of ice and loaded into refrigerated trucks that speed their way to the capital by dawn, and to markets and fish shops throughout the North of France.

Salmon, a popular fish in the North, both wild and farmed

Fish from the colder waters of the North Sea, the North Atlantic, the Channel, and farther out (Boulogne's long-distance trawlers fish the waters of Newfoundland and the Norwegian Sea), landed at Boulogne and other less important coastal ports in Flanders and Picardy, can be spectacularly good, prepared simply and creatively in restaurants.

Traditionally *hareng* (herring) has been the fishing fleet mainstay of the North, for this oily and plump fish (best in winter) has long served as a staple for Northern Europeans. Today, there is much less *hareng* about than in the past, as overfishing has depleted the waters of much of Northern Europe, but it is still prepared in a variety of ways in France.

Fishermen at Audresselles, a small fishing town near Boulogne-sur-Mer

Alsace-Lorraine is a region where freshwater fish from the Rhine and its tributary the Ill, and from the Moselle and Meuse in Lorraine, is plentiful and much appreciated.

TRY TO SAMPLE

Anguille Eel, a Flemish favorite, especially prepared *au vert,* i.e., cooked with wine and herbs. When cold, the cooking liquid sets as a tasty gelatin; delicious served with *pommes frites* (French fries).

Bouffi Lightly salted and smoked herring (known as *craquelot* in Dunkerque, the traditional center of its production).

Brochet Pike, an extremely bony freshwater fish, often pounded and made into *quenelles* (dumplings).

Carpe Carp.

Ecrevisse Freshwater crayfish; a delicacy in Alsace-Lorraine.

Gendarme A traditional method of preparing herring: first salted then cold-smoked over a smoldering fire of oak chips until the fish emerges fairly hard and dry.

Matelote Freshwater fish stew containing at least two or three varieties, usually *brochet, tanche,* and *perche,* cooked in Alsace wine and cream.

Moules à la marinière Mussels prepared by the classic method of steaming them in wine, with shallots, and parsley; a favorite served virtually anywhere along the coast — and throughout the nation. The Flemish way to enjoy mussels is with a side order of French fries *(moules-frites).*

Perche Royal perch, a finely flavored freshwater fish.

Rollmop Soused herring marinated in vinegar and spices; a specialty of Boulogne-sur-Mer.

Saumon Salmon.

Sole Flounder or the true Dover sole; one of the most typical, delicious, and expensive fishes of the North; often simply prepared by the classic method, *à la meunière,* dredged in flour, then fried in butter and served with lemon juice and parsley, with the cooking butter poured over.

Tanche Tench.

Truite Trout; outstandingly prepared *"au bleu"* whereby the freshly killed fish is plunged into a wine or vinegar *court bouillon* which turns the fish a striking shade of blue.

Fresh fish and shellfish for sale at a small poissonnerie on the Baie de Somme, Picardy

---

SERGE PERARD'S *SOUPE DE POISSONS*

Serge Pérard has been cooking his famous *soupe de poissons* for over 20 years at his *poissonnerie* in Le Touquet, the fashionable seaside resort which has earned for itself the sobriquet "Paris-Plage" due to its popularity with the capital's *beau monde* who descend here in summer as well as on weekends. When they depart, they inevitably load up with crates of Serge's concentrated essence of the sea to take back with them, not only because it is excellent, but also as *un bon souvenir* of good times by the sea.

The secret of the famous *soupe?* Serge shrugs in a rather offhand manner, but you can sense his pride: "We use only the freshest fish daily from Boulogne-sur-Mer and Etaples, some 1,300 kg. (about 2,870 lbs.) per day, to make our *soupe.* It is concentrated in flavor because each jar contains 45 per cent fish and shellfish, a mixture of *dorade* (porgy), *rouget* (red mullet), *merlan* (whiting), *rascasse* (scorpion fish), and *crabe* (crab), flavored with white wine, saffron, tomatoes, fennel, and seasoning. Nothing else."

Beside Serge's *poissonerie,* he also has a lively and popular restaurant serving, of course, tureens of freshly made *soupe de poissons* — as much as you can eat — together with simply prepared fish and excellent *plateaux des fruits de mer* (seafood platters).

Serge Pérard
67, Rue de Metz
62520 Le Touquet
tel: 21 05 13 33
fax: 21 05 62 32
$$

Les Fromages

CHEESES OF THE NORTH

STRONG, POWERFUL, and assertive: these are the cheeses of the North — an outstanding and varied range of farmhouse products, mostly made from *lait cru* (unpasteurized milk). Many of the cheeses of the North are not for the faint-hearted: rind-washed *maroilles* from Nord-Pas de Calais, and *munster* from Alsace, both heavyweight classics in their own right, pale into mildness in comparison with the outrageously pungent *gris de Lille,* known locally as *"vieux puant"* or "old stinker." Milder Dutch-style cheeses, such as *mimolette,* come as some relief on the regional cheese board, while the Ile-de-France that borders Champagne is the source of the finest *brie* in the land.

Munster, *the great cheese from Alsace*

TRY TO SAMPLE

Boulette d'Avesnes (Nord-Pas de Calais) Rejected pieces of *maroilles* cheese mashed with tarragon and black pepper, formed into a cone, and rolled in paprika.

Brie de Meaux AC (Ile-de-France and Champagne) The classic *pâte fleurie* cheese *par excellence. Brie de Meaux* must be made entirely from unpasteurized milk and it takes a full 20 liters (5 gallons) to produce one cheese 35 cm. (13½ in.) in diameter, the largest of all *bries*. The best cheeses are aged for at least two months to develop their deep flavor and creamy texture and consistency. *Brie de Meaux* is typically displayed in *fromageries* on its *paillon* (straw mat).

Carré de l'est or **carré de Lorraine** (Champagne and Lorraine) Small, square, *brie*-type cheese, usually produced industrially. The best *carré de*

Sire de Créquy, *from Pas-de-Calais*

Lorraine benefits from a *Label Rouge* (quality label).

Cendré de Champagne (Champagne) *Camembert*-sized cheese aged in fine ash, an ancient process that adds flavor and reduces the fat content of the cheese. The best comes from Les Riceys, a wine town noted for its *rosé*.

Chaource AC (Champagne) One of the great cheeses of Champagne, a *pâte fleurie* cheese made in a cylindrical form, to be eaten after only a few weeks' aging: rich, creamy, and finely textured.

Coulommiers (Ile-de-France and Champagne) Small, *brie*-type cheese with a high fat content.

Dauphin (Nord-Pas de Calais and Picardy) Another assertive example from the *maroilles* family, mixed with herbs and pepper, and molded into a dolphin shape.

Gérômé (Lorraine) The local name in Lorraine for rind-washed cheese similar to *munster.*

Gris de Lille (Lille and all Nord) An incredibly strong, rind-washed cheese left in a brine bath for up to three months, when it acquires its gray rind and assertive flavor and aroma.

Langres AC (Champagne) Soft, cylindrical, rind-washed cheese with a characteristic orange rind. Softly textured, creamy, usually concave on top.

Maroilles AC (Nord-Pas de Calais) The great cheese of the North, and, in spite of its assertive smell, probably the mildest and most delicate of all the rind-washed family of cheeses. Produced in the Avesnois-Thiérache near the Belgian border, the best *maroilles* comes from small farm dairies using *lait cru*.

Mimolette (Dunkerque and all Nord) Orange, Dutch *gouda*-type cheese from Flanders. Try the aged *vieille mimolette*.

Mont-des-Cats (Nord) Pressed cheese from the Trappist Abbaye de Mont-des-Cats; somewhat rubbery, with a mild, nutty flavor.

Munster AC (Alsace) The great cheese of Alsace; rind-washed with a characteristic orange color, pungent odor, and assertive flavor. Some farm versions have cumin seeds mixed in them.

Rollot (Picardy) Rind-washed cheese from Picardy with a rich, spicy flavor. The heart-shaped version is known as *coeur d'Arras*.

Maroilles, *from near the Belgian border*

Sire de Créquy (Pas-de-Calais) Distinctive rind-washed cheese.

Trappe de Belval (Pas-de-Calais) A mild, creamy pressed cheese made by nuns at the Abbaye de Belval near Hesdin.

Vieux Boulogne (Boulogne-sur-Mer) Farmhouse cheese exclusive to Philippe Olivier, rind-washed in local beer.

PHILIPPE OLIVIER, *FROMAGER-AFFINEUR*

Philippe Olivier, a dynamic *maître fromager* (master cheesemaker), is passionate about cheese, and, consequently, his small shop in the heart of Boulogne-sur-Mer has become famous not only throughout France but around the world for its excellent and comprehensive selection of French farmhouse cheeses. Philippe regularly supplies cheeses not only to restaurants throughout France and London as well as other European capitals, but he even sends French cheese regularly to Japan.

Like the *négociant-éleveur* who purchases young wines and brings them to maturity, Philippe buys farmhouse cheeses direct from a vast number of individual cheesemakers while the cheeses are still immature and not yet ready to eat. Then, in his *caves d'affinage* below the shop, he and his team carefully hand-tend the cheeses until they are mature and in perfect condition.

Each type of cheese requires a different treatment, such as storage at different temperatures and levels of humidity. Some cheeses need to be turned and brushed every day or two, others are washed in mixtures of brine, beer, or alcohol.

This fastidious attention to detail means that cheeses, such as *maroilles, dauphin, boulette d'Avesnes,* and *mimolette,* purchased at Philippe Olivier's are almost always in tip-top condition.

Philippe Olivier
43-45, Rue Thiers
62200 Boulogne-sur-Mer
tel: 21 31 94 74
fax: 21 30 76 57

Pâtisseries et Confiseries
PASTRIES AND CANDIES

COULD IT BE the colder weather, the gray skies, the chill winds that in winter blow across from Siberia which make the people of the North seek comfort and wickedly rich sustenance in the form of delicious *pâtisseries* and *confiseries*? What is certain is that, for those with a sweet tooth, the North of France is little short of heaven.

TRY TO SAMPLE

Berawecka or **bierweck (**Alsace) Sweet bread filled with pears, dried fruits, spices, and flavored with *kirsch*.

Bêtise de Cambrai (Cambrai) Mint-flavored boiled sugar candies sold throughout the North in characteristic cans and boxes. A *"bêtise"* is something wrongly or stupidly done, and legend has it that these sweets were first made by accident by a ham-fisted apprentice *confiseur* in Cambrai.

Biscuit de Reims (Reims and all Champagne) Pale pink sweet biscuit twice-baked in a wood-fired oven; never too sweet, it is delicious with a *coupe* of Champagne.

Bretzels (Alsace) Big Alsatian *bretzels* (pretzels), tender and soft on the inside, crunchy and salty on the outside, are a delicious savory baked food of Alsace; delicious with a glass of local wine.

Chocolat The best chocolate in France comes from the North. It is usually more bitter than Belgian versions, and is hand-made in numerous shops throughout the region. In Champagne, try the liqueur-filled *bouchons,* chocolates in the shape of a Champagne cork.

Dragées (Lorraine) Sugared almonds; made in Verdun since the 13th century.

Kokeboterom (Dunkerque and all Nord) Raisin-studded yeast *brioche.*

Krapfen (Alsace) Fried dough filled with jam.

Kugelhopf or **kouglof** or **gougelhopf** (Alsace) Classic yeast *brioche*-like cake baked in a fluted mold with a hole through the middle, sometimes studded with raisins, covered with icing sugar or almonds. *Kugelhopf* is a breakfast favorite in Alsace together with a tot of *eau-de-vie* or a *grand crème* coffee.

Macaron d'Amiens (Amiens) Almond, egg white, honey, and sugar

Kugelhopf, *the traditional yeast cake, partnered by* eau-de-vie d'Alsace

macaroon, the most famous and delicious of which comes from Amiens.

Madeleines de Commercy (Lorraine) Classic, molded lemon teacakes of Proust's childhood memories.

Rabotte (Picardy) Whole apple baked in pastry.

Strudel (Alsace) Austrian-inspired finely textured, layered pastry filled with apples or other fruits in season.

Succès Berckois (Nord-Pas de Calais) Hand-made boiled sugar candies from the seaside town of Berck-Plage.

Tarte au gros bord (Nord-Pas de Calais) The ubiquitous, but delicious, dessert of the North, a simple pastry tart filled with little more than a mixture of sugar, eggs, and cream. The name comes from the fact that this homemade staple generally has a thick, hand-formed crust.

Tarte aux fruits (Alsace-Lorraine) The profusion of fine fruits from Alsace-Lorraine is used to make superlative sweet *tartes,* available at home, in *pâtisseries,* and from market stalls. Our favorite is the *tarte aux mirabelles,* made with succulent yellow plums.

The King of Wines
CHAMPAGNE

CHAMPAGNE IS THE FINEST sparkling wine in the world, and remains the benchmark against which Old and New World competitors are judged.

The obvious needs to be stated: Champagne (the word alone suffices and does not need to be followed by AC) only comes from the delimited Champagne vineyard, produced from black Pinot Noir and Pinot Meunier and white Chardonnay grapes grown to restricted yields and following a stringent and well-defined method of production.

Champagne is produced by a classic method of secondary fermentation in the bottle. After the still wines have been vinified and assembled into the *cuvée,* the wines are bottled with a small amount of *liqueur de tirage* (pure cane sugar and natural yeast dissolved in still wine). The yeast feeds on the sugar in the wine, causing a slow secondary fermentation which produces carbon dioxide as a by-product which gives Champagne its fine stream of bubbles. The bottles must remain resting on their sides to allow this slow process to take its course over a legal minimum of 15 months (though many large firms age even non-vintage wines for a minimum of three and their vintage Champagnes for over five or six years).

The secondary fermentation, however, leaves behind an undesirable sludgy sediment of dead yeast cells and other solid matter that must be removed in order to render the Champagne crystal-clear. This sticky sediment must be made to slide down toward the neck of the bottle from where it will be finally removed. This is *remuage,* whereby the bottles, placed in slanted racks known as *pupitres,* are gradually riddled, i.e., turned and twisted by skilled *remueurs,* a daily process over a period of six weeks that moves them from an initial near horizontal position to an almost vertical one, and ends with the deposit resting on the crown cork of the bottle. A skilled *remueur* can riddle thousands of bottles in a day. In addition to manual *remuage,* many large and small houses now use automatic, computer-operated machines, called *gyropalettes,* that can turn more than 500 bottles at a time. The automated process can take as little as three days — quality, apparently, is identical.

Before the wines are ready to be released, the collected sediment must be removed. Small *récoltants-manipulants* may do this manually simply through a skillful maneuver that expels the sediment as the bottles are uncorked. Large houses, on the other hand, normally freeze the sediment into a block of ice in the bottle neck, and this is similarly expelled when the wine is uncorked. In both cases, the bottles must be topped up and given their selected *dosage* (a mixture of pure cane sugar and older reserve wine) to produce *brut* (the dryest with the exception of *pas dosage* or *nature* which receive no sweetening at all), *extra-sec* (dry), *demi-sec* (sweet), or *riche* or *doux* (very sweet).

Here are some of the terms you are likely to come across when buying or tasting Champagne:

Grand cru Grapes grown in vineyards classified as such for their excellence. The best Champagnes contain a high percentage of *grand cru* grapes. **Premier cru** is a tier below *grand cru* but still indicates grapes of excellent provenance.
Grandes maisons The world-famous Champagne houses that have created the world image and prestige of Champagne

A remueur riddling Champagne bottles to shift the sediment down to the neck

The moulin à vent, windmill, *at Verzenay, a landmark in the vineyards of Champagne*

maintain centuries-long traditions of producing excellent non-vintage wines, using their formidable stocks of older reserves allied with impeccable modern technology.

Grandes marques Members of the Syndicat des Grandes Marques, not all of them well known.

Propriétaire-récoltant or **récoltant-manipulant** Some of the finest Champagnes are now being produced by individual *récoltants-manipulants,* growers who produce, bottle, and sell their own Champagnes direct to the public.

TYPES OF CHAMPAGNE

Blanc de blancs Literally, "white of whites," i.e., Champagne produced entirely from Chardonnay grapes; resulting often in delicate, light wines. *Recommended producers: Billecart-Salmon, Philipponnat, Mumm (Mumm de Cramant), Ruinart.*

Blanc de noirs A Champagne produced entirely from black grapes, usually Pinot Noir: full-bodied, powerful, rich, though sometimes lacking in delicacy. *Recommended producer: Bollinger (Vieilles Vignes).*

Deluxe *cuvées* Very special Champagnes, almost all of them vintages. They are unique to each of the great houses that make them, using either rare old reserves or the finest selected grapes only from

the best years or from individual vine-yards, vinified and subsequently aged for lengthy periods. *Recommended cuvées: Contes de Champagne (Taittinger), Dom Perignon (Moët & Chandon), La Grande Dame (Veuve Cliquot), Cristal (Louis Roederer).*

Non-vintage Champagne Most Champagnes are produced from a *cuvée* or blend of still wines from different years and from three types of grapes: Pinot Noir, Pinot Meunier, and Chardonnay. *Recommended producers: Bollinger, Joseph Perrier, Louis Roederer, Pol Roger, Veuve Cliquot, Bruno Paillard, Krug.*

Rosé Champagne The best is produced in the classic manner by letting some of the color from the skins of black grapes bleed into the grape must to tint it. In other cases, red wine is added. *Recommended producers: Billecart-Salmon, Pommery, Bollinger (Grand Année).*

Vintage Champagnes Made only in exceptional years, the result of a single year's harvest. (For best years, see Vintage Years for Wines, pp.244≠245) *Recommended producers: Bollinger (Grand Année, RD) Alfred Gratien, Krug, Pol Roger, Salon, Perrier-Jouet, Jacquesson.*

OTHER WINES FROM CHAMPAGNE

Coteaux Champenois AC In addition to Champagne, still white and red wines are produced in the region, notably good Chardonnay whites from the Côte des Blancs and reds from wine towns such as Bouzy and Cumières. *Recommended producers: Bollinger, Laurent-Perrier.*

Marc de Champagne Made from the leftover Champagne grape skins and residue after pressing. A favorite after-dinner drink and also widely used in local *cuisine.*

Ratafia Sweetish *apéritif* made from unfermented juice of Champagne grapes, blended with brandy and aged in oak. *Recommended producers: Beaufort, Geoffroy Laurent-Perrier, Moët et Chandon.*

Les Routes du Champagne
THE CHAMPAGNE TRAIL

THE CHAMPAGNE WINE region offers a chance to combine visits to historical and atmospheric centers, such as Reims and Epernay, with organized tours of underground Champagne *caves* where millions of bottles of wine lie aging. You can stay in some of the most luxurious château hotels in France or in simple country *auberges,* enjoying elegant *haute cuisine champenoise* or the more rustic, but always eminently satisfying, local foods.

Reims and Epernay are the two main towns. The rest of the region is quiet in the extreme, made up mainly of small villages with clusters of stone dwellings set amid the vineyards. Both Reims and Epernay warrant visits, not least because the *grandes maisons* give guided tours of their underground *caves,* in many cases without appointment, but also because of their fine restaurants and food and wine shops. But to gain a true feel of Champagne, try to visit at least one *récoltant-manipulant,* a winegrower who makes and sells his own Champagnes.

REIMS, CAPITAL OF THE REGION
Reims, the *"ville-sainte,"* or sacred city, where, since 496 A.D., almost without exception the kings of France came to be crowned and consecrated, is today a busy and modern metropolis. The city, razed to the ground and rebuilt repeatedly, still manages to give an indication of its historical importance. The greatest monument is the Cathédrale de Notre-Dame, with its superbly decorated west front with hundreds of carved figures.

A visit to a *grande maison* to learn about the process of transforming the still wines of the region into sparkling Champagne, as well as simply to view and experience the sheer scale of the underground Champagne *caves* is fascinating. After the visit, enjoy authentic Champenois foods at Le Vigneron, an old restaurant that is something of a shrine and museum to Champagne *vignerons,* or splash out at Gérard Boyer's Les Crayères, one of the greatest and most luxurious three-star restaurants in France.

EPERNAY — WINE CAPITAL
If Reims is the capital of the Champagne region, Epernay can claim to be the capital of Champagne wine. Considerably smaller than the former, Epernay is a town that seems to live, work, and breathe for the production, sale, and consumption of Champagne.

Moët & Chandon, one of the great houses on the Avenue de Champagne, Epernay

Come to Epernay for no other reason than to enjoy Champagne: to visit as many of the town's *grandes maisons* as you care to; to drink Champagne by the *coupe* or bottle in restaurants, cafés, or bars (the *bar à vins* at Les Berceaux is one of the most welcoming); to begin excursions into the wine country along any of the signposted *Routes du Champagne* here; or to luxuriate in fine country hotels, such as the Domaine Royal Champagne, which overlooks Epernay from its hilltop position amid the vineyards (address, p.104).

LES ROUTES DU CHAMPAGNE

Three signposted wine roads extend through the finest vineyards of Champagne. They provide quiet excursions into the wine country and the perfect excuse for an extended vineyard picnic, while giving the chance to visit one of the scores of *récoltants-manipulants,* growers whose Champagnes are a fascinating contrast to those from the famous *grandes maisons*.

The "Montagne de Reims" route extends in a broad horseshoe from Reims to Epernay across the gentle plateau of the so-called Montagne de Reims through quiet wine towns, such as Jouy-lès-Reims, Rilly-la-Montagne, Verzenay, Ambonnay, Bouzy (what a great name for a wine town!), and Ay. This zone is primarily planted with Pinot Noir, the black grape that adds backbone and body to Champagne, so growers' own Champagnes, in some cases *blanc de noirs*, can be full-bodied and powerful. Growers to visit include the Aubry brothers in Jouy-lès-Reims and Herbert Beaufort in Bouzy, the latter making not only outstanding Champagne but also excellent still Bouzy red wine. Dine at the elegant

Heading for the "capital" of Champagne

winegrowers' favorite, Le Grand Cerf in Montchenot, or at the simple Auberge St.-Vincent, which serves genuine *cuisine champenoise* (addresses, pp.104, 105).

The "Vallée de la Marne" route is perhaps the easiest to follow, extending along the banks of the Marne river east and west of Epernay, with a brief excursion into the wooded hills of St.-Imoges and Hautvillers. To the east of Epernay lies the important wine town of Ay, home to numerous famous *grandes maisons*. To the west, the wine road runs into the hills to Hautvillers, where in the town's abbey the blind cellarmaster Dom Pierre Pérignon perfected methods of producing Champagne in the 17th century — "Brothers," he is said to have cried upon opening a successful bottle, "come quickly! I am drinking stars." From Hautvillers, descend down to Cumières, a town noted both for its Champagnes and the excellence of its still red wines, then follow the valley to Châtillon-sur-Marne (birthplace of Pope Urban II), and on through Vandières to Vincelles. Recommended growers along the way include René Geoffroy at Cumières and Frédéric Nowack at Vandières. Dine underground in the cool, atmospheric Le Caveau in Cumières (address, p.105).

The "Côte des Blancs" route extends in another horseshoe curve south of Epernay. Here, on a deep ridge of chalk, the Chardonnay grape reigns supreme. Visit quiet wine villages such as Cramant, Avize, Oger, Le Mesnil, and Vertus. At Le Mesnil, Bernard Launois and his wife Dany are pleased to receive visitors, and have created a small wine museum. A good base for touring this area is the elegant Hostellerie La Briqueterie at Vinay (address, p.105).

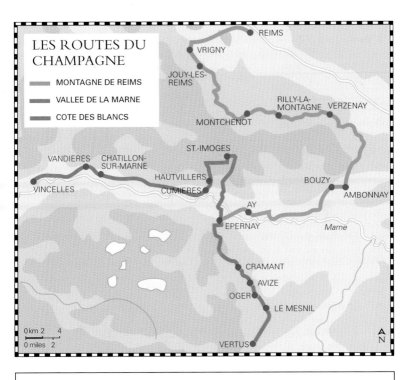

LES ROUTES DU CHAMPAGNE

- MONTAGNE DE REIMS
- VALLEE DE LA MARNE
- COTE DES BLANCS

REIMS
VRIGNY
JOUY-LES-REIMS
RILLY-LA-MONTAGNE   VERZENAY
MONTCHENOT
ST.-IMOGES
VANDIERES   CHATILLON-SUR-MARNE
HAUTVILLERS
BOUZY
VINCELLES   CUMIERES
AMBONNAY
AY
EPERNAY   Marne
CRAMANT
AVIZE
OGER
LE MESNIL
VERTUS

0 km 2   4
0 miles 2

N

INTO CHAMPAGNE COUNTRY

Boyer "Les Crayères"
64, Boulevard Henri-Vasnier
51100 Reims
tel: 26 82 80 80
fax: 26 82 65 52
Elegant château set in its own wooded grounds; a fitting setting for one of the great restaurants of France.
$$$$+

Champagne Herbert Beaufort
32, Rue de Tours
51150 Bouzy
tel: 26 57 01 34
fax: 26 57 09 08
Full-bodied Brut de Noirs Champagne and Bouzy.

Champagne L. Aubry Fils
4 et 6, Grande Rue
51390 Jouy-lès-Reims

tel: 26 49 20 07
fax: 26 49 75 27
The Aubry brothers are great enthusiasts and ambassadors of their region and its wines. Their Champagnes are individual and outstanding.

Champagne Nowack
10, Rue Bailly
51700 Vandières
tel: 26 58 02 69
fax: 26 58 39 62
Pinot Meunier dominated Champagnes with an appealing fruity roundness.

Champagne René Geoffroy
150, Rue du Bois des Jots
51480 Cumières
tel: 26 55 32 31
fax: 26 54 66 50

René Geoffroy still ferments traditional Champagnes in wood casks.

Champagne Taittinger
9, Place St.-Nicaise
51100 Reims
tel: 26 85 45 35
fax: 26 85 84 05
Parts of Taittinger's underground caves date from the 4th century.

Moët & Chandon
18, Avenue de Champagne
51200 Epernay
tel: 26 54 71 11;
(visits) 26 51 20 20
fax: 26 51 20 21
The most visited Champagne house also has the most extensive galeries (28 km. or 17½ miles).

Les Vins

OTHER WINES OF THE NORTH

THE NORTH, unlike the rest of France, is not wholly given over to wine: *bières* (beers) vie for a drinker's affections, and a range of distinctive spirits and liqueurs is also produced.

ALSACE-LORRAINE

This northernmost wine region is the source of a consistently high-quality range of varietal wines, i.e., wines made from single grape varieties. However, in particularly hot summers followed by warm, misty fall weather — conditions that encourage *pourriture noble,* or noble rot *(Botrytis cinerea),* Alsace winemakers produce late-harvested dessert wines, the finest of which can rank among the most exciting in the world.

Alsace AC or **Vin d'Alsace AC**
The basic Alsace *appellation* is generally used with the name of the grape variety. With the exception of small amounts of minor red and *rosé* wines produced

The vineyards of Nothalten, a small town in Alsace in the foothills of the Vosges Mountains

from Pinot Noir, Alsace wines are predominantly dry white wines. Individually named and classified vineyards within the delimited wine region may be designated Alsace Grand Cru AC (together with the *lieu-dit* name), though, more generally, Alsace wines come not from individual *terroirs* but rather from blends of the same single grape grown in various parts of the region.

In certain years only, exceptional *vendange tardive* (late harvest) and *sélection des grains nobles* (individually selected grapes affected by *pourriture noble*) wines are produced. Such great wines are always in demand and extremely expensive. *Recommended producers: Hugel, Dopff au Moulin, Dopff & Irion, Léon Beyer, Kuentz-Bas, Gresser, W. Gisselbrecht, Trimbach, Zind-Humbrecht, Weinbach, caves coopératives de Turckheim* and *Pfaffenheim.*

The principal Alsace grape varieties and blends are:

Edelzwicker Wine made not varietally but from a blend of the so-called noble grapes. In practice, this usually means a high proportion of Sylvaner, with some Pinot Blanc, together with Chasselas. At its best, it is a zesty, refreshing wine.
Gewürztraminer The most recognizable and immediately distinctive grape variety, with an intense, flowery, sometimes spicy character, almost oriental in opulence. Some of the best examples come from north and south of Colmar.
Muscat Produced only in small quantities, Muscat makes the most surprising Alsace wine, flowery and expansively scented, yet bone dry, with a crisp finish.
Pinot Blanc High-quality, clean, dry wines that display a fresh, supple character.
Pinot Gris or **Tokay-Pinot Gris** One of the great grapes of Alsace that can produce the most full-bodied of the region's wines with a warm, spicy bouquet and exceptionally rich flavor. Fine examples of Tokay-Pinot Gris wines come from around Ribeauvillé.

Pinot Noir In this northern vineyard, the Pinot Noir generally ripens only sufficiently to produce light red and rosé wines, though, in exceptional years, surprisingly warm, full-bodied red wines can also result. Pinot Noir from Ottrott, near Obernai, is considered among the best.

Alsace varietals, wines made from "noble" single grape varieties

Riesling The undisputed emperor of Alsace grape varieties; capable of producing outstanding white wines that combine the lusciously appealing and distinctive scent of ripe Riesling with great body and depth of flavor, always underpinned by a firm backbone of fresh, fruity acidity and alcohol. Selected *cuvée* and *réserve* wines from the best houses as well as individual *grands crus* deserve to be aged, for, with time, they emerge with a rich, honeyed character and nuances that only come through bottle aging. Rieslings from Ribeauvillé, Riquewihr, Hunawihr, Kaysersberg, and Andlau are all prized.

Sylvaner Long considered the workhorse of Alsace, this grape produces mainly uncomplicated wines. In certain areas, especially on the *lieu-dit* of Zotzenberg at Mittelbergheim, Sylvaner can yield great wines of depth and finesse.

Other wines in the North are:

Côtes de Toul VDQS The best wines of Lorraine come from vineyards around the city of Toul. Try *vin gris*, a very pale rosé, made mainly from Gamay.

Crémant d'Alsace AC Sparkling wine from Alsace made by the classic method of secondary fermentation in the bottle: refreshing and relatively inexpensive. *Recommended producer: Dopff au Moulin.*

Vin de Moselle VDQS Mainly red wines from Gamay and whites from Pinot Blanc and Sylvaner.

OTHER DRINKS

Eaux-de-vie d'Alsace Strong, clean, clear *alcools blancs* are distilled in Alsace from a range of fruits (see p.103). *Recommended producers: Bertrand, Devoille, Legoll.*

Fine Marne Grape brandy distilled from local Champagne wines then aged in oak casks.

Genièvre A Dutch-style gin from Nord-Pas de Calais with the pungent nose and flavor of juniper berries. *Recommended producers: Persyn (Houlle), Wambrechiés.*

Marc de Gewürztraminer AC The aromatic Gewürztraminer grape makes one of the most distinctive and flavorful of all French *marcs.*

Mirabelle de Lorraine AC One of the great fruit spirits of France: aromatic, powerful, and exceedingly smooth. *Recommended producers: Denizot, DeWeerd.*

BEERS

Au Baron Strong, top-fermented ales from the smallest brewery in France.

Bières d'Alsace A range of nationally and internationally available blond lager-type beers is brewed on a large scale in Alsace. Such beers may be enjoyed draft *(bière à la pression)* — ask for *"un demi"* (25 cl. or ½ pint) — or in bottles *(en bouteille)*. *Recommended producers: Kronenbourg, Mutzig, Fischer, Kanterbräu.*

Jenlain Strong, well-hopped, bottle-conditioned *bière de garde* brewed and sold mainly in Nord.

Pelforth Distinctive, characterful brew from large brewery in Lille.

Trois Monts Dark, artisan-brewed beer from Nord, caramelly but not too sweet, with a distinctive, "irony" finish.

Route du Vin d'Alsace

THE WINE ROAD OF ALSACE

On the well posted Route du Vin *in Alsace*

THE SIGNPOSTED Route du Vin d'Alsace extends for some 125 km. (75 miles) along the eastern flanks of the Vosges Mountains from Marlenheim, in the north near Strasbourg, to Thann, almost at Mulhouse. It is possibly the prettiest and most charming wine road in all France. It meanders along the foothills of the mountains, passing through vineyards where Riesling, Gewürztraminer, Pinot Blanc, Pinot Gris, and other grapes ripen, through half-timbered medieval towns and villages, and past the homes of scores of small winegrowers, most of whom invite you to pause to quench your thirst with a green-stemmed goblet of their cellar-cool wines. Many have brightly colored roadside stands, decorated with boxes of scarlet geraniums, where you can taste and buy; others require no more than a telephone call in advance, or a postcard indicating your likely time of arrival in order to visit the cellars and taste the wines.

A tour of Alsace will probably begin in Strasbourg, capital of the region, headquarters of the Council of Europe, and home of the European Union Parliament. This modern, vibrant, cultural and industrial center still maintains the essential character of a prosperous and wealthy medieval *bourg*. The spiny, sandstone Gothic cathedral dominates an old quarter that is particularly atmospheric, with its dark, stone-paved streets lined with former merchants' houses. The nearby Petite France quarter was once an area of craftsmen and tanners. Today, the restored half-timbered houses overhang a system of quiet canals: come here to sip goblets of wine at terraces overlooking the water, and enjoy local foods such as *choucroute garnie* at the famous Maison des Tanneurs restaurant.

Though the Route du Vin begins at Marlenheim, some 20 km. (13 miles) from Strasbourg, the first wine towns of note are Molsheim and Obernai.

The vineyards above Riquewihr

Molsheim, an ancient university town, is also a convenient starting place for excursions into the beautiful Vosges Mountains. Obernai boasts fine old buildings, such as its 15th-century corn market and a medieval town hall assembly chamber. At weekends, you can enjoy *tarte flambée* cooked in a wood-fired oven in winegrower J. Seilly's rustic Caveau du Vigneron (see p.81).

Villages along the *route,* such as Ottrott, Heiligenstein, Barr, Mittelbergheim, Andlau, and Dambach-la-Ville, all produce fine wines, though so complex is the geology that certain communes specialize in particular grapes: Ottrott is noted for its Pinot Noir reds, Barr for its finely scented Gewürztraminers, Mittelbergheim for its Sylvaner from the *grand cru* Zotzenberg vineyard, and Andlau for its *grands crus* Rieslings. Stop to taste, compare, and buy all three of Andlau's *grands crus* from winegrowers André and Rémy Gresser, and afterward dine at the Restaurant Relais de la Poste, a friendly Alsatian *winstub*. The Hotel-Restaurant Arnold at Ittersviller is another popular restaurant in the thick of the wine country. In Dambach-la-Ville, a signposted footpath leads from the town square into the surrounding vineyards. Willy Gisselbrecht's winery, producing highly regarded wines, is located here.

The heart of the Alsace vineyard is its middle stretch, particularly between Ribeauvillé and Colmar. Ribeauvillé, source of excellent wines, especially from its three *grands crus* sites, is one of the region's principal towns and makes a good touring center. Riquewihr, to the south, is the finest and most perfectly preserved village along the *Route du Vin.* This ancient walled town, with its numerous medieval and Renaissance half-timbered houses and stone-paved streets, is the home of some of the region's best-known *propriétaires-négociants* — grower-shippers — such as Jean Hugel et Fils and Dopff au Moulin.

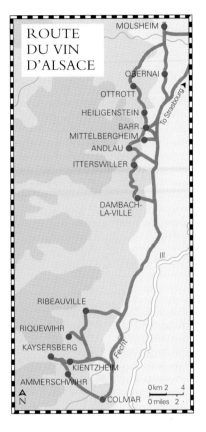

Enjoy simple foods at Riquewihr's Winstub Au Tire-Bouchon. Not far from Riquewihr, on the banks of the Ill, the Auberge de l'Ill is one of the great three-star restaurants of France.

Below Riquewihr, both Kientzheim and Kaysersberg lie in a deep valley that pierces the broad flank of the Vosges. This flank shelters the steep, south-facing and well-exposed slopes of vineyards such as the *grand cru* Schlossberg, noted for its Riesling. Kientzheim is the headquarters of the Confrérie St.-Etienne, an important wine fraternity whose headquarters are located in the town château, where there is also a good wine museum. Another fine, famous restaurant, Aux Armes de France (address, p.105), is at nearby Ammerschwihr.

The largest town along the wine road is pleasant, atmospheric Colmar. Here, as much as anywhere else, the unique fusion of German and French tradition, architecture, and culture is evident. Explore Colmar's medieval quarter, with its intricately carved houses and shops, and the area known as "Petite Venise," lined by a small, pretty winding canal. Visitors should not miss the Unterlinden Museum, with its superb Issenheim altarpiece. The restaurant Au Fer Rouge (address, p.105) serves innovative modern cuisine in the old part of town.

Wine producer's wheelbarrow inviting visitors to stop to taste and buy

The wine country continues south of Colmar. It is worth continuing to Turckheim, where the highly regarded *cave coopérative* makes excellent and affordable wines. Eguisheim is another pretty wine village and there are good views across the Rhine to Germany's Black Forest from Husseren-les-Châteaux. Pfaffenheim has one of the finest *caves coopératives* in the region.

ALONG THE ALSATIAN WINE ROAD

André & Rémy Gresser
2, Rue de l'Ecole
67140 Andlau
tel: 88 08 95 88
fax: 88 08 55 99
Champion of Andlau's grands crus *Rieslings.*

Auberge de l'Ill
Rue de Collonges
68970 Illhaeusern
tel: 89 71 89 00;
89 71 83 23
fax: 89 71 82 83
One of the finest restaurants in France. Classic and innovative cuisine.
$$$$+

Cave Vinicole de Turckheim
16, Rue des Tuileries
68230 Turckheim
tel: 89 27 06 25
fax: 89 21 35 33
Highly regarded cave coopérative.

Dopff au Moulin
2, Rue J. Preiss
68340 Riquewihr
tel: 89 47 92 23

Long-established grower-shipper noted for still wines, as well as fine Crémant d'Alsace.

Hôtel-Restaurant Arnold
98, Route du Vin
67140 Itterswiller
tel: 88 85 50 58
fax: 88 85 55 54
Old favorite serving all the Alsatian classics: baeckenoffe *(Thu and Sat).*
$$

Jean Hugel & Fils
3, Rue de la Première
Asmée Française
68340 Riquewihr
tel: 89 47 92 15
fax: 89 49 00 10
Jean Hugel, Alsace's most famous grower-merchant is a great ambassador for the region, its traditions, culture, and wines.

Maison des Tanneurs
42, Rue Bain-aux-Plantes
67000 Strasbourg
tel: 88 32 79 70
fax: 88 22 17 26

Highly regarded restaurant, in centuries-old workshop, serving Alsatian specialties.
$$–$$$

Restaurant Relais de la Poste
1, Rue des Forgerons
67140 Andlau
tel: 88 08 95 91
Authentic winstub.
$–$$

Willy Gisselbrecht & Fils
5, Route du Vin
67650 Dambach-la-Ville
tel: 88 92 41 02
fax: 88 92 45 50
Full range of Alsace wines, including Crémant d'Alsace and vendange tardive.

Winstub Au Tire-Bouchon
29, Rue du Gén. de Gaulle
68340 Riquewihr
tel: 89 47 91 61
fax: 89 47 99 39
Small winstub: *local foods and wines of Preiss-Zimmer.*
$

Eaux-de-vie des Fruits

FRUIT LIQUEURS FROM ALSACE-LORRAINE

DISTILLING FRUITS into fiery, alcoholic *eaux-de-vie* is a skill that thrives particularly well in Alsace-Lorraine, with a tradition that dates back for centuries. *Mirabelles* (yellow plums), *quetsches* (blue plums), *poires Williams* (Williams pears), *cerises* (cherries), and *framboises* (raspberries) are all distilled primarily on a small scale by artisan distillers, using traditional pot stills and a lengthy process of double distillation similar to that carried out in Cognac.

Such *eaux-de-vie* are known also as *alcools blancs* because they are rarely aged in wood, but, rather, spend time in stainless steel or glass, and so remain colorless. Their appearance is deceptive, however: the best, always high in alcohol (45 per cent or higher), display the highly perfumed aroma of the fruit, and have long, lingering, ethereal flavors that really are the essence of the fruit in all its concentrated intensity. As huge quantities of fruit are required to produce them, they are always expensive.

René Legoll, a medal-winning distiller, is one of a number in Val de Villé, a small hamlet north of Ribeauvillé, outside Alsace's prosperous winegrowing lands. "The people here have traditionally turned to distilling out of necessity, because we had no vines from which to make our living," the genial, young distiller told me. "What we did have was an innate knowledge of the art of distilling that has been passed down for generations."

"To make good *eau-de-vie*," he explained, "you must begin with fruit of the highest quality and you must pay accordingly for it. Not all that I use is local. The *mirabelle* plums from Lorraine are the best in the world, far superior to ours from Alsace. But our own cherries are finer. I go down to Provence to seek the most finely perfumed *poires Williams*, while much of the wild fruits and berries come from Eastern Europe."

To produce *eaux-de-vie*, the fruits must first be fermented like wine. The whole fruits are pumped into vats, where they ferment naturally for upward of a few weeks, during which time the juice must be continually pumped back over the pulp and other solid matter. Once the fermentation is complete and the solids sink to the bottom, the fruits are ready to be distilled. The entire contents of the vat, including the solid pulp and fruit pits, is then transferred to the copper pot still. At Legoll's, the stills are heated indirectly by a *bain-marie* of hot water in order not to scorch the fruit. The *brouilli*, or first distillation, that results is distilled a second time; in each instance, the volatile *têtes* (heads) and *queues* (tails) are discarded, and only the pure, precious *coeur* (heart or middle cut) is kept.

In addition to distilling fresh fruits, Legoll produces a fine, intensely aromatic Marc de Gewürztraminer, made from the residue left over after the wine-making process, as well as unusual specialties, such as *baie de houx* (from holly berries — incredibly pungent), *gratte-cul* (rosehip), *sorbe* (rowanberries), *sureau* (elderflower), and others. Sample first *poire Williams,* the most approachable, as it remains closest in essence to the fruit itself, then graduate onto an aged *mirabelle vieille réserve*, velvety with the fresh yet intense character of cooked plums.

Distillerie R. Legoll
Route de Villé
67330 Châtenois
tel: 88 85 66 90
fax: 88 85 67 72

An impressive range of eaux-de-vie, *artisan-distilled by René Legoll*

Les Bonnes Adresses
USEFUL ADDRESSES

NORD-PAS DE CALAIS

A L'Huîtrière
3, Rue des Chats-Bossus
59800 Lille
tel: 20 55 43 41
fax: 20 55 23 10
Long-standing Lillois institution in the old part of town serving outstanding seafood, shellfish, and regional and classic cuisine.
$$$$

Auberge de la Grenouillère
Madeleine-sous-Montreuil
62170 Montreuil-sur-Mer
tel: 21 06 07 22
fax: 21 86 36 36
An idyllic small inn with outstanding restaurant serving innovative cuisine.
$$$

Aux Pêcheurs d'Etaples
Quai de la Canche
62630 Etaples
tel: 21 94 06 90
fax: 21 09 79 90
Run by the coopérative maritime étaploise (the local fishermen's coop), this restaurant serves the freshest fish and shellfish.
$–$$

Chocolaterie de Beussent
66, Route de Desvres
62170 Beussent
tel: 21 86 17 62
fax: 21 81 85 49

Typical Alsatian winstub, *for wines and light meals*

Hand-made chocolates of the highest quality by brothers Alain and Bruno Derick, in the beautiful Vallée de la Course.

Ferme Auberge Sire de Créquy
Route de Créquy
62310 Fruges
tel: 21 90 60 24
fax: 21 86 27 72
Source of one of the great cheeses of the North, and a welcoming and popular farmhouse restaurant serving home-cooked meals.
$

Restaurant-Brasserie Au Baron
Place des Rocs
59570 Gussignies
tel: 27 66 88 61
Almost on the frontier with Belgium, Au Baron is a brewery producing distinctive and well-hopped top-fermented ales, most of which are consumed in the café on the premises, or in the adjoining restaurant where meats and fish are grilled over an open fire (restaurant open weekends only).
$

PICARDY

Chocolaterie Jean Trogneux
1, Rue Delambre
8000 Amiens
tel: 22 91 58 27
fax: 22 97 96 96
Jean Trogneux is famous throughout Northern France for macarons d'Amiens *and hand-made chocolates.*

Hôtel de la Baie – Restaurant Mado
6, Quai Léonard
80550 Le Crotoy
tel: 22 27 80 42;
22 27 81 22
fax: 22 27 85 43

Haricots de mer, *samphire, a wild sea plant*

Famous old eating house on the waterfront in quiet resort. Mainly seafood menus.
$$

Les Marrissons
Pont de la Dodane,
Quartier St.-Leu
68, Rue des Marissons
8000 Amiens
tel: 22 92 96 66
fax: 22 91 50 50
Located in a 15th-century boathouse in the atmospheric St.-Leu quarter, serving classic and innovative dishes, as well as the great specialty of Amiens, canard en croûte au foie gras.
$$$

CHAMPAGNE AND ARDENNES

Auberge St.-Vincent
1, Rue St.-Vincent
51150 Ambonnay
tel: 26 57 01 98
fax: 26 57 81 48
Simple two-star logis *with a highly regarded restaurant serving regional foods.*
$–$$

Domaine Royale Champagne
Route Nationale 51
51160 Champillon-Bellevue
tel: 26 52 87 11
fax: 26 52 89 69

One of the most beautifully situated hotels in the region, overlooking the vineyards of Epernay. The restaurant serves haute cuisine champenoise.
$$$

Hostellerie La Briqueterie
4, Route de Sézanne
51530 Vinay Epernay
tel: 26 59 99 99
fax: 26 59 92 10
Elegant hotel-restaurant south of Epernay amid the Côte des Blancs vineyards.
$$$

Hôtel-Restaurant Les Berceaux
13, Rue des Berceaux
51200 Epernay
tel: 26 55 28 84
fax: 26 55 10 36
This old favorite has both an excellent restaurant and an informal wine bar.
$$

La Chocolaterie Thibaut
Zone Artisanale
Rue Max Menu
51530 Pierry
tel: 26 51 58 04
fax: 26 55 39 61
Don't miss Monsieur Thibaut's chocolate Champagne corks filled with marc de Champagne.

Le Caveau
Rue de la Cooperative
51480 Cumières
tel: 26 54 83 23
fax: 26 54 24 56
Fine regional foods served in Champagne cave.
$–$$

Le Grand Cerf
50, Route Nationale
51500 Montchenot
tel: 26 97 60 07
fax: 26 97 64 24
Sophisticated country inn serving good seafood; a long-standing winegrowers' favorite between Reims and Epernay.
$$$

Le Vigneron
Place Paul Jamot
51100 Reims
tel: 26 47 00 71
fax: 26 47 87 66
Authentic foods of Champagne prepared and presented with style. Champagne museum and a great selection of Champagnes and Coteaux Champenois wines.
$$–$$$

ALSACE-LORRAINE
Au Fer Rouge
52, Grande Rue
68000 Colmar
tel: 89 41 37 24
fax: 89 23 82 24
Nouvelle cuisine in the old part of Colmar.
$$$$

Au Vieux Strasbourg
10, Rue de la Division Leclerc
67000 Strasbourg
tel: 88 32 00 88
fax: 88 28 04 39
The range of breads in Alsace is generally superior to most other parts of France. This is one of the best bakeries in Strasbourg.

Aux Armes de France
1, Grand Rue
68770 Ammerschwihr
tel: 89 47 10 12
fax: 89 47 38 12
Famous Alsatian temple of gastronomy serving classic foods with regional accent.
$$$$

Charcuterie Glasser
18, Rue des Boulangers
68000 Colmar
tel: 89 41 23 69
fax: 89 23 55 93
The full range of Alsace charcuterie as well as top-notch foie gras maison.

Gilbert Marx
39, Grande Rue
68420 Eguisheim
tel: 89 41 32 56
fax: 89 24 96 85

Gilbert Marx's delicious bretzels are famous throughout the region, and make an excellent snack.

Jean Lutz
5, Rue du Chaudron
67000 Strasbourg
tel: 88 32 00 64
fax: 88 23 27 79
The address in Strasbourg for terrines of exceptional foie gras de canard or d'oie.

Maison Kammerzell
16, Place de la Cathédrale
67000 Strasbourg
tel: 88 32 42 14
fax: 88 23 03 92
This splendid 15th-century dwelling is a classified historic monument. The foods — local as well as innovative — are worthy of the setting.
$$–$$$

BEST BUYS
- *soupe de poissons* (Le Touquet)
- local beers
- *bêtises de Cambrai* (Cambrai)
- *foie gras* (Alsace)
- Champagne
- *bouchons* (chocolate Champagne corks)
- hand-made chocolates (Nord-Pas de Calais)
- *macarons d'Amiens* (Amiens)
- *jambon d'Ardennes* (the Ardennes)

The medieval clock in Riquewihr, Alsace

The Northwest

BRITTANY

NORMANDY

THE LOIRE VALLEY

POITOU-CHARENTES

WASHED BY THE WATERS OF THE NORTH ATLANTIC, its fertile interior irrigated by great rivers like the Loire and the Seine, Northwest France extends from the country's farthest northwest corner, at Brittany's Finistère — land's end — south along the Atlantic seaboard past Nantes, La Rochelle, and the Cognac vineyards of Poitou-Charentes, as far as the mouth of the Gironde. To the east of Finistère, the north coast of Brittany, with its beaches and fishing ports, leads past Mont-St.-Michel into the lush apple and dairy country of Normandy. Inland, the Seine links Le Havre and Rouen with Paris, while the Loire Valley extends upriver from Nantes, following a profusion of magnificent châteaux past Angers, Tours, Orléans, and into the very heart of France and the higher reaches of the river at Sancerre and Pouilly-sur-Loire.

Great shellfish (outstanding native oysters as well as lobster, scallops, and much else) comes from this region, especially Brittany. Normandy is the source of some of the finest and most famous French cheeses and of rich butter and cream, elements essential to classic French cuisine. The Loire Valley, known as *Le Jardin de la France* — the Garden of France — provides fine fruits and vegetables in addition to grapes for exceptional

The formal vegetable gardens of the Château de Villandry in the Loire Valley

(mainly) white wines virtually all along its considerable length. Poitou-Charentes rivals Normandy for its exquisite unsalted butter, and is famous for the finest melon in the land, the *charentais*. Sea-fresh oysters gain a unique flavor and character by being finished in the *claires* (salt pans) of Marennes and the surrounding Cognac vineyard is the source of the world's greatest brandy. (Not to be outdone, Normandy boasts Calvados, an apple brandy which, at best, is a smooth and distinguished distillation of great character.) For lovers of food and drink, Northwest France satisfies from beginning to end, wherever they are.

BRITTANY — A WORLD APART

Brittany is quite unlike anywhere else in France, its people proud of their Celtic origins, language, and traditions. Along the West Coast, in markets such as at Pont l'Abbé, women wearing the traditional Breton dress and high, white *coiffe* (lace headdress) mingle with vacationers who come to enjoy some of the finest beaches and cleanest waters in Northern Europe. Traditionally, Brittany is a land of fisherfolk and farmers. Lorient and Concarneau are two of the most significant fishing ports in the nation in

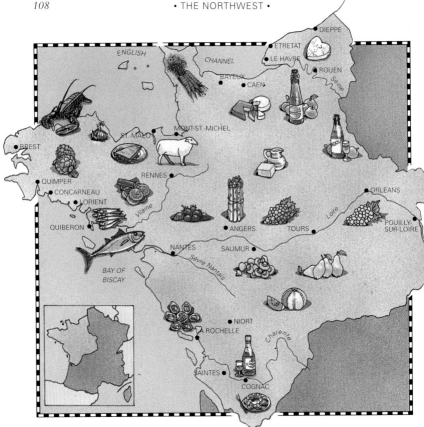

terms of tonnage landed, and all along the coast are smaller ports where local boats land an impressive catch. Inland, Brittany is a harsh country, even bleak in places, but, wherever the soil is arable, farmers grow outstanding vegetables, especially *primeurs* (early ripening young vegetables). But fishing and farming are being supplemented in importance by an ever growing industry: tourism. Brittany in summer is one of the most popular areas in France, with plenty of good, small hotels, inland as well as by the sea, and excellent restaurants and *crêperies*.

NORMANDY — A LUSH, FERTILE DAIRY COUNTRY

With its great, flat beaches that served as the bridgehead for the Allied D-Day invasion, Normandy is today a peaceful, lush, agricultural land. The Pays d'Auge, with its apple orchards, stout half-timbered farms, and pastures where brown and white Norman cattle graze, is about as beautiful a rural idyll as you are ever likely to find. The Cotentin Peninsula is wilder and less ordered, while north of the Seine the Pays de Caux and the Pays de Bray are both rolling, agricultural country and the source of much traditional dairy produce, including superb cheeses, cream, and butter, as well as cider and pork.

Visitors come to Normandy to visit Rouen, one of France's great provincial cities, its old center still hugely atmospheric, especially around the Place du Vieux Marché where the young maiden warrior, Jeanne d'Arc, was burned at the stake by the English in 1431. Many come, too, to pay homage to the soldiers killed on the D–Day beaches of Juno, Gold, Omaha, and Utah. The coast also offers fascinating fishing towns, such as Dieppe and Etretat; Bayeux, with its magnificent tapestry, and Mont-St.-Michel, the magical granite outcrop standing in the Atlantic, are both among the most visited places in France.

THE LOIRE VALLEY

Lined with medieval and Renaissance châteaux, the Loire Valley is one of the most popular regions in France. This is particularly beautiful country, and everything is sweetly in harmony: the weather never too hot, rarely too cold; the villages and châteaux built from the same white tufa that nourishes the vines; the pretty flower and vegetable gardens in front or back of even the smallest house or cottage; the classic foods in perfect partnership with the wines. And everywhere there is the soothing presence of the Loire, the longest river in France.

The scenery of the Loire Valley varies considerably from, say, the Pays Nantais, fanned by Atlantic breezes, through Touraine, the most beautiful part of all, with its magnificent and grandiose châteaux such as Chenonceaux, Loches, Amboise, and Chambord, and on past Orléans into the higher reaches of the Upper Loire leading to the Massif Central, landlocked and continental in feel, with colder, harsher winters and a cuisine to match.

The Marais Poitevin, a secret land of inland waterways, Poitou-Charentes

POITOU-CHARENTES

The western flank of the country between the Loire to the north and the Gironde to the south comprises the region known as Poitou-Charentes. La Rochelle, with its formidable towers protecting the old harbor, is the regional capital, and the beaches to the north and south of the fascinating and historic port are popular with both French and foreign visitors.

Inland, away from the coast, it is altogether quieter. The Marais Poitevin near Niort is a fascinating inland area of secret marshes known as "La Venise Verte" — green Venice — due to its intricate network of canals. The vine-covered Cognac area, especially around Saintes, Cognac, Jarnac, and Segonzac, is quiet agricultural country. Offshore islands deserve to be visited too, among them the Ile d'Oléron for its sandy beaches and the Ile de Ré for its attractive little ports.

Produits Régionaux
REGIONAL PRODUCE

THE WARM WATERS of the Gulf Stream wash the coasts of Northwest France, bringing with them a gentle, mild climate, warm southwesterly winds, and plenty of rain. Brittany particularly benefits from this mild and beneficial influence, and its market gardens, especially in the so-called "golden belt" of St.-Pol-de-Léon, the Pen Arbed and Plougastel Peninsulas, and around

Tresses of garlic on sale in the Breton village of Yffiniac

Concarneau and Audierne, provide a welcome supply of *primeurs* (early fruits and vegetables) and traditional vegetables: large and delicious *artichauts* (globe artichokes), enormous, white *choux-fleurs* (cauliflowers), *oignons* (onions), *poireaux* (leeks), *pommes de terre nouvelles* (new potatoes), *ail* (garlic), and *échalotes* (shallots). Nantes is famous for its delicious, early ripening *carottes* (carrots) and Plougastel is renowned for its early *fraises* (strawberries).

Apple orchards dominate the Norman country. Much of the harvest is of bitter-sweet apples not meant for eating but to be made into *cidre* (alcoholic apple cider) and Calvados, the great apple brandy of Normandy. Pears are also much cultivated, both for eating and to be fermented into *poiré,* a sort of pear cider. Apples and pears are both widely used in cooking, not only for sweet *tartes* and *pâtisseries* but also in savory dishes, such as *porc normande* (pork stewed with apples, cream, and Calvados).

Carrots from Créances and other fresh produce from the market gardens around Mont-St.-Michel are particularly good: soft fruits — *fraises* (strawberries), *fram-*

SEL DE GUÉRANDE: THE SALT OF THE SEA

Just behind the beaches of La Baule in South Brittany, lies a quiet, hidden world: the salt marshes of Guérande, a conservation area. These marshes, a habitat for colonies of birds and other wildlife, flood every fortnight on the highest spring tides. The seawater is trapped in a complex system of salt pans probably first introduced by the Gallo-Romans in the third century, and then evaporates, leaving pure sea salt, which is gathered manually by

paludiers (salt marsh workers). This is *sel de Guérande,* highly valued by gourmets and top chefs throughout France as probably the finest sea salt.

There are two types of *sel de Guérande, gros sel* (known also as *sel gris*) and *fleur de sel. Gros sel* is, in its natural form, coarse in texture with a gray color that is due to its humidity and high magnesium content. *Fleur de sel,* produced in much smaller quantity, has flaky, smaller crystals raked off the top of the salt pans and is the best for the table.

The Maison du Sel provides much interesting information and also sells a variety of outstanding sea salts.

La Maison du Sel
Pradel
44350 Guérande
tel: 40 62 01 25
fax: 40 24 79 84

boises (raspberries), *groseilles* (redcurrants), and *cassis* (blackcurrants).

The Loire Valley is regarded as the Garden of France for its cultivation of superb fruits and vegetables. Fruits from Anjou and Touraine, especially *poires Williams* (Williams pears) and *reinettes,* one of the finest of all eating apples, are superlative.

Poitou-Charentes can rightly claim the finest, sweetest melons in France, the *charentais,* delicious served with a generous measure of Pineau des Charentes.

IN SEASON

Artichaut (St.-Pol-de-Léon and all Brittany)   Globe artichoke (May–Oct).
Asperge blanche (the Loire Valley)   White asparagus, especially the Vineuil-St.-Claude variety grown on sandy soil by the banks of the Loire (Apr–Jun).
Carottes (Nantes and Créances)   Carrots, especially the *nantaise* variety (end Oct–spring).

Echalotes and **ail** (Yffiniac)   Strings of excellent shallots and garlic are sold from roadside stalls in the small Breton town near St.-Brieuc (summer–fall).
Fraises de Plougastel (Brittany)   Strawberries (May–Jul).
Mâche (the Loire Valley)   Corn salad, a deeply flavored, excellent salad vegetable (Apr–Nov).
Melon charentais (Poitou-Charentes)   *Charentais* melon, a type of orange-fleshed cantaloupe (summer).

Artichauts, *artichokes from Brittany, each a first course in itself*

THE MUSHROOM CAVES OF SAUMUR

The French have been cultivating *champignons* (mushrooms) in caves and quarries since the 16th century. Today, nearly three-quarters of the entire national production comes from the deep, cool, dark tufa caves of Saumur, above the banks of the Loire. A visit to Saumur's mushroom caves is as fascinating as a visit to the *galeries* where its famous sparkling wine is produced.

The most common variety cultivated is the so-called *champignon de Paris,*

or button mushroom, which is eaten fresh and also canned. But, today, more exotic varieties, including *pleurottes* (oyster mushrooms), shiitake, the unusual *pied bleu,* and others, are increasingly cultivated.

The mushroom museum is open from mid-February to mid-November. Here, you can not only learn about the cycle of cultivated mushrooms and perhaps buy some, but also enjoy a tasty light meal of mushrooms grilled over a wood fire or fricasseed in olive oil and garlic. The secret world of the mushroom is well worth discovering.
Musée du Champignon
Route de Gennes
St.-Hilaire-St.-Florent
49400 Saumur
tel: 41 50 25 01
fax: 41 50 61 94

Au Marché

MARKETS

BRITTANY

Belle-Ile-en-Mer	Tue, Fri
Brest	Mon–Sat
Cancale	Sun
Carnac	Wed, Sun
Concarneau	Mon, Fri
Dinan	Thu
Dinard	Sat
Douarnenez	Mon, Fri
Guingamp	Sat
Morlaix	Sat
Pont-Aven	Tue
Pont l'Abbé	Thu
Quiberon	Sat
Quimper	Wed, Sat
Rennes	Sat
Riec-sur-Belon	Wed
St.-Brieuc	Wed, Sat
St.-Malo	Tue, Fri
St.-Pol-de-Léon	Tue
Vannes	Sat

NORMANDY

Bayeux	Sat
Caen	Tue–Sun
Cherbourg	Mon–Sat
Deauville	Tue, Fri
Dieppe	Sat
Etretat	Thu
Fécamp	Sat
Granville	Sat
Honfleur	Sat
Le Havre	Sat
Le Tréport	Sat
Livarot	Thu
Neufchâtel-en-Bray	Sat
Pont-Audemer	Mon, Fri
Pont-l'Evêque	Mon
Rouen	Tue, Wed, Fri, Sat, Sun
St.-Valéry-en-Caux	Fri
Trouville-sur-Mer	Sun
Villedieu-les-Poêles	Tue
Vimoutiers	Mon

THE LOIRE VALLEY

Amboise	Sat
Angers	Tue–Sun
Azay-le-Rideau	Wed
Blois	Wed, Sat
Bourgueil	Tue
Chinon	Thu
Loches	Wed
Menetou-Salon	Sun
Montlouis-sur-Loire	Thu
Nantes	Sat
Orléans	Tue, Thu, Sat
Richelieu	Fri
Rochefort-sur-Loire	Wed
Saumur	Sat
Tours	Sat

POITOU-CHARENTES

Angoulême	Sat, Sun
Cognac	Tue, Fri, Sat
Jarnac	Tue, Fri
La Rochelle	daily
Marennes	Sat
Niort	Thu, Sat
Poitiers	Sat
Saintes	Tue–Sun

A stallholder at the market in Dieppe

FETES ET FOIRES FESTIVALS AND FAIRS

BRITTANY

Concarneau *Fêtes des filets bleus (sardine fishing)*
3rd Sun Aug

Le Vivier-sur-Mer (near Cancale) *Fête des moules (mussels)* end Jul

At the Fête de la fouée, *Marson, the Loire Valley*

NORMANDY

Camembert *Fête du camembert (cheese)*
end Jul

Beuvron-en-Auge *Fête du cidre (cider)*
Nov

Le Tréport *Foire aux moules (mussels)*
end May

Vimoutiers *Foire de la pomme (apple)*
3rd weekend Oct

THE LOIRE VALLEY

Souzay-Champigny *Fête de la friture (fried fish)*
mid Jun

Marson (near Saumur) *Fête de la fouée (special bread)* mid Jun

Sancerre *Foire aux huîtres (oysters)*
last week Oct

POITOU-CHARENTES

Rochefort-sur-Mer *Foire aux moules (mussels)*
14 Jul

St.-Georges-des-Coteaux *Foire aux melons (charentais melons)*
end Aug

Crêpes and Galettes
BRETON PANCAKES

Y OU CAN FIND *crêpe* stands and *crêperies* throughout France, but Brittany is the true home of this national fast food.

In Brittany, two types of pancakes are available. *Galettes*, known also as *galettes au blé noir* or *galettes de sarrasin*, are made from buckwheat flour and are always filled with a savory mixture. Buckwheat was the grain of the poor, cultivated in rugged, harsh inland Brittany (known as l'Argoat — the land of the forest — as opposed to l'Armor — the land of the sea) where little else would grow. *Galettes* have a most distinctive, nutty flavor that is outstanding. Ordinary *crêpes*, known also as *crêpes au froment*, are pancakes made with soft wheat flour, eggs, and milk, and are filled with a sweet mixture, sometimes flambéed, and are invariably eaten as dessert, or for a mid-morning, afternoon, or late-night snack.

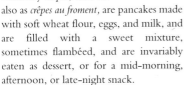

A galette complète, a meal in itself

In *crêperies*, it is quite possible to eat an entire *crêpe* meal, beginning with a *crêpe* appetizer, followed by a substantial main-course *galette*, then finishing with a sweet dessert *crêpe*. The drink to accompany such a rustic but always satisfying feast is rarely wine or beer, but rather a bottle or two of rasping Breton *cidre* (sparkling apple cider) usually served in china cups or mugs not glasses.

It is marvelous to watch a skilled *crêpe* chef at work over a hot griddle. The batter, whether wheat or buckwheat, is poured onto the hot, lightly buttered cooking surface with a ladle, then spread deftly with a wooden T-shaped instrument to result in the thinnest scraping only. As this quickly cooks, a generous knob of good, salted Breton butter is dolloped on, then any number of different toppings might be added: an egg, broken directly onto the *galette* to quickly cook "sunny side up," perhaps

some grated cheese, or a slice of ham. Sweet *crêpes* are topped with jam, chocolate, honey, or hazelnut spread, mixtures of fresh fruit with *crème chantilly* (whipped cream), or flambéed in liqueur.

Once cooked, the *galette* or *crêpe* is folded into a neat square or triangle then presented on a piping-hot plate to be eaten immediately.

Crêpes and *galettes* are a quintessential part of the French food scene. Enjoy them wherever you are, but especially in Brittany. You'll find roadside stands selling them and every Breton town and village has a *crêperie*, often in picture-postcard stone cottages.

CRÊPE AND GALETTE MENU

Crêpe à la banane flambée au rhum
With bananas and flambéed in dark rum; a sensational combination.

Crêpe à la confiture With jam.

Crêpe à l'orange flambée au Grand Marnier With orange slices and a buttery orange sauce and flambéed with Grand Marnier, an orange liqueur.

Crêpe au sucre The simplest, sometimes the most delicious; a thin pancake simply spread with butter and dusted with sugar.

Crêpe normande With homemade apple sauce and flambéed in Calvados, the apple brandy of Normandy.

Galette à l'andouille de Guéméné-sur-Scorff With slices of a rather earthy, smoked, chitterling sausage.

Galette au fromage With grated *gruyère* cheese.

Galette au jambon et oeuf With ham and egg.

Galette aux fruits de mer With shellfish in a creamy white sauce.

Galette complète The Breton favorite; with ham, egg, and grated cheese, filling enough to be a meal.

Les Spécialités
REGIONAL SPECIALTIES

THE *CUISINE* OF the Northwest inevitably centers on the superb fish and shellfish of the Atlantic and Channel seaboards. One of the highlights of a visit to this area of France is to feast on some of the finest and freshest *produits de la mer* — foods from the sea — that you will encounter anywhere in the world.

Brittany is preeminent. Every town has its specialties — Belon and Cancale for *huîtres* (oysters), Camaret-sur-Mer for *langouste* (crawfish), Douarnenez and Quiberon for *sardines* (sardines), and Concarneau for *thon* (tuna).

The cuisine of Normandy is dominated by an ample use of butter and rich, tangy *crème fraîche* (a slightly soured cream) in just about everything — fish and shellfish creations, meat dishes, and desserts.

The Loire Valley is too long and too amorphous to have an identifiable cuisine of its own throughout its entire length. But like the language spoken here, said to be the purest, perhaps the most harmonious in the nation, and like the classic beauty of its châteaux, it is the essential purity of foods that is most noteworthy.

Unloading scallops in the harbor of La Guette, Brittany

The most distinctive foods of Poitou-Charentes come from the Marais Poitevin, the wetlands, where *anguilles* (eels), *grenouilles* (frogs), *lumas* (the local name for snails), even *castor* (beaver) make an appearance on the table. The people of the Cognac region are known as *cagouillards* both for their fondness for *cagouilles* (snails) and for their reputed slow but effective thoroughness.

APPETIZERS AND FIRST COURSES

Araignée de mer (Brittany) Boiled spider crab; fiddly to eat but the sweetest of all crabs.

Artichaut (Brittany) Artichoke. Considering how important this vegetable is to the local economy, it is surprising to find it is offered infrequently in restaurants — a pity. Usually served boiled, with *vinaigrette* dressing.

Assiette de fruits de mer (Brittany, Normandy, and Poitou-Charentes) A smaller version of *le plateau de fruits de mer* (see p.120), usually includes some of the following: raw oysters, mussels, perhaps some sea snails, shrimp, *langoustines,* occasionally a crab leg.

Cagouilles à la charentaise (Poitou-Charentes) Local snails stewed in a casserole with pork, shallots, garlic, and white wine.

Coquilles St.-Jacques au cidre (Brittany and Normandy) Scallops cooked in dry cider and usually finished with cream stirred in.

Crème de cresson (the Loire Valley) Cream of watercress soup.

Eclade de moules (Poitou-Charentes) Mussels, traditionally cooked outdoors over a fire of pine needles. The mussels, once opened, are eaten with the fingers.

Fouée (the Loire Valley) Unleavened flat bread which, after it is baked in a wood-fired oven, is split, then filled with any number of fillings, including goat's milk cheese, *mojettes* (a puree of white beans), *rillettes* (potted meat paste), or sweet fillings and fresh fruits.

Gratin de coquilles St.-Jacques
(Brittany and Normandy) Small scallops
baked on the half-shell in a creamy white
sauce and topped with grated cheese.
Huîtres (Brittany, Normandy, and
Poitou-Charentes) Oysters, both *creuses*
and *plates,* widely available anywhere
near the coast (see p.119).
Lumas (Marais Poitevin) Local snails
prepared in various ways, most typically
stewed with ham and bay leaves.
Melon au Pineau des Charentes
(Poitou-Charentes) *Charentais* melon
(a type of cantaloupe) served filled with
sweet Pineau des Charentes.
Mouclade (Poitou-Charentes) Mussels
cooked in a creamy sauce often flavored,
unusually, with curry powder, saffron,
and turmeric.
Moules à la crème (Normandy)
Mussels served, like almost everything
else in Normandy, in a rich cream sauce.
Pieds de mouton farcis à la
rouennaise (Rouen) Stuffed sheep's
trotters, flambéed and cooked in Calvados.
Praires farcies (Brittany) A typical
and delicious clam, often served topped
with a mixture of finely chopped

Mouclade

shallots, parsley, butter, and breadcrumbs,
baked briefly in a very hot oven.
Rillettes (the Loire Valley) Potted
meat paste of shredded pieces of pork,
sometimes with duck or goose added,
cooked slowly in their own fat.
Delicious spread on bread.
Soufflé au crabe (Brittany) Crab
soufflé; can be an exquisite treat when
well done.
Toast au fromage de chèvre (the
Loire Valley) A sort of French "rare-
bit"; rounds of toasted French bread
topped with disks of melted goat's milk
cheese and usually served with a salad
on the side.

L'OMELETTE A LA MERE POULARD

As you climb up the cobbled path to
Mont-St.-Michel, the rhythmical
sound of eggs being beaten steadily in
copper basins greets you. Here, at the
base of the Mont, for
over a hundred years,
the Restaurant Mère
Poulard (address, p.137)
has captivated its clients
with a traditional menu
that always begins with
its famous omelet.
Cooked over a wood fire
in long handled skillets,
it puffs up like a soufflé.
  So famous is the
omelette à la Mère Poulard

that it has almost become a culinary
cliché, but is no less delicious for that.
Incredibly simple, feather light, and
irresistibly delicious, it is served in the
elegant restaurant as
either a savory first
course or as a sweet
dessert soufflé. In after-
noons, you can come
here just to sample the
omelet, and we urge
anyone visiting one of
France's most popular
tourist sites not to miss
it. Afterward, stroll up
the narrow Grande Rue
to the monastery itself.

Main courses

Agneau de pré-salé (Normandy)
Tasty and highly prized lamb from the
salt marshes around Mont-St.-Michel.
Alose à l'oseille (the Loire Valley)
Shad or other fish served in a light
hollandaise sauce to which cooked,
chopped sorrel has been added.
Barbue au beurre blanc (the Loire
Valley) *Barbue* (brill) served with the
magnificent *beurre blanc* — a sauce made
from shallots, a dash of vinegar or wine,
and butter, cooked in a *bain marie*. Enjoy
beurre blanc also with *bar* (sea bass),
saumon (salmon), or *brochet* (pike).
Canard à la rouennaise or **canard au
sang** (Rouen and Normandy)   Duck
from Duclair, a town downriver on
the Seine from Rouen, slaughtered by
smothering to preserve its blood. The
bird, authentically a cross between
domestic and wild, is roasted and
carved, and then the carcass is pressed
to extract cooking juices and blood to
make a rich sauce.
Chaudrée (Poitou-Charentes)   Soupy
stew made with conger eel, whiting,
plaice, or cod, poached in a *court bouillon*
made with white wine. The *court
bouillon,* enriched with butter and cream,
may be eaten as a soup first, or it can be
used to moisten the fish if taken as a
soupy main course.

Barbue au beurre blanc *at the Auberge Jeanne de
Laval, Les Rosières-sur-Loire*

Côte de veau Vallée d'Auge
(Normandy)   Veal chop cooked in
Calvados, *crème fraîche,* and with fresh
apples.
Cotriade (Brittany)   Fish stew made
with mackerel, cod, haddock, hake,
whiting — whatever is available —
cooked with potatoes, leeks, onion,
sorrel, and finished with *crème fraîche.*
Daube santongeaise de boeuf
(Poitou-Charentes)   Piece of beef
slowly cooked with a calf's foot,
carrots and other vegetables, and
Charentes wine, in an earthenware casserole for hours until tender
and rich.
Friture de la Loire (the Loire Valley)
Tiny fish of the Loire, caught either in
enormous nets stationed on winches by
the side of the river, or on a line. The
small fish are simply dredged in seasoned
flour then deep fried.
Gigot d'agneau à la bretonne
(Brittany)   Leg of lamb cooked with
white beans and tomatoes.
Homard grillé (Brittany)   Lobster,
traditionally simply split, doused
generously with *crème fraîche,* then
broiled. **Homard à l'armoricaine** is
stewed in an elaborate sauce of tomatoes,
olive oil, Cognac, and cream (see *Lotte à
l'armoricaine*).
Lapin au sang (Sancerre and the Upper
Loire)   Wild rabbit cooked in red
Sancerre wine, the sauce thickened with
the blood.

"LE TROU NORMAND"
The Normans are nothing if not
hearty eaters, and restaurant meals
are generally robust. During the
course of eating huge cream- and
butter-laden dishes, the *"trou normand"*
has become customary: a tot of
Calvados downed to aid digestion
mid-meal by creating a hole *(trou)* for
a further course or two. These days,
some restaurants offer a lighter, more
elegant alternative, *sorbet au Calvados,*
an apple ice flavored with Calvados.

Lotte à l'armoricaine (Brittany) Monkfish treated in the same way as *homard,* above, i.e., prepared in the rich traditional sauce. Some claim that this is not really a Breton dish (Armorica was the ancient name for Brittany) but was conceived by a Parisian restaurateur for his American clientele, thus, it is sometimes denoted *à l'américaine.*

Marmite dieppoise (Dieppe) Splendid fish stew made with turbot, sole, shrimp, *langoustines,* mussels, poached delicately in a *court bouillon,* then served in a chafing dish in a sauce made from the cooking liquid enriched with cream, curry powder, and other spices.

Matelote d'anguilles à la charentaise (Poitou-Charentes) Eel cooked with leeks and other vegetables, local wine, and Cognac.

Porc aux pruneaux (the Loire Valley) A great regional dish: medallions of pork tenderloin cooked with prunes from Touraine, Vouvray wine, and *crème fraîche.*

Poulet au cidre (Brittany and Normandy) Chicken stewed in apple cider, usually with apples and cream.

Saumon de la Loire (the Loire Valley) A great specialty, now virtually extinct: due to scarcity, there has been a moratorium on salmon fishing, to preserve stocks for the future. Loire salmon may return to menus in a few years' time when stocks have regenerated, but, in the meantime, farmed salmon served in *beurre blanc* is still a delicious alternative.

Sole normande (Normandy) The true or Dover sole, filleted, then poached in cider, garnished with mussels and shrimp, and served with a cream sauce made up with the cooking liquid.

Thon blanc de Concarneau (Concarneau and all Brittany) Albacore tuna; considered the finest flavored and lightest in texture. Most goes to the canning industry, but when fresh, it is enjoyed simply cooked with carrots and peas.

Tripes à la mode de Caen (Caen and all Normandy) Another regional classic: tripe slowly stewed with onions, carrots, cider, and Calvados, with a pig's or calf's trotter thrown in to give the cooking liquid a rich, thick gloss.

VEGETABLES AND VEGETARIAN DISHES

Blanquette de pommes de terre aux poireaux (Normandy) Potatoes and leeks cooked in a buttery white sauce.

Fèves à la tourangelle (the Loire Valley) Tender new season's fava beans simmered with cubes of ham.

Fricassée des pleurottes (the Loire Valley) Oyster mushrooms sautéed in butter, olive oil, garlic, and parsley.

Salade de fonds d'artichauts (Brittany) Artichoke bottoms boiled until tender then mixed with other vegetables and dressed in *vinaigrette.*

DESSERTS

Gratin des pommes Vallée d'Auge (Normandy) Apple crumble for adults — soaked in Calvados and baked with *crème fraîche.*

Poires au vin rouge (the Loire Valley) Pears poached in red wine.

Pruneaux au Vouvray (Vouvray) Prunes steeped in Vouvray wine.

Tarte Tatin (the Loire Valley) Classic caramelized upside-down apple pie, best served hot with lashings of *crème fraîche.*

Torteau fromage (Poitou-Charentes) Cheesecake, usually made with fresh goat's milk cheese, cooked in a very hot oven so that its top emerges puffed up and almost black.

Friture de la Loire

Charcuterie
CURED PORK AND OTHER MEAT PRODUCTS

THE PIG HAS LONG been a staple on the farms of Northwest France, providing much good, rustic *charcuterie*. Once, itinerant *charcutiers* (pork butchers) went from farm to farm first slaughtering the pig, then assisting with salting it and making *boudins, jambons,* or *saucisses;* today, butchers still sell a range of robust tasting *charcuterie* products.

Andouille de Guémené-sur-Scorff

TRY TO SAMPLE
Andouille de Guémené-sur-Scorff (Brittany) Large sausage made from tripe, chitterlings, and pieces of stomach, cooked and sliced, then arranged in the skin so that they show up as concentric rings when the sausage is sliced. Delicately flavored, it is delicious as a filling in a *galette.*

Andouille de Vire (Normandy) Another chitterling sausage, this time rather knobbly and marbled in appearance, lightly smoked, with a black skin.

Andouillette de Touraine (Touraine) Touraine vies with Lyons and Troyes for the supremacy of its chitterling sausages, made, in this case, with the addition of *fraise de veau* (mesentery). *Andouillette,* unlike *andouille,* always needs to be gently fried or grilled.

Boudin blanc (Normandy) Exceptionally delicate "white pudding," eaten poached or lightly fried throughout

Rillettes *from Vouvray, an unctuous meat spread, excellent for picnics*

Normandy; made from finely ground chicken and lean pork mixed with *crème fraîche,* eggs, and salt and pepper.

Boudin noir (Mortagne-au-Perche and all Normandy) Some of the finest blood sausages, made with pork blood, onion, fat, and seasonings, come from Mortagne-au-Perche in Normandy.

Foie gras normand (Normandy) Excellent *foie gras,* more commonly from ducks than from geese, is increasingly being produced in Normandy. Try it in restaurants.

Jambon de Morlaix (Brittany) Local smoked cooked ham.

Jambon vendéen (Poitou-Charentes) Rare but exceptional dry-salted ham from the hinterland of La Rochelle, rubbed in Cognac and spices, then left to air-cure for several months.

Pâté de lièvre (the Loire Valley) In this hunter country, in season, good *pâtés* are made from game including an excellent version made with *lièvre* (hare).

Pâtés de campagne (Brittany) Particularly tasty, coarse, rustic pork *pâtés* are enjoyed throughout Brittany.

Rillettes (Touraine) *Rillettes* are sold by *charcuteries* throughout France. They are usually made from a mixture of lean and fat pork, sometimes with the addition of duck, goose, or rabbit, lightly salted, then slowly cooked for hours until the meat becomes a fibrous but creamy, tasty paste. The finest come from Tours and Vouvray.

Rillons (the Loire Valley) Cubes of belly pork, sometimes still on the bone, lightly salted, then cooked in fat until the meat is tender and caramelized. Can be eaten cold and also delicious warm.

Saucisse au muscadet (Nantes) Meaty pork sausages with Muscadet wine added to the ingredients.

Les Huîtres

O Y S T E R S

THE FIRST THING every visitor to Northwest France should do is buy an oyster knife: Northwest France yields the most varied and the finest harvest of these rare and valued bivalves. There are scores of opportunities to taste and buy them, which on no account should be missed. You can, of course, sample oysters to your heart's content at any number of restaurants, bars, and shellfish stalls without ever having to pry them open yourself. But nothing is nicer than buying a dozen or two to take to the beach for an impromptu picnic, the effort of shucking rewarded by the long, lingering, sea fresh flavor.

You will come across two types of oysters: *huîtres creuses,* the term used to denote both those with the crinkly, flaky, Portuguese shell *(Crassostrea angulata)* and the similar-looking Pacific *(Crassostrea gigas),* and *huîtres plates,* the rounder, flatter, and more rare natives *(Ostrea edulis).* Though it used to be said that oysters could be enjoyed only in those months with an "r" in them, thus excluding May to August, this no longer holds true. Modern refrigerated transport means that oysters can arrive fresh and alive even far inland in the hot summer, although, at this time of year they are not necessarily at their best; some, though, enjoy the intense, concentrated, though milky flavor of summer oysters.

Northwest France has three great oyster centers that are worth visiting. In Brittany, enjoy *creuses* raised in the oyster

Huîtres *from the oyster beds of Belon*

beds of Cancale near St.-Malo, and exceptional, deeply flavored *plates* from Belon, in the west, the preeminent area in the country for *Ostrea edulis.* In the Charentes-Maritime near Cognac, an oyster oasis extends around the small and unprepossessing town of Marennes, where shallow beds washed by the salty tide create a system of *claires* for finishing *creuses* oysters. In the *claires,* which are actually former salt pans, a green algae flourishes which gives the oysters their distinct flavor. Indeed, *fines de claires* from Marennes, with their green tinge and lemony, iodine finish, are exceptional, and, to our way of thinking, can almost match, for sheer sensuous pleasure, the richness, depth, and lingering flavor of native *plates* from Belon.

Whether from stalls or in restaurants, oysters are always sold by the dozen or half-dozen, the price depending on size. Size may be indicated by number, generally from one (the largest) to four, though, if in doubt, ask for *"des moyennes"* or those of medium or average size. A half-dozen makes a good start to a meal, but for oyster lovers, generally no fewer than a dozen will do.

Fines de claires *oysters, cultivated in former salt pans and tinged with algae*

Poissons et Fruits de Mer
FISH AND SEAFOOD

Northwest France is the most important part of the country for fish — more fish is collectively landed at the numerous fishing ports along the Atlantic and Channel coastlines than anywhere else. The region's *criées* — wholesale fish auctions — are among the liveliest in France. They usually take place in the early hours of the morning so that the waiting trucks lined up on the quays can load up their wet, sometimes live purchases and take them to Paris and other cities by daybreak. Though they are not generally open to the public, early birds can usually poke their heads in and

Araignée de mer, *spider crab, with very sweet meat in legs and body*

have a look around. If in doubt, ask for permission from the *directeur.*

The largest *criées* in Brittany are at Lorient, Concarneau, Guilvinec, Douarnenez, St.-Guénolé, and Loctudy. In Normandy, Port-en-Bessin-Huppain, Dieppe, Granville, and Cherbourg are the most active, and in Poitou-Charentes Les Sables-d'Olonne and La Rochelle take top honors.

TRY TO SAMPLE

Amande de mer Dog cockle; a type of bivalve sometimes included in a shellfish platter.

Araignée de mer Spider crab: the meat from the body and long, spindly legs is incredibly sweet. Best from April to July.

Barbue Brill; a fine, large flat fish.

Bigorneau Tiny black sea snail or winkle; a *plateau de fruits de mer* usually includes a pile of these to be pried out with a pin and dipped in shallot vinegar.

Buccin Whelk, something like a large sea snail; rather rubbery once cooked.

LE PLATEAU DE FRUITS DE MER

There are few more enjoyable ways to spin out an afternoon than picking your way through a *plateau de fruits de mer,* accompanied by a bottle or two of Muscadet *sur lie* or tart, lemony Gros Plant du Pays Nantais. There is no point in attempting this shellfish feast unless you have plenty of time to do justice to it: half the fun is prying the tiniest, sweetest morsels from stubborn shells and legs with pins, pincers, crackers, and other suitable tools.

Watch the French at work: they attack their shellfish platters with a real gusto that has to be admired if not emulated. Bits of shell fly across the table; sharp, prickly *langoustines* are peeled and dispatched in a flash; green-tinged oysters are sucked off the half-

shell noisily; sea snails are pried out of shells with pins. Even the most elegantly dressed display no qualms at slurping, cracking with the teeth, extracting the most minuscule tidbits. The true enjoyment of a *plateau de fruits de mer* lies not only in the marvelous freshness of the shellfish but in the uninhibited pleasure of eating with the fingers.

Cabillaud   Cod.
Coquille St.-Jacques   Scallop or great scallop, usually considerably larger than the North American bay scallop. May be cooked and eaten with or without its orange coral. Specialty of Normandy's Dieppe and Brittany's St.-Brieuc.
Homard   Lobster.
Langouste   Crawfish or spiny lobster.
Langoustine   Dublin Bay prawn or Norway lobster; a particularly popular shellfish, *langoustine* is usually boiled and eaten with mayonnaise.
Lotte   Monkfish; densely textured and rich in flavor.
Moules de bouchot   Mussels that have been cultivated on poles fixed in the water, the now standard method for raising this popular and delicious shellfish. La Rochelle remains an important center. Served usually *à la marinière,* "fisherman's style," i.e., steamed in white wine with shallots.
Palourde   Carpet shell clam; enjoyed both raw and stuffed and baked.
Pétoncle   Small scallop.

Amande de mer, *dog cockle*

Pouce-pied   Goose-necked barnacle; considered by the French a great delicacy; the meat to be sucked out raw.
Praire   Small clam with a hard shell with concentric rings. Can be eaten raw, though often stuffed and baked.
Thon blanc or **germon**   Albacore tuna; specialty of Concarneau.
Tourteau   Edible crab; the large, hard-shelled variety with large claws full of deliciously sweet meat. Best May to September.
Turbot   Turbot; considered by the French the finest of all flat fish, and usually the most expensive.

GOURMET SARDINES

Since the 19th century, the coastal towns of Brittany have been important centers of the canning industry, particularly for sardines. In the past, nearly every town in Western Brittany supported at least one *conserverie,* and fishing towns like Concarneau, Douarnenez, and Quiberon had dozens. Today, only a handful remain, but canned sardines from Brittany are one of the great — and still very affordable — delicacies of the region, as different from common, cheap sardines from elsewhere in the world as fine wine is from *vin ordinaire.*

At the Conserverie La Belle-Iloise in Quiberon, fresh sardines are cooked in *huile d'arachide* (groundnut or peanut oil) then trimmed individually and packed by hand in best-quality extra-virgin olive oil, or in wine, tomatoes, or other flavorings and mixtures.

Such fine sardines, especially those preserved in oil, can be aged, like fine wine, and will noticeably improve in flavor and texture after only six months and even up to two or three years. As the fish ages, the oil gradually replaces all its moisture by osmosis, and the result is a deeper, more unctuous flavor and texture of the sardines. (The cans should be turned every now and again to ensure even aging.)

Conserverie La Belle-Iloise
Zône d'activité "Plein-Ouest"
56170 Quiberon
tel: 97 50 08 77

Les Fromages

GREAT CHEESES OF NORTHWEST FRANCE

NORMANDY IS DAIRY COUNTRY *par excellence,* and the characteristic Norman cattle — brown and white with dark markings around their eyes — provide milk so creamy and rich in butterfat that it is transformed not only into an enviable range of superb, mainly rind-washed and rind-ripened cheeses, but also into the finest *crème fraîche* and sweet, unsalted butter, products that dominate Norman cuisine.

Cheese is produced almost throughout Normandy but two centers are the most important for the production of authentic *fromages fermiers* (farmhouse cheeses) made always from *lait cru* (unpasteurized milk). They are the Pays d'Auge, which straddles the *départements* of Calvados, Eure, and Orne, roughly between Pont-Audemer and Caen and extending south to the town of Camembert itself; and the Pays de Bray, lush dairy country located in the Seine-Maritime south of Dieppe towards Rouen. In both areas, there are sign-posted *routes du fromage* ("cheese roads") with opportunities to visit, taste, and buy cheeses direct.

CHEESES OF NORMANDY AND NORTHWEST FRANCE

Brillat Savarin (Normandy) Super rich cheese with a mild, rich flavor, made with triple cream (cream with an outrageously high butterfat content).

Normandy cows, with characteristic coloring, in the high, lush pastures of the Pays d'Auge

Camembert de Normandie AC *Camembert* is the most popular and famous of all French cheeses (even in France). However, most *camemberts* bought from supermarkets do not qualify for this select Normandy *appellation,* for they are not made on farms or in dairies in Normandy or with unpasteurized milk, essential determinants of quality. The *appellation* applies to cheeses made in small or large dairies, not on farms, but the cheeses are still *"moulé à la louche,"* the process whereby the uncut curds are ladled either by machine or hand into the cheese molds in at least four successive passes (see p.124). The French taste is usually for *camembert* that is still quite firm, even chalky in the center. Even extra-ripe and runny *camembert* should never smell overly strong or of ammonia.

Campénéac (Brittany) Semi-hard, pressed cheese from the Trappist Abbey of Campénéac.

Chabicou de Poitou AC (Poitou-Charentes) Outstanding farm-produced goat's milk cheese, usually in a truncated cone or pyramid shape, aged for about three or four weeks, when it develops its characteristic, pungent, goat aroma.

Crottin de Chavignol AC (the Loire Valley) One of the great goat's milk cheeses of France, a small, usually quite hard, dry disk; produced in the Sancerre wine region and superb with the wine.

Livarot AC (Normandy) Known also as *"le colonel"* (the colonel) because of the five bands of sedge reed wrapped around traditional cheeses to retain their shape (today, paper is often used instead). *Livarot AC* is one of the great rind-washed cheeses of France, with a characteristic reddish brown crust, a pungent odor, and a flavor that is deep but not overly strong.

Neufchâtel AC Historic cheese (Normandy's oldest), made in roughly a similar fashion since the 10th century. *Neufchâtel* is a cheese that is produced from drained curds packed into molds by

Cheeses of Normandy (clockwise from top): livarot, camembert fermier, *and* pont l'evêque

hand, then left to rind-ripen like *camembert* so that the cheeses develop a white bloom on their surface, and a rich, creamy, even runny texture. Like *camembert,* the rind of *neufchâtel* is edible. *Neufchâtel* can be formed into a *briquette* (small block), *carré* (square), *bonde* (small bung-shaped cylinder), *double bonde* (large cylinder), *coeur* (heart), and *gros coeur* (large heart).

Pont-l'Evêque AC (Normandy) *Pont-l'Evêque* is produced by first packing curds into square molds, then rind-washing the individual cheeses in salt, leaving them to dry, and stacking them up like books on a shelf to further age and acquire their characteristic yellow-orange rind and a flavor that can be surprisingly delicate for a rind-washed cheese of this type.

Port-Salut Pressed cheese with an orange rind, creamy texture, and mild flavor. Originally made by Trappist monks at Abbaye d'Entrammes in Mayenne, though now made industrially throughout Northwest France.

Ste.-Maure de Touraine AC (the Loire Valley) Creamy, white, cylindrical goat's milk cheese with a pronounced flavor and aroma. Farm versions may have straw through the middle and there is also a *cendrée* version which is dusted with charcoal ash.

Selles-sur-Cher AC (the Loire Valley) Dusted with gray charcoal ash, this small, round goat's milk cheese from Orléans is not overly strong or pungent.

St.-Paulin This mild, smooth cheese with its orange rind is made (usually industrially) throughout the Northwest, particularly in the Loire and Brittany.

CREME FRAICHE AND BUTTER

Butter and *crème fraîche* of outstanding quality are made by hand on farms in Northwest France, and are often sold in markets and *crèmeries*.

Crème fraîche is produced simply by leaving *lait cru* (unpasteurized milk) overnight: the thick cream rises to the top and is scooped up and left to undergo a light lactic fermentation that gives it its characteristic, slightly sour tang.

Crème fraîche is widely used in cooking, and it is also delicious

spooned over desserts or fresh fruit.

Normandy's finest unsalted butter and cream, both entitled to *appellation d'origine* status, come from Isigny. Brittany's butter, by contrast, is always salted, though no less delicious for that. Poitou-Charentes is the source of two outstanding butters: *beurre de Charentes-Poitou AC* and *beurre des Deux-Sèvres AC*. Farm examples from Echiré (near Niort) are especially fine.

Camembert

ONE OF THE GREAT CHEESES OF FRANCE

Accarding to legend, the most popular of all French cheeses, *camembert,* was first created when a rebel priest, fleeing the fury of the French Revolution, was sheltered by a young Norman farm-wife, Marie Harel. In gratitude, he passed on the secret of producing a new type of cheese. Marie Harel began producing the cheese and named it after her village, the small hamlet of Camembert.

Camembert

Vimoutiers, something of a market center for *camembert* country, has a Camembert Museum which is worth visiting. Note also the two statues in the town in homage to Marie Harel. The original was decapitated when the Allies bombed the town in the last war, so a replacement was donated by Americans from Van West, Ohio.

Today, *camembert*-type cheeses are produced not only throughout Normandy, but throughout France and the world, with varying degrees of success. Genuine *camembert,* such as *camembert de Normandie AC* and, even rarer, genuine farmhouse *camembert fermier,* is a unique cheese, made from unpasteurized milk, with an assertive, pungent aroma and flavor, and a rich, creamy texture.

Camembert fermier is made on only a few remaining farms around Camembert itself. We visited young François Durand to witness the laborious and unique process known as *"moulé à la louche"* (molded by ladle) which is essential to produce genuine *camembert.* Once the unpasteurized milk from the herd of his 40 Norman cows has been heated and coagulated with rennet, François, using a ladle no larger than one used in a kitchen, scoops the rich, creamy, lightly cut curds by hand into the *camembert* cheese molds in five successive passes. This is a time consuming but essential task to develop the character of the cheese: a uniform and homogeneously creamy texture through the even distribution of butterfat.

The next day, the cheeses are taken from their molds, dry salted, then sprayed with the bacterium *Penicillium camemberti.* This encourages the cheese to ripen and a white bloom to form on the surface. After about a month, the cheeses should be ripened through to the *coeur* (heart), ready to eat.

How to choose a perfect *camembert?*

"Ah, that's a difficult question," says François. "You must feel the cheese. It should not be too hard, yet neither should it be too soft. It should never smell overly strong. If you can see through the paper wrapping, it should just begin to get yellow around the edges."

François' *camembert fermier* is a superior cheese with a creamy, layered texture which, even when fully ripe, is never gluey, and with a deep, pronounced flavor and aroma.

François Durand
Ferme de la Héronnière
61120 Camembert
tel: 33 39 08 08

Musée du Camembert
10, Ave. Général de Gaulle
61120 Vimoutiers
tel: 33 39 30 29

François Durand making camembert *by the manual process of* "moulé à la louche"

Pains, Pâtisseries, et Confiseries
BREADS, PASTRIES, AND CANDIES

BUTTER IS THE BASIC ingredient of delicious *pâtisseries* throughout the Northwest, which also has some good regional breads and candies to satisfy the sweetest tooth.

TRY TO SAMPLE

Angélique de Niort (Poitou-Charentes) Fragrant stalks of angelica candied in sugar; mainly for use as decoration on cakes, but also to eat as a candy.

Ardoise (Angers) Chocolate-covered nougatine.

Far breton, *a custard flan dessert popular throughout Brittany*

BRETON COOKIES

One of the loveliest souvenirs of a vacation in Brittany is a tin of sweet Breton cookies. Many towns sell their own versions, but those of Pont-Aven are among the most famous, both for the melting quality of the cookies and because this town is so rightly popular with visitors, prettily sited and a mecca for artists and art lovers since Paul Gauguin lived and worked here in 1886.

The Délices de Pont-Aven manufacture their famous cookies in both *épaisses* (thick) and *fine* (thin) versions, using freshly churned unpasteurized butter. Rivals Traou Mad have their devotees, too. Try both and decide for yourself. And long after the cookies are gone, the colorful tins will remind you of happy times in Brittany.

Brioche vendéenne (Poitou-Charentes) Buttery, yeasty *brioche,* with the delicate perfume of orange blossom — a reminder of vacations at La Rochelle and the Vendée Coast. In the region itself, it is traditionally eaten at weddings.

Confiture du lait (Normandy) Thick traditional spread made by simmering milk with sugar until it caramelizes to a deep brown color.

Cotignac (Orléans) Small quince jelly sweets, made in Orléans since the days of Jeanne d'Arc.

Faluche (Normandy) Traditional yeast *brioche* made with butter and *crème fraîche*.

Far breton (Brittany) Batter and egg custard flan; often made with prunes *(far aux pruneaux)*.

Gâteau breton or **petit gâteau** (Brittany) Rich pound cake made with eggs, butter, and sugar.

Kouigh-amann (Brittany) Delectable, light, flaky, and extremely buttery cake; best enjoyed in the afternoon with a glass of Breton *cidre*.

Sucre de pomme de Rouen (Rouen) Apple sugar candies.

Tarte aux pommes (Normandy) Beautiful, glazed apple tarts are found throughout France, but Normandy's are possibly the finest, usually made with Calvados and best served warm with *crème fraîche*.

Teurgoule (Normandy) Thick, sweet rice pudding; traditionally, slowly baked for hours in cooling bread ovens.

Crumbly, buttery, and melt-in-the mouth Breton cookies from Pont-Aven

Les Vins

WINE, CIDER, AND CALVADOS

NEITHER BRITTANY nor Normandy are wine regions (though the former claims Muscadet and Gros Plant, two wines from the Pays Nantais, once linked to Brittany), and cider is the normal drink. Poitou-Charentes produces minor country wines that are worth seeking out if you are staying here.

The Loire Valley, on the other hand, is one of the great wine regions of France, and a wide range is produced along virtually the entire length of the river, including dry, medium, and lusciously sweet white wines, pretty rosés, light and fruity as well as deeper, serious reds, and outstanding sparkling wines.

BRITTANY

Gros Plant VDQS   This bone-dry, extremely crisp, and lemony white wine can be superb with shellfish.
Recommended producers: Château de Cléray, Guy Bossard.

Muscadet AC; Muscadet de Sèvre-et-Maine AC; Muscadet des Coteaux de la Loire AC; Muscadet Côtes de Grand Lieu AC   One of the best-known and popular of all French dry white wines. Straight Muscadet AC is generally a fairly neutral, light wine with little character; wines from the Sèvre-et-Maine (the largest area) as well as certain examples from the Coteaux de la Loire may have more flavor and personality. The term *"sur lie"* indicates that the wines have been left to rest on their barrel sediment (lees), imparting, in theory, rounder, deeper flavor and character.
Recommended producers: Château du Cléray, Guy Bossard, Chéreau-Carré, Château de Goulaine, Métaireau.

THE LOIRE VALLEY

Anjou Blanc AC; Cabernet d'Anjou AC; Anjou Gamay AC   Dry, medium, and sweet white wines are produced almost exclusively from the versatile Chenin Blanc grape, ranging from simple, inexpensive (often raspingly sharp) to luscious dry whites that can age gracefully, as well as distinguished, honeyed sweet wines. Increasingly good, young red wines from both Cabernet Franc and Gamay, to be drunk young and fresh, are also being produced.
Recommended producers: Domaine de Terrebrune, Baumard, Richou, Château de Tigné (owned by actor Gérard Depardieu).

Bonnezeaux AC   One of the marvels of the Loire, a magnificent sweet dessert wine made from Chenin Blanc grapes affected, in the best years, by *pourriture noble* or noble rot.
Recommended producers: Domaine de Terrebrune, Angeli, Château de Fesles.

Bourgueil AC and **St.-Nicolas-de-Bourgueil AC**   The red Cabernet Franc wines of the Loire are too pungent and herbaceous for many people's taste. The best wines, such as good examples from these two *appellations,* manage to overcome this with perfumed raspberry or floral overtones.
Recommended producers: Amirault, Audebert, Druet.

Chinon AC   The Cabernet Franc wines of Chinon are probably the finest red wines of the Loire, more delicate than Bourgueil yet also capable, in the best years, of improving with age.
Recommended producers: Couly-Dutheil, Domaine Baudry, J.-M. Raffault, Joguet.

Coteaux du Layon AC   These generally honeyed, inexpensive medium to sweet white wines can be delightful.
Recommended producers: Domaine des Hauts Perrays, Domaine de la Soucherie, Moulin Touchais, Domaine Ogereau.

Crémant de Loire AC   Sparkling wine made by the traditional method of secondary fermentation in the bottle; made throughout the Anjou and Touraine vineyards to stricter regulations than the more specific Saumur *appellation,* including lower yields and manual harvesting.
Recommended producers: Gratien-et-Meyer, Langlois-Château, St.-Cyr-en-Bourg coopérative.

Jasnières AC   This little-encountered Chenin white can be rather thin and sharp in off years, but examples from a good, hot year can be a revelation, especially after some time in the bottle.
Recommended producer: Gigou.

Menetou-Salon AC   Little-known area near Sancerre producing look-alike Sauvignon wines at more affordable prices. Can be excellent.
Recommended producers: Chavet, Pellé.

Château de Saumur, one of the lovely châteaux of the Loire Valley

Montlouis AC   In the best years, the sweet wines of Montlouis have a tremen-dous capacity to age. In years when the grapes do not reach a full degree of ripeness, zesty sparkling wines are made.
Recommended producers: Delétang, Levasseur, Martin.

Pineau de la Loire   The name given to the Chenin Blanc in this area. The simple, one-dimensional freshness and green apple bite of straight Pineau can be quenching and enjoyable.

Pouilly Fumé AC   One of the great archetypal Sauvignon wines of the world; produced in the Upper Loire opposite its great rival, Sancerre. At best, Pouilly Fumé demonstrates the assertive, gooseberry fruit character of Sauvignon in a restrained and elegant manner.
Recommended producers: Dagueneau, de Ladoucette, Seguin, Château de Tracy.

Pouilly-sur-Loire AC   Light, dis-tinctly forgettable wine produced from Chasselas grapes grown in the same vineyard as Pouilly-Fumé.

Quarts de Chaume AC   Another outstanding honeyed sweet wine of Anjou, produced from selected Chenin Blanc grapes affected by *pourriture noble*.
Recommended producers: Baumard, Château Bellerive, Château de Suronde.

Quincy AC   This rather rustic, pungent Sauvignon wine from the *département* of the Cher can be good value.
Recommended producers: Domaine Jaumier, Rouzé.

Reuilly AC   Another Sancerre or Pouilly Fumé alternative, similarly produced from the Sauvignon grape from vineyards west of Sancerre. Also some good rosés and reds from Pinot Noir.
Recommended producers: Cordier, Lafond, Beurdin.

Rosé d'Anjou AC   This extremely popular but not terribly distinguished rosé is usually too sweet for our taste; medium-dry to medium-sweet, pro-duced primarily from the Groslot grape.

Rosé de Loire AC   A better alter-native to the above, drier, with more character that comes through the obliga-tory use of at least 30 per cent of the Cabernets Franc or Sauvignon.

Sancerre AC   The greatest Sauvignon wines in France, possibly the world, still come from vineyards in the Upper Loire at Sancerre and Pouilly-sur-Loire. Less well-known than the whites are some good (but still relatively expensive) rosés and reds made from Pinot Noir.
Recommended producers: Bourgeois, Cotat, Crochet, Dezat, Mellot, Gitton, Vacheron.

Saumur AC   Dry white and light red wines from vineyards near Saumur. Most of the harvest goes to the making of sparkling Saumur *mousseux* AC.
Recommended producer: St.-Cyr-en-Bourg coopérative.

Saumur-Champigny AC   The best red wines of Saumur come from select vineyards around Champigny and dis-play an attractive raspberry fruit and the characteristic herbaceous overtones of Cabernet Franc.

Pineau des Charentes country

Recommended producers: Domaine des Roches Neuves, Filliatreau.

Savennières AC The finest dry white wines of the Loire, produced from Chenin Blanc grapes, come from a little-known vineyard near Anjou. However, these steely, high in acid white wines need considerable time in bottle to display fully their great character and rounded, honeyed nuances. Worth the wait.
Recommended producers: Baumard, Clos de la Coulée-de-Serrant, Soulez.

Touraine AC This immense *appellation* can apply to vineyards throughout the Central Loire producing white, rosé, red, and sparkling wines. Inexpensive Sauvignons can be good; best reds come from Gamay and Cabernet Franc.

Vin de Pays du Jardin de la France An even broader designation than the above for inexpensive country wines — mainly white, as well as rosé and red — from throughout most of the Loire.

Vouvray AC Another great Loire wine produced from the distinguished and versatile Chenin Blanc in a full range of styles, from sparkling through dry, medium dry, medium sweet, to lusciously sweet. With the exception of the sparkling wines, Vouvrays of all styles from good vintages have a tremendous

capacity to age and develop character in the bottle.
Recommended producers: Brédif, Foreau, Fouquet, Huet, Pichot, Rohart, Vallée Coquette cave coopérative.

POITOU-CHARENTES

Haut-Poitou AC Zesty Sauvignon whites and grapy Gamay reds come from vineyards just north of Poitiers almost bordering the vineyards of Touraine.
Recommended producer: Haut-Poitou cave coopérative.

Vin de Pays Charentais Fresh, light, sometimes sharp wines made from Ugni Blanc grapes from the Cognac vineyards.
Recommended producers: Château de Didonne, Domaine de la Chauvillière.

OTHER DRINKS

Bénédictine World-renowned herbal liqueur, made with the essence of 27 plants, roots, and herbs to a recipe from the former Abbey of Fécamp. B. & B. is Bénédictine blended with Cognac.

Calvados AC; Calvados du Pays d'Auge AC Apple brandy produced from the distillation of apple cider followed by aging in wood. The finest Calvados comes from the Pays d'Auge zone (see p.132).

Cidre fermier Farmhouse cider; completely different to the industrially produced (see p.132).

Cognac AC The world-famous brandy, made in Poitou-Charentes, is aged to minimum requirements and usually blended (see p.134).

Pineau des Charentes AC Fresh, unfermented grape juice mixed with young *eau-de-vie* or Cognac to result in a fruity *apéritif*.

Poiré Pear-based equivalent to cider; sweet and rather soft.

Pommeau AC Fresh unfermented apple juice blended with Calvados then aged for at least 18 months in oak casks. Sweet, with the distinct flavor of apples, it is a delicious Norman *apéritif*.

A Great River of Wine

A JOURNEY ALONG THE LOIRE VALLEY

THE LOIRE VALLEY is so fertile that the vine flourishes all along its length, from the center of France down to where the river empties into the Atlantic near Nantes, and in adjacent valleys above its tributaries. This is not one wine region, but many, all with their own character, cuisines, and distinctive wines. For wine lovers, as well as those who appreciate beautiful, rural country interspersed with quiet villages and grand châteaux, a tour of the vineyards of the Loire Valley is never less than fascinating and enjoyable.

This is by no means a journey that has to be done in its entirety; rather, dip into wine country wherever you are and for as long as you want.

THE PAYS NANTAIS

The Pays Nantais is primarily Muscadet country. The most important part of the vineyard is to the south and east of Nantes, an elegant city whose 18th-century prosperity was based on the profits of seafaring merchants and slave traders. A signposted *route du vin* leads into the Sèvre-et-Maine area, beautiful country that is little visited compared to the well trodden wine roads further up the Loire. Head down to Vertou, where

vineyards have been cultivated by monks since the 11th century, then down to La Haie-Fouassière, an unassuming village that is home to the Maison des Vins, where wines can be tasted, maps bought, and visits to châteaux arranged.

Continue to Clisson and then to Le Pallet where, in 1079, the ill-fated Pierre Abélard was born. Vallet, which claims the title of *"capitale du Muscadet,"* has a welcoming tasting room, the Maison du Muscadet, and the Château de Cléray, home of the Sauvion family, who are important and well-respected wine producers and who can be visited by appointment. The Restaurant Don Quichotte (address, p.137) is popular with local winegrowers for its seafood.

ANGERS TO SAUMUR

The Anjou vineyard (see map) extends from west of Angers to upriver of Saumur, two towns that both deserve visits, not least for their contrasting châteaux. Begin in Angers at the welcoming Maison du Vin opposite the entrance to the château. Here you can learn about — and taste — the remarkable range of Anjou wines, including dry white, luscious, sweet white, fruity red,

Château de Chenonceau in Touraine

medium-dry rosé, and sparkling. Then strike into the wine country, heading west first to Savennières, source of outstanding dry white wines made from the Chenin Blanc. The Château de la Roche aux Moines is a most welcoming estate. It makes two rare (and very expensive) wines, La Coulée de Serrant and La Roche aux Moines, from grapes cultivated by *"méthode biodynamique"* — the most natural methods possible, in conjunction with phases of the moon and stars.

From Savennières, cross the Loire to Rochefort-sur-Loire where, along the lovely Layon Valley, the same grape, Chenin Blanc, can reach, in the best years, a rare degree of ripeness that results in some of the greatest and most honeyed sweet wines in the world. Only the exceptional *crus* Quarts de Chaume and Bonnezeaux are capable of reaching such heights, but the less-exalted *demi-sec* (medium dry) wines of the Coteaux du Layon can be delightful.

The wine road crosses this gentle country through the wine villages that are entitled to append their names to the general Coteaux du Layon *appellation:* Rochefort-sur-Loire, St.-Aubin, Chaume, St.-Lambert-du-Lattay, Beaulieu, Rablay-sur-Layon, and Faye d'Anjou. After Bonnezeaux and Thouarcé comes Martigné-Briand, a wine town that specializes in Cabernet d'Anjou. Tigné's château is now owned by the French film star Gérard Depardieu, and he has already succeeded in making some high-quality Anjou wines.

Next, continue to Montreuil-Bellay, a fine old Saumurois town, then to Saumur itself by way of wine towns such as St.-Cyr-en-Bourg (excellent *cave coopérative*) and Champigny, source of some of the finest Loire Valley reds, made from Cabernet Franc. Saumur, of

On the way to Pouilly along the Route du Vin

course, is most famous for its traditional sparkling wines. Many of the large companies have extensive caves tunneled into the tufa cliffs at St.-Hilaire-St.-Florent, and provide guided tours.

WINES AND CHATEAUX OF TOURAINE

Touraine is a vast and beautiful section of the Loire, and, with its profusion of fairytale castles, has much more to offer the visitor than merely wine. Two areas deserve to be singled out. Chinon, the town where young Jeanne d'Arc met and recognized the disguised Dauphin, and Bourgueil are both famous for outstanding red wines. Vouvray and Montlouis-sur-Loire, on opposite sides of the river, produce outstanding white wines from the versatile Chenin Blanc, including sparkling, dry, *demi-sec,* and lusciously sweet.

THE CENTRAL VINEYARDS

Sancerre and Pouilly-sur-Loire lie far beyond the châteaux country of the mid-Loire. Sancerre is a remote, fortified hill town. A "wine and cheese" road winds its way through the hilly country that surrounds it, and you can not only buy Sancerre rosé and red, as well as the more usual and famous white, but also one of the great goat's milk cheeses of France, *crottin de Chavignol,* outstanding, accompanied by Sancerre.

Pouilly-sur-Loire is the source of the equally prestigious Sauvignon wine, Pouilly-Fumé. A *route du vin* leads from Pouilly through little wine hamlets such as Les Loges and Les Girarmes to Tracy-sur-Loire, then around to Bois Fleury, Le Grand Soumard, Le Petit Soumard, and St.-Andelain, a popular meeting place for people from the surrounding country.

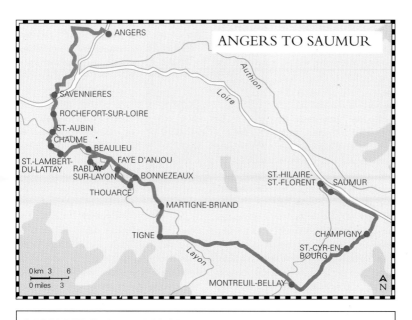

ANGERS TO SAUMUR

RECOMMENDED WINE PRODUCERS AND RESTAURANTS

PAYS NANTAIS
Château du Cléray
Le Cléray
44330 Vallet
tel: 40 36 22 55
fax: 40 36 34 62
*Good range of wines
mainly from own vineyards.*

**Maison des Vins du Pays
Nantais**
"Bellevue"
44690 La Haie-Fouassière
tel: 40 36 90 10
fax: 40 36 95 87
Wines of the Pays Nantais.

ANGERS TO SAUMUR
Coulée de Serrant
Château de la Roche aux
Moines
49170 Savennières
tel: 41 72 22 32
fax: 41 72 28 68
*Outstanding and historic
crus Savennières.*

Langlois-Château
3, Rue Léopold Palustre
St.-Hilaire-St.-Florent
49400 Saumur

tel: 41 50 28 14
fax: 41 50 26 29
*High-quality sparkling
wines.*

Maison du Vin de l'Anjou
5 bis, Place Kennedy
49100 Angers
tel: 41 88 81 13
fax: 41 86 71 84
Official maison *with full
range of wines on display,
literature, and maps.*

TOURAINE
**Auberge de La Cave
Martin**
66, La Vallée Coquette
37210 Vouvray
tel: 47 52 62 18
fax: 47 52 79 34
*Good, simple farm
restaurant serving meals
outdoors in fine weather.*
$

Couly-Dutheil
12, Rue Diderot
37500 Chinon
tel: 47 93 05 84
fax: 47 93 28 58

*Outstanding Chinon,
especially Clos de l'Echo.*

Grands Vins de Vouvray
Manoir du Haut Lieu
37210 Vouvray
tel: 47 52 78 87
fax: 47 52 66 51
*Gaston Huet is Vouvray's
most famous producer.*

THE CENTRAL
VINEYARDS
Didier Dagueneau
Rue de L'Ecole
St.-Andelain
58150 Pouilly-sur-Loire
tel: 86 39 15 62
fax: 86 39 07 61
*Considered by many to be
the most brilliant producer
of Pouilly-Fumé.*

Domaine de la Moussière
Rue Porte César
18300 Sancerre
tel: 48 54 07 41
fax: 48 54 07 62
*Alphonse Mellot is one of
Sancerre's leading
producers.*

Cidre et Calvados

CIDER AND CALVADOS

Norman cider is produced from special varieties of cider apples harvested in the fall when fully ripe and mature, then left to age for at least a month. These apples are very high in both sugar and acid so they are not suitable for eating. The apples are ground into a pulp in a granite trough, then this pulp is layered into burlap and pressed to extract the juice. The pure apple juice ferments naturally in wooden casks and is eventually bottled just before the fermentation is complete.

Pierre Huet of Cambremer, whose family have been making Calvados for generations

This is *cidre bouché,* the bottles sealed with a Champagne-type cork held down with a wire muzzle. Fermentation continues in the bottle resulting in a lively sparkle (there is always a residue of yeast cells left behind, so be careful when pouring). True *cidre fermier* can be raspingly bitter and dry, but it should always display the delicious smell and flavor of freshly picked apples.

Calvados is an apple brandy produced by distilling that same *cidre.* Traditionally, in the Pays d'Auge, the zone entitled to its own *appellation d'origine contrôlée,* the distillation begins the June following the harvest, so the ciders have had a chance to age and ferment to full dryness.

Within the Pays d'Auge, it is obligatory to produce Calvados by a process of double distillation carried out in the traditional manner using discontinuous pot stills — beautiful, immense copper cauldrons, in some cases, still heated directly by wood fires. The discontinuous system of distillation requires the stills to be recharged after each batch, but this system undoubtedly yields the finest results.

Once distilled, the raw, colorless spirit must age in wooden casks to temper its youthful, raw fire and gain fine, round flavors and a supple character that gets smoother with age. Minimum statutory guidelines for aging have been laid down (*Trois étoiles,* or three stars, indicates the minimum age of two years), but the finest old Calvados are aged for several decades.

In Normandy, there are three occasions when Calvados is enjoyed: first thing in the morning added to coffee (*café-Calva),* mid-meal as the *trou normand,* (see p.116), and after dinner, when you can best truly savor an old and rare — and very expensive — Calvados.

LA ROUTE DU CIDRE

This is a sign-posted route through some of the most congenial and pleasant country of the Pays d'Auge. Begin in Cambremer and head for Beuvron-en-Auge (a lovely town with half-timbered houses and a good restaurant), then east across to Beaufour-Druval, Bonnebosq, and back to Cambremer by way of La Boissière and Grandouet. Along the way, producers who have been selected from annual tastings display the sign *"cru de Cambremer"* indicating that they are open to the public for direct sales of cider and Calvados Pays d'Auge.

LA ROUTE DU CIDRE

N

BEAUFOUR
DRUVAL
BONNEBOSQ
BEUVRON-EN-AUGE
Dorette
MONTREUIL-EN-AUGE
GRANDOUET
CAMBREMER
LA BOISSIERE

0 km 2 4
0 miles 2

Lush orchards of Normandy in the Pays d'Auge, source of the finest cider and Calvados

CIDER AND CALVADOS PRODUCERS AND RESTAURANTS

Auberge "La Route du Cidre"
14340 Montreuil-en-Auge
tel: 31 63 00 64
fax: 31 63 12 27
Charming farmhouse restaurant in the heart of the apple country serving local homecooked foods. Mountain bikes for hire to tour the Route du Cidre.
$

Calvados Pierre Huet
Manoir la Brière des Fontaines
14340 Cambremer
tel: 31 63 01 09
fax: 31 63 14 02
The Huets have been distilling and bottling their own Calvados Pays d'Auge for five generations, using only their own harvest from the family orchards. There is a welcoming caveau for tasting and an excellent range of fine old Calvados, as well as Pommeau and good farmhouse cider.

La Ferme de Beuvron
14430 Beuvron-en-Auge
tel: 31 79 29 19
Beuvron-en-Auge is the most charming town along the Route du Cidre and it is well worth coming here to visit this outstanding farmhouse outlet which stocks the produce of about a dozen agriculteurs. This provides a one-stop shopping opportunity for all the best farm goodies of Normandy: farmhouse cider and Calvados, farmhouse cheeses, confiture de lait, and plats cuisinés.

Le Pavé d'Auge
Place du Village
14430 Beuvron-en-Auge
tel: 31 79 26 71
fax: 31 39 04 45
A fine regional restaurant on Beuvron-en-Auge's pretty town square serving the foods of the Pays d'Auge with style and imagination.
$$$

Madame Louise Foucher
Rout de Rumesnil
14340 Cambremer
tel: 31 63 01 71
Deliciously quenching cidre bouché *produced by traditional methods.*

Robert Turmel
St.-Laurent-du-Mont
14340 Cambremer
tel: 31 63 04 74
Monsieur Turmel's Pommeau is deliciously smooth, fruity, yet powerful. Also good cider and Calvados.

Y. & F. Grandval
Grandouet
14340 Cambremer
tel: 31 63 08 73
fax: 31 63 12 43
Family cider produced in the heart of the Pays d'Auge along the Route du Cidre.

Cognac

THE WORLD'S FINEST BRANDY

THE TOWN OF COGNAC not only lives by its most famous product, it, literally, breathes it: sweet, intoxicating aromas hang above the buildings of the old town, whose walls are blackened with an alcohol-hungry fungus. An enormous quantity of Cognac escapes into the atmosphere, evaporating from the many thousands of wooden casks that lie in the aging *chais* (warehouses) of the town's great Cognac firms, a loss they philosophically and poetically describe as *"la part des anges"* — the angels' share.

Cognac is the world's finest brandy. The thin wines of Charentes, unremarkable in themselves, become, through a unique process of double distillation in pot stills, followed by lengthy aging and blending, a fiery, yet ultimately velvety-smooth spirit. To find out more and to sample Cognac you need do no more than point your nose in the direction of this otherwise unassuming Charentais market town.

The River Charente at Jarnac

Park along the riverside *quai,* then explore the *vieille ville* (old town) on foot, following its medieval stone-paved lanes.

The Château de Cognac deserves to be visited. The oldest part of this historic landmark dates from the 9th century. During the course of the Hundred Years' War (1337–1453), the château changed hands many times. The Black Prince, son of Edward III of England, came here several times to retreat from battle and Bertrand du Guesclin, a brilliant French strategist, recaptured it from the English in 1375. The château was enlarged and rebuilt during the 15th century, and, in 1795, was bought by Baron Otard, an exiled Scotsman, who began to trade in Cognac. The château is still owned by Cognac Otard, who offer a fascinating tour of the aging *chais* located in the castle.

Two other expatriates, Richard Hennessy, an Irish mercenary, and James Martell, who came from the Channel Islands, had already settled in Cognac earlier in the 18th century and begun to ship casks of brandy back to Ireland and Britain, a trade which, particularly in the 19th century, expanded to all the corners of the world. Today, Société Hennessy, linked with Champagne Moët & Chandon, is one of the most important drinks companies in France. Both Hennessy and Martell offer fascinating tours of their warehouses in the town without appointment through the year.

Essentially, Cognac is produced from a distillation of wines that may come from various zones within the vast Cognac vineyard that extends even to offshore islands and includes the zones of Grande Champagne, Petite Champagne, Borderies, Fins Bois, Bons Bois, Bois Ordinaires, and Bois à Terroir (Fine Champagne Cognac indicates Cognac produced from wines only from the first two zones).

Distillation must take place twice in discontinuous Charentais pot stills that need to be recharged after each batch. As the wines are distilled, the alcohol vaporizes and then condenses. The first (*têtes* or heads) and last (*queues* or tails) parts of the distillation are discarded as they contain undesirable volatile elements. Only the middle or heart of the distillation, known here as *la bonne chauffe,* is kept.

Afterward, the resulting colorless spirits are aged in oak casks made with wood from the Limousin or Tronçais forests. Only after considerable aging are both these young and old reserve brandies blended together to produce the consistent brands that are the hallmark of each house. These include *Trois étoilles* or VS (three stars or "very special"), which indicates that the youngest brandies in the blend are at least two-and-a-half years old and usually upward of four or five from the large houses; VSOP ("very superior old pale"), a high accolade for cognacs containing percentages of reserves that are a minimum of four-and-a-half and often upward of 15 to 20 years or older; and XO, *Vieille réserve,* or *Grande réserve,* terms applied to the finest, oldest, and smoothest Cognacs.

Visiting the large Cognac houses, which have created the image of this great brandy worldwide, is fascinating, but equally enjoyable is traveling out into

Madame Forgeron in her caves

wine country, to such prestigious areas as the Grande Champagne vineyard which lies to the south of Jarnac, Cognac's second major town.

This is essentially quiet country, hilly and open, a land that is pleasant simply to meander through. In towns such as Segonzac or Barbezieux, you may still come across women wearing the *quichenotte,* the typical Charentaise *coiffe* (headdress). What is particularly fascinating is the chance to visit a Cognac *propriétaire-récoltant,* a winegrower who, on his own premises, also vinifies then distills Cognac himself, both to sell to the large firms who age and blend it, and to age and bottle himself for sale direct to the public. Such single-vineyard Cognacs, especially from Grande Champagne, can be both superb in quality and highly individual in character.

RECOMMENDED COGNAC DISTILLERS

Cognac Otard
Château de Cognac
127, Boulevard Denfert-Rochereau BP3
16101 Cognac
tel: 45 82 40 00
fax: 45 82 75 11
Enjoyable tour explains history of Cognac.

La Cognathèque
8, Place Jean Monnet
16100 Cognac
tel: 45 82 43 31
fax: 45 82 53 97
Large stock of Cognac and Pineau des Charentes.

Courvoisier
2, Place du Château
16200 Jarnac
tel: 45 35 55 55
fax: 45 35 55 00

Courvoisier's Cognac museum also displays one of Napoleon's hats and a greatcoat.

La Ribaudière
Place du Port
16200 Bourg-Charente
tel: 45 81 30 54
fax: 45 81 28 05
Between Cognac and Jarnac, serving stylish local foods on a terrace by the banks of the Charente.
$$

Michel Forgeron
Chez Richon
16130 Segonzac
tel/fax: 45 83 43 05
Michel Forgeron's Grande Champagne Cognac is outstanding, and Madame

Forgeron is passionate about explaining its production process.

Société Hennessy
1, Rue de la Richonne
16101 Cognac
tel: 45 35 72 72
fax: 45 82 49 01
Tour includes a boat ride across the Charente to the vast aging chais.

Société Martell
7, Place Edouard Martell
16101 Cognac
tel: (visits) 45 36 33 33
fax: 45 36 33 99
The oldest of the grandes maisons. Visitors are shown the aging chais, blending room, and bottling plant.

Les Bonnes Adresses
USEFUL ADDRESSES

BRITTANY

Abbaye La Joie Notre-Dame
56800 Campénéac
tel: 97 93 42 07
fax: 97 93 11 23
Cheeses and baked goods, as well as hand-made products from other abbeys throughout France.

Chez Jacky
Rive Droite
Port du Belon
29340 Riec-sur-Belon
tel: 98 06 90 32
Quite simply one of the finest places in the world to enjoy the freshest shellfish, especially Belon oysters.
$$

Crêperie des Remparts
31, Rue Théophile Louarn
Ville Close
29900 Concarneau
tel: 98 50 65 66
In the walled Ville Close, serving exceptional crêpes and galettes au blé noir.
$

Ferme Auberge de Kerambosser
Route de Bannalec
29340 Riec-sur-Belon
tel: 98 06 07 43
*Simple farmhouse restaurant serving own-produced terrines, lamb, and far breton, accompanied by good farmhouse cider.
2 km. (1 1/4 miles) from Pont-Aven.*
$

Ferme Auberge de Pors Klos
Trédudon-Le Moine
29690 Berrien
tel: 98 99 61 65
fax: 98 99 67 36
In the rugged Parc d'Armorique, a professionally run farmhouse restaurant serving excellent local foods. Rooms available.
$–$$

Huîtrières du Château de Bélon
Port de Belon
29340 Riec-sur-Belon
tel: 98 06 41 43
Excellent oysters. Enjoy them with house Muscadet.

La Cotriade
16 Quai Armand Dayot
22500 Paimpol
tel: 96 20 87 08
On Brittany's north coast, an exceptional seafood and shellfish restaurant.
$$–$$$

Le Continental
4, Quai Albert-Thomas
35260 Cancale
tel: 99 89 60 16
fax: 99 89 69 58
Impeccable fish and shellfish and a dining terrace overlooking the oyster beds.
$$

Louis Le Moigne
86, Avenue de la Gare
29100 Tréboul-Douarnenez
tel: 98 74 01 07
Kouigh-amann *made by the Le Moigne family for four generations.*

Musée de la Pêche
Rue Vaubon BP118
(Ville Close)
29181 Concarneau
tel: 98 97 10 20
Interesting museum of the fishing industry in Brittany.

Oysters for sale at Huîtrières du Château de Belon

NORMANDY

Auberge de Beau Lieu
Le Fossé
D915
76440 Forges-les-Eaux
tel: 35 90 50 36
fax: 35 90 35 98
This stylish country auberge warrants a detour for its innovative cooking.
$$

Domaine de la Coudraye
27370 La-Haye-du-Theil
tel: 32 35 52 07
fax: 32 35 17 21
High-quality Norman foie gras. Chambres d'hôte à la ferme.

Four à Pain
Musée de la Boulangerie Rurale
27350 La Haye-de-Routot
tel: 32 57 07 99;
35 37 23 16
fax: 35 37 39 70
This 19th-century rural bread oven is open daily July to August; other times by appointment. Breads and pâtisseries baked on the premises; bakery workshops by reservation.

Hotel Restaurant Belle-Isle-sur-Risle
112, Route de Rouen
27500 Pont-Audemer
tel: 32 56 96 22
fax: 32 42 88 96
Charming, luxurious hotel with a great restaurant, just outside the atmospheric tanners' town.
$$$

La Couronne
31, Place du Vieux Marché
76000 Rouen
tel: 35 71 40 90
fax: 35 71 05 78
The oldest auberge in France, founded in 1345 in the square where the English burned Jeanne d'Arc at the stake. Stylish regional fare.
$$

La Mère Poulard
Grande Rue
50116 Le Mont-St.-Michel
tel: 33 60 14 01
fax: 38 48 52 31
This restaurant has become a culinary landmark, and it is worth coming here for not only the famous omelet *and ambience but also for its exceptional* cuisine du terroir.
$$$$

Palais Bénédictine
110, Rue Alexandre Le Grand
76400 Fécamp
tel: 35 10 26 00
fax: 35 28 50 81
Tour the incredible neo-Gothic palace where Bénédictine is produced and afterward enjoy a tasting.

THE LOIRE VALLEY
Auberge Jeanne de Laval
54, Rue Nationale
49350 Les Rosiers-sur-Loire
tel: 41 51 80 17
fax: 41 38 04 18
The finest beurre blanc *we have ever tasted was in this stylish country restaurant.*
$$

Charcuterie Hardouin
Virage Gastronomique
BP8
37210 Vouvray
tel: 47 40 40 40
fax: 47 52 66 54
Outstanding charcuterie, *especially creamy and delicious* rillettes *and* rillons.

Au Marais
46–48 Quais Louis-Tardy
79510 Coulon
tel: 49 35 90 43
fax: 49 35 81 98
In the heart of the Marais Poitevin, serving cuisine du terroir.
$$

La Couronne, Rouen

Hostellerie Gargantua
73, Rue Voltaire
37500 Chinon
tel: 47 93 04 71
Located in the 15th-century Palais du Baillage, serving traditional specialties, including "la fameuse omelette garganelle."
$$

Le Relais Fleuri
42, Avenue de la Tuilerie
58150 Pouilly-sur-Loire
tel: 86 39 12 99
fax: 86 39 14 15
Charming petite auberge with a flowered terrace, a good base for touring the Upper Loire. Reliable restaurant.
$$

Les Caves de Marson
Rue Henri Fricotelle
49400 Rou-Marson
tel: 41 50 50 05
fax: 41 50 94 01
In a trogolodyte house above Saumur, meals based on fouées— *flat breads with fillings — cooked in a wood-fired oven. Open only in season.*
$

Les Tuffeaux
21, Rue Lavoisier
37000 Tours
tel: 47 47 19 89
Atmospheric restaurant serving good food at fair prices.
$$

Restaurant Don Quichotte
35, Route du Clisson
44330 Vallet
tel: 40 33 99 67
fax: 40 33 99 72
Good fish and shellfish, including huîtres chaudes au Muscadet.
$$

Serre Auberge de la Tuilerie
3, La Tuilerie
Route du Perreau
37510 Savonnières
tel: 47 50 00 51
In the heart of the "Jardin de la France"; dine on local produce, especially fresh vegetables from the farm.
$–$$

POITOU-CHARENTES
Château de Didonne
17120 Semussac
tel: 46 05 18 10
fax: 46 06 93 93
A museum of rural life with a good restaurant. Alternatively, bring a picnic to enjoy in the grounds.

Restaurant le Cayenne
Musée Artisanal Ostréicole
Route du Port
17320 Marennes
tel: 46 85 01 06
fax 46 85 66 04
Amid the oyster beds, this little oyster museum is also the place to sample the famous fines de claires *of Marennes with Vin du Pays Charentais.*
$

BEST BUYS
- cookies from Pont-Aven (Brittany)
- canned sardines (Brittany)
- *sel de Guérande* (Brittany)
- Calvados *Hors d'age* (Normandy)
- wine (Loire Valley)
- Cognac and Pineau des Charentes (Poitou-Charentes)

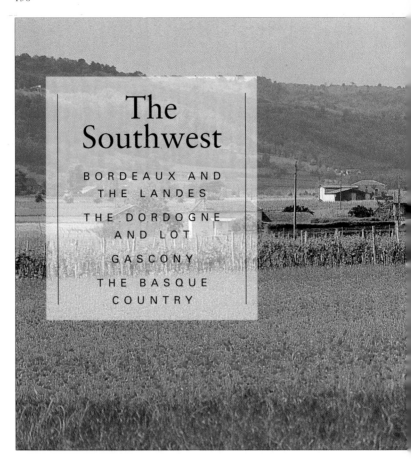

The Southwest

BORDEAUX AND
THE LANDES

THE DORDOGNE
AND LOT

GASCONY

THE BASQUE
COUNTRY

SOUTHWEST FRANCE is a well-fed, comfortable corner of the country, a vast region that exudes a sense of well-being and plenty. For lovers of classic French food and wine, few other regions can match its bounty, its supply of world-class produce and products as well as simpler, yet equally abundant and satisfying, foods and wines.

From the Atlantic seaboard to the heights of the Pyrenees, and from the sluggish banks of the Gironde up into the rural hinterlands of the Dordogne, Lot, and Garonne Rivers, Southwest France continues today, as in the past, to attract thousands of visitors who come for a variety of reasons: to enjoy the quintessential "French experience" that is the Dordogne and Périgord, or to explore less well-traveled rural areas such as Lot and Gers, to surf and sunbathe on the beaches of the Landes and the Basque Country, to walk or cycle through quiet rural landscapes and in the hills and mountains, or to taste, drink, and buy wines from the greatest quality vineyard in the world, Bordeaux. Whatever the reason, it is certain that the visitor in any part of Southwest France will eat well and enjoy exceptional wines — with its rich duck and goose based cuisine and equally rich wines, we suggest you leave any thought of diets behind.

Summer landscape in the Lot Valley

SOUTHWEST FRANCE — THE ENGLISH CONNECTION

When in 1154, Eleanor of Aquitaine married Henry of Anjou, later to rule England as Henry II, most of Southwest France came under the sovereignty of the English Crown. This corner of the country subsequently became the central battlefield in the conflict known as the Hundred Years War (1337–1453), as the English vied with the French for supremacy over the region (legacies of this are the fortified *bastide* towns that are found throughout the area). Eventually, the English were driven out, but the connection with England established by Henry, great-grandson of William the Conqueror, remains even today. It was in Eleanor's day, certainly, and in the decades and centuries afterward, while Aquitaine remained part of England, that the Bordeaux wine trade became so important. Indeed, the English predilection for claret, which is their name for Bordeaux red wine (taken from *"clairet,"* which once referred to a light red wine), was an indication of that country's historic fondness for and association with the region. Even today, the Southwest is still probably the most popular part of France with British tourists, not to mention American, as well as Dutch, German, and other foreign visitors.

BORDEAUX — WORLD CAPITAL OF WINE

We associate Bordeaux primarily with the wines to which it grants its name, but the city itself, the fourth largest in France, is a vast urban sprawl of trade, industry, and culture. Wine has been produced in the region since at least the days of the Romans; moreover, the city's location on the Gironde, the vast waterway formed by the convergence of the Dordogne and Garonne Rivers, meant that it became the natural shipping center for wines not just from its surrounding vineyards but from its vast hinterland too, as far upriver as Bergerac, Cahors, and elsewhere. Today, wine lovers will wish to visit not just the city of Bordeaux but its surrounding principal wine zones, including the Médoc to the north, with its magnificent profusion of mainly 18th-century châteaux, the Sauternais, source of the greatest sweet wines in the world, and St.-Emilion, one of the great wine towns of France. Bordeaux serves, too, as the springboard for exploring both the Dordogne and Périgord, as well as the pine-covered Atlantic seaboard of the Landes leading down to the Basque Country.

THE DORDOGNE AND LOT — A FAT, RICH HINTERLAND

Stone Age people settled in the Dordogne as we know from the paintings left on cave walls and ceilings at places such as Les Eyzies-de-Tayac and Lascaux. Visitors throng the prehistoric sites in summer, and, indeed, the whole region is hugely popular with holidaymakers. The Dordogne River is one of the longest in France. It springs to life in the highest peaks

At the Sarlat-la-Canéda market in the Dordogne

of the Massif Central, then it passes through some of the most beautiful and varied landscapes in the country, dotted with scores of historic towns and villages. The Dordogne in its upper reaches pierces the limestone plateau of Quercy, then passes through the rich and historic countryside of Périgord before leveling out at Bergerac and the broader, vine-covered plains where it eventually joins the Garonne to form the Gironde above Bordeaux. The Lot Valley similarly extends from the Massif Central across the stony uplands of Quercy, a high and dramatic land, less visited perhaps but still popular with vacationers in search of peace and natural beauty.

GASCONY — THE SPIRIT OF THE SOUTHWEST

To the south of the Garonne River, Gascony extends across the *département* of Gers, and comprises the hilly region known as Armagnac, source of France's second great brandy, as well as parts of the low-lying, sandy Landes. A large region almost wholly given over to agriculture, this

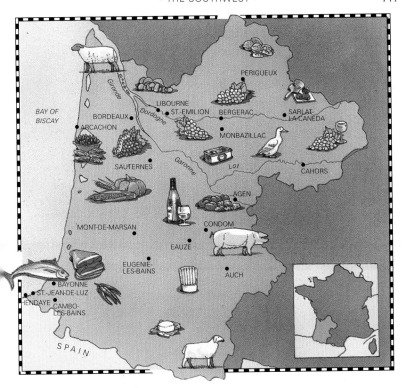

can be a particularly satisfying, wholly rural area to visit. Auch, the capital of Gers, is a fine provincial town; the Armagnac country is genuine and welcoming (visit market towns such as Condom and Mont-de-Marsan); and the otherwise unassuming Landes spa town of Eugénie-les-Bains has become something of a mecca for both gourmets and slimmers who come to Les Prés d'Eugénie to enjoy Michel Guérard's celebrated *cuisine gourmande* (classic gourmet cuisine) as well as his equally delicious *cuisine minceur* (gourmet slimming cuisine).

THE BASQUE COUNTRY

The far southwest corner of France is known as the Basque Country, a unique and fascinating area with its own culture, language, traditions, and foods, more akin to Northwest Spain than to France. Biarritz and Bayonne retain the (now somewhat faded) atmosphere of the grand international resorts that they were in their heyday earlier this century. The rest of the region looks inward, insular and jealous in safeguarding its Basque heritage. People come to some of the finest beaches in Europe to body-surf and to sit out at sidewalk cafés in Biarritz and Bayonne; but visitors should also find the time to travel inland, to explore and experience such typical Basque towns as little Espelette, Cambo-les-Bains, and St.-Jean-Pied-de-Port. The *piment*-tinged foods of the Basque Country are among the most colorful and appetizing of all France's many and varied regional cuisines.

Produits Régionaux
REGIONAL PRODUCE

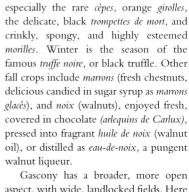

MUCH OF SOUTHWEST FRANCE is hilly, often rugged and wooded, but nonetheless much agricultural produce is grown here.

The fertile Lot and Garonne Valleys, with their mild climate, are ideal for the cultivation of fruit trees. Southeast of Bordeaux, especially between Marmande and Agen, the plains are planted extensively with neat, espaliered orchards. Agen is famous for its Ente plums, picked when almost overripe and dried in ovens to become the succulent *pruneaux d'Agen,* considered the finest prunes in the world.

In addition to plum orchards, the Garonne Valley is the source of peaches, pears, apples, and Chasselas grapes, the latter cultivated around the town of Moissac, which has earned the title "capital of the Chasselas" and boasts an annual grape festival in September. There is also a health center here which administers a dietary regime based on fresh grapes.

The Dordogne is the source of fine early

Girolles *mushrooms*

ripening spring vegetables, and, in late summer and fall, wild mushrooms, especially the rare *cèpes,* orange *girolles,* the delicate, black *trompettes de mort,* and crinkly, spongy, and highly esteemed *morilles.* Winter is the season of the famous *truffe noire,* or black truffle. Other fall crops include *marrons* (fresh chestnuts, delicious candied in sugar syrup as *marrons glacés*), and *noix* (walnuts), enjoyed fresh, covered in chocolate *(arlequins de Carlux),* pressed into fragrant *huile de noix* (walnut oil), or distilled as *eau-de-noix,* a pungent walnut liqueur.

Gascony has a broader, more open aspect, with wide, landlocked fields. Here are found great tracts of grain — wheat, maize (mainly to feed animals), millet — as well as tobacco. Millet was once a staple for the poor people of the region, eaten as a rather mushy porridge known as *millas* or *broye.* Today, it is more often made with coarsely ground white corn and is similar in consistency to Italian

BLACK TRUFFLES

Les truffes noires du Périgord — black truffles — are one of the most famous and expensive luxury foods of France. They are also one of the most over-rated. The so-called "black diamond" of Périgord these days is as likely to come from the Vaucluse *département* of Provence or from Italy as it is to be found locally.

Nonetheless, black truffles continue to be in great demand as it is still considered almost *de rigueur* to use them as a garnish in restaurants throughout the Dordogne and all of France.

Preserved black truffles (bottled in salt water) are not worth the money or the fuss, and the minuscule black specks of mushy truffle garnishing dishes in restaurants leave us stone cold. But *fresh* truffles can be another thing altogether, although only rarely in France do they receive the treatment they deserve — unlike in Italy. If you are in the region from about mid-December to February and encounter fresh truffles in the markets of Sarlat-la-Canéda, Lalbenque, or Périgueux, buy one to try for yourself. A truffle lover from the Dordogne advises, "Clean, then chop coarsely and add to beaten egg. Leave to macerate for an hour or so to let the flavors develop, then cook as an omelet. *Délicieux!*"

Fresh walnuts, a winter treat in Périgord

polenta. Potiron (pumpkin) is another fall vegetable of Gascony, added to stews, used to flavor and color breads, or made into a local dessert, *mesturet* — pumpkin pulp cooked in sugar and flavored with lemon rind.

The Basque Country is a land of small market gardens where a bit of this and a bit of that is grown whatever the season. Tomatoes and red peppers are the most commonly grown vegetables; stewed slowly together, they form *pipérade,* one of the tastiest and most colorful foods of the region.

IN SEASON

Asperge blanche   Big, fat spears of white asparagus, grown underground, come from the Garonne Valley, especially around Marmande (May–Jun).

Cèpes   The finest and most prized of all wild mushrooms, gathered throughout the region (Sep–mid Oct).

Fraises   Strawberries from Périgord (mid May–end Jun).

Légumes de primeur   Baby spring vegetables — *haricots verts* (green beans), *carottes* (carrots), *pommes de terre de primeur* (new potatoes), *courgettes* (zucchini) — grown under glass (early spring and fall) and outdoors (summer).

Marrons   Chestnuts (Sep–Oct).

Noisettes   Hazelnuts (Sep–Oct).

Noix   Walnuts (mid Sep–early Nov).

Pruneaux d'Agen mi-cuits   The great bulk of the *prune d'Ente* (Ente plum) harvest is dried to make the famous *pruneaux d'Agen.* Best are the *pruneaux d'Agen mi-cuits,* which spend only a few hours in the sun or in special drying ovens, and emerge still incredibly moist and succulent (Jul–Oct).

Truffes noires   Fresh black truffles may be worth buying in season if you encounter them in markets (mid Dec–Feb).

PIMENT D'ESPELETTE

Fresh, dried, or coarsely ground into powder, red chili peppers are the most characteristic feature of the foods of the Basque Country. The finest is the famous *piment d'Espelette,* which comes from the eponymous village, a proud Basque town in the hilly hinterland behind St.-Jean-de-Luz. Here, peppers strung into garlands are hung up to dry from balconies and windows throughout the town and surrounding country. Indeed, this gaily colored sight has come to take on something of the significance of a national symbol of the Basque Country.

The *piment d'Espelette* is hot, but never overly so, with a piquant after-bite that draws itself smartly to your attention without hanging around. Apart from its wide use in cooking, it is one of the characteristic spices used in the curing process of *jambon de Bayonne.* You can purchase bags of this classic Basque condiment in markets.

Les Marchés
MARKETS

BORDEAUX AND THE LANDES

Aire-sur-l'Adour	Tue, Sat
Arcachon	Wed, Sat
Bordeaux	Mon–Sat
Castelnau-de-Médoc	Sun
Lesparre-Médoc	Tues, Sat
Libourne	Tue, Fri
Mont-de-Marsan	Tue
Pauillac	Sat
Sauveterre-de-Guyenne	Tue
St.-Emilion	Sun
Ste.-Foy-la-Grande	Sat

THE DORDOGNE AND LOT

Agen	Wed, Sat, Sun
Bergerac	Wed, Sat
Brantôme	Fri
Cahors	Wed
Castelnau-Montratier	Tue, Thu
Lalbenque *Marché aux truffes* (truffle market)	Mon (Dec–Mar only)
Les Eyzies-de-Tayac	Mon
Montignac	Wed, Sat
Périgueux	Wed, Sat
St.-Cyprien	Sun
Sarlat-la-Canéda	Wed, Sat
Sorges	Fri (summer only)
Souillac	Fri
Terrasson-la-Villedieu	daily
Villeneuve-sur-Lot	Tue, Sat

Enjoying market day

Saturday market in Sarlat-la-Canéda

GASCONY

Aignan	Mon
Auch	Thu, Sat
Cazaubon	Sat
Condom	Wed
Eauze	Thu
Plaisance	Thu
Riscle	Fri

THE BASQUE COUNTRY

Bayonne	Mon–Sat
Biarritz	Mon–Sat
Espelette	Wed
Hendaye	Wed, Sat
St.-Jean-de-Luz	Tue, Fri
St.-Jean-Pied-de-Port	Mon

FETES ET FOIRES FESTIVALS AND FAIRS

BORDEAUX AND THE LANDES

Gujan-Mestras (near Arcachon) *Foire ostréicole* (oysters)
1st fortnight Aug

Pissos *Foire au miel* (honey)   Aug

St.-Emilion *Proclamation du ban des Vendanges* (start of harvest)
3rd Sun Sep

THE DORDOGNE AND LOT

Monségur *Foire au gras* (fattened duck and goose)
mid Dec

Nontron *Foire aux châtaignes* (chestnuts)
mid Oct

Villefranche-du-Périgord *Foire aux châtaignes* (chestnuts)   3rd Sat Oct

GASCONY AND THE BASQUE COUNTRY

Eauze *Foire aux eaux-de-vie d'Armagnac* (Armagnac)
early Jun

St.-Jean-de-Luz *Fête du thon* (tuna)   1st week Jul
Fête du ttoro (fish soup),
early Sep

St.-Jean-Pied-de-Port *Foire aux fromages* (cheese fair)
two Thus Aug

Samatan (near Auch) *Foire nationale au foie gras*
end Aug

MARCHES AU GRAS
Ducks and geese are raised and fattened in France on small farms and on an industrial scale, mainly for the production of *foie gras*. Countless stores sell *foie gras* and other duck and goose derivatives, but the best places to buy are the *marchés au gras* — special duck and goose markets usually attached to regular weekly markets, where both fresh and preserved duck and goose products are brought for sale.

Les Spécialités
REGIONAL SPECIALTIES

SOUTHWEST FRANCE is the undisputed kingdom of the fattened duck and goose. *Foie gras de canard* and *d'oie* (see p.151) may be their most famous by-products, but duck and geese feature in many other ways, too. *Graisse d'oie* (goose fat) is the cooking medium of the Southwest, and foods gain a rich flavor and unctuous texture when prepared with it. Legs of both duck and goose are first salted, then cooked slowly in their own fat to become meltingly delicious *confits*. *Magrets de canard* (the plump breasts of duck) are char-grilled over wood fires and eaten rare like steak, *aiguillettes* (long, thin pieces of meat from the back of the carcass) are threaded onto skewers together with *coeurs de canard* (duck hearts), and anything left over is made into the most delicious range of *pâtés,* often studded with truffles. We have enjoyed *cou farci* — the neck of duck stuffed with *foie gras* — and happily munched on *fritons,* little bits of left over skin and meat fried in duck fat to make a crispy drinking nibble. Virtually everything is utilized: the carcass is used to make *garbure,* the hearty vegetable soup of Gascony, while even the down and feathers are used to fill duvets and quilts.

The Southwest is a land of enthusiastic eaters, and the true country foods here are always filling and plentiful, rarely

Arcachon oysters for sale at a roadside stand

delicate or fussy. Hearty vegetable, bread, and bean soups are often the start to meals. Game from the forests is enjoyed in season, lamb from the salt marshes of Pauillac is considered among the finest in the country, and the Blond d'Aquitaine is one of France's preeminent breeds of beef cattle. The Atlantic seaboard supplies excellent oysters from the Arcachon Basin, as well as a superlative catch of deep-sea fish, such as *thon rouge,* from the Basque fishing ports.

If the Bordelais prefer their foods basically simple and unadorned so that they do not overly compete in attention with their famous wines, the foods of the Basque Country come as something of a shocking contrast, their names as different as their aspect — *ttoro* (chili-tinged fish

---

"VINE"-FLAVORED FOODS

Throughout the wine country of the Southwest, the most characteristic method of cooking meat is grilling it over fires made from pruned vine shoots *(sarments), ceps de vigne* (old, uprooted vines), and the wine-drenched staves from discarded *barriques* (wine casks). For *vignerons,* this

was a way of getting rid of the unwanted wood, but now restaurants throughout the wine country, such as the farmhouse restaurant of Château Cros-Figeac in St.-Emilion (left), cook *grillades aux sarments* — meats grilled over vine shoots, one of the simplest but most delicious specialties of the region.

soup), *tripoxa* (a type of mutton blood sausage), or *axoa d'Espelette* (cubes of veal sautéed in — what else? — *piment d'Espelette*).

APPETIZERS AND FIRST COURSES

Assiette fermière or **assiette paysanne** (Gascony)   A mixed platter of duck meat appetizers which can include a morsel of *foie gras*, a few slices of *magret séché* (cured duck breast), some *pâté* or *rillettes de canard,* and some warm *gésiers confits* (conserved gizzards), served with bread and salad.

Brochette des coeurs de canard (the Dordogne and Lot, Gascony) Skewered duck hearts grilled over charcoal (much better than it sounds).

Crudités (Bordeaux and all France) Raw vegetables and salads; served as a starter throughout the nation, this simple first course is particularly favored by the Bordelais. A good selection may include grated carrot and celeriac; beet with chopped shallots in a cream dressing; sliced tomatoes in *vinaigrette;* perhaps a slab of homemade *pâté* with some crunchy, vinegary *cornichons* (pickles); or some tiny gray shrimp and a pile of sea snails complete with pin to extract them.

Feuilleté au foie gras

Elzekaria (the Basque Country) Hearty vegetable soup made with potatoes, onions, leeks, carrots, cabbage, and pumpkin.

Feuilleté au foie gras (Gascony) Rich puff pastry tart layered with sausage meat, *magret de canard* (duck breast), and slices of *foie gras,* baked, and served as an extravagant first course.

Foie gras de canard or **d'oie** (all Southwest)   Fresh, home-prepared and -cooked *foie gras* — the fattened liver of duck or goose — is undoubtedly one of the finest luxury foods of the region. Enjoy hot *(foie gras chaud)* or cold *(froid),* set in shimmering aspic. A rich classic not to be missed.

Garbure (Gascony)   Hearty bean, potato, and cabbage soup cooked with duck fat and often with a piece of *confit de canard* added for richness and flavor. A classic winter warmer.

Huîtres d'Arcachon (Arcachon, Bordeaux, and the Atlantic seaboard) Oysters from Arcachon are usually served raw with just a wedge of lemon, though the Bordelais are said to be fond of them served with the hot local sausages, *louquenkas*.

Jambon de Bayonne (the Basque Country)   Real *jambon de Bayonne* is one of the great food products of the Southwest. Enjoy a thick slice as a first course (see p.150).

Magret de canard séché (all Southwest)   Duck breast, dry-salted, then air-cured like ham; served raw in thin slices, or added to salads.

Moules d'Arcachon (Arcachon and the Atlantic seaboard)   Farmed mussels; served steamed in white wine with shallots.

Pâté du Périgord (Périgord)   Usually means a coarse, homemade *pâté* made from duck, goose, or pork livers, sometimes studded with black truffle.

Pipérade au jambon (the Basque Country)   *Pipérade,* a tasty vegetable stew made from tomatoes, red bell peppers, onions, garlic, and seasoned with *piment d'Espelette*, is cooked with scrambled eggs and served on a thick slice of *jambon de Bayonne*.

Rillettes de canard or **d'oie** (all Southwest) Potted meat paste of shreds of duck or goose slowly cooked in their own fat.

Salade aux gésiers confits (all Southwest) Fresh green salad topped with conserved duck gizzards fried in duck fat and sprinkled with vinegar.

Salade aux noix (the Dordogne and Lot) Fresh green salad sprinkled with walnuts and dressed in walnut oil.

Soupe des vendangeurs (Bordeaux and the wine country) At harvest time, substantial vegetable and meat soup is prepared to satisfy appetites made keen from picking grapes: the custom, once the soup is finished, is *"faire le chabrot"* — to swill out the remaining dregs of soup in the bowl with a glass of red wine and drink it.

Soupe paysanne du Périgord (Périgord) Hearty, homemade vegetable soup, made with root vegetables, duck or goose fat, white beans, and thickened with bread.

Tourin blanchi (the Dordogne and all Southwest) Classic onion soup thickened with country bread and enriched with egg yolk.

Tripoxa or **tripotcha** (the Basque Country) Basque blood sausage made from mutton or veal and spiced with *piment d'Espelette*.

Ttoro (the Basque Country) Atlantic fish soup/stew made with meaty white fish such as *baudroie* (monkfish), *merluche* or *merluza* (hake), and *colin* (pollack), cooked with onions, tomatoes, and red chili pepper and sometimes garnished with *langoustines* and mussels.

Tourin blanchi

MAIN COURSES

A la périgourdine

When this term is appended to a dish, it usually means that the dish is served either with truffles or with *foie gras* or with both.

Axoa d'Espelette (the Basque Country) Cubes of veal cooked with onions and red bell peppers, spiced with *piment d'Espelette*.

Chipirons à l'encre (The Basque Country) Squid cooked in its own ink.

Civet de chevreuil (Gascony) Rich venison stew with wine and vegetables; sometimes thickened with blood.

Confit de canard (all Southwest) Salted pieces of fattened duck cooked slowly in their own fat to conserve them. To prepare, *confit* is usually either fried or broiled.

Daube d'oie (Gascony) Goose, flambéd in Armagnac, then slowly braised with wine and vegetables: a classic.

Entrecôte à la bordelaise (Bordeaux) Char-grilled rib steak served with a classic sauce made of red Bordeaux wine, shallots, and bone marrow.

Estouffat de porc (the Dordogne and Lot) Pork cooked in a sealed pot together with white beans, wine, herbs, and vegetables: classic country cooking of the Southwest.

Foie de canard aux raisins (Gascony and all Southwest) A rich and extravagant main course: fresh *foie gras* first flambéd in Armagnac, then sautéed lightly with fresh grapes.

Gigot d'agneau pré-salé (Pauillac and Bordeaux) *Agneau "pré-salé"* is lamb that has grazed on the salt marshes, here, particularly on the banks of the Gironde around Pauillac. The local method is usually to roast a leg on a bed of spring vegetables with red Bordeaux wine added to make a tasty sauce.

Gigot de sept heures (all South-west)   Classic method of cooking a leg of lamb or mutton: first mari-nated in wine, garlic, and herbs, then slowly braised with vege-tables in a low oven for, yes, as long as seven hours.

Thon rouge

Lamproie à la bordelaise (St.-Emilion and all Bordeaux)   Pieces of Gironde lamprey stewed in red wine with shallots, leeks, and tomatoes, and enriched with the lamprey's own blood.

Lapin aux pruneaux (Agen and all Southwest)   Rabbit (usually wild) stewed in wine with *pruneaux d'Agen*.

Magret de canard grillé au feu de bois (all the Southwest)   The large breast of fattened duck is delicious grilled like steak over an open wood fire, then thinly sliced and fanned out on the plate. It will be cooked rare unless you specify otherwise (*bien cuit* for well done).

Merlu à la koskera or **merluza in salsa verde** (the Basque Country) Hake and potatoes baked in an earthenware *cocotte* with asparagus tips, green peas, and plenty of chopped parsley and seasoned with garlic and chili pepper: virtually the national dish of the Basque Country.

Omelette aux truffes (The Dordogne) The best way to taste fresh black truffles in season is finely chopped in an omelet.

Poulet basquaise (the Basque Country) Classic stew of chicken with *jambon de Bayonne,* tomatoes, bell peppers, and *piment d'Espelette.*

Rognons à la bordelaise (Bordeaux) Veal kidneys sautéed in red wine with *cèpes* (*Boletus edulis* or cepe mushrooms).

Salmis de palombe (the Basque Country and all Southwest)   Wood pigeon stewed in red wine with onions and nuggets of *jambon de Bayonne.*

Thon rouge (the Basque Country) Fresh bluefin tuna, landed at St.-Jean-de-Luz and other Basque ports; superlative grilled like meat over charcoal. **Thon à la basquaise** is cooked in a casserole with tomatoes, onions, and red bell peppers.

Truite arc-en-ciel (the Landes)   Farmed rainbow trout, often cooked with *lardons* (bacon cubes) or simply pan-fried.

VEGETABLES AND VEGETARIAN DISHES

Cèpes à la bordelaise (Bordeaux) *Cèpes* (*Boletus edulis* or cepe mushrooms) stewed in olive oil with chopped shallots, and parsley.

Haricots verts à la landaise (Bordeaux and the Landes)   Green beans braised in goose fat with *jambon de Bayonne.*

Poireaux des vignes (Bordeaux and the wine country)   Wild leeks, with their strong, assertive flavor, grow in the vineyards of the region; a favorite vegetable of the region.

Pommes de terre sarladaise (the Dordogne)   Potatoes sautéed in duck or goose fat and garlic; sometimes truffles are added.

Salades   Salads, often dressed with *huile de noix,* are usually offered as a separate course after the main course and before the cheese or dessert.

Basket of cèpes

Charcuterie

CURED PORK AND OTHER MEAT PRODUCTS

IN ADDITION TO PORK, Southwest France's *charcuterie* centers on the duck and goose, highlighted and intensified with the *truffes* of Périgord. This is a region with a great tradition of producing such *charcuterie* on a small-scale and producers who make it at home and on farms offer it for sale to those passing by. It is worth visiting too the *marchés au gras* that take place in towns and villages, where duck and goose farmers bring their prized products to market (see p.144).

TRY TO SAMPLE

Chichons   Type of Basque *rillette* made with goose, duck, and/or pork preserved in its own fat; an unctuous meat spread.

Confit de canard et d'oie   Conserved duck and goose (see below).

Cou farci   The neck of duck or goose stuffed with *pâté* and *foie gras*.

Foie gras de canard et d'oie   Fattened liver from duck or goose; a great regional and national delicacy (see p.151).

Jambon de Bayonne   This term has come to be used for any *jambon cru* (raw, cured, Parma-style ham), but the finest examples still come from the Basque Country (see p.150).

Pâté   An outstanding range of *pâtés* is produced and enjoyed throughout the Southwest, all made to individual recipes: **pâté du Périgord** usually made from a coarse mixture of pork and duck or goose liver, with truffles; **pâté de perdrix**   partridge *pâté;* **pâté basquais piquant** pork *pâté* spiced with *piment d'Espelette;* **pâté à l'armagnac**   pork with duck or goose liver macerated in Armagnac; **pâté de foie de volaille**   chicken liver *pâté.*

Rillettes de canard or **d'oie**   Goose or duck meat slowly cooked in its fat until the meat becomes extremely tender; to be eaten spread on bread.

Sanguette   Local blood pudding made from duck's blood, onions, and fat and fried like a pancake.

Saucisse basquaise   Piquant pork sausage.

Tripoxa   Basque blood sausage, flavored with *piment d'Espelette.*

Food shop in St.-Jean-de-Luz

LES CONFITS — CONSERVED DUCK AND GOOSE

In the Southwest, a traditional method of conserving meat and poultry (especially fattened duck or goose leftover from birds raised especially for their *foie gras*) is the *confit:* legs and thighs of duck or goose, or pieces of pork, are first salted for a day or so, then they are slowly cooked in large quantities of their own fat until the flesh is meltingly tender. Afterward, the meat can be packed into jars or crocks, topped up with fat, and will conserve well for months if kept in a cool place.

Confits are widely used in the cooking of the area, added to soups and stews to add rich flavor and texture. They can also be eaten on their own.

To cook *confit de canard,* fry it in its own fat until the skin is crispy (on not too high a flame or for too long or else it will dry out). Served with *pommes de terre sarladaise,* it is the unmistakable taste of the Southwest.

Le 'Véritable Jambon de Bayonne'

IN SEARCH OF REAL BAYONNE HAM

THE FRENCH can be so overly protective of their rights to regional and local *appellations,* that it is curious and sad that they have allowed the term *jambon de Bayonne,* one of the nation's greatest regional delicacies, to be applied to any number and types of hams made by a variety of methods, produced virtually anywhere in France, and even made from pigs raised and imported from abroad.

Real *jambon de Bayonne* can still be found in its traditional heartland, the Basque Country and parts of the Landes extending from Bayonne to the area to the south of the Adour River basin, past Tarbes, Pau, and down to the frontier with Spain.

Jambon de Bayonne is a type of raw, air-cured ham produced by a process of dry-salting (as opposed to salting in brine or injecting with brine), followed

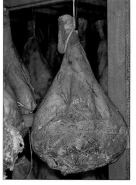

Jambon de Bayonne

by a lengthy period of air-drying, often in mountain outposts where the air is fresh and dry. The local wind from the south, the *funn,* which blows at least every few days throughout the year, provides the conditions, even in coastal Bayonne itself, for drying these delicious hams. Every producer has his or her own recipe for the salting process, which may combine coarse sea salt with mixtures of *piment d'Espelette,* garlic, vinegar, and other seasonings. An average sized ham weighing about 10½ kg. (23 lbs.) is salted for about two weeks, then hung up to dry and cure for up to nine or ten months. The period of salting is the most critical, for, during this time, the hams develop their flavor and their ability to be conserved. Hams not salted sufficiently may spoil; but overly salted hams become tough, no longer sweet and fragrant.

Plans have been made recently to protect the name *jambon de Bayonne,* though, at the time of writing, this has not yet come about, nor indeed is it likely that the ham will be granted an official *appellation d'origine contrôlée.* However, there have been some moves within the Basque Country to create a new label for genuine *jambon de Bayonne* produced from the Large White breed of pig, salted and air-dried to stringent traditional methods: such select hams may be entitled to the label *"Ibaïaona";* if you see this name, you can be sure it is a mark of quality.

Ibaïaona or not, good, traditional, and authentic *jambons de Bayonne* produced by artisan *charcuteries* can be tasted and bought throughout the Southwest. Whole *jambons de Bayonne* are sold either with or without the bone. The bone makes the ham more difficult to slice, but as a trade-off the ham keeps much better. Hams that have been de-boned must be kept refrigerated as opposed to being left to hang in a dry, cool larder. You can also buy good sliced *jambon de Bayonne* in vacuum-packs.

Pierre Chabagno, a young, committed producer of traditional *jambon de Bayonne,* is passionate about safeguarding this great regional product. He would like to see, at the least, a label that distinguishes genuine *jambon de Bayonne* from the industrial versions produced anywhere in France. "Here in the Basque Country," he explained, "we have always had the artisan *savoir-faire* as well as the unique microclimate to gain expertise in air-drying hams. Our traditional *jambons* are still the best."

Pierre d'Ibaïalde
41, Rue des Cordeliers
64100 Bayonne
tel: 59 25 65 30
fax: 59 25 61 54

Fois Gras de Canard et d'Oie

FATTENED DUCK AND GOOSE LIVER

ONE OF THE GREAT national treasures of gastronomic France, *foie gras* is the liver of specially raised ducks or geese that are force-fed so that their livers become swollen and fattened. It is a specialty of Périgord, Gascony, and the Landes, areas that have long enjoyed great expertise in raising such birds (usually *en plein air,* i.e., allowed to wander and feed outdoors), the eventual force-feeding known as *le gavage,* and the final preparation of the livers themselves.

Foie gras is a delicacy that was enjoyed by the ancient Greeks, Egyptians, and Romans, and later by Jews who used goose fat as an alternative to pork lard. So even if you are uneasy about the process of its manufacture, remember, it is a food that is deeply rooted in Western gastronomic traditions.

Whereas, in the recent past, most *foie gras* came from geese, today, the *canard* (duck) has largely supplanted the former throughout the Southwest, though goose *foie gras* is still available and preferred by traditionalists. However, ducks can be farmed all year round, and their fattened livers, claim connoisseurs, have both more finesse and complexity of flavor.

The finest *foie gras* — whether duck or goose — is that which is prepared fresh, cooked at a relatively low temperature to preserve its taste, delicate aroma, and texture, and served still just pink in the center. Either cold as a *terrine* or warm

Ducks roaming free before le gavage, *the force-feeding necessary for* foie gras

sliced onto a *salade tiède* (warm salad), or pan-fried gently with fresh grapes, it is certainly a great and rich delicacy. Most visitors to Southwest France will not want to miss it.

Throughout the Southwest, restaurants offer *terrine de foie gras maison* (own-cooked fresh *foie gras*) on their menus, farms sell their own-produced *foie gras*

Fattened ducks

direct, and stores and markets in most towns have it on sale. The finest is always *foie gras entier,* i.e., a whole liver still in one piece, preferably cooked at low temperature *(mi-cuit)* and conserved *en bocal* (bottled). *Foie gras mi-cuit,* however, though more delicate in flavor and texture, must be kept refrigerated, so it may not be practical for taking home. Conserved whole *foie gras* can still be very fine, either in bottles or cans. *Bloc de foie gras* indicates pure *foie gras* but put together from different pieces and categories of liver. *Parfait de foie gras* should contain 75 per cent *foie gras,* bulked out usually with chicken livers, while *pâté de foie gras* consists of about 50 per cent *foie gras* mixed with pork *pâté.* Conserved *foie gras aux truffes* (with truffles), we consider, commands an unreasonably high premium.

The most usual accompaniment to *foie gras* is a sweet wine, a rather curious combination that actually works very well, richness complementing richness. While a top-class Sauternes or Barsac is the classic choice, the Southwest is the source of some fine, undervalued sweet wines that can also partner this great luxury extremely well, including Monbazillac and Jurançon Moelleux, as well as the lesser Bordeaux sweet wines such as Loupiac and Ste.-Croix-du-Mont.

Poissons et Fruits de Mer

FISH AND SEAFOOD

THE BASQUE fishing ports of St.-Jean-de-Luz and Hendaye are among the most important in France for landing Atlantic tuna, both the prized *thon blanc* or *germon* (albacore tuna) and the delicious red-fleshed *thon rouge* (bluefin tuna). The Basque fleet goes out in search of tuna during summer months only, from June to August, when the fish are crossing the Bay of Biscay. The finest are caught by line, not net. While much of the albacore catch is sent to the canneries, this fish is delicious fresh, though we ourselves are partial to the more robustly flavored *thon rouge*. If you have cooking facilities, buy a steak or two, brush with olive oil, stud with a little garlic, and grill over hot coals for a real treat.

Unloading crates of sardines in St.-Jean-de-Luz

Arcachon, which lies to the west of Bordeaux, is most famous for its cultivated *huîtres* (oysters) — *creuses* or *gigas* varieties, and *moules de bouchot* (mussels) raised on poles in the basin. If you are vacationing on the beaches of

the Atlantic Coast during the summer, oysters are available during this period, but, remember, at this time of year, they are rarely at their best. Mussels, on the other hand, are usually at their plumpest and most delicious in summer.

Freshwater fish is caught in the fast streams that tumble down from the Pyrenees, though most of that which you will encounter in restaurants is farmed these days, notably throughout the Landes.

TRY TO SAMPLE

Alose Shad, a bony but delicious seawater fish that enters rivers in spring to spawn. Usually cooked *à l'oseille* (poached), then served on a bed of sorrel.

Ecrevisses Freshwater crayfish; a favorite Bordelais delicacy.

Germon or **thon blanc** Albacore tuna; considered to have the finest flavor.

Huîtres d'Arcachon Oysters from the Arcachon Basin are widely available even in inland towns.

Lamproie Lamprey; a gruesome-looking fish caught in the Gironde. The lamprey has a poisonous vein running down its back which must be removed (England's King Henry I was reputed to have died from eating lamprey), so home preparation is not advised.

Merlu or **merluza** Hake, a firm-fleshed white fish that is a favorite with the Basques.

Pibales Small-fry eels from the Sargasso Sea return to their native estuaries in the Basque Country where they are netted. Usually served fried in olive oil with garlic.

Thon rouge Bluefin tuna.

Truite arc-en-ciel Rainbow trout; introduced into France from the United States; the most widely farmed variety.

Thon rouge, *bluefin tuna, a meaty, red fish, ideal for grilling*

Les Fromages
CHEESES OF THE SOUTHWEST

THE SOUTHWEST is not a great area for cheese. This is not intensive dairy country, and many of the region's best cheeses, made with unpasteurized milk from herds of goats and sheep, come from small individual farms and dairies.

While red Bordeaux wine is considered by many to be a great accompaniment to cheese, curiously, in the wine country itself, the cheese most widely eaten is not even French but the bland, rubbery, red-rind Dutch *edam,* known locally as *holland.* This habit is a legacy from the time when the Dutch were important trading partners and often part-exchanged consignments of their own cheeses for Bordeaux wine.

The finest cheeses of the Southwest come from the Basque Country, where upland traditions remain strong and *bergers* (shepherds) still take their flocks into the mountains to graze in the higher, fresher meadows in summer. Here, outstanding cheeses continue to be produced, usually on a small scale.

TRY TO SAMPLE

Ardi gasna (the Basque Country)   The name means "local cheese" in Basque, but usually applies to homemade ewe's milk cheese; served fresh, often with a *confiture* (jam) made from black cherries.

Bleu du Quercy (Lot)   Softly textured blue-veined cheese made from cow's milk in the uplands of Quercy; rich and assertive in flavor.

A selection of goat's milk cheeses, to be eaten on their own or warmed, with salad

Brebis fermier de montagne (The Basque Country)   Characterful and individual cheese made from unpasteurized ewe's milk traditionally transformed in *cayolars* or remote mountain huts where the shepherds go during the summer transhumance: hard-pressed, salty, and nutty. Some of the most distinctive cheeses indicate their provenance, including the outstanding Vallée d'Aspe and the Vallée d'Ossau.

Various brebis fermiers

Cabicou or **chabichou** or **cabécou** (the Dordogne)   Small white disk of goat's milk cheese; enjoyed after meals, sometimes hot as *cabicou chaud,* when it is baked and served with salad. Can be fresh or quite hard and dry; sometimes it is wrapped in vine leaves or macerated in local liqueur.

Echourgnac (the Dordogne)   Soft semi-pressed cheese from the Trappist Abbaye d'Echourgnac.

Fromage des Pyrénées (the Basque Country and the Pyrenees)   Mild mountain cheese made in two versions: that with a lightish red-colored rind is made from ewe's milk, the other, with a distinctive black rind, from cow's milk.

Ossau-iraty-brebis-pyrénées AC (the Basque Country)   This mouthful of a name applies to ewe's milk cheeses protected by an *appellation* but mainly made in industrial dairies. Often, handmade examples sold simply as *brebis fermier* have more character.

Rocamadour (the Dordogne)   The finest *cabicou* goat's cheese, delicious and flavorful when aged until fairly hard.

Vache brûlée (the Basque Country) Round cow's milk cheese with a hard rind that is singed over a wood fire to add a distinctive, slightly smoky taste.

Pâtisseries & Confiseries
PASTRIES AND CANDIES

SOUTHWEST FRANCE offers a delightful range of pastries, confectioneries, and candies. Some have their origins in the many monasteries and abbeys of the region; others are simply the elaborate creations of housewives and farmers' wives who, on isolated farms, used their own produce, especially fruit, to create a range of pastries that were traditionally sold on market days in the main towns.

Macarons de St.-Emilion

TRY TO SAMPLE

Arlequins de Carlux (the Dordogne) Fresh walnut kernels in chocolate.

Cannelé (Bordeaux) Little, moist, molded cake flavored with cinnamon.

Chocolats de Bayonne (Bayonne) Bayonne has been famous for its hand-made chocolates since the Spanish first brought cocoa here centuries ago. There are plenty of opportunities to buy choc-olates and don't miss the town's specialty, *chocolat chaud,* whipped hot chocolate — a real treat!

Fruits à l'armagnac (Gascony) Fresh local fruits, such as *fraises* (strawberries), *cerises noires* (black cherries), *reines-claudes* (greengages), and dried *pruneaux d'Agen* are macerated in Armagnac and sold in jars or bottles: an exquisite (if powerful) instant dessert.

Gâteau aux noix (the Dordogne and Lot) Walnut cake, a typical traditional dessert of Périgord and Quercy.

Gâteau basque or **pastiza** (the Basque Country) Cream- or black-cherry-filled buttery Basque tart (see opposite).

Macarons de St.-Emilion (St.-Emilion) St.-Emilion's delightful almond macaroons, not too sweet, and delicious with a lightly honeyed Ste.-Croix-du-Mont or Loupiac wine.

Mesturet (Gascony) Thick candied pumpkin pulp flavored with lemon.

Noix au café (Bayonne) Pieces of walnut wrapped in *turron* (marzipan) which is then covered with coffee-flavored chocolate.

Pastis gasconne or **croustade** (Gascony) An exquisite creation of the finest paper-thin pastry (something like phyllo), folded and layered repeatedly with butter and vanilla sugar, then topped with apple slices soaked in Armagnac.

Pruneaux fourrés (Agen) Local prunes stuffed with a puree of prunes and almond paste.

Tarte aux pruneaux (all Southwest) Puff pastry tart made with local prunes.

Turron or **touron** (Bayonne and all Basque Country) A vast range of different marzipan sweets is produced and enjoyed in the region; made with pastes of ground almonds, pistachios, hazelnuts, sometimes with the addition of candied fruits, sometimes covered with chocolate or with mocha.

Pastis gasconne

Le Moulin de Bassilour

A COUNTRY MILL IN THE BASQUE COUNTRY

PERHAPS MORE THAN anywhere else in France, the Basque Country jealously guards its rural traditions. Throughout France, country and village mills once supplied stone-ground flour to local bakeries and often baked breads and cakes on their own premises.

At the Moulin de Bassilour, in the midst of rural country inland from Bidart, beside a fast-flowing millstream, Jacques Inchaurraga and Gérard Lhuillier continue to stone-grind wheat, white and yellow corn, and rye into flours that are used in an outstanding range of Basque breads, cakes, and cookies made at the mill.

The Inchaurraga family have been working here since the 1930s, though the lovely water mill dates from 1741. In addition to milling flours, they bake the *gâteau basque* and other cakes and breads to take to sell in local markets. Baking is still carried out on the mill premises, so you can buy not only stone-ground flours but also breads, tarts, and cookies straight from the oven. As you enter the mill and pass the slowly revolving granite millstones to reach the small shop, the aromas of slightly singed cornmeal, anise seeds, and rich, buttery yeast pastries baking in the oven are irresistible.

Corn flour is typical of the Basque Country, and the favorite bread here is still the *méture,* a round, yeast corn bread, made with either white or yellow corn flour, depending on the market (white is preferred in Bayonne, yellow in St.-Jean-de-Luz). *Miche,* also made with corn

Méture, *the typical Basque corn bread fresh from the oven*

The gâteau basque, *known also as* pastiza, *filled either with cream or cherry jam*

flour, is a typical Basque cake flavored with anise seeds, dense, heavy, and moist.

The great specialty of the Moulin de Bassilour, and one which people come from, literally, miles to sample and buy, is its famous *"véritable pastiza"* or *gâteau basque*. This is a meltingly delicious buttery tart filled with either black cherry *confiture* (jam) or simply cream and eggs. The *gâteau basque* is the sort of baked tart that once every housewife used to make , jealously guarding the family recipe and passing it down the generations.

Breads, cakes, *sablés* (butter cookies), and, of course, the *gâteau basque* baked at the Moulin are still taken to weekly markets. But try to hunt out the mill (it is not all that easy to find) for a *gâteau basque* hot from the oven to enjoy by the banks of the lovely millstream.

Le Moulin de Bassilour
Zone Artisanale de Bassilour
64210 Bidart
tel: 59 41 94 49

Buttery sablés *(cookies) and large and small* pastiza *at the Moulin de Bassilour*

Les Fermes Auberges
FARMHOUSE RESTAURANTS

SOUTHWEST FRANCE is the foremost area for farmhouse tourism in France. Throughout Périgord and Gascony especially, there are scores of opportunities to enjoy home-cooked meals in *fermes auberges* (farmhouse restaurants), sleep on farms in *chambres d'hôte à la ferme* (farmhouse bed and breakfast), involve yourself in "hand's-on" *stages de cuisine* (cooking courses), and buy *produits de la ferme* (farm products) directly at source.

Simple advertisement for a farmhouse restaurant

As this is duck and goose country *par excellence,* most *fermes auberges* serve enormous meals squarely based around these meats. Thus, for lovers of *foie gras, confits,* or *magret de canard,* a visit to at least one *ferme auberge* is virtually obligatory.

Fermes auberges adhere to rigid conditions laid down by their respective Chambres d'Agriculture. These include, among other things, that, in addition to serving meals of farm and local produce with local wines, the *ferme auberge* meet necessary hygiene requirements. Farms are also encouraged to respect local architecture and to convert traditional buildings wherever possible. Equally important, the essential family ambience of the *ferme auberge* must be maintained, which usually means that whole families work together. At some *fermes auberges,* guests eat with the family, and, at others, guests can eat communally.

Though a *ferme auberge* is never the same as a professional restaurant, many

---

HUILE DE NOIX — WALNUT OIL FROM PERIGORD

The Dordogne and Lot Valleys are one of the most important sources in France for *noix* (walnuts), gathered in the forests from mid–September to early November. Apart from being eaten fresh, they are used widely in the kitchen: added to *pâtés,* as an ingredient in *gâteaux,* macerated in syrup and alcohol to make the local firewater — *eau-de-noix,* turned into an imaginative range of confectionery (the finest are the delicious chocolate-covered

arlequins de Carlux), and, not least, transformed into *huile de noix,* walnut oil, a characterful condiment much prized for dressing salads or seasoning white meats and fish.

Only a handful of traditional walnut mills, such as the Moulin de la Tour, still exist in the region. Here, the shelled walnuts are ground to a paste by slowly revolving granite stones; the paste is then heated in small cauldrons to release the oil, which is extracted by pressing — emerging fragrant with the rich flavor of roasted walnuts.

Keep walnut oil refrigerated and use it up quickly as it tends to go rancid quite rapidly.

Moulin de la Tour
Ste.-Nathalène
24200 Sarlat-la-Canéda
tel: 53 59 22 08
fax: 53 31 08 33

are excellently run and some even go on to become full scale restaurants, such as Pierette Sarran's Auberge du Bergerayre, which we originally visited when it was a *ferme auberge*. But precisely because such establishments are run not by professional restaurateurs but by *agriculteurs* (farmers), there is always an engaging personal touch to a *ferme auberge*.

A visit to a good *ferme auberge* is one of the best ways of placing food and drink within their regional context. The chance to eat local specialties, prepared and served by the people who produced, grew, or raised them, provides a rare opportunity to eat totally fresh food, whether a *salade* picked

A genuinely warm welcome at a ferme auberge

from the garden, own-produced *foie gras,* a home-killed chicken, or a loaf of still-warm, freshly baked bread.

From the point of view of the farmer, farmhouse tourism provides an opportunity to supplement farm income. But much more than that, we have found, particularly in the Southwest, that running a *ferme auberge* is valued as an important chance for people living in rural areas to make contact with others from outside their own limited *milieu*. The welcome that you will receive, especially as a foreign visitor, will be as warm, satisfying, and genuine as the food itself.

To avoid disappointment always telephone in advance.

FERMES AUBERGES — FARMHOUSE RESTAURANTS

THE DORDOGNE AND PERIGORD
Ferme Auberge Le Colombier
24250 La Roque Gageac
tel: 53 28 33 97
Genuine cuisine du terroir with all the specialties of Périgord on a lovely farm 7 km. (4 miles) outside Sarlat-la-Canéda.
$

Marie-Jeanne et Marie-Thérèse Archer
La Barabie
24520 Lamonzie-Monastruc
tel: 53 23 22 47
fax: 53 22 81 20
Farmhouse bed and breakfast; also stages de cuisine on how to prepare foie gras, pâtés, confits, and rillettes.
$

GASCONY
Auberge du Bergerayre
St.-Martin d'Armagnac
32110 Nogaro
tel: 62 09 08 72
fax: 62 09 09 74
Very pretty and friendly auberge with chambres d'hôte around a swimming pool. Excellent Gascon cuisine, with pastis gasconne as Pierrette Sarran's pièce de résistance.
$$

Ferme Auberge La Cave
32290 Aignan
tel: 62 09 23 17
fax: 62 09 20 65
Outstanding farmhouse foods of Gascony: own-produced foie gras, magret, confit de canard (can also be bought to take away); excellent cassoulet and croustade. Near the Mairie.
$$

Ferme Auberge aux Cerfs et aux Sangliers
32460 Le Houga
tel: 62 08 92 15
fax: 62 08 92 10
Deer and wild boar are raised here along with ducks and geese. Walk around the grounds and visit the animals. Alternatively, telephone for a goûter à la ferme, a visit to the farm followed by a substantial afternoon goûter or snack.
$$

THE BASQUE COUNTRY
Ferme Auberge Xixtarteko Borda
64250 Cambo-les-Bains
tel: 59 29 85 36
fax: 59 29 29 43
Country cooking in the Basque mountains.
Chambre d'hôte *available.*
$

Les Vins

WINES, ARMAGNAC, AND OTHER DRINKS

For centuries, Aquitaine has been France's greatest and most important wine region. Bordeaux, of course, dominates. This is the greatest single wine region in the world for three reasons. First, it is the source of the most prestigious red wines in the world, *grands crus classés* that are classics and the benchmarks against which all great red (especially Cabernet based) wines are measured. Second, Bordeaux boasts a remarkable variety of wines, not just great and everyday reds, but also the finest sweet wines, from Sauternes and Barsac, as well as outstanding and everyday dry white wines and good rosés. Last, but most important, Bordeaux is the greatest wine region in the world because of its ability to satisfy with wines which are available at all price levels.

Beyond the Bordeaux vineyard, up-river along both the valleys of the Dordogne and Garonne, there is plenty of interest too, with good country wines coming from Bergerac, Cahors, the Côtes du Marmandais, Côtes de Duras, and Buzet. Gascony has traditionally grown grapes for distillation into the fiery, pungent brandy, Armagnac, but, today, it is increasingly turning to the production of sound table wines, such as zesty white Côtes de Gascogne, red and white Côtes de St.-Mont, and sturdy red Madiran. Good, if rarely encountered wines come from the foothills of the Pyrenees and the Basque Country, notably both sweet and dry Jurançon, Pacherenc du Vic-Bilh, and the characterful red Irouléguy.

Though the choice of wines throughout the Southwest is great indeed, this can pose its own difficulties, especially when presented with seemingly baffling wine lists consisting of little more than châteaux names with no descriptions. If you want to drink a good Bordeaux red but are unsure of what to choose, decide on how much you wish to pay, then ask the wine waiter to recommend something in that bracket.

BORDEAUX

Bordeaux AC Bordeaux's broadest and most general *appellation* can apply to red, white, and rosé wines made from permitted grape varieties grown throughout the vast Bordeaux vineyard. In itself, the *appellation* may mean little, for it applies to quite ordinary wines as well as to great and expensive wines which, for whatever reason, are not entitled to a more particular communal *appellation*. Red Bordeaux is produced from a blend of Cabernet Sauvignon, Cabernet Franc, Merlot, and Malbec. White comes from Sauvignon, Sémillon, and Muscadelle. Wines designated *supérieur* have a slightly higher alcohol content.

Cadillac AC; Loupiac AC; and **Ste.-Croix-du-Mont AC** These three *appellations* apply to sweet wines pro-

---

BORDEAUX'S CLASSIFICATION OF 1855

In Bordeaux, the terms *cru classé* or *grand cru classé* refer to a historic classification of wine estates that dates from 1855, when wines from the Médoc (and one from Graves) and Sauternes were placed in a hierarchy based on the prices that the wines had historically fetched. In the case of the Médoc and Graves, five superlative tiers of *grands crus* were established, and wines on that original list may still be referred to as *premiers* (first), *deuxièmes* (second), *troisièmes* (third), *quatrièmes* (fourth), or *cinquièmes* (fifth) *crus* or growths. The finest wines of Sauternes were classified as *premiers* and *deuxièmes crus,* with one exceptional wine, Château d'Yquem, classified on its own as *grand premier cru*.

The wines of St.-Emilion have their own classifications, as do those of Graves, but, curiously, Pomerol has never been classified.

duced from vineyards on the opposite bank of the Garonne from Sauternes. Though rarely reaching the heights of that great sweet classic, some excellent, honeyed, and usually lightly sweet wines are made in these zones.
Recommended producers: Château du Cros, Clos Jean, Château de Ricaud, Château La Rame.

Côtes de Blaye AC and **Côtes de Bourg AC**   Good, sometimes excellent, sometimes merely sound but good-value red and white wines come from these two wine zones on the right bank of the Gironde.

Bergerac's town quay on the banks of the Dordogne

Entre-Deux-Mers AC   Fresh, fruity, still mainly inexpensive dry white wine made from Sauvignon grapes (mainly) grown in the undulating country between the Dordogne and Garonne.
Recommended producers: Château Bonnet, Château Launay.

Fronsac AC; Canon Fronsac AC
Mainly red wines from these lesser-known zones near Pomerol; can be satisfying and good value.
Recommended producers: Château Fontenil, Château La Rivière, Château Canon, Château Canon de Brem, Château Villars.

Graves AC   This large, prestigious wine zone was split in 1987, its northern half, containing its most famous wine estates, renamed Pessac-Léognan. Graves is still the source of both outstanding dry white wines and fruity, and in some cases, long-lived reds.
Recommended producers: Carbonnieux, Domaine la Grave, Rahoul.

Lalande-de-Pomerol AC   North of Pomerol, producing less distinguished but more affordable wines with a similar if lighter ripe, fleshy style.
Recommended producers: Château Bel Air, Bertineau-St.-Vincent.

Margaux AC   Many consider the wines of Margaux to be the most elegant of all the great communes of the Médoc.
Recommended producers: Château Margaux, Château Palmer, Château Rausan-Ségla,
Château Prieuré-Lichine, Château d'Angludet, Labégorce-Zédé, Lascombes.

Médoc AC; Haut-Médoc AC   The Médoc peninsula, extending northwest from Bordeaux to where the Gironde meets the Atlantic, is the source of many of Bordeaux's greatest and most prestigious wine estates. Wines bearing the simpler *appellation* or the superior Haut-Médoc generally are full, tannic wines the best of which have the capacity to age and further develop in the bottle.
Recommended producers: Château Loudenne, Château La Tour-de-By, Château Les Ormes Sorbet, Potensac, Cantemerle, Sociando-Mallet, La Lagune.

Pauillac AC   For lovers of Cabernet Sauvignon, the vineyards that rise from the estuary town of Pauillac are something close to paradise: for the greatest, longest-lived, and most intense Cabernet wines in the world come from here, from its three *premiers crus classés* estates, Mouton-Rothschild, Latour, and Lafite-Rothschild. Pauillac is home to some 15 further classed growth estates, and even wines from its *coopérative* demonstrate the power and pedigree of the commune. The finest wines from the best years can need decades before they are ready.
Recommended producers: Château Mouton-Rothschild, Château Latour, Château Lafite-Rothschild, Château Lynch-Bages, Château Pichon-Longueville, Château Haut-Batailley,

Château Pichon-Longueville-Lalande, Château Pontet-Canet, Château Clerc-Milon, Batailley.

Pessac-Léognan AC   The greatest wines of Graves were granted their own *appellation* in 1987, extending over the extremely gravelly soil of northern Graves nearest Bordeaux. This is the source of both exceptional *crus classés* red wines as well as outstanding *crus classés* whites.

Recommended producers: Château Haut-Brion, Château Pape Clément, Château Smith-Haut-Lafitte, Château Malartic-Lagravière, La Mission-Haut-Brion, Domaine de Chevalier, Laville Haut-Brion.

Pomerol AC   The fleshiest, ripest, juiciest, most appealing — and, in some cases, the most expensive — wines of Bordeaux come from this tiny, Merlot-dominated enclave extending across a low plateau northeast of Libourne.

Recommended producers: Château Pétrus, Vieux-Château-Certan, Château Gazin, La Conseillante, Château L'Evangile, Château L'Eglise-Clinet, Château de Sales, Le Pin, Trotanoy, Lafleur.

St.-Emilion AC   The softer and less tannic Merlot in combination with Cabernet Franc results at St.-Emilion in generous, full-bodied, and round wines that can be superb for drinking within years, not decades, of the vintage. The finest are classified as *premiers grands crus* and *grands crus*.

Recommended producers: Château Ausone, Château Cheval Blanc, Château Pavie, Château Magdelaine, Château Canon, Château Figeac, Château La Gaffelière, Château Troplong Mondot, Château Belair.

St.-Estèphe AC   Wines from this commune north of Pauillac are considered by many to be the toughest and longest-lived of the great wines of the Médoc.

Recommended producers: Château Calon-Ségur, Château Cos d'Estournel, Château Montrose, Château Les Ormes-de-Pez.

St.-Julien AC   Beautifully balanced wines come from the mid-Médoc, combining the ripe elegance of Margaux with the power of Pauillac.

Recommended producers: Château Gruaud-Larose, Château Beychevelle, Château Talbot, Château Gloria, Château Léoville-Las-Cases, Château Léoville-Poyferré, Château Léoville-Barton, Ducru-Beaucaillou.

Château de Monbazillac

Sauternes AC; Barsac AC Sauternes and Barsac produce, in the best years, the most luscious, rare, and prestigious sweet dessert wines in the world, often sold by the glass in restaurants — a dessert in itself. In this famous vineyard, Sémillon, Sauvignon, and Muscadelle grapes can be affected by *pourriture noble* or noble rot, when conditions are favorable, whereby a beneficial fungus, *Botrytis cinerea,* helps dry out the grapes, thus concentrating sugar and glycerin, and at the same time imparting intense flavors, bouquet, and texture to the finished wines. In general, the wines of Barsac are considered slighly lighter and less opulent than those of Sauternes.
Recommended producers: Château d'Yquem, Château Rieussec, Château Suduiraut, Château Guiraud, Château Coutet, Château Climens, Haut-Marbuzet, Lafon-Rochet, Lafaurie-Peyraguey.

THE DORDOGNE AND LOT

Bergerac AC and **Côtes de Bergerac AC** The Dordogne Valley inland and upriver from Bordeaux is the source of a fine range of good country wines. The general Bergerac *appellation* applies to sound red (from Cabernet Sauvignon, Cabernet Franc, Merlot, and Malbec), dry white Bergerac *sec* (crisp, clean Sauvignon based examples can be good), and small quantities of rosé wines. Côtes de Bergerac AC for reds indicates a higher alcohol content; Côtes de Bergerac *moelleux* AC applies to sweet wines.
Recommended producers: Château de La Jaubertie, Château Le Barradis, Court des Mûts, Bergerac and St.-Laurent-des-Vignes caves coopératives.

Buzet AC Plentiful, still inexpensive Bordeaux-style red wines from vineyards along the Garonne near Agen.
Recommended producer: Buzet-sur-Baïse cave coopérative.

Cahors AC One of the great country wines of Southwest France, Cahors was celebrated even in Roman days. Malbec

> ## FIRST CLASS SECONDS
>
> The finest estates in Bordeaux maintain consistent quality and concentration by a ruthless process of selection whereby only the finest vats of wine are assembled to make the *grand vin*. Lesser wines (perhaps from younger or less well-exposed vineyards) may be made into a second wine that, while undoubtedly lighter in character, is nonetheless a reflection of its respected pedigree. Such second wines, such as Château Margaux's Pavillon Rouge, Château Latour's Les Forts de Latour, and Château Lafite-Rothschild's Carraudes de Lafite-Rothschild, and others, have two considerable advantages: they are less expensive than the estate's *grand vin* and they are also usually ready to drink at a far younger age. Try examples from any top *crus classés* estates.

grapes (known locally as Auxerrois) together with Merlot, Tannat, and Jurançon Noir can result in immense, dark, and hugely tannic wines that have traditionally required lengthy bottle age to soften. Today's style is altogether more supple and approachable.
Recommended producers: Château de Haute-Serre, Château St.-Didier-Parnac, Clos Triguedina, Côtes d'Olt cave coopérative.

Côtes de Duras AC The sound red, white, and rosé wines from Lot-et-Garonne have a lengthy pedigree as the preferred wines of François I.
Recommended producer: Landerrouat cave coopérative.

Côtes du Marmandais AC The Marmandais is a virtual extension of the Bordeaux vineyard beyond Entre-Deux-Mers, and is the source of some good fruity reds and clean, well-made whites.
Recommended producers: Cocumont, Beaupuy caves coopératives.

Monbazillac AC   As in the Sauternes vineyard, fall mists followed by warm sunshine can encourage formation of *pourriture noble* at Monbazillac, and thus this wine zone is the source of sweet, and sometimes exceptional dessert wines with the concentrated aromas and character of *Botrytis cinerea*.
Recommended producers: Château Theulet, Hébras, Château de Monbazillac cave coopérative.

Montravel AC; Côtes de Montravel AC; and **Haut-Montravel AC**   Dry, *demi sec,* and sweet white wines from gentle hill country. The latter two *appellations* apply only to sweet wines.
Recommended producers: Château Pique-Segue, Château Le Raz, de Krevel.

Pécharmant AC   Perhaps the finest wine of the Bergerac vineyard, a rich, full-bodied red of real character, with the capacity to age further in bottle.
Recommended producers: Domaine du Haut Pécharmant, Clos les Côtes, Château de Tiregand.

GASCONY AND THE BASQUE COUNTRY

Béarn AC   The best wines from this strictly minor zone are the delicately perfumed rosés.
Recommended producer: Les Vignerons de Bellocq.

Côtes de St.-Mont VDQS   Sound, full-flavored red (something like a lighter Madiran), fresh, zesty white wines, and fruity rosés.
Recommended producer: Plaimont cave coopérative.

Irouléguy AC   The only true wine of the Basque Country, but noteworthy nonetheless. Reds, mainly from Cabernet and Tannat, can be robust and full-flavored if bordering on the rustic, while whites are similarly full in body and character.
Recommended producers: Domaine Brana, Domaine Ilarria.

Jurançon AC   The historic dry and sweet wines of Jurançon are certainly worth sampling; the dry as an *apéritif,* the sweet *moelleux* with *pâté* or *foie gras.*
Recommended producers: Cauhapé, Clos Vroulat, Bru-Baché.

Madiran AC   Another distinguished country red wine of the Southwest, sturdy, full-bodied, and excellent with *garbure* (bean and vegetable soup, see p.146) and other hearty foods.
Recommended producers: Château Bouscassé, Château Montus, Château d'Aydie.

Pacherenc du Vic-Bilh AC Mouthful of a name for mainly dry and sometimes sweet wines made from a cocktail of local grapes.
Recommended producers: Château Bouscassé, Château Montus.

Vin de Pays des Côtes de Gascogne Zesty, inexpensive white wines from the Armagnac vineyard have gained in popularity in recent years.
Recommended producers: Plaimont cave coopérative, Château Monluc, Grassa.

OTHER DRINKS

Armagnac AC   Pungent and characterful grape brandy distilled from St.-Emilion (Ugni Blanc), Colombard, and Folle Blanche grapes grown in Gascony (see p.167). Try old vintage Armagnacs for a real after dinner treat.

Eau-de-noix   Liqueur, often home-produced, made by infusing green walnuts in alcohol.

Floc de Gascogne   A mixture of unfermented grape juice and young Armagnac aged in wood for two to three years. This sweet, fortified *apéritif* should be drunk chilled. Try it: it can be delightful.

Izarra   Highly distinctive Basque liqueur made from an infusion of plants and herbs, mixed with acacia honey and fruits macerated in old Armagnac. The yellow version is made with 32 different plants, the green with some 48.

Vieille Prune   This sweet, dark plum liqueur is often brought out at the end of meals in the Dordogne.

La Route des Châteaux

CHATEAUX AND VINEYARDS OF THE MEDOC

BORDEAUX'S Route des Châteaux is the most famous and well-traveled of all of France's wine roads, leading from Bordeaux north through the wine country of the Médoc. The profusion of elegant 17th- and 18th-century châteaux, their names famous and familiar from padded, leather-bound wine lists, really does have to be seen to be believed. For the wine lover, especially the lover of the classic red wines of Bordeaux, it can be a rare experience to pay homage to the most hallowed and famous concentration of vineyards in the world.

Bordeaux is an international city, its prosperity no longer wholly dependent on the vast quantities of wine once transported by boat from its riverside quays. The old quarter of the city, Le Vieux Bordeaux, is appealing, and the Quai des Chartrons is reminiscent of a time when its pavements were crowded with barrels full of wine. Bordeaux is worth visiting if only to get information, maps, and other literature from the Maison du Vin (or write for help with arranging visits to châteaux). Opposite the Maison du Vin,

La Vinothèque de Bordeaux (address p.165) is one of the city's finest wine shops.

To tour the Route des Châteaux, leave Bordeaux on the D2 north. Cantenac is the first wine commune of note, for, together with Labarde and Margaux, it makes up the communal vineyard of Margaux, one of the most prestigious in the world. The great Château Margaux is of course the flagship, its wine considered by many the most elegant and harmonious of all the five *premiers grands crus classés*. It is not easy to visit many of the region's top properties, but one that is always open to visitors without appointment is Château Prieuré-Lichine, owned today by the family of the late wine writer, Alexis Lichine. Other well-known Margaux properties include Châteaux Palmer, d'Angludet, and d'Issan. The Relais de Margaux, incidentally, is a good, stylish restaurant and the Lion d'Or at nearby Arcins offers a simpler but excellent lunchtime menu.

Between Margaux and St.-Julien, there are plenty of good, if not internationally famous, wine châteaux at Arcins,

Château Margaux

LA ROUTE DES CHATEAUX

ST.-YZANS-DE-MEDOC

ST.-ESTEPHE

Gironde

PAUILLAC

ST.-JULIEN-BEYCHEVELLE

CUSSAC

LAMARQUE

LISTRAC-MEDOC

ARCINS

Dordogne

MOULIS-EN-MEDOC

MARGAUX

CANTENAC

LABARDE

Garonne

D2

BORDEAUX

0 km 2   4
0 miles   2

N

Relais du Médoc, in Lamarque near where the ferry crosses the Gironde to Blaye, is a good, family-style restaurant.

St.-Julien-Beychevelle lies in the heart of the mid-Médoc, a wine commune with an astonishing concentration of great wine properties — Léoville-Barton, Châteaux Beychevelle, Gruaud-Larose, Talbot, Léoville-Las-Cases, Léoville-Poyferré, Gloria, to name but a few. The wines of St.-Julien are generally considered, at best, to combine the elegance and harmony that are the hallmarks of Margaux with the power and backbone of Pauillac. Apart from its profusion of stunningly beautiful châteaux, there is very little of a town here at all.

For lovers of Cabernet Sauvignon, Pauillac comes as something of an El Dorado, notwithstanding that the riverside town itself is — what shall we say? — just a little rough around the edges, with an unsightly oil refinery on its outskirts. No matter: this is hallowed ground all the same, for Pauillac is the home of no fewer than three of the five *premiers grands crus classés,* Châteaux Mouton-Rothschild, Lafite-Rothschild, and Latour.

The late Baron Philippe de Rothschild was one of the great personalities of the wine world, and at Château Mouton-Rothschild he created a wine museum that is one of the most fascinating in the world, not merely a collection of old tools and instruments, but a homage to the cultivation of the vine as part of Western civilization and art. This museum can be visited only by appointment, preferably made in writing as far in advance as possible. In addition to its top three châteaux, other highly regarded *crus classés* include Châteaux Lynch-Bages, Pichon-Longueville, Pichon-Longueville-Lalande, Haut-Batailley, Pontet-Canet, and Clerc-Milon. The local *cave coopérative,* La Rose Pauillac, produces good, relatively inexpensive wines.

Beyond Pauillac, St.-Estèphe is the last great wine commune of note and the

Lamarque, Cussac, Moulis-en-Médoc, and Listrac-Médoc. Many smaller properties may offer signs to *"visitez les chais"* (visit the wine cellars). Take pot-luck: this is privileged wine country and you are hardly likely to go too far wrong.

The Fort Médoc near Lamarque is a fascinating 17th-century moated ruin; walk beyond it through the salt pastures to the Gironde River, a good place for a picnic or to spin out a bottle of wine. The

largest in Haut-Médoc. Traditionally, its wines have been considered among the hardest, dark in color, rich in tannin, and in need of considerable age before they come around. Modern vinification means that more supple styles of wines are being produced today, but wines from great properties such as Cos d'Estournel (the château an outrageously whimsical 18th-century French pagoda), Châteaux Montrose, Calon-Ségur, and Phélan-Ségur are still, in the best years, hugely powerful, well-structured wines that demand time and patience.

North of St.-Estèphe, the Haut-Médoc gives way to the gentler Médoc. Wines and wine estates still abound, but the great concentration of beautiful and famous châteaux is now mainly finished. Château Loudenne, at St.-Yzans-de-Médoc, is worth visiting for its well-balanced wines and its wine museum. If you write in advance, you may have the opportunity to lunch at the château.

RECOMMENDED WINE CHATEAUX AND RESTAURANTS

Château Loudenne
St.-Yzans de Médoc
33340 Lesparre
tel: 56 09 05 03
fax: 56 09 02 87
Wine museum and lunch at château *(write well in advance).*

Château Mouton-Rothschild
Le Pouylaet
33250 Pauillac
tel: 56 59 22 22
fax: 56 73 20 44
Almost a national monument. Write as far in advance as possible for an appointment.

Château Prieuré-Lichine
34, Avenue de la 5ᵉ République
33460 Cantenac Margaux-en-Médoc
tel: 57 88 36 28
fax: 57 88 78 93
Always open for visits. Tastings for purchasers.

Conseil Interprofessionel du Vin de Bordeaux
1, Cours du XXX Juillet
33075 Bordeaux
tel: 56 00 22 66
fax: 56 00 22 77
Information center for wines from throughout Bordeaux. Write or fax for specific requirements.

Groupement de Producteurs la Rose Pauillac
44, Rue du Maréchal Joffre
BP 14
33250 Pauillac
tel: 56 59 26 00
fax: 56 59 63 58
Good value wines.

La Vinothèque de Bordeaux
8, Cours du XXX Juillet
33000 Bordeaux
tel: 56 52 32 05
fax: 56 51 23 46
Long established, well-regarded wine shop.

Le Lion d'Or
Place de la République
33460 Arcins-en-Médoc
tel: 56 58 96 79

Tonnelier *(cooper)* at work at
Château Margaux

Friendly restaurant serving seasonal foods.
$$

Maison du Vin de Margaux
Place la Trémoille
33460 Margaux
tel: 57 88 70 82
fax: 57 88 38 27
Display and sale of wines from the commune.

Maison du Vin de St.-Estèphe
Place de l'Eglise
33780 St.-Estèphe
tel: 56 59 30 59
fax: 56 59 73 72
Good range of wines from the commune.

Relais de Margaux
Route de l'Ile Vincent
33460 Margaux
tel: 57 88 38 30
fax: 57 88 31 73
Imaginative cuisine, served outdoors in fine weather. Great wine list.
$$$

Relais du Médoc
70, Rue Principale
33460 Lamarque
tel: 56 58 92 27
fax: 56 58 95 67
Local foods served family-style. Near the ferry.
$–$$

St.-Emilion

A GREAT MEDIEVAL WINE CAPITAL

ST.-EMILION, with its steep cobbled streets, mellow, picturesque, ocher houses, and atmospheric medieval churches and monuments is one of the great wine towns of France.

The origins of this ancient town date at least from the Romans, who probably first planted the vines that surround it, but the town is named for the saint who journeying along the pilgrim's route to Santiago de Compostela in Spain, stayed here, and lived as a hermit in a cave. The town, built on top of a limestone plateau, is, in fact, riddled with caves — the town's unique Eglise Monolithe, hollowed out of the limestone, is the largest cave church in Europe. The town's caves have traditionally been used, as they are used today, as repositories for wine.

On Sundays, a lively market sprawls through the streets by the church. Good restaurants serve local specialties — *entrecôte aux sarments* (steak cooked over vine shoots) and *lamproie à la bordelaise* (lamprey stewed in

St.-Emilion, one of the great wine towns of France

Bordeaux wine). St.-Emilion's *macarons* — little almond pastries — are almost as famous as its wine. And the town makes an excellent base to further explore St.-Emilion and Pomerol wine country.

St.-Emilion's Maison du Vin is one of the region's best organized and most helpful. It has plenty of free literature, English is spoken, and visits to properties can be arranged. The Syndicat d'Initiative (tourist office) also arranges tours to wine properties and excursions into vineyards.

The vineyards of St.-Emilion begin on the very edge of the medieval town. Along its southern flank, the vineyards, known as the Côtes, extend over a well-exposed limestone flank and include the great Château Ausone. To the west and north of the town, the Graves vineyards extend over a flatter, richer terrain that leads to Pomerol. Château Cheval Blanc is the great flagship of this zone — "the land of a thousand châteaux" — with opportunities to taste and buy everywhere.

RECOMMENDED WINE ESTATES AND RESTAURANTS

Château Cros Figeac
Route de Libourne (D243)
33330 St.-Emilion
tel: 57 24 76 32
This grand cru wine estate not only produces superb St.-Emilion but has a farmhouse restaurant. Not to be missed.
$$

Daniele Blanchez
9, Rue Guadet
33330 St.-Emilion
tel: 57 24 72 33
The best macarons de St.-Emilion in town.

Hostellerie de Plaisance
Place du Clocher
33330 St.-Emilion
tel: 57 24 72 32
fax: 57 74 41 11
Best hotel in town, worthy of its Michelin rosette.
$$$

L'Envers du Décor
Rue du Clocher
33330 St.-Emilion
tel: 57 74 48 31
fax: 57 24 68 90
Welcoming wine bar. Wines by the glass with simple, well-prepared foods.
$–$$

Logis de la Cadene
3, Place du Marché-au-Bois
33330 St.-Emilion
tel: 57 74 71 40
fax: 57 74 42 23
Good home cooking.
$–$$

Maison du Vin de St. Emilion
Place Pierre-Meyrat
33330 St.-Emilion
tel: 57 55 50 55
fax: 57 24 65 57
The place to begin for an introduction to the wines of St.-Emilion.

Armagnac

THE FIRE AND SOUL OF GASCONY

ARMAGNAC, the distinctively pungent and flavorful distillation of the grape, comes from the equally singular and distinctive country of Gascony.

France's second brandy (after Cognac) is as different from that smooth, suave aristocrat as rugged Gascony is from the bucolic, rural Charentes. True, Armagnac, like Cognac, is a liquor produced by distilling wine, but there the similarity ends. For Armagnac is unique and individual, produced not by large merchants or internationally known companies but primarily on a small scale, in farmhouses. The wine is distilled in an *alambic armagnaçais*, a still that employs a continuous form of distillation as opposed to the *alambic charentais* or pot still favored in Cognac (see p.134). The spirit that results, though more rustic and robust in character, retains a high degree of individual personality unique to each farm.

While Cognac is essentially a blended spirit, Armagnac is often aged and bottled on the farm where it is produced. Many producers bottle single vintage Armagnacs, and connoisseurs of old brandies (as well as those in search of year-of-birth bottles) come to the region to visit dusty, cobwebbed farmhouse

An old alambic armagnaçais (still), once transported from farm to farm to distill Armagnac

cellars and buy at source.

A fascinating tour can be made from Condom to Eauze. Condom is a fine old wine town, the low-lying *chais* of large producers of Armagnac lining the stone-paved *quais* of the Baïse River. A visit to the largest producer, Janneau, is a must.

Eauze, capital of the Bas–Armagnac, is a busy market town. Merchants used to come here and sample Armagnacs simply by rubbing a few drops in their hands and smelling them — now a thing of the past. However, plenty of Armagnac still gets drunk in the bars of the town which surround the market square.

STOPPING OFF IN ARMAGNAC COUNTRY

Armagnac Marcel Trépout
Château Notre Dame
22, Rue Notre Dame
32190 Vic-Fézensac
tel: 62 06 33 83
fax: 62 64 40 95
Specializes in old single vintage Armagnacs.

Auberge de Guinlet
Guinlet
32800 Eauze
tel: 62 09 85 99
fax: 62 09 84 50
Just outside Eauze, a friendly auberge serving all the specialties of Gascony.
$

Château de Cassaigne
Cassaigne
32100 Condom
tel: 62 28 04 02
fax: 62 28 41 43
Thirteenth-century château with an extensive range of single vintage Armagnacs.

Ferme Auberge du
Château de la Hitte
32330 Gondrin
tel: 62 28 28 23
fax: 62 28 36 26
Good farmhouse restaurant with gîtes and chambres d'hôte.
$

Janneau Fils SA
50, Ave d'Aquitaine
32100 Condom
tel: 62 28 24 77
fax: 62 28 48 00
The oldest Armagnac house and market leader is most welcoming to visitors.

La Table des Cordeliers
1, Rue des Cordeliers
32100 Condom
tel: 62 68 28 36
fax: 62 68 29 03
Stylish restaurant set in a 14th-century Gothic chapel.
$$

Les Bonnes Adresses
USEFUL ADDRESSES

BORDEAUX AND THE LANDES
Chez l'Ahumat
Rue des Ecoles
40800 Aire-sur-l'Adour
tel: 58 71 82 61
Good, inexpensive country cooking of the Southwest in this rural market town in the Landes.
$

Francis Goullée
27, Rue Gaudet
33330 St.-Emilion
tel: 57 24 70 49
fax: 57 74 47 96
Fine restaurant serving creative, regional foods.
$$–$$$

Hostellerie des Criquets
130, Avenue du XI Novembre
33290 Blanquefort
tel: 56 35 09 24
fax: 56 57 13 83
Well-equipped hotel, with highly regarded restaurant, at the start of the Route des Châteaux; an alternative to Bordeaux.
$$$

Hôtel-Restaurant La Renaissance
43, Rue du Général de Gaulle
33112 St.-Laurent-Médoc
tel/fax: 56 59 40 29
Small hotel-restaurant recommended by the local winegrowers for its simple, well-prepared foods.
$

La Ferme aux Grives
40320 Eugénie-les-Bains
tel: 58 51 19 08
fax: 58 51 10 10
Michel Guérard's restored country restaurant near Les Prés is a delight, serving authentic cuisine du terroir — *meats grilled over an open fire, old-fashioned* terrines, *and vegetables from the garden.*
$$

La Ferme aux Grives

Le Chapon Fin
5, Rue Montesquieu
33000 Bordeaux
tel: 56 79 10 10
fax: 56 79 09 10
Long considered one of the top restaurants in Southwest France, serving regional and inventive cuisine in a luxury setting.
$$$

Le Patio
10, Boulevard de la Plage
33120 Arcachon
tel: 56 83 02 72
fax: 56 54 89 98
Fish and shellfish from the Bassin prepared stylishly and with care.
$$–$$$

Les Prés d'Eugénie
40320 Eugénie-les-Bains
tel: 58 05 06 07;
58 05 05 05
fax: 58 51 13 59
The great chef Michel Guérard's delightful hotel is a real luxury. Come here for both the exquisite cuisine gourmande *(creative classic cuisine) as well as the lighter* cuisine minceur *(gourmet slimming cuisine).*
$$$$+

Pâtisserie Bonnaud
260, Boulevard Wilson
33000 Bordeaux
tel: 56 81 45 06
Reputed to make the best cannelés *in town.*

Restaurant Auberge Les Vignes
23, Rue Principale
33210 Sauternes
tel: 56 76 60 06
fax: 56 76 69 97
Charming auberge in town famous for its luscious dessert wines. Grillades aux sarments *and* Sauternes *by the glass.*
$

THE DORDOGNE AND LOT
Aux Armes du Périgord
1, Rue de la Liberté
24200 Sarlat-la-Canéda
tel: 53 59 14 27
This is the place to buy fresh truffles (winter only). Stock up also on foie gras, confits, *and other excellent* plats préparés *in cans or jars to take home for an instant taste of Périgord.*

Château de Mercuès
Mercuès
46090 Cahors
tel: 65 20 00 01
fax: 65 20 05 72
The château, once part of the fief of the Bishops of Cahors, is now a luxury hotel-restaurant owned by renowned wine producer, Georges Vigouroux. The restaurant serves classic cuisine.
$$$

Château Le Barradis
24240 Monbazillac
tel: 53 58 30 01
fax: 53 58 26 13
One of our favorite sweet wines of the Southwest, produced from organically cultivated grapes. For non-drinkers, the jus de raisin *is a delicious tonic.*

Confiserie Boisson
20, Rue Grande Horloge
47000 Agen
tel: 53 66 20 61
fax: 53 87 76 64
The pruneau d'Agen *is rightly regarded as a great*

regional specialty. Come here to taste the most delicious pruneaux d'Agen fourrés (stuffed prunes) and other prune sweets.

Distillerie La Salamandre
Temniac
Les Tissanderies
24200 Sarlat-la-Canéda
tel: 53 59 10 00
fax: 53 28 39 16
Distillery producing eaux-de-vie from fresh local fruits, as well as the distinctive eau-de-noix. Guided visits for groups of ten or more.

Domaine du Haut-Pécharmant
Pécharmant
24100 Bergerac
tel: 53 57 29 50
fax: 53 24 28 05
Pécharmant is the finest Bergerac wine; come here for one of the best examples.

La Ferme
24200 Caudon-de-Vitrac
tel: 53 28 33 35
It's worth hunting out this genuine farm restaurant (about 12 km. or 7½ miles S.E. of Sarlat-la-Canéda) for its tasty regional foods made with produce from the farm.
$$

Le Cyrano
2, Boulevard Montaigne
24100 Bergerac
tel: 53 57 02 76
fax: 53 57 78 15
The classics of the Périgord — rillettes de canard, foie gras chaud, pigeon aux cèpes — handled with a stylish, light touch. Rooms available.
$$

Pierre Champion
21, Rue Taillefer
24004 Périgueux
tel: 53 53 43 34
fax: 53 04 25 56

One of the best sources for all Périgord specialties: foie gras mi-cuit, confits de canard, and plats préparés such as salmis de canard, cassoulet, and pâtés. There are branches throughout France and all are reliable.

GASCONY
Restaurant Daguin
Hôtel de France
2, Place de la Libération
32003 Auch (Cédex)
tel: 62 61 71 84;
62 61 71 71
fax: 62 61 71 81
Quite simply one of the greatest restaurants of the Southwest. André Daguin has put the foods of Gascony on the culinary map of France.
$$$$

See also *Fermes Auberges,* p.156.

THE BASQUE COUNTRY
Chocolaterie Cazenave
19, Arceaux, Port-Neuf
64100 Bayonne
tel: 59 59 03 16
fax: 59 59 32 97
If you are visiting Bayonne it is virtually obligatory to sit out under the arcades with a whipped hot chocolate so frothy and delicious, it has to be tasted to be believed. Buy chocolate bars to make your own.

Chocolaterie Cazenave

Euzkadi
Rue Principale
64250 Espelette
tel: 59 93 91 88
fax: 59 93 90 19
In the town famous for its chili peppers, an outstanding restaurant serving authentic foods of the Basque Country.
$$

La Grillerie de Sardines
Port de Pêche
64500 St.-Jean-de-Luz
tel: 59 51 18 29
fax: 59 26 21 47
In summer, the local tourist office runs this simple but good grill by the quay, serving sardines, thon rouge à la pipérade, and wines by the carafe.
$

Restaurant Arrantzaleak
Avenue J. Poulou
64500 Ciboure
tel: 59 47 10 75
By the fishermen's quay, this is the place to enjoy the freshest fish served Basque style.
$$

BEST BUYS
• *macarons* (St.-Emilion)
• wines from throughout Bordeaux, especially from the Médoc and Sauternes
• *huile de noix* walnut oil (the Dordogne)
• *arlequins de Carlux* (the Dordogne)
• *foie gras de canard* and duck *rillettes* (the Dordogne, Lot, and Gers)
• chocolate (Bayonne)
• *confits de canard* and *plats cuisinés* based on duck and goose, packed in jars or cans (all the Southwest)
• Armagnac and Floc de Gascogne (Gascony)
• Jambon de Bayonne (the Basque Country)
• Pruneaux d'Agen (Agen)

The East & Center

BURGUNDY

LYON AND HINTERLAND

FRANCHE-COMTE, SAVOIE, AND DAUPHINE

CENTRAL FRANCE

EASTERN AND CENTRAL FRANCE, extending from the French Alps across the fertile Saône and Rhône valleys, and from the borders with Switzerland and Italy way onto the high plateau of the Massif Central, is the domaine of France's farmers, who collectively create an abundance of the finest foods and wines that are cornerstones of French national gastronomy. Wheat for bread is grown across this region, while Charolais beef from Burgundy, Limousin beef from the center, and Bresse chickens from the Lyonnais are all raised here. This area, too, is the source of great mountain cheeses — *comté, reblochon fermier, beaufort, cantal,* and *salers* — as well as great wines to accompany them, including Chablis, Nuits-St.-Georges, Pommard, and others from Burgundy; Beaujolais, the local wine of Lyon; and hefty and prestigious reds and whites from the Northern and Central Côtes du Rhône.

BURGUNDY — HISTORY, FOOD, AND WINE

Burgundy is, of course, famous for its wines, which rank among the greatest in the world. Wine lovers certainly will wish to tour the small, unassuming wine hamlets whose names are so well-known. Beaune is the

The vineyards of Meursault, one of the most famous white wine communes in Burgundy's Côte d'Or

undoubted wine capital of Burgundy, with no shortage of excellent restaurants. Dijon is the true capital of the region, former seat of the Dukes of Burgundy who, in the 14th and 15th centuries, oversaw an empire that extended to the lowlands of Belgium and Holland. Few who come here to visit their Gothic palace (don't miss the vaulted kitchen with its enormous chimneys for roasting whole animals) that houses a fine Musée des Beaux Arts leave the city without buying a pot of Dijon mustard, sampling a *kir* (the blackcurrant liqueur and white wine *apéritif* named for a former mayor), or enjoying a slice of *pain d'épice,* delicious, spicy gingerbread.

Burgundy, like its foods and wines, is expansive and ample. The region extends from the small wine "island" of Chablis south of Paris, through the Côte d'Or and the vineyards of Beaujolais, virtually to Lyon, and from the manicured, pampered wine country into the dense and wild forests of the Morvan. Wherever you are and whatever you are doing, from touring Romanesque abbeys, such as Cluny and Vézelay, to lazing on boats and barges along the region's extensive canals, what is certain is that you will always eat — and drink — well.

LYON AND HINTERLAND

France's second city considers itself second to none as a center of gastronomic excellence. Lyon is well worth visiting for no other reason than to dine in its simple *bouchons* (working-class cafés) and its elegant temples of gastronomy, such as Restaurant Paul Bocuse. Lyon is fortuitously situated from a gastronomic point of view, able to claim as its own, superlative produce from its surrounding country: chickens from nearby Bourg-en-Bresse, cheeses from Savoie and Franche-Comté, excellent fruits and vegetables, freshwater fish from the Saône and Rhône Rivers, an abundance of *charcuterie,* and, of course, wines from both Beaujolais to the north and the Rhône to the south.

In spite of initial impressions, this sprawling, sometimes messy metropolis has a compact historical heart located mainly on the spit of land between the two rivers. This quarter, once home to the silk weavers upon whom Lyon's prosperity was based, is atmospheric and full of character.

The Lyonnais hinterland extends into the lush Bresse country to the northeast, the vineyards and granite hamlets of Beaujolais, to the north, the Roannais to the northwest leading up into the Massif Central, and the wine country of the Northern and Central Côtes du Rhône. These are all smug, prosperous areas, and there are great, starred restaurants to explore, including Troisgros in Roanne and La Pyramide in Vienne.

FRANCHE-COMTE, SAVOIE, AND DAUPHINE —
THE MOUNTAIN TRADITIONS

East of Burgundy, and to the south, the land gradually rises toward the snow-covered peaks of the French Alps. These eastern lands include three separate regions, Franche-Comté to the north and Savoie and Dauphiné to the south, all of which have their own history and traditions.

Besançon, east of Dijon, is the capital of Franche-Comté. The birthplace of the writer Victor Hugo (1802–85), this is a town with a glorious and vivid past, its prosperity evident in the old town with its fine 16th-, 17th-, and 18th-century houses. Arbois, to the south, is a small wine town that is also worth visiting. The center of the region's minor wine industry, Arbois, is where Louis Pasteur made a study of fermentation and aging of wines, the results of which paved the way to modern winemaking.

The beautiful, deep alpine lake at Annecy, Savoie

Savoie and Dauphiné extend across the French Alps, and towns such as Grenoble and Chamonix are familiar to winter sports enthusiasts. Summer is also a good time to visit the mountains, to walk on the high slopes or relax around beautiful lakes like those at Annecy and Evian-les-Bains. In summer, herdsmen still take their animals to the *alpages* — high, alpine meadows — where the animals can feed on lush, fresh grass redolent of mountain herbs and wild flowers.

CENTRAL FRANCE — HIGH, WIDE, AND LONELY

France has at its heart a high, central plateau known as the Massif Central. This vast area runs well to the north, but for our purposes we include here the regions of the Auvergne and Limousin. Hellishly hot in summer, when much of the land is planted with wheat, corn, and other grains, and bitterly cold in winter, these are areas where hearty, country foods sustain the appetites of people who spend long days outdoors.

The Auvergne is particularly rich in volcanic thermal springs, and towns such as Vichy and Volvic are now internationally famous for their mineral waters as well as nationally for their spa facilities where people come for a *'cure'* (treatment that involves both drinking and bathing in the waters). The Limousin is most famous for its superlative breed of cattle, as well as for lamb and *veau sous la mère* (milk-fed veal). But perhaps the Limousin's greatest contribution to French gastronomy is the fine Limoges porcelain, produced in Limoges itself, an essential element in stylish dining anywhere in France.

Produits Régionaux
REGIONAL PRODUCE

THE HUMBLE *POMME DE TERRE* (potato) unites the regions of Eastern and Central France, for this basic root vegetable is cooked in different ways everywhere. Dauphiné's *gratin dauphinois* (sliced potatoes baked in cream and *gruyère* or *beaufort* cheese) has become an international dish. Franche-Comté's version uses nutty *comté* cheese and adds cubes or slices of smoked ham, and, in the central Auvergne, the local *bleu d'Auvergne* or *bleu des Causses* cheeses might be used instead. Lyon's restaurants and cafés serve potatoes in all guises, the

Local cherries, at their best in summer, especially from the Yonne département

gratin, of course, and *pommes à l'huile* (warm potato salad), *gâteau de pommes de terre* (a thick, potato "cake"), *galette lyonnaise* (a fritter of waxy potatoes and onions), and the crisp-fried *pommes paillasson* (straw potatoes, emerging from the pan like a lacework pancake). The Limousin is known for its unusual but delicious *pâté de pomme de terre* (potato pie with other vegetables, cream, and sometimes cubes of meat).

Eastern and Central France are propitious zones for growing fruit, and Savoie benefits from a *Label Régional* for its fine profusion of fruit. Burgundy is most famous for its *cassis* (blackcurrant), for the bushes that yield this juicy fruit were planted to replace vineyards wiped out by the phylloxera catastrophe that devastated the wine industry at the turn of the century. Today, *cassis* is used to make *crème de cassis* (blackcurrant liqueur) which when mixed with white Aligoté wine becomes *kir*. In the Auvergne, local fruits such as *abricots* (apricots), *poires*

POULET DE BRESSE AC

The French passion for giving labels to their finest products is legendary, but in the case of *poulet de Bresse* (Bresse chicken) it is certainly well deserved, for this is a superior bird.

The quality of a Bresse chicken comes from the particular breed, a handsome white cockerel with blue feet and a five-pointed crest. It must be raised *en plein air* (outdoor) in the Bourg-en-Bresse country, and fed on milk, corn, and other cereals.

Poulet de Bresse is the only chicken in France that has been granted its own *appellation d'origine contrôlée,* and it is usually sold with the feathered head and blue feet still

attached as a way of proving its authenticity. Furthermore, it sports three badges of identification, a red, white, and blue sticker on its breast, a metal clip on its neck, and a metal band around its left foot.

This select bird is considerably more expensive than ordinary chicken, and restaurateurs proudly proclaim its prove-

nance on their menus. Once cooked, it may be impossible to verify this, but there are strict penalties for passing off the inauthentic.

An authentic *poulet de Bresse* is notable for its firm but tender, pale, white flesh and its intense flavor, and is best simply roasted or sautéed *à la crème*.

(pears), and *fraises* (strawberries) are used by *confiseurs* (candy makers) to produce a wide range of delicious fruit candies.

One of the most typical products of this part of France is the *lentille verte du Puy,* a green, marbled-with-turquoise lentil grown on rich volcanic soil which is so fine in flavor that it has earned its own *appellation d'origine contrôlée.*

Red onions, mild in flavor

IN SEASON

Cardon Cardoon, an edible thistle much loved in Savoie (Sep–Nov).

Cerises Cherries from the Yonne *département* of Burgundy (May–Jul).

Champignons sauvages Wild mushrooms, particularly from the forests of the Limousin, including **morilles** (morels; Mar–Apr), **girolles** (orange mushrooms; Jun), and **cèpes** (*Boletus edulis),* most prized of all (Jul–Sep).

Châtaigne Chestnut, particularly from the Limousin and Northern Rhône (Sep–Nov).

Fruits rouges Soft red fruits including cassis (blackcurrants), **groseilles** (redcurrants), and **framboises** (raspberries) (May–Jul).

Lentilles vertes du Puy Green lentils; best are *lentilles nouvelles* from the new harvest (Oct–Nov).

Noix de Grenoble Walnuts from Grenoble benefit from an *appellation d'origine contrôlée* (Sep–mid Oct).

Oignons rouges Red onions from the Côte d'Or *département,* mild in flavor and delicious raw (summer).

Poires and **pommes** Pears and apples from Savoie (Aug–Nov).

MOUTARDE DE DIJON

Dijon mustard was first mentioned in an account of a banquet given by the Dukes of Burgundy in 1334. Made from finely ground mustard seed mixed with *verjus* (sharp, unfermented grape juice) or white wine, it remains a condiment much loved locally.

The Grey-Poupon mustard shop has been a Dijonnais landmark since its foundation in 1866, and, today, visitors from all over the world come here not only to buy mustard but also to see the collection of antique mustard pots and period reproductions. Earlier this century, it was but one of scores of *moutardiers* in the city, most of whom produced mustard to be sold *à la louche,* ladled into the customers' own pots.

The Grey-Poupon mustard available in the shop itself, made with finely ground mustard seed and white wine, is outstanding, and is still supplied fresh weekly, an important factor, since a mustard's potency and aroma diminish with age. Any mustard, once opened, should always be kept refrigerated and is best consumed within six months.

Grey-Poupon
32, Rue de la Liberté
21000 Dijon
tel: 80 30 41 02

Lyon

THE BELLY OF FRANCE

LYON LIVES AND EATS well. It may be France's second city but it is the undoubted capital of French gastronomy. Sited at a confluence of rivers and regions, it has long benefited from some of the finest produce in the country, and it puts them all to good use. Above all, Lyon is the kingdom of the pig, its *charcuterie* possibly the most varied in France.

Lyon's best outdoor market, held along the Quai St.-Antoine

To gain an appetite-whetting understanding and impression of Lyonnais gastronomy, visit one of the city's great markets, such as the open-air one along the Quai St.-Antoine, or the indoor, modern Les Halles.

Lyon is a haven for *bons viveurs,* and more restaurants here hold the coveted Michelin rosettes than anywhere else but Paris. Just as important is the tradition of small *bouchons* — picturesque, lively, and informal restaurants serving the basically homey, unfussy, and delicious dishes of Lyon. *Bouchons* were originally inns where working folk, especially grooms and horsemen, stopped to have their horses tended and to grab a *mâchon* — a quick bite, perhaps a plate of *charcuterie* and a *pot* of wine. Today, characteristic *bouchons* in Vieux Lyon serve informally and in large portions the typical, mainly *charcuterie*-based foods of the city. In such places, a plate of crunchy *grattons* — nibbles of fried pork skin — might be

RESTAURANT PAUL BOCUSE

The most famous *grand restaurant* in France is just north of Lyon. Through the force of his larger-than-life personality, his energy and passion, but most of all through his supreme skill and regard for classic cuisine, Paul Bocuse has made his restaurant into something of a gastronomic shrine, where food lovers come to pay homage not only to the man but to the entire tradition of *haute cuisine française.*

Trompe-l'œil murals in the courtyard trace the history of French *haute cuisine,* beginning with Carême and Auguste Escoffier, and passing by way of Fernand Point to his disciples, Jean Troisgros, Alain Chapel, Jacques Pic

(even paying homage to our own James Beard and Julia Child), and ending with Bocuse himself and his magnificent *équipe* (team).

Restaurant Paul Bocuse is a *grand restaurant* of the highest order, but it is never a stuffy one. The excellence of its cooking, with its intense flavors, classically based on the tradition of *terroir* (local produce and traditions), and the friendly professionalism of its service make eating here always a marvelous experience.

Restaurant Paul Bocuse
69660 Collonges-au-Mont-d'Or
tel: 72 40 90 90
fax: 72 27 85 87
$$$$

offered to be washed down with the traditional 46-cl. *pot* (a refillable, thick glass bottle containing 1 pint) of young, fruity Beaujolais or Côtes du Rhône, followed by a plate of *charcuterie* or a *salade lyonnaise,* the curly endive lettuce or *pissenlits* (dandelion leaves) topped with fried *lardons* (cubes of smoked bacon), fried *croûtons* and a softly poached egg, all dressed in a sharp, mustardy *vinaigrette.* Typical Lyonnais main courses include *tablier de sapeur* (marinated, breaded, and fried tripe), *poulet au vinaigre* (chicken stewed in vinegar), *boudin aux pommes* (blood sausage served with pan-fried apple slices), accompanied by *pommes paillasson* (a sort of crispy potato pancake) or

One of the most welcoming of all Lyon's characteristic bouchons

gratin dauphinois (creamy potato gratin). Finish with a slice of *tarte aux pommes* and a strong, black *café.* This, essentially, is simple, working-class fare for a hard-working city, and we suggest that you take your jacket off, roll up your shirtsleeves, and chow down.

Lyon has no shortage of fine and tempting food shops. Three are worth singling out: Charcuterie Reynon for the full range of local Lyonnais cured pork products; Fromagerie Renée Richard for the best selection of cheese in town; and Pâtisserie-Chocolaterie Bernachon (address, p.203) for the most wickedly delicious and beautiful pastries and hand-made chocolates you will ever taste.

LYON

**Bouchon Lyonnais
Chez Hugon**
12, Rue Pizay
tel: 78 28 10 94
One of the oldest bouchons *in Vieux Lyon, this rough-and-ready place around the corner from the Hôtel de Ville serves hearty and authentic local foods and good wines by the* pot.
$

Brasserie Georges
30, Cours de Verdun
tel: 72 56 54 54
fax: 78 42 51 65
This immense Lyonnais eating house has been a city landmark since 1836.
$$

Café des Fédérations
8, Rue du Major-Martin
tel: 78 28 26 00
Authentic bouchon *with an informal atmosphere serving the classic foods of Lyon. Excellent* charcuterie *(especially* rosette), tablier de sapeur, *and house Morgon by the* pot.
$$

Charcuterie Reynon
13, Rue des Archers
tel: 78 37 39 08
The place to buy the finest Lyonnais charcuterie.

Fromagerie Renée Richard
Les Halles
102, Cours Lafayette
tel: 78 62 30 78

Renée and Renée Richard (mother and daughter) are fromagers-affineurs *and supply cheese to Lyon's finest restaurants (including Restaurant Paul Bocuse). Come here to sample the classic cheese of Lyon,* St.-Marcellin.

Le Petit Léon
3, Rue de Pleney
tel: 72 00 08 10
fax: 78 39 89 05
Next door to its grander, famous sister establishment, Léon de Lyon, this small, inexpensive bistro serves imaginative foods (lunch only) based on whatever is fresh from the market.
$$

Au Marché

MARKETS

BURGUNDY

Auxerre	Tue, Fri
Beaune	Sat
Chablis	Sun
Chagny	Thu, Sun
Chalon-sur-Saône	Wed, Fri, Sun
Dijon	Tue, Fri, Sat, Sun
Fleurie	Wed
Gevrey-Chambertin	Tue
Mâcon	Wed, Sat
Nuits-St.-Georges	Fri

LYON AND HINTERLAND

Bourg-en-Bresse	Wed, Sat
Lyon	Tue–Sun
Nantua	Sat
Roanne	Tue, Fri
Romans-sur-Isère	Tue
Valence	Tue, Thu, Sat
Vonnas	Thu

FRANCHE-COMTE, SAVOIE & DAUPHINE

Aix-les-Bains	Sat
Annecy	Tue, Sun
Arbois	Fri
Besançon	Fri
Dole	Sat
Evian-les-Bains	Tue
Le Grand-Bornand	Wed
Grenoble	Tue, Fri, Sun
Lons-le-Saunier	Thu
Montbéliard	Sat
Morteau	Tue, Sat

CENTRAL FRANCE

Aurillac	Wed, Sat
Clermont-Ferrand	Mon–Sat
Laguiole	Wed, Sat
Limoges	Tue–Sun
St.-Flour	Sat
St.-Nectaire	Sun (summer only)
Salers	Wed
Vic-sur-Cère	Tue

FETES ET FOIRES FESTIVALS AND FAIRS

BURGUNDY

Dijon: *Foire internationale gastronomique*
1st fortnight Nov

Macôn: *Foire nationale des vins de France (important wine trade fair)*
May

Vougeot, Beaune, Meursault: *Les trois glorieuses: (annual three-day event includes feast in Clos du Vougeot, auction of wines of the Hospices de Beaune in Beaune, and the Paulée de Meursault literary prize)*
3rd Sat, Sun, and Mon Nov

Chablis: *Fête des Vins (wine)*　3rd Sun Nov

LYON AND HINTERLAND

Bourg-en-Bresse: *Salon de la gastronomie et des produits régionaux (regional gastronomy)*
end Oct

Bourg-en-Bresse: *Les trois Glorieuses de Bresse (poultry festival)*　Dec

Curis-au-Mont-d'Or (north of Lyon): *Foire au boudin (blood sausage)*　Sep

FRANCHE-COMTE, SAVOIE & DAUPHINE

Arbois: *Fête de la vigne et du vin (wine)*
3rd week Jul

La Clusaz: *Fête du reblochon (cheese)*
mid Aug

Cordon (near Sallanches): *Fête du pain (bread)*
end Aug

Lebetain (near Delle): *Fête de la tarte aux prunes (plum pie)*　3rd Sun Sep

Poligny: *Fête du comté (cheese)*　end Jul

CENTRAL FRANCE

Vieillevie (south of Aurillac): *Fête des cerises (cherries)*　early Jun

Billom: *Foire à l'ail (garlic)*
1st weekend Aug

Brive-la-Gaillarde: *Foire aux noix fraîches (new walnuts)*　end Sep

Limoges: *Journées Internationales de l'Elevage Limousin (beef)*　Sep

Annecy's Sunday market, one of the best in Eastern France

Les Spécialités
REGIONAL SPECIALTIES

THROUGHOUT THIS VAST and varied section of the nation, wherever you happen to find yourself, you will be able to eat satisfying and filling country foods. In both the grandest, starred restaurants and in simple city bistros or country inns in the vineyards, the finest produce of these rich, agricultural lands is put to good use.

Burgundy probably boasts the richest, most ample cuisine of all the French wine regions, a fitting partner to its grand white and red wines, as well as to humbler and more affordable wines from the Chalonnais and Mâconnais. Wine, not surprisingly, finds its way into the cooking pot. In Chablis, slabs of ham are braised on the lees of wine, the natural sediment left in the barrels after the wines have been racked (transferred to clean barrels). The classic yet essentially humble *coq au vin* in Burgundy can sometimes emerge as an ultra-extravagant *coq au Chambertin* (but who would really use that great *grand cru* for cooking?). Eggs, considered by many to be incompatible with wine, are here poached in a thick, dark wine sauce and are all the more delicious for it. And freshwater fish from the Saône and other rivers are poached in wine for the classic *pochouse*.

If Burgundy relies essentially on a wine based cuisine, the food of Franche-Comté, Savoie, and Dauphiné is based on mountain traditions, with cheese taking pride of place. *Fondue savoyarde* (cheese fondue), *raclette* (*raclette* cheese melted onto potatoes), *tartiflette* (*reblochon* cheese with potatoes, bacon, and onions), *pommes dauphinoise* (potato *gratin* made with cheese and *crème fraîche*): these are all foods of mountain herdsmen.

The essentially working-class, *charcuterie* based foods of Lyon have their roots in kitchens of bistros and *bouchons* made famous by formidable women cooks who established many of the city's best-known eating establishments at the turn of the century. These women were

Lunch at a bouchon

known by their surname prefaced by the word *mère* (mother) as in Mère Fillioux, one of the most celebrated, who, in her now defunct *bouchon*, served such classics as *potage velouté aux truffes, quenelles de brochet au beurre d'écrevisses,* and *poularde demi-deuil.* Such foods are still served in simple and grand establishments, for the tradition of Lyon's *mères* influenced not only the simpler eating houses of the city but also the *grandes cuisiniers* who went on to establish the famous starred restaurants of Lyon and its surroundings.

Central France is not a uniform or homogeneous region by any stretch of the imagination, but whether in the Auvergne, the Limousin, the Berry, or Nivernais (the latter two areas stretch across the center of the country, linking the Upper Loire with Burgundy), the foods on offer are essentially warming, country fare. This is meat-rearing country, the beef and veal from the Limousin some of the best in France, and it is served in generous portions. Good lamb comes from the Limousin, too, while the forests of the Auvergne yield plenty of game, served often on a bed of *lentilles vertes du Puy.*

APPETIZERS AND FIRST COURSES
Assiette lyonnaise (Lyon) Plate of Lyonnais *charcuterie,* including *rosette, cervelas, tête de veau,* and other specialties (see pp.186–187), along with *carottes* or *celeri-rave râpés* (grated carrot or celeriac), or perhaps a plate of *lentilles du Puy* in a vinegar and mustard dressing.

Escargots à la bourguignonne (Burgundy) Snails, a vineyard pest, are much loved in Burgundy, enjoyed in the classic fashion: first simmered in wine, then stuffed back into their shells

Escargots à la bourguignonne

with a pungent garlic and parsley butter, and baked in a hot oven.

Grattons (Lyon) Bits of pork skin fried until crisp, a typical nibble with a glass of Beaujolais.

Jambon persillé (Burgundy) Exquisite *terrine* of chunks of ham marbled with a gelatin made from chopped parsley, white wine, garlic, and shallots (see p.186).

Museau de boeuf à la vinaigrette (Lyon) Gelatinous *terrine,* made from ox muzzle, which is served in slices with a vinegary dressing.

Oeufs en meurette (Burgundy) Eggs poached in a rich, thick sauce made from red Burgundy wine.

Pâté de pommes de terre (the Limousin) Vegetable terrine made from cooked potatoes, *crème fraîche,* and sometimes nuggets of cured ham or bacon.

Rosette (Lyon) Probably France's finest air-cured salami-type sausage, made with pure pork and garlic, served sliced.

Salade lyonnaise (Lyon) Salad of *frisée* (chicory) or *pissenlits* (tender dandelion leaves) dressed in a mustardy *vinaigrette,* and topped with fried *lardons* (cubes or strips of bacon), fried

Diot au vin blanc

croûtons, and a warm poached egg.

Tourte au reblochon (Savoie) Cheese tart made with creamy *reblochon,* a cheese particularly well-suited for cooking.

MAIN COURSES

Andouillette à la moutarde (Lyon and Burgundy) *Andouillette,* that popular gutsy sausage made from cooked pork tripe and chitterlings, is widely enjoyed in Lyon and Burgundy where it can also be made with *fraise de veau* (veal mesentery). Usually served broiled, sometimes with a creamy mustard sauce, or just with Dijon mustard on the side.

Boeuf bourguignon (Burgundy) The classic beef and wine stew, here, quite properly, made with good red Burgundy wine: rich, thick, and flavorful.

Civet de porc (the Limousin) Pork from the Limousin benefits from a quality *Label Rouge* and is enjoyed slowly stewed in red wine.

Coq au vin (Burgundy) Another Burgundian classic enjoyed throughout France, but always delicious on home ground: chicken cooked with red Burgundy wine, bacon, and onions, often served with fried garlic *croûtons.*

Côte de boeuf au gros sel (Lyon) Large piece of beef rib, boiled, and served with coarse sea salt.

Diot au vin blanc (Savoie) This meaty, ungreasy sausage is classically placed on a bed of vine shoots in a pot, then steamed in white Savoie wine.

Entrecôte de boeuf charolais, sauce marchand de vin (Burgundy) Rib steak from prized Charolais cattle, served with a rich wine sauce made from red Burgundy, bone marrow, meat stock, and shallots.

Filets de sole nouilles Pyramide (Lyon and Northern Rhône) A classic dish created at the famous La Pyramide restaurant south of Lyon: pan-fried sole fillets served on a bed of light, fine homemade egg noodles.

Fondue bourguignonne (Burgundy and Savoie) Meat *fondue:* a communal pot of oil kept hot over a special burner, thin slices of meat (usually beef, sometimes also pork and chicken), and a selection of sauces mainly based on mayonnaise. Individual portions of meat are dipped into the hot oil until they are cooked and then into a sauce.

Fondue savoyarde (Savoie) The classic cheese fondue of the mountains, normally made with a selection of different cheeses including *beaufort, comté,* and *gruyère,* cooked in a pot with local white wine until melted and creamy, and served in the same pot kept hot at the table with a flame underneath. Diners, each with their own long fork, spear cubes of bread and dip them into the bubbling mixture.

Fondue savoyarde

Fricassée de caïon (Savoie) Cubes of pork first marinated then cooked in red Savoie wine.

Friture du lac (Savoie and Dauphiné) Small fry from the freshwater, alpine lakes of Savoie and Dauphiné, generally dredged in flour and deep fried.

Gâteau de foies de volaille (Lyon) Mousse of finely chopped chicken livers, eggs, herbs, and garlic; cooked in a *bain-marie* till set, then turned onto a plate and usually served with a simple tomato sauce.

Jambon au Chablis (Chablis) Ham braised on the lees of Chablis wine.

Lapin à la moutarde (Burgundy and Lyon) Rabbit (usually wild), roasted or pan-fried, then served in a piquant mustard and cream sauce.

Omble chevalier (Savoie and Dauphiné) Char, a freshwater fish of alpine lakes related to salmon, caught at great depth and highly prized for its delicately flavored, firm flesh; served poached or grilled.

Petit salé aux lentilles (Lyon and Central France) Piece of lightly salted, unsmoked pork slowly cooked with lentils — a warming, satisfying classic.

Pochouse or pauchouse (Burgundy) Freshwater fish stew made from a selection of fish, including pike, perch, trout, and eel, poached in a white Burgundy wine.

Pormonier (Savoie) Pork cooking sausage made with cabbage and other green vegetables.

Potée auvergnate (Auvergne) Substantial one-pot dish containing salted pork, cabbage, potatoes, turnips, carrots, and other vegetables slowly cooked in stock. The liquid can be served as a first course, followed by the meat and vegetables as a main course.

Poularde demi-deuil (Lyon) Mature chicken with black truffles inserted under the skin, gently poached and served with *sauce velouté* (white sauce made from the cooking liquid).

Poulet au vinaigre d'estragon (Lyon) Chicken stewed in tarragon wine vinegar: classic bistro fare of Lyon.

Poulet de Bresse (Lyon and Burgundy) Bresse chicken, best enjoyed simply roasted. **Poulet de Bresse à la crème** Stewed in a rich cream sauce.

Coq au vin

Tablier de sapeur

Quenelles de brochet, sauce Nantua
(Lyon and Burgundy) The flesh of very
large pike, the fearsome freshwater
predator which can reach a length of up
to 1½ m. (about 5 ft.), is mainly good
for quenelles and mousses. Boned and
sieved, it is mixed with eggs and *crème
fraîche* to make light, poached dumplings
which are usually served with *sauce
Nantua,* a cream sauce made with
freshwater crayfish.

Raclette (Savoie) Classic food of the
mountains: a piece or wheel of *raclette*
cheese is heated in front of a fire
(restaurants have special tabletop grills
for this) and, when the cheese is melted,
you scrape it off to eat with boiled
potatoes, raw onions, and *cornichons*
(pickles).

Saucisson chaud à la bourguignonne
(Burgundy) Meaty cooking sausage
poached in red Burgundy and served in
the rich wine sauce.

Tablier de sapeur (Lyon) Beef tripe,
first marinated in wine and
mustard, then breaded and
fried. The dish gets its name
because the large slab of
meat is supposed to look
like a fireman's apron.
Usually served with *sauce
gribiche,* a mayonnaise made
with chopped pickles.

**Tête de veau, sauce
gribiche** (Lyon) Boiled
meat from the head of a calf
served with sharp
mayonnaise with pickles.

VEGETABLES AND VEGETARIAN DISHES

Aligot (Auvergne) Cooked, pureed
potatoes, young *cantal* or *salers* cheese,
and *crème fraîche* beaten together and
heated through so that the cheese forms
long, stringy ribbons.

Carottes à la Vichy (Vichy) Carrots
cooked in Vichy water and glazed in
butter and sugar.

Cèpes à la limousine (the Limousin)
Cepe mushrooms stewed in garlic and
oil, then finished in *crème fraîche.*

Cervelle de canut (Lyon) Silk weavers
(*canuts*) were considered to be brainless
— hence the name of this mixture of
fromage blanc (fresh, white cheese), chives,
and herbs served in a small bowl.

Lentilles vertes du Puy (Central
France) Green lentils from Le Puy,
cooked, then dressed in a mustardy
vinaigrette, or served as a bed on which
main-course meats are placed.

Pommes dauphinoise (Lyon,
Dauphiné, and everywhere else) Waxy,
sliced potatoes baked with *crème fraîche*
and cheese.

Tartiflette (Savoie) Boiled potatoes,
sliced or cubed, layered with creamy
reblochon cheese, garlic or scallions,
lardons, and *crème fraîche,* and baked.

DESSERTS

Bugnes (Lyon) Yeast-dough fritters.

Clafoutis limousin (Limousin) Pie of
cherries baked in batter.

**Fromage blanc à la
crème** (Lyon and
Burgundy) White cheese
with a dollop of *crème fraîche*
and sugar to taste, often
eaten instead of a selection
of aged *fromages.*

Gâteau grenoblois
(Dauphiné) Walnut cake.

Mont Blanc (Savoie and
Dauphiné) Mound of
pureed chestnut topped
with whipped cream.

Saucisson chaud à la
bourguignonne

Les Fromages

CHEESES OF THE EAST AND CENTER

Cows TAKEN UP TO the high pastures of the French Alps or the plateaus of Central France provide milk that is the source of scores of distinctive and flavorful mountain cheeses, ranging from creamy *reblochon* and semi-pressed *tomme de Savoie,* to hard, mountain cheeses like *beaufort, comté,* and *cantal.* Many such cheeses also benefit from select *appellation d'origine* status.

The cheese selection at Restaurant Paul Bocuse

TRY TO SAMPLE

Abondance (Savoie) Firm, smooth, round, pressed cheese with a compact interior with hardly any holes. Made from milk from the Abondance breed of cattle, the cheese is usually aged for a minimum of three months.

L'ami du Chambertin (Burgundy) Small, wrinkled, orange, rind-washed cheese flavored with *marc de Bourgogne.* Creamier, less strong, but similar in character to *époisses.*

Beaufort (Savoie) Great *gruyère*-type cheese made from cooked, hard-pressed curds of cow's milk, produced in huge rounds, and aged for upward of a year, during which time the sides of the cheese become concave. Best cheeses may be labeled *beaufort d'alpage,* indicating that they have been made with summer milk from the high pastures and so have a richer flavor.

Bleu d'Auvergne AC (Auvergne) Blue cheese of great character from the Auvergne, similar to *roquefort* but made with cow's milk. Sharp and pungent, it should never be too salty or runny.

Bleu de Bresse (Bresse) Small, cylindrical factory-made blue cheese from dairies around Bourg-en-Bresse.

Bleu de Gex or **du Haut-Jura AC** (Franche-Comté) Made in the Jura since the 13th century; this blue cheese has a compact texture, and is only lightly veined.

Epoisses de Bourgogne AC

Bleu des Causses (Rouergue) Similar to Bleu d'Auvergne, with lighter, finer blue veins and a less assertive flavor.

Cancoillotte franc-comtoise (Franche-Comté) Specialty of Franche-Comté, made from skimmed milk curd cheese mixed and cooked with butter, milk, spices, and wine, then packed into pots. Eaten spread on bread or used in cooking.

Cantal AC (Auvergne) Classic, huge wheel of mountain cheese from Central France, traditionally made in *burons* (mountain huts) from unpasteurized milk virtually straight from the cow, curdled (but not cooked), then drained, hard pressed and aged for upward of a year.

Cervelle de canut (Lyon) *Fromage blanc* (fresh white cheese) mixed with chives, herbs, and cream.

Cîteaux (Burgundy) Fine, semi-pressed cheese from the once-powerful Abbaye de Cîteaux, which, at one time, owned fine vineyards in the Côte d'Or.

Comté AC (Franche-Comté) Another, classic, *gruyère*-type cheese made like *beaufort* from cooked, pressed cow's milk curds. Comté has a fine, distinctive, nutty flavor and dense texture.

Emmental Grand Cru (Franche-Comté and Savoie) Based on the classic Swiss prototype with large holes, this cooked, pressed cheese should have a slightly grainy (not rubbery) texture and a fine, nutty flavor.

Beaufort, *with characteristic concave sides*

Epoisses de Bourgogne AC
(Burgundy) One of the great rind-washed cheeses of the East, with an orange rind, and a pungent aroma and flavor. Washed in *marc de Bourgogne*, this assertive cheese is a classic partner to big, warm, silky red Burgundy wine.

Fourme d'Ambert AC (Auvergne)
Another great blue cheese of Central France, tall and cylindrical in shape, made from unpasteurized cow's milk on small farms. Known also as *fourme de Montbrison*.

Fromage blanc à la crème (Lyon and Burgundy) Fresh, white cheese mixed with *crème fraîche* and sugar to taste.

Gougère (Burgundy) *Choux* pastry filled with nuggets of *gruyère* cheese, baked, and served hot as an appetizer with Beaujolais or Burgundy.

Gruyère (Franche-Comté and Savoie)
Family of cooked and pressed cheeses that includes *beaufort, abondance,* and *comté*. Good French *gruyère,* simply labeled as such, is widely made in these areas, the classic cheese for grating or cooking.

Laguiole AC (Auvergne) Large, pressed mountain cheese of great character, similar to *cantal* and *salers*.

Mont d'Or or **Vacherin du Haut-Doubs AC** (Franche-Comté) Soft, creamy cheese, runny when ripe, made from unpasteurized milk, traditionally in mountain chalets in the Haut-Doubs, only from August to March. After three months, when the cheese develops an orange crust, it is packed in spruce boxes that lend a characteristic resiny flavor.

Montrachet (Burgundy) Small, cylindrical goat's milk cheese wrapped in chestnut or vine leaves. Usually fairly fresh, soft, and mild.

Morbier (Franche-Comté)
Traditionally made in two steps with milk from separate milkings: the cheese from the first is protected with a layer of spruce ash spread on top, then the curds from the next milking are added to this, thus leaving a fine line of gray ash through the middle of the cheese. Authentic farmhouse *morbier* has a fine, slightly smoky flavor.

Picodon de l'Ardèche and **picodon de la Drôme AC** (Northern Rhône)
Two great goat's milk cheeses of the Northern Rhône, these small, hard disks gain an assertive but not overly sharp flavor with age.

Reblochon AC (Savoie) Creamy, hand pressed mountain cheese of Savoie (see opposite).

Rigotte de Condrieu (Northern Rhône) Small, mild cow's milk cheese with a reddish-orange crust.

St.-Marcellin (Lyon) The great cheese of Lyon, a small, flat disk made from cow's milk with a rind that turns orange as it ages. When perfectly aged, should be smooth, creamy, even runny, but never overly pungent or strong.

St.-Nectaire AC (Auvergne) Flat, circular, semi-pressed cheese, made from uncooked, unpasteurized milk on upland farms around the town of St.-Nectaire. As it ages, the crust takes on a moldy bloom, but the flavor remains mild.

Salers AC (Auvergne) Hard-pressed mountain cheese of the Auvergne made in huge wheels, traditionally in mountain *burons* (huts) using unpasteurized milk from Salers cattle. Aged cheeses are sharp and nutty.

Tomme de Savoie (Savoie) Small, circular mountain cheeses usually made from cow's milk or goat's (*tomme de chèvre*). Lightly pressed, with fine holes; such cheeses can be excellent.

Reblochon Fermier

MOUNTAIN CHEESE FROM THE HIGH PASTURES

Iɴ Mᴀʏ or early June (depending on when the winter's snows have finally melted), the herdsmen of the Vallée de Thônes, east of Annecy, begin the annual transhumance to the *alpages* — the high pastures. They take with them their families, their herds of

Young reblochon fermier

cows, their *reblochon* cheeses that will continue to age in the mountains, and all their cheesemaking equipment. There they will stay for up to five months, living in simple, isolated chalets on slopes that in winter are alive with the cries of skiers; in summer, the only noise is the ever present clank from the large bells around the necks of the cows, a gentle, if discordant, symphony of the Alps.

Here in the mountains, the cows benefit from a rich supply of grass redolent of wild flowers and herbs, and the milk that they yield is particularly rich in butterfat. This is transformed into one of the great cheeses of Savoie, *reblochon fermier*. *Reblochon* was first made in the 14th century. At that time, the farmers worked under a system of tenancy whereby they had to pay the landowner in proportion to the amount of milk their cows produced. When the landowner's henchmen came to check the amount,

the crafty herdsmen would only partially milk the cows, returning to milk them a second time after the men had gone, a process known as *reblocher*. This milk was even richer, thicker, and tastier than the first, and it was from this that *reblochon* cheese originally was made.

Today, *reblochon fermier* continues to be made by hand. So essential is the freshness of the milk that in the *alpages* (the name signifies the mountain chalets as well as the high pastures) the cheesemaking room always adjoins the stalls where the cows are milked, because the cheese is made almost immediately the milk emerges from the animal, a process undertaken twice daily, from both the morning's and the evening's milkings.

The fresh, coagulated curds are pressed lightly by hand into molds, salted, then aged for about a week. The cheeses are next washed in water then left to age in damp, unpaved cellars below the chalets. As the cheeses age, *reblochon* develops a light bloom on the surface, a soft, creamy texture, and a deliciously fragrant flavor redolent of the mountains.

The annual transhumance in the Vallée de Thônes represents a traditional way of life that has changed little for centuries. It is heartening to see that the younger generation is prepared to continue that tradition.

Visitors to the Vallée de Thônes can hike into the mountains to buy cheese direct from the producers as well as to witness a unique life *dans l'alpage*.

Marguerite et Alain Deloche
Les Languières
74450 Le Grand-Bornand
tel: 50 27 00 20
Telephone before visiting. You can buy cheeses here, and, if there is time, you can also watch the cheese being made in the afternoon.

Vallée de Thônes and its high mountain pasture

Charcuterie

CURED PORK AND OTHER MEAT PRODUCTS

THE RURAL MOUNTAIN traditions of Eastern France have resulted in a range of outstanding, artisan-cured pork products, in the past, mainly made on upland farms. In Franche-Comté, most farmhouses had (and, in many cases, still have) their own *tuyé,* a small, pitch-blackened smoke room usually sited next to the kitchen. Here, hams, tongues, sausages, beef tenderloin, and bacon would be hung up to smoke over smoldering fires of pine, spruce, and aromatic juniper sawdust.

A selection of salaisons de Savoie *at a market stall*

In Savoie, by contrast, the cool, dry, fresh mountain air has resulted in a range of salted, air-cured meats that may or may not be smoked, depending on taste.

The popularity of pork in Eastern France is nowhere more evident than in Lyon, where an entire repertoire of *charcuterie* specialties has developed, and where such foods can be enjoyed with gusto in the *bouchons* or bistros of the city.

In Central France, good rustic *charcuterie* comes from both the Auvergne and Limousin, especially outstanding air-cured hams and sausages. Pork liver *pâtés* and *crépinettes* are also popular, as are *boudins noirs* (blood sausages).

TRY TO SAMPLE

Andouillette (Lyon) Sausage made from cooked pig's tripe, chitterlings, or sometimes from *fraise de veau* (veal mesentery). Sold already cooked, to be broiled or gently pan-fried.

Boudin aux châtaignes (the Auvergne and Limousin) Blood sausage flavored with bits of chestnuts.

JAMBON PERSILLE

One of the prettiest and most delicious of all French regional *charcuterie* products is Burgundy's *jambon persillé*. Though *charcuteries* throughout the region may offer their own versions, it is most at home in the Côte d'Or.

Roger Batteault makes *jambon persillé* daily, using lightly cured ham and pork shoulder slowly cooked in a *court bouillon* (stock) made with white wine, vegetables, and seasoning, together with a few veal trotters to render the gelatin necessary to set the mixture. He leaves the meat in large chunks, then mixes plenty of freshly chopped parsley and garlic with more white wine and the concentrated cooking liquid. Next, he layers the meat and parsley mixture carefully into white china bowls to get a marbled effect, and then lets the mixture set to a shimmering aspic jelly.

You can buy *jambon persillé* by the slice, together with Roger's *rosette de Beaune* (the meaty pork sausage, in this case, flavored with *marc de Bourgogne*), for a superior picnic in the vineyards of the Côte d'Or.

Charcuterie Batteault
4, Rue Monge
21200 Beaune
tel: 80 22 23 04

Brésis (Franche-Comté) Similar to Swiss *viande des Grisons* and Italian *bresaola, brésis* is a boneless tenderloin of beef which is cured in salt and spices, then usually smoked.

Caillette (Dauphiné and Northern Rhône) Type of *pâté* made with pork liver, herbs, and cooked vegetables such as spinach or Swiss chard.

Cervelas truffé et pistaché (Lyon) The finest and most prized of Lyon's *charcuterie* specialties, this meaty cooking sausage is studded with pistachio nuts and pieces of black truffle, the dark slices of that expensive delicacy visible under the skin.

Crépinette (the Auvergne and Limousin) Mixtures of pig's liver, meat, seasonings, and cooked vegetables, wrapped in lacy caul fat, to be cooked in the oven.

Diot (Savoie) Meaty, not too fatty, pork sausage, traditionally placed on a bed of vine shoots and steamed in wine.

Jambon d'Auvergne (the Auvergne) Rustic, air-cured mountain ham; eaten raw in slices.

Jambon de Luxeuil (Franche-Comté) Outstanding, air-cured ham from the Luxeuil region, made by first marinating local hams in wine and seasoning, then dry-salting. Once cured, the meat is usually lightly smoked over pine, spruce, and wild cherry sawdust. The whole process must take at least six months.

Jambon persillé (Burgundy) Ham set in parsley aspic (see box opposite).

Jésus (Lyon) Plump, air-cured pork sausage to eat cold in slices.

Noix de jambon de Savoie (Savoie) Boneless cut of ham, salted and air-dried in the Alps; sometimes smoked.

Pormonier (Savoie) Rustic homemade sausage made with pork and cooked vegetables.

Rosette (Lyon and Burgundy) The finest French *saucisson sec,* made from pure pork, seasoned with salt, pepper, spices, a little garlic, and red wine, air-cured for at least two months. *Rosettes,* always made with a natural skin, are irregular in shape (one end is always more bulbous), and can be up to 1½ m. (5 ft.) in length. Hanging in *charcuteries* and from ceilings of *bouchons,* they have become a symbol of Lyon.

Sabodet (Dauphiné) Rustic sausage made from meat from a pig's head, shoulder, tongue, and pieces of skin, served hot with *gratin dauphinois.*

Salaisons de Savoie (Savoie) *Salaisons* is the general term for salted meats.

Saucisse de Montbéliard (Franche-Comté) Meaty pork sausage flavored with garlic and cumin seed and smoked over a smoldering fire of juniper berries and pine sawdust. Needs to be boiled before eating.

Saucisse or **Jésus de Morteau** (Franche-Comté) Another fine, coarsely ground pork sausage from the mountain zone of Franche-Comté. Genuine *saucisse de Morteau* always has a wooden peg at one end from which it is suspended to smoke in the *tuyé* (smoke house).

Saucisson à cuire (Lyon and Burgundy) Fat, cooking sausage to be boiled, or served hot in a wine sauce.

Saucisson sec (Savoie) Air-cured *saucisson* to eat sliced. Can be flavored with hazelnuts, mushrooms, cheese, or wine or *marc.*

Saucisson sec d'Auvergne (the Auvergne) Air-cured *saucisson,* the best of which is hand-made, with the meat chopped by knife, not machine.

Cervelas truffé et pistaché, *boiling sausage with black truffles and pistachio nuts*

Pâtisseries et Confiseries
PASTRIES AND CANDIES

THIS REGION is not renowned for its desserts and candies, but, like anywhere in France, there are always local treats to indulge in. Lovers of chocolate, cakes, and *pâtisseries* should not miss paying a visit to Bernachon in Lyon (address, p.203), one of the finest *pâtisseries-confiseries* in the nation.

TRY TO SAMPLE

Bourrioles (Central France) Thick buckwheat pancakes sprinkled with sugar or spread with jam.

Boursadas (Limousin) Boiled chestnuts; often made into a sweet puree, or eaten as a savory.

Bugnes (Lyon) Large, batter fritters.

Clafoutis (Limousin) Pie of black cherries baked in batter. The cherries are usually left unpitted, as the pit is deemed to give flavor, so be careful when you take a bite.

Escargots en chocolat (Burgundy) Those who can't bring themselves to eat snails might prefer the chocolate versions.

Fruits à l'eau-de-vie (Franche-Comté, Savoie, and Dauphiné) Fruits such as cherries, pears, or plums conserved in fruit- or grain-based liqueurs.

Gâteau de noix (Dauphiné) Walnut cake — a favorite in the Alps.

Gâteau de Savoie (Savoie) Feather-light sponge cake, enjoyed on its own or used as a base for *pâtisseries*.

Marrons glacés (Dauphiné and Northern Rhône) Fresh chestnuts candied in sugar syrup, a great seasonal delicacy.

Matafan or **matefaim** (Lyon and Franche-Comté) Thick pancake usually served with fruit or *confiture* (jam).

Pastilles de Vichy (Vichy) Mints made with Vichy water, to suck after you've taken the waters.

Pâté de fruits (the Auvergne) Fruit candies made with fruit pulp.

Pêches en Chartreuse (Dauphiné) Fresh peaches marinated in Chartreuse.

Pogne (Dauphiné) Round *brioche*-type cake filled with fruits or jam.

Pommes farcies (Central France) Whole apples stuffed with nuts and fruits, and baked.

Roseaux du Lac (Annecy) Exquisite coffee-filled chocolate batons.

PAIN D'EPICE

Dijon's *pain d'épice,* or spiced gingerbread, is as famous as the town's mustard, and no visitor should leave here without sampling it.

This sweet bread dates probably from the 15th century, when spices from the Orient reached the capital of the Dukes of Burgundy on their way to Northern Europe. It grew in popularity not just at court, where Marguerite de Valois was said to enjoy it, but with the common people too, and, as spices became more available, dozens of firms sprang up in Dijon specializing in

its manufacture. The family firm of Mulot et Petitjean was founded in 1796, and still bakes the most exquisite gingerbread, made with honey, anise, ginger, and cinnamon.

Pain d'épice lasts well, and acts rather like a barometer: in hot, settled weather, the loaf will tend to dry up, but when it rains, the *pain d'épice* absorbs moisture from the atmosphere like a sponge. If kept properly, *pain d'épice* will last for months.

Mulot & Petitjean
13, Place Bossuet
21000 Dijon
tel: 80 30 07 10
fax: 80 30 18 03

Les Vins

WINES OF THE EAST AND CENTER

BURGUNDY IS THE GREAT wine region of Eastern France, the source of a superlative range that includes silky, voluptuous reds from Pinot Noir grapes grown on the fabled Côte d'Or; exceptional white Chardonnays from the Côte de Beaune, Chablis, and Pouilly-Fuissé; good, sound everyday reds and whites from the Hautes-Côtes, Mâconnais, and Chalonnais; and exuberant Beaujolais (the world's most gulpable wine).

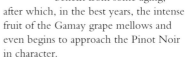

Going home for lunch in the vineyards of the Côte de Beaune

Jura, in Franche-Comté, and Savoie are both only minor wine regions, but visitors will find some satisfying and unique wines here. Lyon claims the wines of the Northern and Central Rhône as its own.

BURGUNDY

Aloxe-Corton AC One of the few wine communes of the Côte d'Or producing both exceptional red and white wines of *grand cru* quality. Corton *grand cru* is mainly red and Corton-Charlemagne *grand cru* is one of the great white wines of the world, golden, full-bodied, with a long, lingering finish.
Recommended producers: Château de Corton-André, Jadot, Latour, Senard, Voarick.

Beaujolais AC; Beaujolais–Villages AC Fruity, gulpable Beaujolais is produced from Gamay grapes grown on rugged granite soil vineyards that extend from south of Mâcon almost to the outskirts of Lyon. While Beaujolais *nouveau* is meant to be drunk within weeks of the harvest, more serious Beaujolais-Villages wines from vineyards in the north of the zone can improve with age. Straight Beaujolais is almost always drunk well chilled, in Lyon, from 46-cl. *pots* (almost 1 pint). Relatively rare, white Beaujolais is made from Chardonnay grapes.

Recommended producers: Duboeuf, Drouhin, Jaffelin, Large, Château de Lacarelle.

Beaujolais Crus Ten superior villages in the north of Beaujolais are entitled each to their own communal *appellations* for the production of red wines from the Gamay grape: *Brouilly AC, Chénas AC, Chiroubles AC, Côte de Brouilly AC, Fleurie AC, Juliénas AC, Morgon AC, Moulin-à-Vent AC, Regnié AC, and St.-Amour AC.* Such wines, at best, are considerably more full-flavored and complex than straight Beaujolais, and all benefit from some aging, after which, in the best years, the intense fruit of the Gamay grape mellows and even begins to approach the Pinot Noir in character.
Recommended producers: Duboeuf, Hospice de Beaujeu, Champagnon, Lapierre.

Beaune AC Burgundy's great wine capital is surrounded by vineyards, and is the largest single wine commune in the Côte d'Or, producing mainly red wines of a high overall standard.
Recommended producers: Jadot, Latour, Germain, Drouhin, Tollot-Beaut, Hospices de Beaune.

Bourgogne AC The broadest regional *appellation*, applied to red and rosé wines from Pinot Noir and white from Chardonnay produced within the vineyard following certain regulations. At best, these are sound varietals, if usually light in character.
Recommended producers: Faiveley, Jadot, Jaffelin, Latour, Coche-Dury, Drouhin, Caves des Hautes-Côtes cave coopérative.

Bourgogne Aligoté AC White Burgundy produced not from the noble Chardonnay but from the lesser Aligoté. High in acid, light, and crisp, it is the classic wine to mix with *crème de cassis* (blackcurrant liqueur) to make *kir*. The

best Aligoté comes from the village of
Bouzeron.
Recommended producer: De Villaine.

Bourgogne Grand Ordinaire AC
The lowest *appellation* in Burgundy: reds
and rosés may contain Gamay as well as
Pinot Noir, and the white is made with
other grapes in place of or in addition to
Chardonnay. Rarely worth buying.

**Bourgogne Hautes-Côtes de Beaune
AC** Wines from the higher slopes above
the Côte de Beaune can be good
examples of Burgundy at affordable
prices. Red wines are fleshy, warm, but
always on the light side and generally
ready to drink while still young.
*Recommended producers: Joillot, Cave des
Hautes-Côtes cave coopérative.*

**Bourgogne Hautes-Côtes de Nuits
AC** Mainly red wines from the higher
slopes above the Côte de Nuits. Best
wines display an attractive raspberry fruit
and are more long-lived than examples
from the Hautes-Côtes de Beaune.
*Recommended producers: Thomas-Moillard,
Cornu, Cave des Hautes-Côtes.*

Bourgogne Irancy AC The best red
wine from the Yonne, usually rather
light in character but finely scented.
Recommended producer: Simonnet-Febvre.

Bourgogne Passe-Tout-Grains AC
Red blend of about two-thirds Gamay
to one-third Pinot Noir, an inexpensive,
fruity wine to drink young.
Recommended producer: Buxy cave coopérative.

Chablis AC Probably the best-known
white wine in the world produced from
vineyards around the quiet, eponymous
town in Yonne. In contrast to the richer
styles of white Burgundy from the Côte
d'Or or Mâconnais, Chablis' style is
fresh, crisp, vividly focused; it used to be
marked by characteristic mineral aromas
though many wines are now oak-aged.

PROPRIETAIRE-RECOLTANT OR NEGOCIANT-ELEVEUR

In Burgundy, wines may be produced
by individual *propriétaires-récoltants,*
growers who make, bottle, and market
their own wines from their own
harvested grapes, or by *négociants-
éleveurs. Négociants-éleveurs* are the large,
sometimes internationally known firms
that purchase both grapes and finished
wines from growers and wine brokers
to account for the bulk of their production, even though some of them
have their own vineyards.

They subsequently
assemble wines in their
own cellars, blending,
balancing, aging them —
in short, "rearing" the
wines to maturity — then
eventually bottling and
selling them under the
house's own label.

The argument in favor
of wines from individual

growers is that they may have more
character, more individual personality,
and in the best years are able to reach
higher peaks than wines assembled
from various sources by merchants.
The *négociants-éleveurs,* on the other
hand, may claim that by skillful
selection of wines from each vintage,
village, or individual *climat* (single
vineyard) they are able to produce
wines that, once assembled and aged,

are greater and more
balanced than any of
their individual
components.

While good (and,
sadly, mediocre) wines
can come from both
négociants-éleveurs and
individual growers, the
reputation of each
merchant or *domaine* is
most important.

Finest *grands* and *premiers crus* come from vineyards rich in chalk and fossils and have an intensity of scent and flavor. *Recommended producers: Defaix, Drouhin, Louis Michel, Chablisienne cave coopérative.*

Chambolle-Musigny AC Wine commune in the Côte de Nuits famous for its red wines that combine power, delicacy, and fine scent. The commune has two *grands crus*: Les Musigny and Les Bonnes-Mares. *Recommended producers: Drouhin, Hudelot-Noëllat, Roumier, Mugnier.*

Chassagne-Montrachet AC Chassagne is one of the great white wine communes of the Côte de Beaune, sharing with its neighbor Puligny the *grand cru* Le Montrachet. Chassagne's simpler white Burgundies are always full, nutty, and rich in style, and the commune is the source of excellent, undervalued red wines too. *Recommended producers: Pillot, Bachelet, Gagnard, Jadot, Ramonet.*

Côte de Nuits-Villages AC The *appellation* applies only to wines from the communes of Fixin, Brochon, Prissey, Comblanchien and Corgoloin. Wines from the extreme southern end of the Côte, in particularly, at Corgoloin and Comblanchien, can be very good. *Recommended producer: De L'Arlot.*

Crémant de Bourgogne AC High-quality white or rosé sparkling wine made by the classic method of secondary fermentation in the bottle. *Recommended producers: Simonnet-Febvre, Bailly and Lugny caves coopératives.*

Fixin AC Unfashionable wine commune at the northern end of the Côte de Nuits near better-known Gevrey-Chambertin. Meaty red wines are often relative bargains. *Recommended producers: Berthaut, Gelin.*

Gevrey-Chambertin AC Classic red Burgundy from the Côte de Nuits, with a concentration of classified great vineyards, including *grands crus* Chambertin and Chambertin-Clos-de-

A winegrower's farm in Chassagne-Montrachet

Bèze, and a further 11 *premiers crus*. Gevrey-Chambertin wines are noted above all for their power and perfume. *Recommended producers: Rousseau, Bachelet, Jadot, Faiveley.*

Givry AC Mainly red and some white wines from the center of the Côte Chalonnaise. Reds are marked by their attractive, light, delicate fruit. *Recommended producers: Lumpp, La Renarde, Pelletier, Ragot, Thenard.*

Hospices de Beaune Each year, wines made from vineyards belonging to the Hospices de Beaune, a charitable hospital founded in 1443, are sold in what is called the "biggest charity auction in the world." Such wines are entitled to a special, distinctive label and usually denote the name of the donor who originally granted the lands to the Hospices, as in Cuvée Nicolas Rolin (the founder) or Cuvée Docteur Peste.

Mâcon AC; Mâcon-Villages AC The Mâcon vineyard is the source of sound red and rosé (from Gamay as well as Pinot Noir) and white Chardonnay wines. Best whites are entitled to Mâcon-Villages *appellation*, sometimes qualified by the name of the village, as in Mâcon-Lugny, Mâcon-Chardonnay, Mâcon-Viré. Much of the production is in the hands of *caves coopératives*, and the wines can be excellent value. *Recommended producers: Lugny, Mancey caves coopératives, Chardonnay.*

Mercurey AC Historic vineyard in a sheltered part of the Côte Chalonnaise, where good, solid red wines exclusively from Pinot Noir are produced.
Recommended producers: Faiveley, Juillot, Rodet.

Meursault AC One of the great white wine communes of Burgundy, source of rich, powerful, dry wines with nuances of butter and honey that are accentuated with age. No *grands crus* but some 13 *premiers crus*. The standard even of the village wines is very high. Small amount of red wines also produced.
Recommended producers: Coche-Dury, Lafon, Matrot, Château de Meursault, Drouhin, Jadot.

Montagny AC Outstanding and still affordable white wines from the Côte Chalonnaise. Best wines spend some time in new oak, and gain intensity of flavor and richness.
Recommended producers: Buxy cave coopérative, Vachet.

Monthélie AC Tiny village lost between the famous wine communes of Volnay and Meursault producing some light, generally well-made red wines.
Recommended producer: Monthélie-Douhairet.

Morey-St.-Denis AC Côte de Nuits wine commune of exceptional concentration and excellence, with five *grands crus* and 23 *premiers crus*. Best wines are well balanced and display an intense raspberry fruit.
Recommended producers: Faiveley, Dujac, Marchand-Grillot, Rodet, Drouhin.

Nuits-St.-Georges AC Nuits lies at the southern half of the Côte to which it gives its name; it produces deep, sturdy, classic red Burgundies that should age well. The commune has no *grands crus* vineyards, but it has no fewer than 37 *premiers crus*.
Recommended producers: Drouhin, Faiveley, Thomas-Moillard, Jayer, Méo-Camuzet.

Pommard AC Classic red wine of the Côte de Beaune, traditionally dark, chewy, and mouth-filling.
Recommended producers: Château de Pommard, de Montille, Mussy, Pousse d'Or.

Pouilly-Fuissé AC The greatest white wine of the Mâconnais, sometimes on a par even with Meursault and the Montrachets in terms of quality and (sadly) price. More affordable examples come from adjoining communes of Pouilly-Loché, Pouilly-Vinzelles, and St.-Véran.
Recommended producers: Château de Fuissé, Jadot, Drouin.

Puligny-Montrachet AC Probably the greatest white wine commune in Burgundy, famous not only for its *grands crus* Le Montrachet, Bâtard-Montrachet, Chevalier-Montrachet, and others but also for village white wines that combine elegance with extremely rich, long, and lingering flavors.
Recommended producers: Latour, Drouhin, Jadot, Carillon, Sauzet, Ramonet, Chartrou, Faiveley.

Rully AC Côte Chalonnaise commune that is the source of both outstanding, oak-aged white wines and light Pinot Noir reds.
Recommended producers: La Renarde, Faiveley, Rodet.

Savigny-lès-Beaune AC Wine commune in the valley between Corton and the Montagne de Beaune: good, sometimes undervalued red (mainly) and some white wines.
Recommended producers: Bize, Girard-Vollot, Tollot-Beaut.

Volnay AC Volnay's red wines are noted above all for their light delicacy and exquisite perfume and are considered among the most elegant of the Côte de Beaune.
Recommended producers: Bitouzet-Prieur, Lafon, Lafarge, Pousse d'Or, Montille.

Vosne-Romanée AC Luscious, highly elegant red wines are produced in this famous wine commune, possibly the greatest in the Côte de Nuits. Vosne-Romanée's *grands crus* — Romanée-Conti, La Romanée, Romanée-St.-

Vivant, Richebourg, La Tâche, La Grande Rue, Les Echézeaux, and Les Grands-Echézeaux — rank among the most prized and expensive wines in the world.

Recommended producers: Jadot, Domaine de la Romanée-Conti, Thomas-Moillard, Gros, Grivot, Drouhin, Engel, Méo-Camuzet.

Vougeot AC Burgundy's most famous single *climat* (vineyard) is Vougeot's Clos de Vougeot, a *grand cru* vineyard first planted in the Middle Ages by the monks of Cîteaux. Today, there are scores of different owners making and selling their own wines, so quality can be variable.

Recommended producers: Arnoux, Château de la Tour, Faiveley, Drouhin, Leroy, Gros, Grivot.

THE NORTHERN AND CENTRAL COTES DU RHONE

Château-Grillet AC One of the smallest *appellations* in France, pertaining to a single estate, producing compact, concentrated, very expensive dry white wine from the Viognier grape.

Recommended producer: Château Grillet.

Clairette de Die AC Outstanding, undervalued, and refreshing sparkling wine made from both Clairette and fragrant Muscat grapes in the Drôme

Valley. *Tradition* style, which preserves the grape-fresh character of the Muscat and remains just off-dry, is the best.

Recommended producers: Clairette de Die cave coopérative, Raspail.

Condrieu AC Great, but very expensive, dry white wine produced from Viognier grapes grown on the steep granite terraces of the Northern Rhône. The Viognier is one of the great white grapes of the world, capable of producing wines with a heady, musky scent of violets.

Recommended producers: Guigal, Vernay, Dumazet, Pinchon.

Cornas AC A mighty red wine made from the Syrah, the great grape of the Northern Rhône. Traditionally vinified wines are thick and concentrated, with deep, rasping fruit and tannin, and need plenty of time to mature.

Recommended producers: Jaboulet, Clape, Voge, Verset.

Côte-Rôtie AC One of the greatest of all Rhône reds, produced from Syrah grapes (with some Viognier) grown on well-exposed, terraced vineyards opposite the town of Vienne. Best wines have concentration of flavor and scent, combining power with elegance.

Recommended producers: Guigal, Vernay, Jamet, Jasmin, Rostaing.

The Château de Clos du Vougeot amid vineyards of the Côte de Nuits

Hermitage vineyards in the Central Rhône

Côtes du Rhône AC Great torrents of straight Côtes du Rhône (often served in the ever present 46-cl. Lyonnais *pot*) find their way into the bars and *bouchons* of Lyon and its surrounds, providing a more beefy alternative to Beaujolais.

Crozes-Hermitage AC Extensive vineyards to both the north and south of the famous hill of Hermitage are the source of good meaty red and full-bodied white wines.
Recommended producers: Jaboulet, Graillot, Chapoutier.

Hermitage AC One of the most famous, indeed, legendary, red wines of France, produced from Syrah grapes grown on the steep flank of Hermitage, above the town of Tain-l'Hermitage. Wines combine immense power with a famous rich flavor and bouquet, and often need years to come around. White Hermitage can be equally long-lived.
Recommended producers: Chave, Jaboulet, Chapoutier, Grippat, Guigal, Belle, Delas, Sorrel.

St.-Joseph AC Another ripely fruity pure Syrah. Wines are often undervalued and should be tried.
Recommended producers: Chapoutier, Chave, Jaboulet, Coursodon, Grippat, Graillot, St.-Désirat coopérative.

St.-Péray AC Undervalued sparkling wine produced by the classic method of secondary fermentation in the bottle from grapes grown opposite Valence.

Some still wines are produced from Marsanne and Roussanne.
Recommended producers: Chaboud, Thiers.

Vins de Pays des Collines Rhodaniennes Inexpensive country wines from the traditional grapes of the Northern Rhône, including Syrah and Viognier as well as Merlot and Gamay.
Recommended producer: St.-Désirat coopérative.

Vin de Pays des Coteaux de l'Ardèche Particularly good Gamay and Cabernet Sauvignon varietal wines are produced from vineyards in Ardèche.

FRANCHE-COMTE AND SAVOIE

Arbois AC; Arbois Pupillin AC
Arbois' mountain vineyards are the source of red, white, and rosé wines. The whites, made from the distinctive Savagnin grape, are generally preferred aged, even oxidized, during which time they gain a characteristic nutty flavor. Best reds are produced from the local Trousseau grape. Rosés from the nearby commune of Pupillin are worth sampling.
Recommended producers: Henri Maire, Fruitière Vinicole d'Arbois, Fruitière Vinicole de Pupillin, Rolet, Tissot.

Château Chalon AC The most famous — and expensive — Vin Jaune (see below).
Recommended producers: Henri Maire, Macle, Bourdy, Courbet.

Côtes du Jura AC All-embracing regional *appellation* for all the styles of wines of Jura, including red, white, rosé, Vin Jaune, sparkling wines, and *Vin de Paille*. The taste locally is for wines that have aged often far too long.
Recommended producers: Henri Maire, Rolet, Grand Frères, Bourdy, Clavelin.

Crépy AC Vineyards planted around Lake Geneva mainly with Chasselas provide light, sharp, quenching wines that are enjoyed locally.

Seyssel AC Light, refreshing sparkling wine from Savoie.

Recommended producers: Maison Mollex, Varichon & Clerc.

Vin de Paille Unique Jura specialty: produced (like Italian Vin Santo) from grapes laid out to dry on straw mats to concentrate sugar levels. The sweet, luscious wine that results has an intriguing, nutty aftertaste.

Recommended producers: Tissot, Henri Maire, Grand Frères, Courbet.

Vin de Savoie AC The regional *appellation* applies to red, rosé, and white wines produced on the alpine vineyards of Savoie, mainly planted at low altitudes. Best reds are the beefy Mondeuse and the fruity Gamay. The most distinctive whites are produced from the Apremont *oue* (zesty, appley, and light), and made from Roussette (fruity, fragrant, with a nutty flavor), and Chardonnay (dry and fruity).

Recommended producers: Boniface, Quénard.

Vin Fou This branded sparkling wine is not entitled to an *appellation,* but examples made from Chardonnay can be refreshing.

Recommended producer: Henri Maire.

Vin Jaune Another unique Jura specialty, made from Savagnin grapes fermented in sealed wooden barrels. As with *fino* sherry, a film of yeast develops on the surface of the wine and protects it from oxidizing. The wine is not racked (transferred to clean barrels) or topped up for at least six years, and the wines that eventually emerge are intriguing, with intense, nutty flavors and aromas.

Recommended producers: Henri Maire, Tissot, Caveau des Jacobins, Macle, Fruitière Vinicole d'Arbois.

Other drinks

Chambéry vermouth France's driest vermouth, and the only one to have *appellation d'origine* status, is made in Savoie with local wild herbs and other flavorings.

Chartreuse Herbal liqueur still made by monks from some 130 aromatic plants and herbs grown in Dauphiné. Two versions are made: Chartreuse *verte* (green) is the stronger and more aromatic of the two; Chartreuse *jaune* (yellow) is sweeter.

Eaux-de-vie de Fougerolles Good fruit brandies, especially *kirsch* produced from cherries, come from Franche-Comté.

Macvin The Jura's answer to Pineau de Charentes: unfortified grape juice blended with local Franche-Comté grape brandy, then aged in wood. A sweet, deceptively strong *apéritif.*

Marc de Bourgogne One of the best of all French *marcs,* produced by distilling the mass of grape skins and pips left over after the wine-making process.

Verveine du Velay Pungent herbal liqueur from the Upper Loire.

CREME DE CASSIS

Crème de cassis is made by infusing blackcurrants in alcohol and sugar. The result is a concentrated fruit liqueur that contains 16–20 per cent alcohol, which is the base for making the favorite French *apéritif, kir,* named for Félix Kir, a mayor of Dijon.

In Burgundy, *kir* is usually made by mixing about one-third *crème de cassis* with two-thirds white Aligoté wine, but that proportion may be too sweet. Experiment for yourself (we find approximately a finger of *cassis* just about right).

Beaune

BURGUNDY'S WINE CAPITAL

BEAUNE IS ONE OF THE GREAT wine capitals of France. This small town in the center of the Côte d'Or, roughly dividing the Côte de Nuits from the Côte de Beaune, is seemingly devoted entirely to good living Burgundian-style. Wine-tasting (and buying) opportunities abound around every corner and down every lane; beautiful, exclusive shops offer not just wine but also crystal goblets, silver *tastevins,* and other wine accessories; there are scores of fine shops selling good things to eat, from puffy, cheesy *gougères* to *jambon persillé* and fruit-filled *pâtisseries;* and there is no shortage of restaurants offering the hearty, typical foods of Burgundy as well as more refined, inventive fare.

Beaune's most famous building, the Hôtel-Dieu, is itself inextricably linked to

Beaune's Hôtel-Dieu with its magnificent glazed tile roof

wine. As part of the Hospices de Beaune, founded in 1443 by Chancellor Nicolas Rolin as a hospital for the poor, it became through donations one of the most important vineyard proprietors in Burgundy, and so it remains today. Every year since 1859, the wines from these vineyards are auctioned to the public on the third Sunday in November, which marks the start of a great celebration known as *Les Trois Glorieuses.* This is, it is claimed, the greatest annual charity auction in the world.

Many who arrive in Beaune may feel overcome by an immediate thirst to sample Burgundy wines. The best place to go is the Marché aux Vins, located opposite the Hôtel-Dieu. This is run by a group of about a dozen *négociants-éleveurs* whose wines are on display. The entrance fee includes a *tastevin* you can keep, and then you simply wander through atmospheric, candlelit cellars sampling wines that include even exalted *premiers* and *grands crus.*

Wine lovers should also check with Beaune's Syndicat d'Initiative (tourist office) for details on wine happenings. Often, there are guided group tours of the cellars and vineyards as well as courses in wine tasting and appreciation on offer.

BEAUNE

Chez Félix
5, Rue Ziem
tel: 80 22 66 29
fax: 80 22 37 08
Bar à vins *serving a good range of Burgundies by the glass and simple Burgundian foods.*
$

Le Vigneron
6, Rue d'Alsace
21200 Beaune
tel: 80 22 68 21

Excellent shop for wine accessories.

Marché aux Vins
Rue Nicolas Rolin
tel: 80 22 27 69
fax: 80 22 75 72
Entrance fee includes taste-vin *for tasting wines.*

Patriarche Père & Fils
5, Rue du College
21200 Beaune
tel: 80 24 53 01
fax: 80 24 53 03

The largest cellars in Beaune. Guided tour includes opportunity to taste the wines.

Restaurant Le Jardin des Remparts
10, Rue de l'Hôtel-Dieu
tel: 80 24 79 41
fax: 80 24 92 79
Light, imaginative cooking in a pleasant garden just up from the Hôtel-Dieu.
$$$

The Côte d'Or

BURGUNDY'S FABLED GOLDEN SLOPE

THE CÔTE D'OR, possibly France's most famous stretch of vineyards, extends in a mainly north–south orientation from just below Dijon past Beaune to south of Santenay, a distance of about 50 km. (30 miles). The land is unprepossessing, never dramatic, the flanks of east-facing manicured vineyards gently sloping up towards the tops of the heavily wooded hills. Millions of visitors traveling along the A6 *autoroute* that leads to the South of France speed by without a second glance, never even realizing that they have passed the vineyards that produce some of the most prestigious and expensive wines in the world.

Fixin and its vineyards

Wine lovers, though, will certainly wish to drive along the so-called Route des Grands Crus that leads through tiny villages whose names are a familiar roll call from the pages of exclusive wine lists. Apart from viewing the well-tended vineyards at close hand, you can taste and buy wines as well as eat Burgundian foods in charming restaurants.

THE COTE DE NUITS —
LA ROUTE DES GRANDS CRUS

The Côte de Nuits (see map) begins just south of Dijon, virtually in its suburbs. Chenôve, Marsannay-la-Côte, and Fixin are the first three wine communes you come across. Chenôve has virtually been swallowed up by Dijon. Marsannay produces what many consider Burgundy's finest rosé wine. Fixin has a number of *premiers crus* vineyards.

The first great wine commune of note is Gevrey-Chambertin. The wines of *grand cru* Le Chambertin, Gevrey's most famous vineyard, were a favorite of Emperor Napoleon. Chambertin-Clos-de-Bèze is another magnificent *grand cru*. A further six *climats* (vineyards) are entitled to append the Chambertin name after (not before) their own. La Rôtisserie du Chambertin is a superlative restaurant in town right on the wine road, in an old wine *cave*.

From Gevrey, the Route des Grands Crus continues south for about 3 km. (1½ miles) to Morey-St.-Denis, a town whose vineyards, enclosed by dry-stone walls, indicate ecclesiastical origins. Indeed, a nunnery was established here in the seventh century, and, like the Cistercian brothers at Vougeot, the devoted sisters furthered the cause of medieval viticulture through the careful tending of such vineyards as the Clos de Tart, Clos St.-Denis, Clos de la Roche, and Clos des Lambrays.

Chambolle-Musigny, which comes next on the route, is a particularly pretty little hamlet. Nearby Vougeot is dominated by its great *clos,* the enclosed, walled monastic vineyard known as the Clos de Vougeot. The only producer actually located within the walled *clos* is the Château de La Tour, but no fewer than 70 growers and *négociants* own or control parcels of land here, all making and selling Clos de Vougeot AC wine. Undoubtedly, the vineyard is a great one, but it is not at all surprising to find that quality within the *appellation* can vary considerably.

The Château du Clos de Vougeot is an imposing medieval building where the Cistercian monks once undertook the vinification of their prestigious wines. Today, it is the property of the most famous wine fraternity in the world, the Confrérie des Chevaliers du Tastevin.

LA ROUTE
DES GRANDS
CRUS

DIJON

CHENOVE

MARSANNAY-
LA-COTE

FIXIN

GEVREY-CHAMBERTIN

MOREY-ST.-DENIS

CHAMBOLLE-
MUSIGNY

VOUGEOT

VOSNE-ROMANEE

NUITS-ST.-
GEORGES

COMBLANCHIEN

CORGOLOIN

Meuzin

N

0 km   2   4
0 miles   2

BEAUNE

come from this southern end of the Côte, notably from the Clos des Langres, an excellent and welcoming walled property at the very end of the Côte de Nuits. Beyond it begin the vineyards of the Côte de Beaune.

THE COTE DE BEAUNE

While the wines of the Côte de Nuits are almost exclusively classic red Burgundy from the Pinot Noir, the Côte de Beaune is the source of both outstanding reds and some of the most famous and finest of all white Burgundies, produced from Chardonnay grapes. North of Beaune, the first great wine commune of the Côte, Aloxe-Corton, epitomizes this: it is the only wine commune that boasts both red and white *grands crus* wines: Le Corton (mainly red) and Corton-Charlemagne (white). Aloxe-Corton's Château de Corton, with its characteristic particolored roof, is a source of both the *grands crus*.

Beaune itself is the single greatest wine commune of the Côte de Beaune, and the broad flank of vineyards that lie above the town produce a number of superlative *premiers crus*. One of the best chances for buying affordable Burgundies, mainly from the higher Hautes-Côtes (vineyards in the higher ground above the Côte de Nuits and Côte de Beaune), is the Cave des Hautes-Côtes, a well-regarded cooperative on the road to Pommard.

Pommard's wines are among the most loved of the Côte de Beaune: juicy, ripe,

Beyond Vougeot, the vineyards of Vosne-Romanée begin, a tiny wine hamlet with such a reputation that its wines rank among the finest, most expensive, and sought after in the world, especially those from the Domaine de la Romanée-Conti.

Nuits-St.-Georges is the largest town in the Côte de Nuits and it is home to a number of fine *négociants-éleveurs* and growers. In addition to wine, Nuits is the source of fine *crème de cassis*. Nuits-St.-Georges, the wine, represents the archetypal red wine of the Côte de Nuits, meaty, mouth-filling, rather hard, and powerful.

Below Nuits, the marble quarries at Comblanchien and Corgoloin take over from the vineyards, but some fine wines

Wine tasting in the cellars of Ropiteau Frères, Meursault

weighty, the Pinot Noir at its most seductive and rich. Pommard's Clos du Château is the largest *monopole* (vineyard owned by a single owner) in the Côte de Beaune, owned by the Château de Pommard. The cellars can be visited (for a charge), and its (expensive) wines tasted and purchased.

Neighboring Volnay produces red Burgundies which are considerably lighter, and usually more elegant if less powerful. Meursault, the largest town along this wine road, is the first great white wine commune. From Meursault, two other great white wine communes deserve to be visited, Puligny-Montrachet and Chassagne-Montrachet. Chassagne has a welcoming municipal *caveau* and Puligny a fine hotel-restaurant, Le Montrachet.

RECOMMENDED ADDRESSES

Caveau du Chapitre
1, Rue de Paris
21220 Gevrey-Chambertin
tel/fax: 80 51 82 82
Tasting caveau for a group of about seven producers who vinify and market their wines collectively. Good range of wines on offer.

Caveau Municipal de Chassagne-Montrachet
Centre Ville
21190 Chassagne-Montrachet
tel: 80 21 38 13
fax: 80 21 35 81
The caveau presents an excellent opportunity to taste and buy wines from Chassagne's individual growers.

Château de Corton-André
21420 Aloxe-Corton
tel: 80 26 44 25
fax: 80 26 43 57
Source of Aloxe's grands crus Corton and Corton-Charlemagne and other well-made wines.

Château de La Tour
Clos de Vougeot
21640 Vougeot
tel: 80 62 86 13
fax: 80 62 82 72

This is the only property that can claim that its wine is harvested, vinified, and bottled within the Clos de Vougeot.

Château de Meursault
21190 Meursault
tel: 80 21 22 98
fax: 80 21 66 77
Broad range of wines, including premiers crus. Entrance fee includes tastevin.

Château de Pommard
Route d'Autun
21630 Pommard
tel: 80 22 12 59
fax: 80 24 65 88
Charge for visit includes dégustation.

Hotel-Restaurant Le Montrachet
Place des Marronniers
21190 Puligny-Montrachet
tel: 80 21 30 06
fax: 80 21 39 06
Stylish classic and regional foods.
$$$

La Grande Cave
RN74
21640 Vougeot
tel: 80 62 87 13
fax: 80 62 82 46

On the main road, near the Clos de Vougeot, with extensive 17th-century cellars.

La Rôtisserie du Chambertin
Rue Chambertin
21220 Gevrey-Chambertin
tel: 80 34 33 20
fax: 80 34 12 30
Great regional restaurant in an elegant caveau. There is a small wine museum and their Le Bonbistrot at the back serves simpler foods at lower prices.
$$$$

Les Caves des Hautes-Côtes
Route de Pommard
21200 Beaune
tel: 80 24 63 12
fax: 80 22 87 05
Best cave coopérative in the Côte d'Or, with excellent, affordable Burgundies.

Ropiteau Frères
13, Rue du 11 Novembre
21190 Meursault
tel/fax: 80 21 24 73
fax: 80 21 20 57
Well-regarded négociant with particular expertise in fine white Burgundies.

Vichy
A SPA TOWN IN THE AUVERGNE

THE ROMANS, of course, were right; wherever hot thermal waters emerge naturally from the bowels of the earth, there are to be found centers of leisure, health, and relaxation. The Auvergne, on France's great central plateau, is riddled with the remains of long-extinct volcanoes, and intense thermal activity below the surface of the earth makes this little-visited region the richest source of natural thermal springs. The waters, high in natural bicarbonates and other minerals, are captured and bottled, and sold internationally (Vichy, St.-Yorre, Volvic, and others), and people still come to the region's numerous spa towns to drink the waters and to bathe in them.

Sources des Célestins, Vichy

Vichy is the Auvergne's most famous thermal spa. At the heart of Central France not far from Clermont-Ferrand, it was known as Aquis Caladis during Roman times, but gained most fame during its heyday from the 17th to the 19th centuries. In the 17th century, Madame de Sévigné, the brilliant woman of letters, extolled her *"cure vichyssoise,"* and a century later, the daughters of Louis XV spent the summer of 1785 in Vichy. Under Napoleon III, the Parc des Sources was established, and the beautiful wrought-iron arcades were added during the *belle époque* earlier this century. During World War II, Vichy became notorious as the seat of the much-hated German-backed Pétain government. Vichy today is a stylish, popular spa town, with fine recreational facilities, that is well worth visiting even if you are not in need of treatment.

Vichy's waters are considered particularly beneficial for those suffering from that peculiarly French malady, a *"crise de foie"* — a liver crisis that comes, we suppose, from overindulgence in rich *cuisine française*. Drinking Vichy waters in prescribed doses, together with bathing in the waters, thermal showers, massage, and a number of other related treatments are said to aid numerous problems relating to digestion. Moreover, bathing in the waters combined with a range of other treatments is also said to be beneficial for those suffering from rheumatic ailments.

A number of different Vichy waters emerge from individual, named sources, each with its own concentrated mineral makeup and curative properties. Anyone may enter the Halle des Sources and for a small fee sample all the waters: Parc, rich in calcium; Lucas, good for those suffering from allergies; Hôpital, quite pungent, with a high carbonic acid content; Grande Grille, most concentrated of all, to be sampled only under prescription. Remember, these are *eaux médicales* (medicinal waters) and should be sampled only in the tiniest quantity unless you know what you are doing. *Curistes* — those who have come to Vichy for a thermal cure — carry special glasses in wicker baskets and measure out medically prescribed doses. The only water that is safe to drink as table water is from the Source des Célestins, which has its own separate elegant tap house along the Avenue des Célestins. Here, you can sample and bottle the water for yourself (but taste it first, for its high mineral content makes it pretty unpalatable).

Apart from its famous water, Vichy is associated with two other specialties: *pastilles de Vichy,* mints rich in mineral salts sold from a kiosk in the center of the Parc des Sources, and *vichyssoise,* the leek and potato soup that we have never seen offered — hot or cold — in Vichy itself.

Bienvenue à l'Alpage

WELCOME TO THE HIGH PASTURES

IN WINTER, the high slopes of the French Alps provide some of Europe's best winter sports facilities, and resorts such as Megève, Chamonix, Flaine, and Albertville are internationally known. Summer, by contrast, provides tourists with superb, unspoiled, cool mountain country for trekking, climbing, cycling, and other outdoor pursuits.

Summer is the time, too, of the annual transhumance, when families and herds leave the valleys and climb into the *alpages* — high mountain pastures at between 1,000–2,000 m. (about 3,300–6,500 ft.) above sea level. Throughout the Savoie, *agriculteurs* still participate in this traditional migration. Indeed, it must bring great annual relief, after a long winter when the goats and cows do not leave their stalls for months at a time and the valleys are locked under snow.

Visitors, through a scheme known as *"bienvenue à l'alpage"* — "welcome to the high pastures" — can make mountain treks to isolated chalets where such outstanding cheeses as *reblochon* and *beaufort* are produced, to see how they are made, and to buy them direct, as well as to enjoy simple afternoon *goûters en alpage*

(farmhouse snacks consisting of hot drinks, cheeses, bread, and a dessert) or full meals of local specialties (generally cheese-based) served in *auberges d'alpage* (farmhouse restaurants located in the high slopes). Generally, you arrive at the *alpage* by foot, though, in some cases, you can take a cable car for part of the way. To our mind, there is little that can match the satisfaction of a rigorous mountain trek followed by an ample, informal snack or meal prepared by the *alpagistes* themselves. Remember: such places are usually open only during summer, and it is essential to telephone in advance.

Grazing in the high summer pastures of the Massif des Aravis

BIENVENUE A L'ALPAGE

AUBERGES D'ALPAGE
Alpage de Doran
Route de Doran
74700 Sallanches
tel: 50 58 27 13
Open in summer for lunches only; reserve the night before. Specialty: Tome de Savoie *and* chevrotin des Aravis *cheeses.*

Auberge d'Alpage de l'Airon
Route de Flaine
74300 Araches les Carroz
tel: 50 90 03 31

One of the best auberges d'alpage *for traditional mountain foods.*

Le Grand Montaz
74170 St.-Gervais
tel: 50 93 12 29
Specialty: steak au fromage.

Liliane et André Berthet
Charmy-l'Envers
74360 Abondance
tel: 50 73 02 79
Mme Berthet's specialty is berthoud *made with the local* abondance *cheese.*

GOUTERS EN ALPAGE
Au Coeur des Myrtilles
Le Petit Châtel (in Aug:
Alpage des Grands Plans)
Route de Bassachaux
74390 Châtel
tel: 50 73 27 59
Goûter *with fresh produce.*

Marie-Louise & Bernard Donzel
Alpage Les Corbassières
Massif de Beauregard
74220 La Clusaz
tel: 50 32 63 81
Hike up for an outstanding goûter *with hot chocolate.*

Les Bonnes Adresses

USEFUL ADDRESSES

BURGUNDY
Abbaye Notre-Dame de Cîteaux
Cîteaux
21700 St.-Nicolas-les-Cîteaux
tel: 80 61 11 53
Not much is left of the glory of Cîteaux, once the most powerful abbey in the world, but monks still live and work here, producing a good, tasty cheese.

Au Bon Accueil
La Montagne
21200 Beaune
tel: 80 22 08 80
fax: 80 22 93 12
Rustic country cooking outside town on a mountain overlooking the vineyards.
$

Cassis Védrenne
BP70 Zone Industrielle
21700 Nuits-St.-Georges
tel: 80 61 10 32
fax: 80 61 02 64
Source of one of the finest of all crème de cassis — go for the "supercassis," made with twice the amount of blackcurrants.

Caveau St.-Pierre
71260 Lugny
tel: 85 33 20 27
fax: 85 33 20 23
Located above the town, with splendid views, this welcoming caveau serves good foods and Lugny coop wines. You can purchase here at the same prices as at the coop.
$

Hostellerie des Clos
Rue Jules Rathier
89800 Chablis
tel: 86 42 10 63
fax: 86 42 17 11
This beautiful old hospice is a hotel with a first-class restaurant serving innovative cuisine. Great list of Chablis, including many wines by the glass.
$$$

Hotel-Restaurant Lameloise
36, Place d'Armes
71150 Chagny
tel: 85 87 08 85
fax: 85 87 03 57
One of the great restaurants of Burgundy, serving classic and innovative dishes.
$$$$

La Cave de Lugny
71260 Lugny
tel: 85 33 22 85
fax: 85 33 26 46
This immense cave coopérative in the heart of Mâconnais wine country is one of the most important in the country, and the source of well-made white, red, and sparkling wines.

La Chablisienne
8, Boulevard Pasteur
89800 Chablis
tel: 86 42 89 89
fax: 86 42 89 90
Chablis' cave coopérative is well run and the source of superlative white wines up to grand cru level.

Le Cellier Volnaysien
21190 Volnay
tel: 80 21 61 04
fax: 80 21 21 95
Simple restaurant serving good Burgundian foods and its own wines.
$

Kiosk in Vichy with the spa town's famous mints

Le Relais de la Diligence
23, Rue de la Gare
21190 Meursault
tel: 80 21 21 32
fax: 80 21 64 69
An old favorite, by the station, serving lots of different regional menus.
$$

Maison Mâconnaise des Vins
484, Avenue de Lattre de Tassigny
71000 Mâcon
tel: 85 38 36 70
fax: 85 38 62 51
Simple Mâconnais dishes are served in this large house by the river, together with a full range of Mâcon wines.
$

Restaurant Au Pouilly-Fuissé
71960 Fuissé
tel/fax: 85 35 60 68
An old favorite at the heart of the finest vineyards of the Mâconnais, source of exquisite Pouilly-Fuissé. Restaurant serves cuisine au vin using local products.
$-$$

Rôtisserie de la Paix
47, Rue du Faubourg Madeleine
21200 Beaune
tel: 80 22 33 33
fax: 80 22 84 39
Just outside the center of Beaune; serves Burgundian classics and meats grilled over a wood fire.

LYON AND HINTERLAND
(see also p.177)
Brasserie-Rôtisserie Le Nord
18, Rue Neuve
69002 Lyon
tel: 78 28 24 54
fax: 78 28 76 58
Paul Bocuse's new restaurant serves classic brasserie foods.
$$

La Pyramide
14, Boulevard Fernand Point
38200 Vienne
tel: 74 53 01 96
fax: 74 85 69 73
Earlier this century, this was one of the most influential restaurants in France, and, under the tutelage of the great Fernand Point, the inspiration for a whole generation of super-star chefs. Come here to pay homage as well as to sample brilliant, modern cuisine of the highest order.
$$$$

Pâtisserie-Chocolaterie Bernachon
42, Cours Franklin Roosevelt
69006 Lyon
tel: 78 24 37 98
fax: 78 52 67 77
A must for lovers of the finest pâtisseries and hand-made chocolates.

Troisgros
Place de la Gare
42300 Roanne
tel: 77 71 66 97
fax: 77 70 39 77
One of the great restaurants of France, just west of Lyon in the Upper Loire.
$$$$

FRANCHE-COMTE, SAVOIE, AND DAUPHINE
Chocolaterie-Confiserie Bernard Laurent
6, Rue du Lac
74000 Annecy
tel: 50 45 04 70
Don't leave Annecy without sampling Laurent's roseaux du lac — exquisite chocolate batons filled with espresso coffee.

Coopérative Fromagerie d'Arbois
Rue des Fosses
39600 Arbois
tel: 84 66 09 71

Rosettes *over the bar at the Café des Fédérations (see p.177)*

Come here early to watch cheesemaking.

Fromagerie Coopérative du Beaufortain
73270 Beaufort-sur-Doron
tel: 79 38 33 62
fax: 79 38 33 40
Source of genuine beaufort d'alpage (best is aged for upward of 12 months) and other cheeses and local specialties.

Henri Maire S.A.
Aux Deux Tonneaux
Place de la Liberté
39600 Arbois
tel: 84 66 15 27
Henri Maire is the most important private producer of Arbois wines. Film, tasting, and guided tour of wine country.

Hôtel Les Célestins — Restaurant L'Empereur
111, Boulevard des Etats-Unis
03200 Vichy
tel: 70 30 82 00
fax: 70 30 82 01
Vichy's most chic modern hotel has its own spa center; its restaurant is probably the best and most stylish in town.
$$$$

La Cave de la Ferme
Rue du Grand Pont
74270 Frangy
tel: 50 44 75 04

Frangy is famous for its Roussette wine: come here to taste a fine, home-grown example together with Savoie foods.
$

La Finette Taverne Arbois
22, Ave Pasteur
39600 Arbois
tel: 84 66 06 78
Mountain foods and wines of Jura.
$

Le Clos des Sens
13, Rue Jean-Mermoz
74940 Annecy-le-Vieux
tel: 50 23 07 90
fax: 50 66 56 54
Probably the best restaurant in town, with a pleasant shaded terrace. Imaginative, creative foods.
$$$

Les Caves de la Chartreuse
10, Boulevard Edgar-Kofler
38500 Voiron
tel: 76 05 81 77
fax: 76 66 19 35
Reputed to be the most beautiful and extensive caves à liqueur in the world.

Le Tuyé "Papy Gaby"
25650 Gilley
tel: 81 43 33 03
fax: 81 43 30 26
All the cured meat products of Franche-Comté.

BEST BUYS
• Lyonnais *charcuterie* (vacuum-packed *rosette, Jésus)*
• Vichy *pastilles*
• Bags of *lentilles vertes du Puy* (Auvergne but available everywhere)
• wines from Burgundy and the Northern Rhône
• cheeses from Savoie, Franche-Comté, and the Auvergne
• *crème de cassis* (Dijon)
• *moutarde de Dijon*
• *pain d'épice* (Dijon)

The South

LANGUEDOC-
ROUSSILLON

PROVENCE AND THE
COTE D'AZUR

CORSICA

THE SOUTH OF FRANCE: how the very phrase transports us to sun, sea, and azure skies; to walks in mountains and across the scrubby limestone plateaus, *garrigues,* alive with the clicking of a thousand cicadas; to the noise, color, scents, and excitement of endless outdoor street markets; to hours wasted watching and sometimes playing that laziest yet most serious of games, *pétanque,* under the dappled shade of plane trees; to the keen anticipation of an appetite-whetting *pastis,* the anise drink made cloudy by an ice cube or just a dash of tap water; and to dreams of the intense and direct flavors of its *cuisine du soleil,* its sun-ripened foods and wine that are among the most appealing and delicious on earth.

THE MIDI — LAND OF THE MIDDAY SUN
The South of France is known as the Midi, the land of the midday sun, where, in high summer, it is often far too hot to even think about doing anything. At such times, the locals retire to bed after lengthy, garlic-laden midday repasts; shops close their faded and peeling shutters to the world, only to reopen again in the late afternoon when it is cooler and there is a breath of fresh air; and the thousands of visitors (French and foreign alike) head for beaches to lie down like so many sardines side by side and roast in the coruscating afternoon heat.

Sunflower fields in Provence

Yet, the South of France, unlike Southern Italy or Southern Spain, is not a torpid land of *"demain,"* where everything only happens tomorrow, if even then. Away from the fashionable resorts of the Côte d'Azur, the enormous yachts and motor cruisers bobbing up and down in ports and harbors, one senses a new energy at work. Along the fertile littoral, in isolated upland farms, or in vineyards planted since Roman days, locals as well as newcomers diligently set about providing a wealth of fine and sometimes innovative produce and products alongside the traditional. The local wine industry, long considered the source of only bulk wines, is being transformed, as new ideas and new technologies have shown that the South of France can compete in quality and price with offerings from classic and New World wine regions.

LANGUEDOC-ROUSSILLON

Extending along the northern Mediterranean shore from the Spanish frontier as far as the mouth of the Rhône, Languedoc-Roussillon is an area that has always stood apart from the rest of France. The very name, Languedoc, indicates its separateness: this was where the *langue d'oc* (the language of *oc,* the word for yes) or *occitan,* was spoken, whereas the *langue d'oïl* (the language that had *oïl* — the precursor of modern *oui* — for yes) came to dominate the rest of France. Roussillon itself once formed part of a Catalan kingdom whose influence extended throughout much of Northern Spain and the Balearic Islands.

Today, Languedoc and Roussillon are linked administratively and politically, though each retains its own character. Tourism and development may have come to coastal areas, but this is not the fashionable or chic Mediterranean encountered farther east. Cities such as Toulouse, Narbonne, Montpellier, and Béziers all have a no–nonsense and hard–working attitude; rugby is the favorite sport and *pieds-noirs* (French nationals born in Algeria) and immigrants from North Africa have settled in search of a better life. Here, robustly satisfying foods, such as *cassoulet* (the great beanfeast of the Midi), couscous (a North African staple that has been adopted by the French), or *gardiane* (bull stewed in red wine and olives) are the order of the day.

PROVENCE AND THE COTE D'AZUR

Between mid-July and mid-August, Provence and the Côte d'Azur heave with humanity. Not only does half of France descend *"plein sud"* (straight down to the South) by Bastille Day, July 14, the traditional start of the French summer break, but also much of Northern Europe — British, German, Scandinavian, Dutch, and Belgian — arrives here, all in search of sun, sea, and the glamor of Europe's most popular playground.

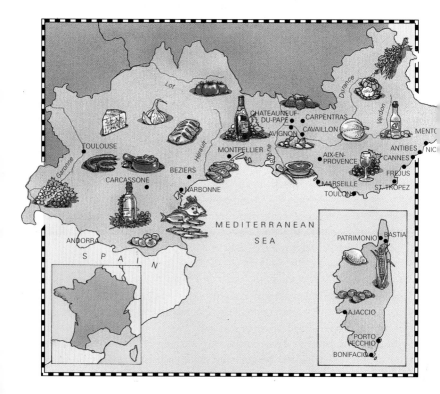

Houses shuttered and shaded from the midday sun in the South of France

But even at its busiest, away from hot spots such as Antibes, Cannes, Menton, Fréjus, St.-Tropez, anywhere even just a few miles inland, lies another, genuinely French, but no less vivid world. The climate, the quality of brilliant sunlight (even in winter), the relaxed, outdoor way of life, the reminders of ancient history, the landscapes and colors straight from a canvas by Cézanne or Van Gogh (to witness sunflowers in Provence is to experience nature imitating art), and, not least, the intense flavors of its foods and wines: all these can combine to create rare and memorable experiences.

CORSICA — "*ILE DE BEAUTE*" OR BEAUTIFUL ISLAND

The third largest island in the Mediterranean (after Sicily and Sardinia), Corsica lies some 170 km. (105 miles) south of the mainland, a harshly beautiful, mountainous, mainly wooded land carved by gorges and covered by its characteristic *maquis,* a dense scrub brush of myrtle, heather, and sweet smelling herbs. In many ways, Corsica is closer to Italy than to France, geographically, just a stone's throw from Sardinia. Though French is widely spoken, most inhabitants speak Corsican, a dialect closely related to Italian. This rugged island, still largely undiscovered, presents an island cuisine that is distinctive and robust, based on superb fish and shellfish and rustic ingredients such as goat and mutton. It also has excellent *charcuterie* derived from Italian traditions, and a range of cheeses made from ewe's and goat's milk.

THE MEDITERRANEAN — SOURCE AND INSPIRATION

Languedoc-Roussillon, Provence, the Côte d'Azur, and Corsica are united by the Mediterranean, which exudes its influence on all the lands its waters lap. These regions certainly have their own individual character, traditions, and identity, but they are merely variations on a subtly changing, always beautiful theme that runs elsewhere from the Straits of Gibraltar to the Bosporus. The Midi is Mediterranean France, a far cry from Paris and the gray North, from the western and northwestern coasts with their cold North Atlantic waters, and from the alpine mountain ranges of the landlocked East. At times, the Midi seems more a dream than reality, glimpsed in the mind's eye through a curtain of mist or dull rain, vividly reappearing through memories and re-creations of its rich and flavorful cuisine. It is, above all, a place we return to forever and again for what the poet Keats so poignantly expressed: "Provençal song, and sunburned mirth … a beaker full of the warm South."

Les Produits Régionaux
REGIONAL PRODUCE

PROVENCE IS THE LAND of mild, sweet garlic, of the best French *huile d'olive extra vierge* (extra-virgin olive oil), of Mediterranean vegetables such as *aubergines* (eggplants), *courgettes* (zucchini), *tomates* (tomatoes), *poivrons* (bell peppers), and *oignons* (onions), and of nuts, wild mushrooms, and pungent, aromatic herbs, gathered in the scrubby upland *garrigues*. Much of this bountiful, sun-soaked produce forms the mainstay of the Mediterranean diet, French-style.

Fruits ripen almost all year round, starting in the new year with an early

Apricots from Roussillon, small but concentrated in flavor and scent

crop of citrus fruits and *kiwi*, followed by early ripening *fraises* (strawberries), then a glorious summer procession of first *cerises* (cherries), then *abricots* (apricots), *pêches* (peaches), *brugnons* (nectarines), *melons* (melons), *poires* (pears), and *prunes* (plums). Fall brings a new harvest of *pommes* (apples), *raisins* (grapes), and *châtaignes* (chestnuts). During this annual and abundant glut, such fruits have traditionally been conserved in sugar into beautifully glazed *fruits confits* (see p.226).

Languedoc-Roussillon's most distinctive feature agriculturally is its vines that spread almost as far as the eye can see across the interior of the region. Other crops too are grown here, not just table grapes and those for wine. The best garlic in France, it is generally agreed, is the *ail rose* from the Tarn *département*. This pink variety is mild in flavor and also particularly hard and so can be conserved when hung in a cool, dry spot for upward of several months (purchase a string or two to take home). The Languedoc is a great region for vegetables, and a similar crop is cultivated here as in Provence,

---

LES HERBES DE PROVENCE

Locally grown herbs give life and character to Provence's *cuisine du soleil*, its foods of the sun.

The best are gathered wild from upland *garrigues*, and walkers will know that the *sentiers* (footpaths) of the Alpilles and those that lead to the summit of Mont Ste.-Victoire are indeed covered with bush-sized plants of *thym* (wild thyme), *romarin* (rosemary), and *lavande* (lavender), the source of exceptional honey, and whose flowers are used mainly for perfume. Peppery, small-leaved *basilic* (basil) is essential to the Provençal favorite, *pistou*, the pounded basil and garlic paste similar to Genoese *pesto*, while *sarriette* (summer savory) is

another characteristic flavor and *verveine* (verbena) is popular as a *tisane*, an infusion taken instead of tea.

The rather anonymous dried mix sold as *herbes de provence* in markets is good only if the herbs are reasonably fresh and still retain their essential aromatic oils. Rub a bit between your fingers then smell, before buying.

Cavaillon melons, considered among the finest, sweetest, and most perfumed in France

sometimes on a large commercial scale (even under plastic tunnels) to be sold to the markets of Northern France and Europe. Around the fertile mouth of the Rhône, especially in the marshes of the Camargue, rice is grown extensively.

Inland, in the rugged Cévennes or in the hinterland between Toulouse and Albi, flocks of sheep graze on the limestone plateaus, their milk transformed into some of France's greatest ewe's milk cheeses, including the magnificent *roquefort.* Elsewhere, wide stretches of land are given over to the cultivation of grains, including wheat and corn, the latter to be made into *millas,* a sort of cornmeal mush similar to Italian *polenta.*

Corsica's harsh, mainly mountainous terrain has never made life easy for its inhabitants. For long, one of its most important staples was the chestnut, its flour used to make a range of local breads and cakes. Today, wheat and corn and a good range of fruits and vegetables are grown on reclaimed lower grounds that were once a breeding place for malaria spreading mosquitoes.

MESCLUM

Mesclum is the most fashionable salad in France, a marvelous mixture of at least half a dozen different tender, young lettuce leaves and herbs, grown and gathered separately, then mixed and sold as a *mélange.* Varieties may include (depending on the season) arugula, oak leaf lettuce, curly endive, *mâche* (known also as corn salad), the red-leaved *radicchio,* and sprigs of basil or tender dandelion leaves. Sold in markets by the 100 g. (3½ oz.), no more than a generous handful, *mesclum* is rightly considered a delicacy, and, when dressed with fine *huile d'olive extra vierge* and just a dash of wine vinegar, can be one of the finest salads in the world.

IN SEASON

Abricot Apricot; the best is the *rouge du Roussillon,* small and intensely flavored (Jun–Jul).

Ail rose Pink garlic from the Tarn (Jul–Aug, but available throughout the fall).

Asperge Both white and green asparagus are available from late spring to early summer (Apr–Jun).

Mesclum, *a delicious mix of tender salad leaves*

Aubergine Eggplant, one of the most characteristic and delicious of all vegetables of the South (summer).

Fraises Strawberries from the Bouches-du-Rhône and Carpentras (Apr–May).

Melon Ogen melon; the best comes from Cavaillon (Jun–Sep).

Pêche Peach, especially the white variety from the Bouches-du-Rhône (Jun–Sep).

Poivron Red, green, and yellow bell pepper (summer).

Raisins Table grapes (Aug–Nov).

Tomate Vine-ripened tomatoes with the intense flavor that only the Mediterranean sun can produce (Jun–Sep).

Les Olives et l'Huile d'Olive Extra Vierge
OLIVES AND EXTRA-VIRGIN OLIVE OIL

THE OLIVE TREE IS the single most characteristic feature of Mediterranean France. These tenacious trees seem to grow where other plants fail, and, for centuries, their fruit, the olive, has been harvested both for its *huile d'olive* (olive oil) and for eating.

Olive trees in the Vallée des Baux, source of some of the best olives and olive oils in France

Olive oil, especially extra-virgin olive oil, is probably the most important element of the Mediterranean diet. The finest oils are produced by traditional methods: the olives harvested, crushed by granite millstones, then pressed only once to extract both olive oil and vegetable water that is subsequently separated, usually by means of a centrifuge. This is *huile d'olive extra vierge,* the best quality, containing the lowest oleic acidity, which is guaranteed to be no more than one per cent. *Vierge fine* can also be good, containing up to 1½ per cent oleic acidity.

The arrival of each year's new oil is an event of importance equal to the arrival of the new wine. If you are in the South of France in December or January, visit an olive oil mill and taste and buy direct.

The range of olives on display in any southern market throughout the year is quite remarkable. Both green and black olives (black are fully ripe) must be treated before they are edible, by soaking either in caustic soda or brine. Our favorite olives are the *olives cassées* from Les Baux-de-Provence, fresh, new-season olives that are split and still vividly green, firmly toothsome, and deliciously bitter. But they last only a few months, so try to enjoy them in October or November. *Picholines du Gard,* flavored with fennel, are also excellent and last well so they can be taken home in jars. The mahogany-brown olives of Nyons are delicious, while the small, shiny black olives of Nice add an almost nutty taste to dishes such as *salade niçoise.* Olives are given added treatments, infused with chilies or garlic, flavored with spices and herbs, or pitted then stuffed with anchovies or pieces of bell pepper. Ground into a paste as *tapénade,* they make a delicious spread to enjoy on crusty bread.

Our favorite olive mill for both oil and olives is:

Coopérative Oléicole de la Vallée des Baux
Rue Charloun-Rieu
13520 Maussane-les-Alpilles
tel: 90 54 32 37
fax: 90 54 30 28

Black olives marinated in herbes de Provence

Olives à trois épices, *with fennel, coriander, and thyme*

Olives marinated in lemon juice with pieces of lemon

Les Marchés
MARKETS

PROVENCE AND THE COTE D'AZUR

Aix-en-Provence	Tue, Thu, Sat
Antibes	Tue–Sun
Apt	Sat
Arles	Sat
Avignon	Sat
Banon	Tue
Bonnieux	Fri
Cagnes-sur-Mer	Fri
Cannes	Tue–Sun
Carpentras	Fri
Cassis	Wed, Fri
Cavaillon	Mon
Châteauneuf-du-Pape	Fri
Fontvieille	Mon, Fri
Gigondas	Wed
Grasse	Tue–Sat
L'Isle-sur-la-Sorgue	Sun
Lambesc	Fri
Marseillan	Tue
Maussane-les-Alpilles	Thu
Menton	daily
Montélimar	Wed, Thu
Nice	Tue–Sun
Nyons	Thu
Orange	Thu, Fri
St.-Rémy-de-Provence	Wed, Sat
St.-Tropez	Tue, Sat
Salon-de-Provence	Wed
Vaison-la-Romaine	Tue
Vence	Fri

LANGUEDOC-ROUSSILLON

Aigues-Mortes	Wed, Sun
Banyuls-sur-Mer	Sun
Béziers	Fri
Carcassonne	Sat
Castelnaudary	Mon
Collioure	Wed, Sun
Frontignan	Thu
Le Grau-de-Roi	Tue, Sat
Lézignan-Corbières	Wed
Montpellier	Mon–Sat
Narbonne	Thu
Nîmes	Fri
Perpignan	daily
St. Cyprien-Plage	Fri
Sète	Wed

CORSICA

Ajaccio	daily
Bastia	Tue–Sun
Bonifacio	Wed
Calvi	daily

FETES ET FOIRES
FESTIVALS AND FAIRS
PROVENCE AND THE COTE D'AZUR

Alicoque: *Fête de l'huile nouvelle (new olive oil)*   Feb

Hyères: *Foire à l'ail (garlic)*   end Aug

Menton: *Fête du citron (lemons)   Mardi Gras (Shrove Tue)*

Nyons: *Fête de l'huile d'olive nouveau (new olive oil)*   end Jan

LANGUEDOC-ROUSSILLON

Bonnieux: *Fête de la Soupe au pistou (basil soup)*   Jun

Fitou: *Fête du Cru Fitou (Fitou wine)*   1st week Aug

Lautrec: *Foire à l'ail (garlic)*   mid Aug

Perpignan: *Foire au miel (honey)*   Sat in Oct

Rivesaltes: *Fête de l'abricot (apricots)*   mid-Jul

Lazing away the hours with a game of pétanque *in the Midi*

Au Marché en Provence

THE COLORFUL MARKETS OF PROVENCE

THE MARKETS OF Provence are undoubtedly one of the highlights of any visit to the South of France. In big cities and in small towns, they remain a focus of local life, a weekly event that is eagerly looked forward to, almost a social event, providing the opportunity for people not just to buy good food but to see and be seen, to haggle with the market stallholders, and to be in touch with the changing seasons. The French, as much as any nation in Europe, have embraced the concept of one-stop shopping in *hypermarchés* (great superstores) but *non,* never (or only under rare and unusual circumstances) on local market days.

Fresh figs at a market stall, to be eaten or conserved

Zucchini flowers, delicious stuffed, coated in batter, and deep fried

Visiting any of the markets of Provence provides a wonderful assault on the senses. The colors of the striped

Shopping for lunch outdoors, one of the pleasures of Provence

awnings and sunshades clash with the bright hues of the fruits and vegetables on display, made vivid under a sun that shines brightly on most days of the year. The sweet, honeyed perfume of ripe and overripe melons and strawberries overlayered by the savory scent from a bank of revolving *poulets rôtis* (spit-roasting chickens) and the sea-fresh aromas from a stall of fish and shellfish cannot help but whet the appetite in anticipation of the midday meal. The noise and activity of the stallholders, haranguing you demonically but in a friendly fashion, urging you to buy, all in their quick, persuasive, Italianate Provençal accents; the feel of enormous, taut-bellied *aubergines,* firm, tight heads of fat garlic, and furry, fresh-off-the-tree *pêches* (peaches); the taste of briny *olives aromatisées* (infused with sprigs of fennel), or a nugget of hard, pungent goat's cheese, a morsel of *saucisson* preferred as an enticement to buy as you stroll past: all these and more are part of the rich and satisfying sensuous experiences of going to market in Provence.

Of course, it makes perfect sense for visitors to shop in markets if they have access to cooking facilities (even a one-ring stove or the tiniest camp cooker), for it allows them to *profiter* (benefit) from the wide variety and invariably inexpensive seasonal foods at their disposal. This is the greatest lesson of going to market: the produce on sale, good, ripe, and fresh, comes from local sources and is available only seasonally. Those delicious, dark red, intensely flavored *fraises de Carpentras* that we enjoyed last week may

The immense range of olives on offer everywhere

jars of local honey and artisan-made *confitures* (jams), bottles of green extra-virgin *huile d'olive* and vinegars infused with *herbes de Provence*. When we're in Provence, we eat fresh fruit until it comes out our ears and buy vegetables by the kilo, enjoying them raw, grilled over charcoal, or stewed in olive oil.

Meat? Who needs it? But we can rarely resist passing by a fish stall offering a selection of *poissons des roches* (rock fish) to throw into the pot together with sprigs of fennel and a half bottle or so of wine to make a concentrated fish soup, or great slabs of *thon rouge* (bluefin tuna) to rub with garlic and grill like steak.

And we can never resist the stall selling beautiful Provençal table linen: table-cloths and napkins are among the best, and most easily packed, gifts to take home.

Even the smallest local markets are excellent anywhere in Provence. It may be useful to remember that the market traders move on from neighboring town to town on the different days of the week. So if that cheesemonger sold you a *banon* cheese that was overly ripe on Monday, chase him down in the next town on Wednesday and let him know. Do, also, try to visit at least one of the region's great markets, such as those at Arles, Aix-en-Provence, Antibes, Avignon, Carpentras, Cavaillon, St.-Rémy-de-Provence, Cannes, and Nice — truly an experience in itself.

now be gone; not to worry, in their place we can enjoy instead the first ripe, oozing melons from Cavaillon, the delicious *rouges du Roussillon* apricots from just down the coast. Indeed, for those of us who have become mainly used to shopping in supermarkets where we can find strawberries or asparagus all year round, it is wonderful to rediscover the enjoyment of seasonal foods.

What to buy in the markets of Provence? For picnics, we purchase ready-to-eat or already prepared foods to take with us to the beach or for long walks in the mountains or hill country, for Provence is truly a land where outdoor eating is a way of life. Thus, we pause at the stall selling a range of home-baked breads and purchase a twisted *fougasse* or two, that unique regional bread, almost a meal in itself, studded with *grattons* (crunchy bits of meat) or olives, then pick up a meaty, chewy *saucisson d'Arles,* and a couple of hard, pungent disks of *fromage de chèvre* (goat's cheese), a tub of mixed olives, or one of the aforementioned *poulets rôtis.* Purchase

Pots of pungent, small-leaf basil, one of the many fresh Provençal herbs

Les Spécialités
REGIONAL SPECIALTIES

Foods of the sun — *cuisine du soleil* — are the essence of the cooking and local and regional specialties of the South of France. Yet there are considerable variations reflecting the separate cultures and histories of the regions and smaller areas.

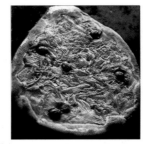
Pissaladière, *the Provençal* pizza

Roussillon, for example, bordering the frontier with Spain, still maintains its strong Catalan heritage, and this is reflected in its exuberant foods. The love of anchovies, fresh, semi-conserved, or salted, is a taste shared with its Spanish neighbors, and *paella* is a favorite fast food of the region, which also has a penchant for strong, sweet, fortified wines — *vins doux naturels* — that are exactly similar in style to the old-style *vinos rancios* of Catalonia.

The foods of Languedoc reflect the influences of both mountain and sea. The region's most famous dish, *cassoulet* (see p.218), is a hearty winter warmer from inland Castelnaudary, Toulouse, and Carcassonne, and the last thing on earth you would care to eat in the heat of mid-summer. By contrast, the coastal areas, especially around *étangs* — shallow saltwater lakes separated from the sea — are the source of fine shellfish, including oysters and mussels, so such sea-fresh and other summer foods satisfy appetites made keen from lazy days in the sun.

Provençal cuisine has a rich style of its own which has now extended well beyond the borders of the region itself and embraces many elements considered essential to the Mediterranean diet. Extra-virgin olive oil and the excellent seasonal produce combine with local meat and fish — lamb from the Alpilles, Mediterranean fish and shellfish — to result in one of the most colorful and tasty of all French regional cuisines. On the other hand, the proximity to Italy's Liguria is evident along the Côte d'Azur, in the love of dishes such as *pissaladière* (a sort of French *pizza*), *pistou* (the same pungent basil and garlic sauce as Ligurian *pesto*), and that favorite of Nice, *la socca,* a fast-food pancake equally loved in Genoa, where it is known as *farinata.*

Corsica also demonstrates its proximity to Italy and Sardinia. *Stufatu,* a hearty beef stew, is served with *macaroni* on the side, *polenta,* the cornmeal mush of Northeast Italy, is much loved, and the *charcuterie* is influenced more by Italian prototypes than French.

But many of the best foods encountered in the South of France may not be precise regional or local specialties; rather, they are dishes that use the superb produce and products of the region in both traditional and imaginative ways.

APPETIZERS, BREADS, AND FIRST COURSES

Aïgo bouïdo (Languedoc and Provence) Garlic and bread soup; sometimes topped with a poached egg.

Anchoïade (Provence and Corsica) Pungent mixture of anchovies, olive oil, olives, and lots of chopped garlic, served as a dip with raw vegetables or spread onto toasted bread.

Anchois de Collioure et poivrons rouges (Roussillon) Platter of *anchois*

Paella

Anchois de Collioure *with roasted peppers: a classic*

de Collioure (see p.221) laid out like the spokes of a wheel with strips of roasted red bell pepper, topped with *vinaigrette,* chopped parsley, and quartered or chopped hard-boiled eggs.

Anchois frais au vinaigre de Banyuls (Roussillon)   Fresh, boned anchovy fillets lightly cured in a vinegar made from rich Banyuls wine.

Brandade de morue (Languedoc)   Creamy emulsion made from soaked and boiled salt cod beaten together with olive oil, garlic, and milk or cream.

Cargolade (Roussillon) Snails gathered locally, grilled over charcoal or stewed in white or red wine.

Escargots à la languedocienne (Languedoc) ·   Tasty snails gathered from the *garrigues,* cooked in a piquant, crunchy sauce of tomatoes, anchovies, and finely chopped walnuts.

Fougasse (Languedoc)   Characteristic flat bread cut into a sort of skeleton lace pattern; usually made with olive oil, and often topped with ingredients such as *grattons* (crunchy bits of meat), *olives* (olives), or *anchois* (anchovies). At Christmas, especially in Marseilles, *fougasse à l'anis* is made using anise seeds and local *pastis*.

Anchoïade

Huîtres du Bassin de Thau (Languedoc)   Some of the finest French oysters (*gigas* or *creuses* varieties) come from Languedoc's Bassin de Thau. Enjoy them raw or hot, covered in bread crumbs and lemon juice, then briefly baked.

Michette antiboise (Antibes)   Small, flat bread with fillings such as anchovies, tuna, *ratatouille, pistou, roquefort,* and olives; specialty of Antibes.

Moules à la catalane (Roussillon) Mussels, steamed and served in a tomato and bell pepper sauce.

Pan bagnat (Provence)   Special rolls or loaves are baked for this Provençal specialty: the bread is split then soaked in extra-virgin olive oil and piled with a salad of lettuce, onions, anchovies, olives, and bell peppers, then dressed in *vinaigrette.*

Pissaladière (Provence)   Provençal *pizza,* a flat yeast dough topped with plenty of sliced onions stewed in olive oil, black olives, and anchovies. Good hot or cold.

Ravioli à la niçoise (Nice and all Provence) The proximity to Italy means that fresh *pasta* is characteristic of the Côte d'Azur. *Ravioli* stuffed with spinach and cheese, or with meat, is common; usually served with tomato sauce.

Salade niçoise (Provence)   Like many dishes that have become internationalized, it is something of a pleasant surprise to enjoy the real thing *in situ,* a simply delicious salad usually made with lettuce, boiled green beans, hard-boiled eggs, boiled potatoes, anchovy fillets, tomatoes, and sometimes tuna.

Socca (Nice)   The classic street food of Nice, something like a thick batter pancake made from chickpea flour, cooked in an extremely hot oven, seasoned liberally with black pepper, and served piping hot.

Soupe au pistou (Provence)   Soup made with seasonal vegetables such as zucchini, green beans, tomatoes, carrots, potatoes, dried haricot beans, and vermicelli noodles, served with a dollop or more of *pistou,* a sauce of small-leaved basil, garlic, extra-virgin olive oil, and pine nuts, added at the end: summer fare.

Socca, *Nice's favorite fast food*

Soupe de poissons (Provence)   The rich, pureed fish soup flavored with tomato and saffron may even today be encountered in the North of France (made from different Atlantic varieties of fish), but this classic is still best in Provence, where it is made with small, bony Mediterranean *poissons des roches* (rockfish). The soup is served always with toasted rounds of bread or fried *croûtons, rouille,* a fiery mayonnaise made with red chilies, and plenty of grated *gruyère* cheese. You can either spread the *rouille* onto the bread, then ladle the soup over it, or you can add the bread or *croûtons* to the soup, stir in a dollop of *rouille,* then pile on the cheese.

Agneau à la ficelle, *lamb from the Alpilles hung on a string in front of a wood fire*

Tapénade (Languedoc and Provence)   Coarse paste made from chopped black olives, capers, anchovies, and olive oil — delicious spread onto toasted bread or mixed with hard-boiled egg yolks, then stuffed into the whites to make *oeufs durs farcis à la tapénade*.

Tellines persillés (Camargue and Languedoc Coast) Tiny, smooth-shelled clams cooked in olive oil with garlic and plenty of finely chopped parsley.

MAIN COURSES

Agneau à la ficelle (Provence)   Some of the tastiest lamb in France comes from the Alpilles, where it is fed on wild herbs and grasses. In this simple preparation, small legs are hung by the shank with a piece of string and roasted in front of a wood fire.

Aïoli (Languedoc and Provence)   A pungent mayonnaise made with plenty of crushed garlic. The name also refers to a complete meal consisting of a platter of boiled vegetables, poached salt cod, hard-boiled eggs, perhaps even snails, served with *aïoli*.

Bouillabaisse (Provence)   The classic and famous fish soup/stew of Provence, an expensive but delicious delicacy (see p.222).

Bourride (Languedoc)   Languedoc's answer to Provençal *bouillabaisse:* a substantial fish soup/stew made with firm-fleshed white fish, such as conger eel, sea bass, whiting, or bream, poached in a concentrated fish stock with plenty of garlic, and thickened toward the end with *aïoli*.

Cassoulet (Languedoc)   Great regional specialty of boiled haricot beans cooked with pork, sausages, mutton, and preserved duck or goose (see p.218).

Civet de lapin (Provence and Languedoc)   Wild rabbit stewed in red wine and herbs, the sauce thickened at the end with the blood of the rabbit.

Couscous (Languedoc)　North African classic of steamed semolina served with a spicy lamb or fish stew on top.

Daube de boeuf à la provençale (Provence)　Beef stew marinated in red wine with garlic, vegetables, and orange rind, then slowly cooked and flavored with an anchovy puree.

Gardiane de taureau (Camargue) Something of a specialty in this bull-raising country: rather tough bull meat, marinated in wine, then slowly stewed with olives in a rich, thick sauce, and served always with *riz de Camargue,* rice from the surrounding paddies.

Gardiane de taureau – *beef stewed with olives and wine, a specialty of the Camargue*

Paella (Roussillon)　Spanish-inspired rice and shellfish dish usually cooked outdoors in immense flat pans. Often available in markets and from stands to take away ready to eat.

Pebronata (Corsica)　Kid stewed in wine with bell peppers and tomatoes; a classic dish of inland Corsica.

Pieds et paquets (Marseilles and all Provence)　Little "packets" of lamb's or mutton tripe cooked with lamb's feet together with garlic, wine, tomatoes, and *petit salé* (cured, unsmoked pork) until tender, thick, and gooey — a delicious classic not to be missed.

Stufatu (Corsica)　Rich stew made from beef or occasionally *sanglier* (wild boar) slowly cooked in wine and tomatoes until thick. The rich sauce can be served over *pasta* as a starter or with the meat as a main course.

VEGETABLES AND VEGETARIAN DISHES

Aubergines à la provençale (Provence)　Char-grilled eggplant served with tomato and basil sauce.

Bohémienne (Camargue and Languedoc)　Chunks of eggplant with plenty of sliced garlic slowly stewed in olive oil until almost caramelized, then mixed with tomatoes and extra-virgin olive oil, and eaten tepid.

Fleurs de courgette farcies (Provence and Languedoc)　Zucchini flowers filled with a mixture of pureed zucchini and herbs, dipped in batter, and deep fried.

Légumes grillés à l'huile d'olive (Provence and Languedoc)　Mixed vegetables — slices of eggplant, zucchini, onions, tomatoes — brushed with olive oil and grilled over charcoal. Alternatively, the grilled vegetables can be pureed with roasted garlic afterward to make a delicious spread.

Ratatouille (Provence)　Classic Mediterranean vegetable stew of eggplant, zucchini, onions, tomatoes, bell peppers, and herbs slowly cooked in olive oil.

Tian des légumes (Provence) Casserole of vegetables and eggs baked in an earthenware dish (itself known as a *tian*). There are many local variations.

DESSERTS

Crème catalane (Roussillon)　Rich custard flavored with lemon and vanilla.

Mesturet (Languedoc)　Thick, dense, slabs of candied pumpkin pulp traditionally eaten as a dessert.

Millas (Languedoc)　The once ever present staple, a sort of French *polenta* made from coarse white cornmeal, is also enjoyed as a dessert, sautéed in butter and with fresh orange juice added.

Nougat glacé (Provence)　Delicious frozen honey and almond dessert.

Tarte au citron (Corsica)　The typical Corsican finish to a meal, this lemon tart is made with the fresh lemons that grow on the island in abundance.

Le Cassoulet

THE FAMOUS BEAN STEW OF THE LANGUEDOC

SO GREAT AND FAMOUS a French regional specialty is *cassoulet,* that when you encounter it for the first time, you may well wonder what all the fuss is about. For *cassoulet* is essentially French country cooking at its simplest and most basic: white haricot beans *(lingots)* soaked and cooked with wine, herbs, garlic, onions, tomatoes, and meats such as fresh or cured pork, sausages, and/or conserved duck or goose, and sprinkled with a layer of coarse breadcrumbs.

As with all great French regional dishes, however, something of a cult has developed over its preparation and consumption, and arguments rage throughout Languedoc over which is the most authentic or original version.

The purist's version is probably that of Castelnaudary, a small town between Toulouse and Carcassonne (the two other centers that claim this dish as their own). Castelnaudary has been at the heart of a pottery industry for centuries, and the name *cassoulet* probably comes from the earthenware *cassole* traditionally made in the nearby village of Issel — the *cassole's* sloping sides presenting just the right amount of surface area for creating the crunchy *croûte,* or crust, so loved by *cassoulet* connoisseurs. Indeed, *cassoulet de Castelnaudary* was documented as long ago as the 17th century, a dish enjoyed weekly as the inhabitants of the town took their *cassoles* filled with *lingot* beans, *coustelous* (blade) and *baticol* (neck) of fresh pork, sausages, and *couenne* (pork skin) to the local bakeries to slowly cook in the still-warm bread ovens. As the dish cooked, the famous crust would form on the surface, and this would be broken and stirred back into the bubbling mixture — three times, five times, some say even seven times, in order for the *cassoulet* to acquire the right creamy consistency.

Cassoulet de Carcassonne (a much later creation, sneer the connoisseurs of Castelnaudary, though we have enjoyed delicious versions) may contain leg of lamb (some say even partridges), while that of Toulouse, the most elaborate of all, has lamb as well as *confit d'oie* or *canard* (conserved pieces of goose or duck), in addition to fresh pork and, of course, *saucisses de Toulouse.*

Restaurants throughout the Languedoc offer *cassoulet* on their menus all year round, though it is probably the last thing you would care to eat in the midsummer heat of the Midi. Winter, though, is another kettle of beans, and there are few more satisfying dishes than a well-prepared steaming pot of *cassoulet* accompanied by a hearty red wine from Corbières or Minervois, the beans creamy and unctuous, the cured meats literally falling off the bones, the texture just slightly crunchy from the exquisite baked *croûte.* One place where you can be sure of enjoying the real thing, made with care and the proper ingredients, is the Auberge de Poids Public, a small but charming hotel-restaurant near Castelnaudary, where chef Claude Tafferello serves not only this great regional dish but also other traditional foods, such as *millas* and *mesturet,* and imaginative dishes using the fine local ingredients of Haut-Languedoc.

Auberge du Poids Public
31540 St.-Félix de Lauragais
tel: 61 83 00 20
fax: 61 83 86 21
$$-$$$

Cassoulet de Castelnaudary, *one of the great regional dishes of France*

Charcuterie
CURED PORK AND OTHER MEAT PRODUCTS

The South of France does not strike you immediately as one of France's great regions for *charcuterie,* but, nonetheless, a good range of cured pork products is on offer, and picnickers are rarely short of choice.

Charcuterie *from Arles*

Haut-Languedoc is virtually contiguous with Gers, an area where ducks and geese are raised and fattened to provide *foie gras* as well as to be preserved as delicious *confits* and *pâtés.* Toulouse, a great gastronomic city, offers an impressive range of both duck and goose as well as pork *charcuterie.*

Provence's *charcutiers* produce good air-cured *saucisson* and *plats cuisinés* (prepared dishes) to take out, including *pieds et paquets* and *daube de boeuf.*

Corsica presents an imaginative and tasty range of cured pork products that display the influence of Italy and Sardinia.

TRY TO SAMPLE

Caillettes or **gayettes** (Provence) Finely ground pork liver, fat and lean pork, mixed with herbs, garlic, and blanched spinach, then wrapped in caul fat into "meatballs" and sold ready cooked. Can be eaten cold, as unusual but tasty picnic fare.

Confit de canard (Haut-Languedoc) Legs of duck cooked and conserved in duck fat — delicious char-grilled or fried.

Figatelli (Corsica) Pork liver sausage flavored with pepper, paprika, and other spices, smoked and cured.

Grattons (Languedoc) Bits of pork skin and meat fried until crunchy, and nibbled as a snack or to accompany drinks.

Jambon cru de Lacaune (Haut Languedoc) Excellent if somewhat tough and chewy air-cured ham from the Plateau de Lacaune. Air-cured hams are also made from wild boar (*jambon cru de sanglier*).

Lonzo (Corsica) Tenderloin of pork, macerated in local wine and herbs and spices, then salted and air-dried.

Megisca (Corsica) Air-dried goat tenderloin.

Panzetta (Corsica) Cured belly of pork.

Pieds et paquets (Marseilles and all Provence) *Charcuteries* sell this great regional delicacy prepared and ready to cook.

Prisuttu (Corsica) Raw, air-cured ham (like Italian *prosciutto crudo*).

Sanguette (Haut Languedoc) Type of "pancake" or *galette* made from fresh pig's or duck's blood cooked with garlic and parsley; sold cooked and ready to be warmed up.

Saucisse de Toulouse (Toulouse) The name of this great regional sausage has come to be used to represent a type, usually sold in a coil, made from coarsely chopped lean pork mixed with hard back fat and seasoned with salt, plenty of black pepper, and nutmeg. In Toulouse, the sausage is never labeled as such (it is simply called *saucisse*). Excellent grilled over charcoal.

Saucisse mise en l'huile d'olive (Provence) Small, usually fairly spicy sausages, conserved in jars with olive oil.

Saucisson d'Arles (Camargue) One of the great air-dried sausages of France, a true artisan product made from lean, finely ground beef, pork and pork fat, salt, garlic, whole black peppercorns, cured and air-dried in *séchoirs* (drying rooms), to be eaten in slices. Traditionally, *saucisson d'Arles* was made with the addition of a small percentage of *cheval* (horse) or *viande d'âne* (donkey meat) though many versions forgo these today. Ask, if you are worried.

Poissons et Fruits de Mer
FISH AND SEAFOOD

FISH AND SEAFOOD from the Mediterranean are, in many cases, unique to this great body of water. Fresh fish is widely available throughout the whole of the South of France, even in markets inland.

The Bassin de Thau, source of superlative oysters and mussels

TRY TO SAMPLE

Chapon   Local name for *rascasse rouge*, red scorpion fish, an ugly brute, but one of the tastiest fishes of the coast, an essential ingredient of *bouillabaisse*.

Denté   Dentex, a member of the porgy or sea bream family.

Dorade royale or **daurade royale** Gilt-head porgy or sea bream, one of the most highly valued of local fish. It has a gold band, hence the name. **Dorade commune** refers to red porgy or sea bream, less prized but still a tasty if coarser fish.

Galinette   Red gurnard.

Huîtres du Bassin de Thau   Oysters (Pacific *gigas* or *creuses*) raised in the Bassin de Thau are among the finest in France. No oysters are at their best in summer, when they tend to be milky and rather thin in flavor.

Lotte   Monkfish or anglerfish; **lotte à la provençale** is monkfish stewed in tomatoes and garlic.

Loup   Sea bass, one of the great and most prestigious of all Mediterranean fish; **loup flambé au fenouil** is sea bass stuffed with sprigs of fennel and flambéed in *pastis* (anise-flavored liquor).

Marbré   Striped porgy or sea bream.

Pageot   Bronze or Spanish porgy or sea bream.

Poissons des roches   Mixed selection of small rockfish; for *soupe de poissons* or *bouillabaisse*.

Rascasse noire   Brown scorpion fish (there are several varieties of *rascasse*); **rascasse en papillote** is whole fish baked in parchment with herbs, olive oil, and tomatoes.

Rouget   Goatfish or red mullet.

St.-Pierre   John Dory.

Sar   Sheepshead porgy or sea bream.

Telline   Tiny, smooth-shelled clam, either steamed in wine or boiled and served with *aïoli*.

Thon rouge   Bluefin tuna.

MORUE — SALT COD

Throughout the South of France, the custom remains of enjoying *morue* (salt cod) on Fridays and feast days. Caught

off the coast of Newfoundland, cod has traditionally been preserved in salt, then transported to France.

 Morue is not necessarily overly salty; the best is only lightly salted, its flesh still moist and soft, not rock hard. Soaked in several changes of water, then cooked and beaten into an emulsion with olive oil, milk, and plenty of garlic, it becomes *brandade de morue,* light and creamy in texture, and deliciously delicate in flavor.

Les Anchois de Collioure

PRESERVED ANCHOVIES

PEOPLE OF THE CATALAN region of Roussillon have a passion for anchovies. Fresh, semi-conserved in vinegar, or packed in salt or in oil, *anchois de Collioure* are one of the great, simple treats for visitors to this friendly corner of France.

In the little fishing village of Collioure, made famous by Fauvist and other painters such as Matisse, Derain, Picasso, and Dufy, the shimmering, silver-blue fish, landed at nearby Port-Vendres, are still prepared by hand. It is fascinating to come here and visit the *ateliers de fabrication* where women sit at benches, gossiping, singing, nibbling as they work, packing the salted anchovies into jars or stuffing olives, one by one, with little bits of the famous *anchois de Collioure*.

Packing salted anchois de Collioure *at Société Roque's* atelier de fabrication

Collioure has long been a center for anchovy fishing. The small boats still go out from June to October in fine weather in search of this elusive but highly profitable small fry. Anchovies, unlike easier-to-catch sardines, are fished in shoals far from the coast, the fishermen using lamps at night to attract the fish.

This fishing port has been conserving anchovies since the Middle Ages, when King Louis XI granted Collioure a charter giving it the right to make *salaisons de poissons* — salt-cured fish. Not that long ago, there were 30 *maisons* in Collioure salting and conserving anchovies and other fish, but today, there are only three.

If you are in Collioure, visit the Société Roque's remarkable *atelier de fabrication* to see them being processed and to buy fresh, semi-conserved, and salt-cured *anchois* by the jar. *Boquerones* (even the Spanish word is used) are fresh

anchovies that are not salted but rather soaked overnight in vinegar, then packed in oil. They should be consumed quickly. Semi-conserved are salted anchovies that have been first de-salted, then packed in jars of vegetable oil. They must be kept in the refrigerator and will last for upward of six months. Traditional, conserved anchovies by contrast come packed in salt, and must be soaked before using to de-salt them; however, they will last for upward of a year.

After viewing the *atelier* repair to any one of a number of excellent fish restaurants, such as the quayside Les Templiers (its walls adorned with paintings both by the famous and less so) for a plate of fresh anchovies seasoned with vinegar made from old Banyuls wine, followed by excellent *grillade de poissons de la côte* (char-grilled fish).

Société Roque
17, Route d'Argelès
66190 Collioure
tel: 68 82 04 99
fax: 68 98 01 25

Les Templiers
12 Quai de l'Amirauté
66190 Collioure
tel: 68 98 31 10
fax: 68 98 01 24
$$

Collioure, a lovely old fishing village popular with artists

La Bouillabaisse
PROVENCAL FISH STEW

FULL OF THE SCENTS of saffron and the sea, *bouillabaisse* has become synonymous with the South of France. This great *spécialité* is served all along the coast, always at a high, sometimes an exorbitant, price.

Yet, *bouillabaisse* was once a humble dish, the classic one-pot preparation of the fishermen of Marseilles, who would prepare it on board their boats, throwing the bony, often tiny (and thus unsalable) rockfish of the coast into the ever present cooking pot. This *soupe* was consumed with gusto, together with rounds of stale bread rubbed with garlic and fried in olive oil, then spread with a fiery chili mayonnaise known as *rouille*.

Rouille *and* croûtons — *the traditional accompaniment to* bouillabaisse

Adrien Sordello, of the Restaurant de Bacon at Cap d'Antibes, goes to the Cannes fish market every morning to inspect and buy the freshest fish, just landed, still glistening, and virtually alive.

"Our Mediterranean fish is excellent, but, unfortunately, it has become very expensive due to the high demand. That is why *bouillabaisse,* essentially a *plat pauvre* of the fishermen, is such an expensive dish everywhere today. But to be good, it must be made with absolutely fresh fish from this coast." The implication is that many restaurants clearly do not take the trouble to use fresh local fish.

We inspected Adrien's daily purchase as he handled the still-wet fish: ugly red *chapon* ("one of the finest of all of our fish"), *St.-Pierre,* the fish that is supposed to have the imprint of St. Peter's thumbs on its sides, the spiny *galinette,* and the tiny *poissons des roches* that give concentrated flavor to the cooking liquid of *bouillabaisse.*

At Bacon, *bouillabaisse* is prepared by first making a concentrated *soupe de poissons* with tomatoes, wine, fennel, olive oil, saffron, and fish stock. Then a selection of whole fish, such as *rascasse, chapon, St.-Pierre,* and others, is gently poached in the *soupe.* The *soupe* can be eaten first, followed by the boned fish, or it can be enjoyed as a main course, the fish served in chunks in the *soupe* itself; otherwise, the two can be served *côte à côte* (side by side) so that you can enjoy first a spoonful of *soupe,* then a bite of fish moistened in it, and so on.

The freshness and texture of such fish are remarkable — the *chapon* as dense and fine as lobster claw, the *St.-Pierre* firm yet delicate in taste — while the *soupe* is almost intoxicating in its richness. The perfect wine to accompany *bouillabaisse?* The classic accompaniment is a good bottle of Cassis, produced from grapes grown just around the coast from Marseilles and, at best, a forceful white wine that is crisp, full-bodied and assertive enough to stand up to the rich symphony of flavors from the sea that is *bouillabaisse.*

Restaurant de Bacon
Boulevard Bacon
06160 Cap d'Antibes
tel: 93 61 50 02
fax: 93 61 65 19
$$$$

Bouillabaisse *as served at Restaurant de Bacon, Cap d'Antibes*

Les Fromages

CHEESES OF THE SOUTH OF FRANCE

CHEESES MADE FROM goat's milk (*fromages de chèvre*) and ewe's milk (*fromages de brebis*) are more distinctive in the South of France than those made from cow's milk. Pungent, sometimes assertive in flavor, such cheeses vary considerably in character depending on the milk and time of year they are made.

Fromages de chèvre, *goat's milk cheese, in olive oil*

TRY TO SAMPLE

Banon (Provence)   One of the great cheeses of Provence, a small disk made from ewe's or goat's milk; sold both young and old, the latter wrapped in chestnut leaves tied with raffia. Because the cheese is not visible, make sure it is not overripe (smell it, feel it), especially in summer when the cheeses can age and get runny and smelly quite quickly.

Bleu de Corse (Corsica)   Ewe's milk cheeses from Corsica used to be sent to Languedoc to be made into *roquefort*, but, today, the island makes its own blue cheeses that are excellent.

Bleu des Causses (Languedoc)   This fine cow's milk blue cheese is made in caves near the Gorge du Tarn.

Brousse (Provence)   Fresh, light, creamy cheese to eat with fresh fruits or as a spread mixed with garlic or *fines herbes*.

Cabecou (Languedoc)   Small, usually firm, sometimes hard, goat's milk cheese.

Cachat   Fresh, creamy cheese made from goat's or ewe's milk.

Fromages de chèvre (Provence) Many goat's milk cheeses produced on individual farms have no particular name. Such cheeses can be excellent, available sometimes *au poivre* (covered with black, green, and red peppercorns), *aux herbes de Provence* (with dried Provençal herbs pressed into the surface), or *à l'huile* (conserved in olive oil).

Fromage fort (Provence)   *Cachat* cheese mixed with pepper, salt, herbs, and *marc,* then packed into pots and left to further ferment until very strong and pungent.

Gardian or **tomme de Camargue** (Camargue) Fresh ewe's milk cheese rolled in thyme and other fragrant herbs.

Pélardon (Provence and Languedoc)   Firm, small, white disk of goat's cheese, available either *frais* (young and fresh), *demi-affiné* (medium, aged for a month or two), or *affiné* (hard, piquant, aged for some months). *Pélardon des Cévennes* is a particularly tasty version.

Picodon (Provence)   Another great goat's milk cheese of Provence: a flat, white disk that, when only days old, can be extremely mild and fresh, or when aged, hard and pungent. Traditionally, aged cheeses are rubbed with local brandy or *marc* then stored in terracotta pots. Excellent examples include *picodon dromois, picodon de l'Ardèche,* and *picodon dieulefit*.

Poivre d'âne or **pebre d'aï** (Provence) Fresh, young *banon* cheese covered with *sarriette* (summer savory), a fragrant herb known locally as "donkey's pepper."

Roquefort   The greatest blue cheese in the world (see p.224).

Sarriette   Rich cream cheese flavored with *sarriette* (summer savory).

An assortment of fromages de chèvre *on sale at Aigues-Mortes' market*

Roquefort
KING OF CHEESES

THE WORLD'S MOST FAMOUS blue cheese, *roquefort*, is made entirely from unpasteurized ewe's milk. It owes its distinct character to the airy *caves* in which it is left to age and mature, acquiring in the process its blue-green veins, intense aroma, and strong yet not overly assertive creamy, salty taste. It is well worth visiting the eponymous cheese town, located in the Aveyron of the Haut Languedoc above Montpellier, to see these great underground *caves* where, literally, thousands of cheeses lie aging slowly, developing to maturity. Only here, and in a few outlying villages, in natural *caves* formed millions of years ago, do the precise conditions exist for the ripening of this great cheese.

Since time immemorial (Pliny the Elder praised the cheeses of Roquefort), shepherds and cheesemakers have produced blue cheeses from the rich milk yielded by their flocks of hearty Lacaune sheep. Today, the immense Société Roquefort, the largest source of *roquefort* by far, ages some five million *pains* (the local name for individual cheeses) a year, all made by hand. For the *caves* of Roquefort support a valuable natural strain of bacterium, known as *Penicillium roquefortii,* still cultured traditionally on loaves

Roquefort, *the world's finest blue cheese, with its characteristic mold*

of rye bread left to mold in the *caves*. This bacterium is seeded into the young cheeses, and is also wafted through the damp atmosphere of the *caves* by a natural system of ventilation known as *fleurines*. *Fleurines* are crevasses in the *caves* that create natural thermal air currents and regulate temperature and humidity all year round, whatever the outside conditions. This system of ventilation is so important to the development and ripening of *roquefort,* that the *fleurines* are considered the "soul of the *caves*."

Roquefort is unique, the only great French *pâte persillée* (blue cheese) made entirely from ewe's milk, which gives a creamy texture and a particularly rich, tangy taste. Each is turned by hand, wrapped in sheets of thick, malleable tin by skilled *cabanières* to ensure a slow, even development, and tested by the *maître affineur* who oversees the cheeses' development using *la sonde,* a metal instrument with which he extracts a plug of cheese, examines, and replaces it.

Enjoy *roquefort* with an *apéritif* or after a meal, when its pronounced taste and texture can best be savored. Its traditional accompaniment is a luscious sweet wine whose unctuosity matches the creamy richness of the cheese: a great Sauternes or Barsac, or perhaps a Muscat wine from Rivesaltes, Beaumes-de-Venise, or Lunel.

Société Roquefort
12250 Roquefort-sur-Soulzon
tel: 65 58 58 58
fax: 65 59 93 75

Maurice Astruc, maître affineur *of Société Roquefort*

Pâtisseries et Confiseries
PASTRIES AND CANDIES

THE IMAGINATION and exuberance of the South of France are evident in its range of delicious *pâtisseries* and *confiseries*. Most towns and cities of this region have their own specialties.

TRY TO SAMPLE

Brac de gitano (Roussillon)   Jelly-roll-type cake, sometimes with chestnut cream.
Calissons d'Aix (Aix-en-Provence) Little diamond-shaped, sugar-iced cookies made from ground almonds and bits of candied fruit (especially melon).
Cédrat confit (Corsica)   Candied citron, a thick-skinned citrus fruit.
Chichis (Languedoc and Provence) Dough fritters, sometimes filled with jam and rolled in sugar.
Confitures maisons (Provence and Languedoc)   The South of France is the source of exceptional homemade fruit jams, usually available in markets.
Figues séchées   Dried figs; a delicious sweet snack — buy them in the markets.
Fruits glacés (Provence)   Fresh fruits candied in sugar syrup; the best come from Apt and St.-Rémy-de-Provence (see p.226).
Marrons glacés (Provence)   One of the great treats of fall, fresh chestnuts candied in vanilla-flavored sugar syrup.

Marrons glacés, *candied chestnuts — a Provençal delicacy*

Nougat de Montélimar (Montélimar) Another great regional candy, white *nougat* made from ground almonds, egg whites, honey, and sugar syrup.
Nougat noir (Marseilles, St.-Tropez, and all Provence)   "Black" *nougat* made from roasted almonds and caramelized sugar, which gives it a dark color.
Oreillettes de Toulouse (Toulouse and Languedoc)   Flaky fritters made from *feuilleté* (puff) pastry to look like little pig's ears.
Panisses (Provence) Fritters made from chickpea flour and dusted with sugar.
Tarte aux noix et châtaignes (Corsica) Characteristic tart made with walnuts and chestnut flour.
Violettes de Toulouse (Toulouse) Delicately perfumed candied violets.

HONEY

Miel (honey) from the South of France is outstanding. It is designated either by place (*miel des garrigues,* from the herb-scented *garrigues; miel de montagne,* from the mountains; *miel des Cévennes,*

from the Cévennes uplands) or by the plants from which the bees gathered nectar, such as *miel de lavande* (lavender honey), *miel de thym* (wild thyme honey, not too sweet), *miel de romarin* (rosemary honey, particularly good with lamb), and *miel de bruyère* (heather honey, with a dense, jelly-like consistency).

All honeys vary in flavor and the only way to tell what you like is to sample and taste for yourself before you buy. *Bonbons au miel* — candies made from honey — are also delicious.

Fruits Confits
CANDIED FRUITS OF THE SUN

THE ANNUAL harvest of beautiful and delicious fresh fruits in the South of France is one of the great bounties of this region. It comes as no surprise, then, that in the days before freezing and refrigeration, it was necessary to find a way of preserving this sheer abundance of riches in order to enjoy it even in winter. The method that evolved was the conservation of fresh fruits in sugar syrup. Now that fresh fruits are widely available even in winter, they are conserved by these traditional methods only in a few *ateliers*.

Selection of fruits confits *to take home as an extra special food gift*

At the Maison Lilamand in St.-Rémy-de-Provence, fruits are conserved in small batches. When we arrived at the *atelier* one day in June, the fresh apricots known as *rouges de Provence* were in season. Monsieur Lilamand held one up, a pretty, orange fruit with a blushing rose tint to it. "This is the finest variety for conserving," he explained, shaking it vigorously. You could hear the pit rattle. "That is how you tell a perfectly ripe *abricot*," he said.

To preserve the apricots, they are first pitted, then placed in small unlined copper pans containing light sugar syrup, and gently boiled. This process, which evaporates the moisture in the fruit, is repeated at least seven or eight times,

using successively more concentrated sugar syrup. The aim is gradually to replace all the moisture in the fresh fruit with sugar syrup, allowing it to be conserved for months.

Once the fruit has been so conserved, it needs to mature for a further few months to allow it to fully absorb the sugar and develop its flavor and scent. Thus, from fresh fruit to candied ready-to-eat is a time-consuming process that needs at least three months, one reason why these delectable candies are so expensive.

At Lilamand, all types of fruits are conserved throughout the seasons, beginning with citrus fruits in winter (clementines, oranges, and lemons all conserve well), followed by kiwi fruits, cherries, strawberries (very delicate and difficult to keep whole), apricots, melons, plums, pears, and figs.

Whole melons — *canteloupes de Vaucluse* — are one of the most spectacular conserved fruits of all, peeled and seeded by hand, then gradually conserved in the concentrated syrup to emerge a glistening, translucent jack-o'-lantern of candied fruit, far too perfect and beautiful to eat.

Not all preserved fruits are able to maintain their essential character, taste, and perfume, however, no matter how beautiful they look. Apricots, all citrus fruits, and melons are the most successful in terms of flavor.

Lovers of candied fruits should definitely make their way to the *atelier* in this charming Provençal town to see how *fruits confits* are made and to purchase wooden boxes to take home.

Lilamand
Avenue Albert Schweitzer
13210 St.-Rémy-de-Provence
tel: 90 92 11 08

Glistening crystallized melons at the atelier *of* Lilamand, St.-Rémy-de-Provence

Les Vins
WINES OF THE SOUTH OF FRANCE

GENEROUS, EXUBERANT, full-flavored, the wines of the South of France are *vins du soleil* (wines of the sun) — packed with flavor, and peppery, spicy, and herbaceous aromas. White, rosé, and red *vins de pays* as well as fine, prestigious *appellation d'origine contrôlée* wines, especially from the Southern Côtes du Rhône, are all produced here.

Wherever you are, stick to the local wines. In Roussillon, enjoy an *apéritif* of Banyuls, the red, fortified *vin doux naturel*. Good table wines include the robust, tannic Collioure and more supple Côtes du Roussillon-Villages.

The Languedoc is, in many ways, France's greatest vineyard, in sheer size alone if not in quality and prestige. Long the source of bulk wines vinified in antiquated *caves coopératives,* today, this vast region is demonstrating that it is capable of producing modern, fruity wines from both local and international grape varieties, at extremely affordable prices. Corbières, Minervois, Fitou are all good *appellation* wines, and Blanquette de Limoux is an excellent, creamy, and refreshing sparkler. However, don't overlook new wines bearing simpler, humbler tags, such as outstandingly vivid varietal examples of Vins de Pays d'Oc.

Provence is a rewarding region for the wine drinker seeking serious wines, especially if one includes the southern flank of the Côtes du Rhône and prestigious vineyards such as Châteauneuf-du-Pape, Gigondas, Vacqueyras, and Tavel.

The best French rosés come from Provence. Try delicious, fruity examples from Les Baux-de-Provence and the Côtes de Provence.

The enormous number of visitors to the Côte d'Azur means that such rarely encountered wines as the forceful, dry white Cassis; the full-bodied white, sturdy red, and fruity rosé Bandol; or the nearly non-existent Bellet (from vineyards above Nice), and Palette (near Aix-en-Provence) are in considerable demand and are thus correspondingly more expensive than their quality may justify. Nonetheless, you may wish to try such wines, if for no other reason than that you may never encounter them again.

The South of France accounts for an immensely high proportion of French

The vineyards of Caramany in the hills of Roussillon

The terraced vineyards of Banyuls

vins de pays, and sound, usually satisfying, sometimes exciting, wines are produced throughout the zone, entitled to regional designations (as in Vins de Pays d'Oc, which can apply to wines from throughout the South of France), *département* designations (Vins de Pays du Vaucluse, du Var, de l'Aude), or designations by specific zones (Vins de Pays de la Vallée du Paradis, des Sables du Golfe du Lion). Such wines are still extremely inexpensive and can be far better than mere holiday "plonk." If you are staying in a *gîte,* consider buying *en vrac* (see p.61).

Fortified *vins doux naturels,* such as Banyuls, are produced by muting fermentation, by adding either grape brandy or brandy mixed with unfermented grape juice. There are also scores of fortified and extremely fragrant Muscats made throughout the South of France which should be sampled well chilled, either as an *apéritif* or as a dessert wine. A particularly delicious combination is half a ripe *melon de Cavaillon* filled with a glass of Muscat de Beaumes-de-Venise.

LANGUEDOC

Blanquette de Limoux AC   This creamy fizz claims to be the oldest sparkling wine in the world, documented as long ago as 941. It is remarkably clean and refreshing and still quite inexpensive. *Recommended producers: Producteurs de Blanquette de Limoux, Laurens.*

Corbières AC   The *appellation* includes powerful and rich white wines, rosés, and modern, fruity red wines from vineyards planted with the traditional Mediterranean cocktail of Cinsaut, Carignan, Grenache, Mourvèdre, and others — extending over the rugged Corbières *massif* in the Aude. *Recommended producers: Château de Lastours, Val d'Orbieu, Château Ollieux.*

Costières de Nîmes AC   Mainly soft, fruity, easy-to-drink reds and rosés. *Recommended producers: Listel, Paul Blanc.*

Coteaux du Languedoc AC   This *appellation* covers such a vast stretch of the Languedoc that it is difficult to generalize about its wines. White, rosé, and red (fruity, to be consumed young, as well as traditionally vinified) wines are made here, the best of which are entitled to their *appellations,* such as Faugères, a sturdy, robust Midi red, and St.-Chinian, a spicy, fruity red from vineyards above Béziers. In other cases, wines may have the name of a particular *terroir* appended to the Coteaux du Languedoc *appellation:* Picpoul de Pinet, for example, a zesty, fresh, uncomplicated white. *Recommended producers: Abbaye de Valmagne, Pech Redon, Alquier, Château Milhau-Lacugue, caves coopératives of Pinet, Carignano, Montpeyroux.*

Fitou AC   This wine has achieved minor cult status for lovers of tough, dark, traditional reds, produced mainly from the uncompromising Carignan. *Recommended producers: Cellier de la Pierre, Château des Nouvelles.*

Minervois AC   Historic vineyard producing mainly light, supple, raspberry-scented reds, and uncomplicated but tasty whites and rosés, as well as some deeper, more robustly structured reds aged in wood. *Recommended producers: Domergue, Gourgazourd, Ste.-Eulalie.*

Vin de Pays des Sables du Golfe du Lion   Vast, sandy vineyard extending across the alluvial Rhône delta and the

source of white, rosé, and red wines, as well as fine, pale *gris de gris,* a rosé made from free-run grape juice with only the briefest contact with the skin for color.
Recommended producer: Listel.

Vin de Pays d'Oc   Though this immense catchment tag may apply to table wines produced throughout the South of France, it has in recent years been applied to a range of modern, well-made varietal wines produced from both local and international grapes, such as Chardonnay, Cabernet Sauvignon, Sauvignon Blanc, and others. Such wines can be good and good value.
Recommended producers: Fortant de France, Val d'Orbieu.

ROUSSILLON

Banyuls AC   This *vin doux naturel,* made from Grenache grapes grown on steep, terraced vineyards near the Spanish border, can be either fruity and quite sweet when it is young, or, aged in wood, result in a drier, rather austere oxidized style known as *rancio.*
Recommended producers: Cellier des Templiers, Mas Blanc, La Tour Vieille.

Collioure AC   Rather tough, concentrated, red wine from grapes grown on terraced vineyards behind the port.
Recommended producer: Mas Blanc.

Côtes du Roussillon AC; Côtes du Roussillon-Villages AC   Roussillon's hill vineyards are the source of fruity young reds and juicy rosés, as well as well-structured and more serious reds that can age.
Recommended producers: Château de Jau, Domaine Cazes, caves coopératives of Caramany and La Tour de France.

Muscat de Frontignan AC; Muscat de Rivesaltes AC   Full-bodied, sweet, highly perfumed *vins doux naturels* made from the Muscat grape come from Frontignan and Rivesaltes. Enjoy as an *apéritif* with a handful of fresh almonds.
Recommended producers: Domaine Cazes, Château de Jau.

PROVENCE

Bandol AC   One of the great but relatively unknown red wines of Provence, made primarily from the tough, uncompromising Mourvèdre grape, and thus requiring time to soften and develop harmony with age. Good rosé too, but less interesting white.
Recommended producers: Mas de la Rouvière, Domaine Tempier, Château Vannières, Château de Pibarnon.

Cassis AC   Outstanding, but expensive, dry white wine from coastal vineyards near Marseilles. Some rosé and red is also produced but is of less interest.
Recommended producers: Ferme Blanche, Clos Ste.-Magdeleine.

Châteauneuf-du-Pape AC   One of the great, classic wines of France, produced from an exotic *assemblage* of some 13 different black and white grape varieties, from stony vineyards stretching from Orange to the ruins of the summer palace of the Popes. Traditionally, it has been a wine that has required plenty of bottle age, but younger, more supple styles are also being made. Try the less common but fine, full-bodied white.
Recommended producers: Château de Beaucastel, Mont Redon, Vieux Télégraphe, Bosquet des Papes, Rayas.

Coteaux d'Aix-en-Provence AC   Though the *appellation* can apply to white, rosé, and red wines, we consider the rosés of this wine zone to be among

The Crusaders' tower at Aigues-Mortes

Coteaux d'Aix-en-Provence, source of good rosés and reds

the finest in Provence. Some good red wines come from outstanding individual estates, but are not the norm.
Recommended producers: Château Vignelaure, Château de Beaupré, Château de Calissanne, Château de Beaulieu.

Côtes de Provence AC   In addition to the vast quantities of fairly ordinary rosé, sold in curvy, wobbly bottles, this large Provençal vineyard also produces some serious, traditionally vinified reds.
Recommended producers: Ott, Maîtres Vignerons de la Presqu'île de St.-Tropez, Féraud, Richeaume, Jas d'Esclans, Commanderie de Peyrassol.

Côtes du Lubéron AC   The Lubéron is the source of good, rich, traditional reds.
Recommended producer: Château Val Joanis.

Côtes du Rhône AC   Though the *appellation* applies to wines produced throughout the Rhône Valley (including the Northern and Central Rhône, see pp.193–194), wines from its southern half are generous, fruity, sometimes powerful, and tannic. Modern vinification can result in good, clean white wines as well as fruity rosés and reds. Some 17 villages are entitled to add their name to the *appellation,* among them Vacqueyras, Laudun, Rasteau, Beaumes-de-Venise (source of good red wines as well as fragrant Muscat), and Chusclan.
Recommended producers: Fonsalette, Guigal, Grand Moulas.

Gigondas AC   Another warm and generous, peppery Southern Rhône red.
Recommended producers: St.-Gayan, Guigal, Château du Trignon, Cayron.

Les Baux-de-Provence AC   This small but prestigious vineyard centered on Les Baux-de-Provence and the Alpilles around St.-Rémy is the source of outstanding red wines.
Recommended producers: Trévallon, Mas de la Dame, Terres Blanches.

Lirac AC   Source of sturdy reds, outstanding rosés, and forceful, dry whites.
Recommended producers: Château de Ségriès, Château de St.-Rock, L'Assemat.

Muscat de Beaumes-de-Venise AC   The most famous of the southern Muscats is a *vin doux naturel,* delicately fragrant and perfumed, yet powerful through its fortification with grape brandy.
Recommended producers: Durban, cave coopérative of Beaumes-de-Venise, Jaboulet.

Tavel AC   Many consider Tavel France's finest rosé: dry, forceful, yet fruity.
Recommended producers: Les Vignerons de Tavel, Château de Trinquevedel, Château d'Aquéria.

CORSICA

Ajaccio AC   Sturdy red wine from the west of the island.

Patrimonio AC   White, rosé, red, and even fortified Muscat wines produced in the north of Corsica.

Vin de Corse AC   Corsica has an island-wide *appellation* that can apply to white, rosé, and red wines made from both traditional Mediterranean and indigenous grapes.

OTHER DRINKS

Pastis   The *de rigueur* anise-flavored liquor of the South of France.

Pétillant de raisin   Refreshing, sparkling grape juice, from slightly fermented grapes.

Vermouth   Noilly Prat vermouth, with its pungent, herbal flavors, is an excellent, locally made *apéritif.*

Les Baux-de-Provence

HISTORY, WINES, AND OLIVE OIL

THE ALPILLES, a jagged chain of limestone, cleaves the valley floor below St.-Rémy-de-Provence, dramatic in its bare whiteness against the buff green of the olive orchards and the manicured rows of vineyards. This small area is known as Les Baux-de-Provence after the medieval, fortified town built out of and into these same limestone heights. It is one of the most singular and atmospheric corners of Provence, and, a not insignificant bonus, it is also a wine region of considerable note as well as the source of some of the country's best extra-virgin olive oil. Add to that a handful of excellent restaurants (in all price ranges) and you can clearly see that this wine zone is well worth touring around, even for those not just interested in wine.

St.-Rémy is one of our favorite Provençal market towns (the excellent market sprawls through the center on Wednesdays and Saturdays), built near the site of the former Gallo-Roman town of Glanum, on the old imperial road that connected Italy with Spain. The Provençal poet Frédéric Mistral was born in 1830 just north of the town, and Van Gogh was an inmate of the St.-Paul asylum near the Glanum ruins and spent much time painting the surrounding country.

From St.-Rémy, visit Les Baux itself (stopping at the Mas de la Dame *en route*

to taste and buy wine and olive oil), then make a tour of the wine country, first to Maussane-les-Alpilles, a small, charming town that is the center for both wines and outstanding olive oil (purchase oil and olives from the cooperative olive oil mill; see p.210), then on to Fontvieille, another simple, unremarkable, yet wholly typical town. Outside Fontvieille, look out for the big, whitewashed windmill described by Alphonse Daudet in his *Letters from My Mill*. Return to St.-Rémy by way of St.-Étienne-du-Grès.

The Oustau de Baumanière, just outside Les Baux itself, is among France's greatest restaurants. Simpler but still genuine and stylish foods can be enjoyed in St.-Rémy, Maussane, and Fontvieille.

Vineyards of the Mas de la Dame in Provençal country, once painted by Van Gogh

---

RECOMMENDED WINE PRODUCERS AND RESTAURANTS

Mas de la Dame
Les Baux-de-Provence
Maussane-Les-Alpilles
13520
tel: 90 54 32 24
fax: 90 54 40 67
Excellent red and rosé wines, olives, and olive oil.

Ou Ravi Provençau
34, Avenue de la Vallée des Baux
13520 Maussane-les-Alpilles

tel: 90 54 31 11
fax: 90 54 41 03
Well-prepared local foods.
$$

Oustau de Baumanière
Val d'Enfer
13520 Les Baux-de-Provence
tel: 90 54 33 07
fax: 90 54 40 46
Legendary hotel-restaurant with regional cuisine.
$$$$

Domaine de Terres Blanches
D99
13210 St.-Rémy-de-Provence
tel: 90 95 91 66
fax: 90 95 99 04
Outstanding organically produced wines.

The Southern Côtes du Rhône

GREAT WINES OF THE SUN

THE RHONE VALLEY, a great natural corridor, was a historic thoroughfare connecting Northern Europe with the Mediterranean. And so it is today: for in summer, the A7 *autoroute* (dubbed *"l'autoroute du soleil"*) is the way to the sun for, literally, millions of vacationers from Northern France and Northern Europe. Most pass through with hardly a second glance. For those who care to pause awhile, the Rhône Valley is one of the great wine regions of France.

The wines of the Northern and Central Rhône are described in The East & Center (see pp.193–195) as they are the logical extension of the Lyonnais hinterland. The vineyards of the Southern Rhône, by contrast, are undoubtedly part of Provence. For those heading south or north along the Rhône Valley, the vineyards can be dipped into and explored anywhere along the way.

Avignon makes a good base. In the 14th century, it enjoyed a brief heyday as a political capital when the papal seat was transferred here. Today, it is a prosperous town of considerable charm, even elegance,

Nyons, famous for its olives and olive oil and sturdy wines

with its street cafés, atmospheric medieval quarter, Palais des Papes, and Pont St.-Bénézet of nursery-rhyme fame, only half-spanning the Rhône.

On its eastern side (see map), a pleasant route through the wine country leaves Avignon by way of the D942 to Carpentras (an important market town and source of superb early strawberries), then climbs into the hills to Beaumes-de-Venise, famous for its fragrant Muscat wines as well as good sturdy reds. A signposted wine road then leads through Vacqueyras, Gigondas, Sablet, and Séguret, all noted for their fine, peppery red wines (Gigondas and Vacqueyras are entitled to their own *appellations,* while the other two are within Côtes du Rhône-Villages). Vaison-la-Romaine is a charming former Roman town rebuilt as a fortified, perched village in the Middle Ages. From Vaison, go on to Rasteau (excellent fortified wine — taste it at Paul Coulon's private wine museum), Cairanne, and Orange, boasting a well-preserved Roman arch and an amphitheater that is one of the finest and best preserved in the world. South of Orange, visit Châteauneuf-du-Pape, one of the great wine towns of France, riddled with cellars and good wine-tasting and buying opportunities, before returning to Avignon.

A tour of wine country to the west of Avignon is also enjoyable, leading across the Rhône to Villeneuve-lès-Avignon, then north via Sauveterre and Roquemaure to · the important wine towns of Tavel and Lirac. The former is most famous for its forceful, characterful pink wines; Lirac also makes good rosés, but it is also the source of strong dry white and deep red wines. There is much good wine to the north, around wine communes such as Laudun and Chusclan (both Côtes du Rhône-Villages). Less single-minded visitors, however, might prefer at this point to head southwest (on the D976) to Remoulins and the impressive Roman Pont-du-Gard aqueduct, built nearly 2,000 years ago to supply Nîmes with fresh water.

One final suggested tour for lovers of both wine and olive oil is to explore the country between Bollène and Nyons by way of Suze-la-Rousse, whose *cave coopérative* is one of the largest in the southeast and the source of excellent, keenly priced wines; Bouchet, where a 12th-century Cistercian abbey has been turned into a wine store and tasting room; Ste.-Cécile-les-Vignes; St.-Maurice-sur-Eygues; and Vinsobres, all important wine towns. Nyons lies at the end of the Eygues Valley, its surrounding hillsides covered not just with vines but with olive trees, for this is the source of one of the most distinctive olive oils in France, made from the walnut-brown Nyons olive. Both wines and olive oil can be tasted and bought at the *cave coopérative*.

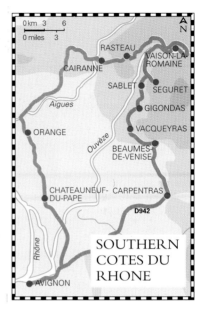

SOUTHERN
COTES DU
RHONE

RECOMMENDED WINE PRODUCERS AND RESTAURANTS

Auberge de Tavel
30126 Tavel
tel: 66 50 03 41
fax: 66 50 24 44
Farmhouse with rooms and regional restaurant.
$$

Cellier des Dauphins
Abbaye de Bouchet
26790 Bouchet
tel: 75 04 83 21
fax: 75 04 84 10
Wines to taste and buy in former Cistercian abbey.

Coopérative Agricole du Nyonsais
Place Olivier de Serres
26110 Nyons
tel: 75 26 03 44
fax: 75 26 23 16
Wines, olive oil, and olives.

Domaine des Bernardins
Ave. Castaud
84190 Beaumes-de-Venise
tel: 90 62 94 13
fax: 90 65 01 42

Fragrant Muscat and sturdy Côtes du Rhône-Villages.

Hostellerie Les Florets
Route des Dentelles
84190 Gigondas
tel: 90 65 85 01
fax: 90 65 83 80
Hotel with a restaurant serving regional dishes.
$$

La Vieille Fontaine
Hôtel d'Europe
12, Place Crillon
84000 Avignon
tel: 90 82 66 92
fax: 90 85 43 66
Classic Provençal cuisine worthy of its Michelin rosette.
$$$$

Les Vignerons de Tavel
Route de la Commanderie
30216 Tavel
tel: 66 50 03 57
fax: 66 50 46 57
Highly respected cave coop.

Moulin del la Gardette
Place de la Mairie
84190 Gigondas
tel: 90 65 81 51
fax: 90 65 86 80
Taste and compare a range of traditionally vinified Gigondas wines.

Paul Coulon & Fils
Musée du Vigneron
Route de Vaison
84110 Rasteau
tel: 90 46 11 75
fax: 90 83 78 06
Private wine museum and good local wines.

Père Anselme
Musée des Outils de Vignerons
Route d'Avignon
84230 Châteauneuf-du-Pape
tel: 90 83 70 07
fax: 90 83 74 34
Excellent wine museum explaining vine cultivation in this unique terroir.

Les Bonnes Adresses
USEFUL ADDRESSES

LANGUEDOC

Côte Bleue
34140 Bouzigues
tel: 67 78 31 42
fax: 67 78 35 49
Sample shellfish from the Bassin de Thau, some of the best in the Mediterranean, accompanied by local Picpoul de Pinet.
$$$$

Domaine de Jarras
30220 Aigues-Mortes
tel: 66 53 63 65
fax: 66 53 66 04
Les Salins du Midi produce sea salt and wine — and plenty of it — from vineyards planted in the mainly sandy soil of the Camargue. Good tour with wine-tasting.

Ferme Auberge Domaine de La Tour du Cazeau
Le Sambuc
13200 Arles
tel: 90 97 21 69
fax: 90 97 20 70
In the heart of the Camargue amid the rice paddies, this farmhouse restaurant serves outstanding local food made almost exclusively with its own produce. Also accommodation with swimming pool.
$

La Barbacane
Place l'Eglise
La Cité
11000 Carcassonne
tel: 68 25 46 47
fax: 68 71 50 15
Carcassonne's medieval Cité may have been reconstructed over-zealously but it is worth visiting all the same, especially to dine in this splendid and atmospheric luxury restaurant.
$$$$

La Cave d'Agnès
11510 Fitou
tel: 68 45 75 91

Barrels of Noilly Prat vermouth under the Midi sun

At the top of the wine town, a friendly, informal restaurant serving grillades au feu de bois.
$–$$

La Maison du Saucisson d'Arles
3, Ave de la République
13310 St.-Martin-de-Crau
tel: 90 47 30 40
fax: 90 47 03 90
Located on the road between Arles and Salon-de-Provence, a good source of this great charcuterie product of the region.

Le Musée de la Vigne et du Vin
Caves Saury-Serres
RN113
11200 Lézignan-Corbières
tel: 68 27 07 57
Excellent and informative wine museum tracing the life of the viticulteur (wine-maker) in Languedoc.

Maison Escourrou
30, Rue de Dunkerque
11400 Castelnaudary
tel: 68 23 13 93;
68 23 16 88
fax: 68 23 30 56
Castelnaudary's famous cassoulet ready prepared and bottled to take home with you together with other specialties of Languedoc.

Noilly Prat & Cie
1, Rue Noilly
34340 Marseillan
tel: 67 77 20 15
fax: 67 77 32 22
Lovers of vermouth should come to Marseillan to see how this great fortified wine is made.

Restaurant La Camargue
19, Rue de la République
30220 Aigues-Mortes
tel: 66 53 86 88
fax: 66 53 72 69
This off-beat bistro serves good food — tellines, anchoïade, and gardiane — on an outdoor patio accompanied by hectic flamenco music.
$–$$

Source Perrier
30310 Vergèze
tel: 66 87 62 97
fax: 66 87 62 30
Perrier mineral water bubbles up from its source at Vergèze between Nîmes and Lunel. Tours of the automated bottling plant.

ROUSSILLON

Brasserie Le Vauban
29, Quai Vauban
66000 Perpignan
tel: 68 51 05 10
Old style city center brasserie.
$$

Cellier des Templiers
Route du Mas Reig
66650 Banyuls-sur-Mer
tel: 68 88 31 59
fax: 68 88 53 56
Banyuls vin doux naturel and aged vinaigre de Banyuls, one of the best of all French vinegars.

La Casa Sansa
2, Rue Fabriques-d'en Nadal
66000 Perpignan
tel: 68 34 21 84
Good Catalan cooking and lively atmosphere.
$$

Le Moulin du Meunier
Allée des Chênes
Parc Ducup
66000 Perpignan
tel: 68 54 61 60
*Best bread in town — try
the* fougasse aux grattons.

Restaurant L'Almandin
Hotel L'Ile de la Lagune
Les Capellans
66750 St.-Cyprien Sud
tel: 68 21 01 02
fax: 68 21 06 28
*Superlative seafood with a
Catalan accent.*
$$$

PROVENCE
Auberge de la Loube
84480 Buoux
tel/fax: 90 74 19 58
*Old favorite in the Lubéron,
serving regional foods in
the garden in fine weather.*
$$

Auberge La Rigalido
Rue Frédéric Mistral
13990 Fontvieille
tel: 90 54 60 22
fax: 90 54 64 29
*Pretty auberge serving
authentic cuisine du terroir.*
$$–$$$

La Michette Antiboise
8, Rue Sade
06600 Antibes
tel: 93 34 78 46
*Home of the original
michette antiboise.*

*Fancy bottles of deliciously
fragrant Muscat wines*

La Presqu'île
Quartier Port-Miou
13260 Cassis
tel: 42 01 03 77
fax: 42 01 94 49
*Stylish restaurant serving
superb fish and shellfish
and the best Cassis wines.*
$$$

Le Bistrot des Alpilles
15, Boulevard Mirabeau
13210 St.-Rémy-de-
Provence
tel: 90 92 09 17
*Sidewalk bistro serving
good vegetarian dishes
and the house specialty,
gigot d'agneau à la ficelle.*
$$

Le Fournil des Augustins
51, Rue Espariat
13100 Aix-en-Provence
tel: 42 27 85 02
*Excellent selection of
Provençal breads,
including fougasse.*

L'Oustau de la Mer
20, Quai des Baux
13260 Cassis
tel: 42 01 78 22
fax: 42 73 02 15
*Outdoor tables overlook
the port. Closed Thu. all
day and Fri. lunchtime.*
$–$$

Le Bacchus Gourmand
Maison des Vins des
Côtes-de-Provence
RN7
83460 Les Arcs-sur-Argens
tel: 94 47 48 47
fax: 94 47 55 13
*Regional foods and wines
in restaurant of the Maison
des Vins, a good place to
taste and buy local wines.*
$$

Musée de la Boulangerie
12, Rue de la République
84480 Bonnieux
tel: 90 75 88 34
*Village bakery transformed
into a shrine-cum-museum
dedicated to the art of
traditional bread.*

A selection of michettes *with a
variety of fillings*

CORSICA
Le Lucullus
17, Rue Général de-Gaulle
20137 Porto Vecchio
tel: 95 70 10 17
fax: 95 73 03 12
*Genuine Corsican cuisine,
including roast kid and
fresh fish.*
$$

Restaurant Stella d'Oro
7, Rue Doria
20169 Bonifacio
tel: 95 73 03 63
fax: 95 73 03 12
*Local food in a converted
olive oil mill.*
$–$$

BEST BUYS
• *anchois de Collioure*
(Roussillon)
• honey (Provence)
• Montélimar nougat
(Rhône Valley)
• wine (Côtes du Rhône)
• Noilly Prat vermouth
(Languedoc)
• jars or cans of ready-
made *cassoulet*
(Languedoc)
• Muscat wines
(Beaumes-de-Venise,
Rivesaltes, Lunel,
Frontignan)
• *fruits confits* (Apt, St.-
Rémy-de-Provence)
• *calissons d'Aix* (Aix-en-
Provence)
• olive oil (Les Baux-de-
Provence and Nyons)

Basic English-French Food Glossary

Almond Amande.
Anchovy Anchois.
Apple Pomme.
Apricot Abricot.
Artichoke Artichaut.
Asparagus Asperge.
Bacon Poitrine salée; **smoked bacon** poitrine fumée.
Banana Banane.
Beef Boeuf; **rib steak** entrecôte.
Beer Bière.
Bell pepper Poivron.
Bread Pain.
Butter Beurre.
Cabbage Chou.
Cake Gâteau.
Can Boîte; **canned** en boîte.
Caper Câpre.
Carrot Carotte.
Cauliflower Chou-fleur.
Celeriac/celery root Céleri-rave.
Celery Céleri.
Charcoal Charbon de bois.
Cheese Fromage; **goat's milk cheese** fromage de chèvre; **ewe's milk cheese** fromage de brebis.
Cherry Cerise.
Chestnut Marron.
Chicken Poulet.
Chocolate Chocolat.
Chop Côtelette.
Cod Cabillaud.
Coffee Café; **coffee beans** café en grains; **coffee pot** cafetière.
Cookie Biscuit.
Cornflakes Flocons de maïs.
Crab Crabe.
Cream Crème.
Cucumber Concombre.
Date Datte.

Dessert Dessert.
Duck Canard.
Egg Oeuf.
Eggplant Aubergine.
Fava bean Fève.
Fennel Fenouil.
Fig Figue.
Fish Poisson.
Flour Farine.
Fruit Fruit.
Game Gibier.
Garlic Ail.
Grapefruit Pample-mousse.
Grapes Raisins.
Green bean Haricot vert.
Ham Jambon.
Hamburger/ground beef Bifteck haché.
Honey Miel.
Ice cream Glace.
Lamb Agneau.
Leek Poireau.
Lemon Citron.
Lemonade Citron pressé.
Lentil Lentille.
Lettuce Laitue.
Liver Foie.
Lobster Homard.
Mayonnaise Mayonnaise.
Meat Viande.
Melon Melon.
Milk Lait.
Monkfish Lotte/baudroie.
Mushroom Champignon.
Mussel Moule.
Mustard Moutarde.
Nectarine Brugnon.
Nutmeg Muscade.
Octopus Poulpe.
Oil Huile.
Onion Oignon.
Orange Orange.
Parsley Persil.

Pasta Pâtes alimentaires.
Pastry Pâtisserie.
Peach Pêche.
Pear Poire.
Peas Pois.
Pepper Poivre.
Pine nut Pignon.
Pineapple Ananas.
Plum Prune.
Pork Porc.
Potato Pomme de terre.
Prune Pruneau.
Rabbit Lapin.
Radish Radis.
Raspberry Framboise.
Rice Riz.
Rosemary Romarin.
Saffron Safran.
Salad Salade.
Salami Saucisson sec.
Salmon Saumon.
Salt Sel.
Sauerkraut Choucroute.
Sausage Saucisse.
Shallot Echalote.
Shellfish Coquillage.
Shrimp Crevette.
Snail Escargot.
Spinach Epinard.
Squid Calmar/encornet.
Steak Biftek.
Strawberry Fraise.
Sugar Sucre.
Tea Thé.
Toast Pain grillé.
Tomato Tomate.
Truffle Truffe.
Tuna Thon.
Turkey Dinde/dindon.
Veal Veau.
Vegetables Légumes.
Vinegar Vinaigre.
Walnut Noix.
Water Eau.
Watermelon Pastèque.
Wild boar Sanglier.
Wine Vin.
Yoghurt Yaourt.
Zucchini Courgette.

French-English Food Glossary

à l'/à la/au/aux In/in the style of.

Abats Variety meats.

Abricot Apricot.

Affiné Aged, particularly cheese.

Agneau Lamb; cuts include: **carré** rack of best end; **épaule** shoulder; **gigot** leg; **noisette** medallion or small steak; **selle** saddle.

Aigre-doux Sweet and sour.

Aiguillette Long strip of poultry or game.

Ail Garlic.

Alose Shad.

Amande Almond.

Amuse-gueule Little savory appetizer.

Ananas Pineapple.

Anchois Anchovy.

Aneth Dill.

Anguille Freshwater eel.

Anis Anise.

Araignée de mer Spider crab.

Artichaut Artichoke.

Asperge Asparagus.

Assiette Plate/dish; **assiette anglaise** plate of cold meats.

Aubergine Eggplant.

Avocat Avocado.

Baguette Long, thin, white bread.

Banane Banana.

Bar Sea bass.

Barbue Brill.

Basilic Basil.

Batavia Broad-leafed lettuce.

Baudroie/lotte Monkfish.

Bavette Beef skirt; a favorite cut for grilling.

Bécasse Woodcock.

Béchamel White sauce.

Beignet Sweet- or savory-filled doughnut.

Belon Famous native oyster from Brittany.

Betterave Beet.

Beurre Butter; **beurre blanc** emulsion of wine vinegar or wine with chopped shallots and sweet, unsalted butter; **beurre maître d'hôtel** savory butter creamed with chopped parsley and lemon juice; **beurre noir** browned butter, vinegar, and capers.

Bien cuit Well-done.

Bifteck Beefsteak.

Bigorneau Periwinkle.

Biologique Organic.

Bisque Thick pureed soup, often based on fish or shellfish.

Blé Corn or wheat; **blé noir** buckwheat.

Bleu Extremely rare or underdone meat.

Boeuf Beef.

Bombe glacée Molded ice cream dessert; usually with two or more flavors.

Bouchée à la reine Small *vol-au-vent* filled with savory mixtures.

Bouilli Boiled; also signifies boiled beef.

Bouillon Broth; **court bouillon** flavored vinegar or wine based stock for poaching fish.

Braisé Braised.

Brioche Rich, yeasted breakfast bun.

Brochette Skewered meat.

Brocoli Broccoli.

Brugnon Nectarine.

Bulot Whelk or large sea snail.

Cabillaud Fresh cod.

Caille Quail.

Calmar Squid.

Canard Duck; **canard de barbarie** Barbary duck; **canard sauvage** wild duck.

Caneton/canette Young duckling.

Cannelle Cinnamon.

Câpres Capers.

Cardon Cardoon.

Carotte Carrot.

Carpe Carp.

Carré Rack, or best end.

Casse-croûte Quick snack.

Cassis Blackcurrant.

Cassolette Small cooking and serving dish.

Caudrée Fish chowder.

Céleri Celery (also used for *céleri-rave* celeriac or celery root); **céleri rémoulade** grated celeriac in mayonnaise.

Cèpe *Boletus edulis* or cepe mushroom.

Cerfeuil Chervil.

Cerise Cherry.

Cervelle Brains.

Champignon Mushroom.

Chanterelle/girolle Yellow, ear-shaped wild mushroom.

Chapon Capon.

Charcuterie Various kinds of pork products.

Charentais Melon, originally from the Charentes region.

Chariot Shopping cart.

Châtaigne Chestnut.

Châteaubriand Thick slice of beef from the tenderloin.

Chaud/e Warm.

Cheval Horsemeat.

Chèvre Goat.
Chocolat Chocolate.
Chorizo Spicy red sausage.
Chou Cabbage.
Chou navet Rutabaga.
Chou-fleur Cauliflower.
Choux de Bruxelles Brussels sprouts.
Ciboule Spring onion.
Ciboulette Chives.
Citron Lemon.
Citrouille Pumpkin.
Cochon de lait Suckling pig.
Cocotte, en Cooked in a small, round/oval dish.
Coeur Heart.
Coeur d'artichaut Artichoke heart.
Coing Quince.
Colin Hake.
Concombre Cucumber.
Confiture Jam.
Congre Conger eel.
Consommé Clarified meat broth.
Contre-filet Cut of beef from the sirloin.
Coq Cockerel.
Coquillage Shellfish.
Coquille Shell; **coquille St.-Jacques** scallops.
Cornichon Small pickled gherkin.
Côte Rib or chop.
Côtelette Cutlet.
Coulis Sweet or savory sauce or puree.
Courgette Zucchini.
Crabe Crab.
Crème Cream; **crème chantilly** whipped cream; **crème fraîche** tangy, slightly sour cream; **crème anglaise** cream custard; **potage crème** cream soup.
Crêpe Large thin pancake.

Cresson Watercress.
Creuse Crinkle shelled Portuguese oyster.
Crevette Shrimp.
Croissant Crescent-shaped, buttery, flaky breakfast roll.
Croque-monsieur Toasted cheese or ham and cheese sandwich.
Croque-madame Open-face cheese, ham, and egg sandwich.
Croustade Feather light layered pastry with sweet or savory fillings.
Cru/e Raw.
Crudités Assorted raw vegetables served as a starter.
Cuit/e à la vapeur Steamed.
Cuit/e au four Baked.
Darne Thick slice, usually of fish.
Datte Date.
Daurade Gilt-head sea bream or porgy.
Délice Dessert concoction or specialty.
Dessert Dessert.
Dinde/dindon Turkey.
Dorade Red sea bream or porgy.
Doux/douce Sweet.
Echalote Shallot.
Ecrevisse Freshwater crawfish.
Eglefin Haddock.
Encornet Squid.
Endive Belgian endive.
Entrecôte Similar to rib or rib-eye steak.
Entremets Dessert.
Epaule Shoulder.
Epice Spice.
Epinard Spinach.
Escalope Thin slice, usually of meat.

Escargot Snail.
Espadon Swordfish.
Estouffade Meat or meat and beans stew.
Estragon Tarragon.
Façon Manner of preparing a dish.
Faisan Pheasant.
Farce Stuffing; **farci/e** stuffed.
Farine Flour.
Faux-filet Cut of steak similar to sirloin.
Fenouil Fennel.
Fève Fava bean.
Ficelle Long, thin bread.
Figue Fig.
Fine de claire Green-tinged oyster.
Fines herbes Mixture of herbs.
Flageolet Flageolet bean, similar to haricot.
Flétan Halibut.
Fleur de courgette Zucchini flower.
Foie Liver.
Fourré/e Stuffed.
Fraise Strawberry; **fraise des bois** wild strawberry.
Framboise Raspberry.
Frisée Chicory.
Frite Fried or deep-fried.
Frites Fried potatoes (short for *pommes frites*).
Friture Fried food.
Froid/e Cold.
Fromage Cheese.
Fromage de tête Brawn/head cheese.
Froment Wheat.
Fruit de la passion Passion fruit.
Fruit Fruit.
Fruits de mer Seafood and shellfish.
Fumé/e Smoked.

Garni/e or **avec sa garniture** Garnished/with vegetables.
Gâteau Cake.
Gaufre Waffle.
Gelée Aspic.
Genièvre Juniper berry.
Génoise Sponge cake.
Gésier Gizzard.
Gibier Game.
Gigot Leg, usually lamb.
Gigue Haunch of game.
Gingembre Ginger.
Girofle Clove.
Girolle (see Chanterelle).
Glace Ice cream.
Glacé/e Iced or frozen.
Glaçon Ice cube.
Goujon/goujonette Small freshwater fish/strip of fish coated in flour or breadcrumbs and fried.
Gousse d'ail Garlic clove.
Gras/graisse Fat.
Gras-double Tripe.
Gratin, au Browned in the oven or under a broiler.
Grenade Pomegranate.
Grenouille Frog; **cuisse de grenouille** frog's leg.
Grillade Grilled steak or other meat.
Grillé Grilled or broiled.
Grillon Crisp pieces of duck, goose, or pork skin.
Grondin Red gurnard.
Gros sel Coarse salt.
Groseille Redcurrant.
Haché Ground or chopped.
Haddock Smoked haddock or cod.
Hareng Herring.
Haricot Dried haricot bean.
Haricot vert Green French bean.

Hollandaise, sauce Hot butter, lemon juice, and egg yolk emulsion.
Homard Lobster.
Hors-d'oeuvre Appetizer or first course.
Huile Oil; **huile d'arachide** groundnut or peanut oil; **huile de noisette** hazelnut oil; **huile de noix** walnut oil; **huile de tournesol** sunflower oil.
Huître Oyster.
Hure de porc Pork head cheese.
Jambon Ham.
Jarret Shank, knuckle, or shin (of beef, veal, or pork).
Julienne Thin strips.
Jus Juice; **jus de viande** pan juices or gravy.
Kaki Persimmon.
Lait Milk.
Laitue Lettuce.
Lamproie Lamprey.
Langouste Spiny lobster or crawfish.
Langoustine Dublin Bay prawn or Norway lobster.
Langue Tongue.
Lapin Rabbit.
Lard Pork fat or bacon.
Lardon Thick-cut bacon cubes or strips.
Laurier (feuille de) Bay (leaf).
Léger/légère Light.
Légume Vegetable.
Lentille Lentil.
Lièvre Hare.
Limande Dab.
Lotte/baudroie Monkfish.
Loup de mer Sea bass.
Macaron Macaroon.
Macédoine Diced fruit salad; diced mixed vegetables.

Mâche Corn lettuce.
Madeleine Small, shell-shaped lemon cake.
Magret de canard Breast of fattened duck; broiled rare like a steak.
Maigre Lean.
Maïs Corn.
Mandarine Mandarin orange.
Mange-tout Snow pea.
Mangue Mango.
Maquereau Mackerel.
Marcassin Young boar.
Mariné Marinated.
Marjolaine Marjoram.
Marmite Small covered pot/the food cooked in it.
Marron Chestnut.
Matelote Freshwater fish stew; **matelote d'anguille** eel stew.
Médaillon Round, oval, or slice of meat.
Mélange Mixture.
Melon Melon.
Menthe Mint.
Merguez Small spicy sausage.
Merlan Whiting.
Merlu Hake.
Meurette Rich, red wine sauce from Burgundy.
Mi-cuit/e Half-cooked.
Miel Honey.
Mignonette Coarsely ground peppercorns.
Mijoté/e Simmered.
Mille-feuille Layers of puff pastry, filled with a savory mixture or cream.
Mirabelle Yellow plum.
Moëlle Bone marrow.
Morille Morel mushroom.
Mornay White, cheese sauce.
Morue Dried salt cod.
Moule Mussel.

Moulin à poivre Peppermill.

Moulu/e Ground.

Mousseline Blended with whipped cream or beaten egg whites; **sauce mousseline** hollandaise sauce with cream.

Moutarde Mustard.

Mouton Mutton.

Mulet Gray mullet.

Mûre Blackberry.

Muscade Nutmeg.

Myrtille Bilberry.

Nage, à la Served in an aromatic poaching liquid.

Nature/naturel, au Plain.

Navarin Lamb or mutton stew.

Navet Turnip.

Noir/e Black.

Noisette Hazelnut. Also medallion of meat; **pommes de terre noisette** small, whole potato balls sautéed in butter.

Noix Walnut/nut.

Noix de coco Coconut.

Noix de muscade Nutmeg.

Nouilles Noodles.

Nouveau, nouvelle New/young.

Oeuf Egg.

Oie Goose.

Oignon Onion.

Omble-chevalier Char.

Omelette Sweet or savory omelet.

Onglet Flank steak, usually beef.

Oreille Ear, usually pork.

Origan Oregano.

Ortolan Tiny game bird.

Os, à l' On the bone.

Oseille Sorrel.

Oursin Sea urchin.

Pagre Mediterranean sea bream or porgy.

Pain Bread.

Palombe Wood pigeon.

Palourde Carpet-shell clam.

Pamplemousse Grapefruit.

Panaché/e Mixed/mixture of.

Pané/e Breaded.

Parfait Rich mousse or ice cream dessert.

Parmentier With potatoes.

Pastèque Watermelon.

Pâte Pastry.

Pâte feuilletée Puff pastry.

Pâtes alimentaires *Pasta,* noodles; **pâtes fraîches** fresh *pasta.*

Pâtisserie Pastry.

Paupiette Veal or beef olive.

Peau Skin.

Pêche Peach.

Perche Perch.

Perdreau Young partridge.

Perdrix Partridge.

Persil Parsley.

Petit/e Small; **petit four** small pastry.

Pétoncle Tiny queen scallop.

Pièce Piece or portion.

Pied de porc Pig's trotter.

Pigeonneau Young pigeon/squab.

Pignon Pine nut.

Pilchard Adult sardine.

Piment Pepper/pimento.

Pintade Guinea hen.

Pintadeau Young guinea hen.

Pistache Pistachio.

Pistou Sauce made with fresh basil, garlic, olive oil, and grated cheese.

Pithiviers Pastry cake with almond cream.

Plat Plate/dish.

Plateau Large platter.

Pleurote Oyster mushroom.

Plie Plaice.

Poêlé Pan-fried.

Point, à Medium.

Poire Pear.

Poireau Leek.

Pois Pea; **petit pois** baby pea.

Poisson Fish.

Poitrine Breast.

Poitrine demi-sel Unsmoked streaky bacon.

Poivre Pepper; **poivre blanc** white peppercorn; **poivre noir** black peppercorn; **poivre vert** green peppercorn.

Poivron Red or green bell pepper.

Pomme Apple.

Pomme de terre Potato (often, just *pomme*); **pommes allumettes** matchstick fried potatoes; **pommes frites** French fries.

Porc Pork.

Porcelet Suckling pig.

Pot-au-feu Boiled beef and vegetables hotpot.

Potage Soup.

Potiron Pumpkin.

Poularde Fattened hen or roasting chicken.

Poule Hen.

Poulet Chicken; **poulet rôti** roast chicken.

Poulpe Octopus.

Poussin Baby or spring chicken.

Praire Small clam.

Praline Ground caramelized roasted almonds.

Profiterole Small, *choux* pastry, usually cream filled.

Prune Plum.

Pruneau Prune.

Quenelle Poached dumpling (usually of fish, shellfish, or poultry).

Quetsche Small blue plum.

Queue Tail; **queue de boeuf** oxtail.

Radis Radish.

Ragoût Meat stew.

Raie Skate.

Raisin Grape; **raisin sec** raisin.

Ramequin Small, individual dish or casserole.

Râpé/e Grated.

Rascasse Scorpion fish.

Reine-claude Greengage.

Rémoulade Mayonnaise with mustard, pickled gherkins, capers, herbs.

Rhubarbe Rhubarb.

Riz Rice.

Rognon Kidney.

Romarin Rosemary.

Roquette Arugula.

Rosbif Roast beef.

Rôti Roast; roast meat.

Rouget Red mullet.

Rouget-grondin Red gurnard.

Rouille Spicy mayonnaise.

Roux Sauce base of flour cooked in butter.

Rumsteck Rumpsteak.

Safran Saffron.

Saignant Rare.

Saindoux Pork lard.

Saint-Pierre John Dory.

Salade Salad; **salade panachée** mixed salad; **salade verte** green salad.

Salé/e Salted.

Salmis Roasted game or poultry in a rich wine

sauce.

Sandre Pike-perch.

Sanglier Wild boar.

Sardine Sardine.

Sarments, aux Grilled over vine shoots.

Sarrasin Buckwheat.

Saucisse Cooking sausage.

Saucisson Cured and air-dried slicing sausage or salami, usually pork.

Saumon Salmon.

Savarin Ring-shaped yeast cake, soaked in rum or liqueur.

Scarole Escarole or batavian endive.

Sel Salt.

Selle Saddle.

Selon grosseur (S.G.) or **selon poids (S.P.)** Sold or priced according to size or weight.

Sole Dover sole.

Sorbet Water ice.

Steak haché Hamburger; **steak tartare** minced raw beef, served with egg yolk, capers, mustard, onions, and parsley.

Sucre Sugar; **sucré/e** sweetened.

Tanche Tench.

Terrine Rectangular earthenware dish/*pâté* of coarsely chopped meat, liver, poultry, vegetables, or fish made in such a dish.

Thon Tuna.

Thym Thyme.

Timbale Round mold filled with vegetable, fish, or *pasta* filling.

Tomate Tomato.

Topinambour Jerusalem artichoke.

Tournedos Small, round tenderloin steak;

Tournedos Rossini served with *foie gras,* truffles, and Madeira sauce.

Tourte Savory tart or covered pie.

Tourteau Large common crab.

Tranche Slice.

Tripes Tripe.

Truffe Truffle.

Truffé/e Garnished with truffles.

Truite saumonée Sea or salmon trout.

Truite Trout.

Turbot Turbot.

Vache Cow.

Vacherin Meringue dessert with whipped cream, fruit, or ice cream.

Vanille Vanilla.

Veau Veal.

Velouté Cream of vegetable or poultry soup; **sauce velouté** white sauce with egg yolk and cream.

Venaison Venison.

Verdure Green vegetables.

Verjus Unripe grape juice.

Viande Meat.

Vichyssoise Cream of potato and leek soup, served chilled or hot.

Vin Wine; **au vin** cooked in wine.

Vinaigre Vinegar.

Vinaigrette Salad dressing made with oil, vinegar, mustard, salt, and pepper.

Vol-au-vent Puff pastry shell with savory fillings.

Volaille Chicken or poultry.

Yaourt Yoghurt.

French-English Drinks Glossary

Apéritif Drink taken before a meal; usually alcoholic.

Appellation d'origine contrôlée (AOC) System of classification that defines over 250 quality wines by their locations and defines rigid strictures.

Armagnac Brandy traditionally distilled from grapes grown in the Gers, Lot-et-Garonne, and Landes *départements*.

Barrique Bordeaux cask of French oak with 225-liter (55-gallon) capacity.

Bénédictine Norman liqueur invented by Benedictine monks, originally flavored with herbs and spices from around the world.

Bière Beer; **bière blonde** light lager beer; **bière brune** dark beer; **bière pression** draft beer.

Blanc de blancs White wine or Champagne made from white grapes only.

Blanc de noirs Champagne made from black grapes only.

Brut Very dry sparkling wine.

Byrrh Bitter herb-flavored *apéritif*.

Café Small cup of strong, black coffee; **café au lait** large milky coffee; **café crème** coffee with milk or cream; **café glacé** iced coffee; **express** *espresso*, a small, very concentrated strong coffee; **faux café/déca** decaffeinated coffee.

Calvados Apple brandy from Normandy.

Cardinal *Crème de cassis* mixed with red wine.

Cave coopérative Cooperative winery.

Chambéry Dry vermouth made in Savoie.

Chartreuse Green or yellow herb- and plant-based liqueur made by Carthusian monks near Grenoble.

Chocolat chaud Hot chocolate.

Cidre Cider.

Citron pressé Freshly squeezed lemon juice, topped up with water, and served with sugar on the side.

Climat Burgundy term for individual vineyard.

Cognac Brandy distilled from grapes grown in the delimited Cognac vineyard to a unique method of double distillation. Almost all Cognacs are blended.

Cointreau Clear, fragrant orange liqueur.

Crémant Term for sparkling wines made by the classic method of secondary fermentation in the bottle.

Crème de cassis Blackcurrant liqueur, used as a base for the cocktail *kir*.

Crème de framboises Liqueur made from raspberries.

Crème de mûres Liqueur made from blackberries.

Cru classé Classed growth; Bordeaux wines mainly from the Médoc classified officially into five tiers of excellence in 1855.

Curaçao Orange-flavored liqueur.

Cuvée Wine blended from either different grape varieties, or grapes from different vineyards or even years.

Demi, un A 25-cl. glass of draft beer (½ pint).

Digestif Alcoholic drink taken after a meal to help digestion.

Doux Sweet.

Dubonnet Brand of wine- and herb-based *apéritif*.

Eau Water; **eau du robinet** tap water; **eau minérale** mineral water; **eau minérale gazeuse** sparkling mineral water; **eau minérale plate** still mineral water.

Eau-de-vie "Water of life," the general term for clear distilled brandy, usually made from a fruit.

Elevé en fûts de chêne Aged in oak barrels or casks.

Fine Grape brandy, distilled either from wine, or from the wine lees — the barrel sediment left over after racking.

Floc de Gascogne *Apéritif* from Gascony produced by mixing unfermented grape juice with Armagnac. Similar to Pineau des Charentes.

Grand cru Great growth or wine; usually refers to wine officially classified as such.

Grand Marnier Cognac-based orange liqueur.

Grand vin The term means "great wine" but has no official standing.

Infusion Herbal tea.

Kir Apéritif made from crème de cassis (blackcurrant liqueur) topped up with Bourgogne Aligoté; named after a mayor of Dijon, Félix Kir.

Kir royal Crème de cassis topped up with Champagne or other sparkling wine.

Macvin Liqueur-like drink made from wine and spirits, macerated with herbs, spices and other flavorings: specialty of Jura.

Magnum Double bottle.

Marc Potent spirit, made by distilling the grape skins, stalks, pips, etc., left over after pressing the grapes.

Mise en bouteille au château/au domaine Château or domaine bottled.

Monopole Burgundy term for vineyard with single owner.

Négociant Wine merchant; **négociants-éleveurs** are wine merchants who purchase, blend, and age wines from individual growers to release under their own house labels.

Noilly-Prat Brand of dry vermouth from the Languedoc.

Panaché Shandy: beer and lemonade.

Pastis Anise-flavored apéritif, usually diluted with water, which turns the drink cloudy.

Pêcher Peach-flavored liqueur.

Pernod Popular brand of anise-flavored apéritif.

Pétillant Slightly sparkling.

Pétillant de raisin Sparkling non-alcoholic grape juice, produced from wine grapes.

Pineau des Charentes Apéritif from Cognac region made with fresh grape juice and young Cognac, aged in wood for a minimum of one year.

Pommeau Similar to above, made by blending sweet apple juice with young Calvados, then leaving it to age in wood casks for a year or longer.

Pourriture noble Noble rot, a beneficial fungus that affects certain grapes in select microclimatic conditions only, resulting in concentrated dessert wines of great quality.

Pousse-Rapière Gascon cocktail of Armagnac based liqueur mixed with sparkling wine.

Propriétaire-récoltant Winegrower who makes wine exclusively from his own grapes.

Ratafia Apéritif made from unfermented juice of Champagne grapes mixed with brandy, aged in wood for at least a year.

Récolte Vintage.

Ricard Brand of anise-flavored apéritif.

Sec Dry; when used for Champagne: slightly sweet.

St.-Raphaël Bitter apéritif.

Supérieur Wines usually with a slightly higher alcohol content than minimum requirement.

Suze Gentian-flavored yellow apéritif.

Thé Tea; **thé au citron** tea with lemon; **thé au lait** tea with milk.

Tisane Herbal infusion

Vendange tardive Late harvested dessert wine, a specialty of Alsace.

Vin de pays Basic classification of table wines (below AOC and VDQS); guarantees that the wine comes from a specific named area and from specific grape varieties.

Vin délimité de qualité supérieure (VDQS) Category of classification below AOC; guarantees that the wine comes from a carefully defined region, and applies strictures regarding grape varieties, methods of production, yield per hectare, and minimum alcohol levels.

Vin doux naturel (VDN) Traditional sweet wine fortified with grape brandy during fermentation.

Vin Wine; **vin blanc** white wine; **vin de table** table wine; **vin mousseux** sparkling wine; **vin ordinaire** usually anonymous wine, often served in carafe; **vin rosé** rosé wine; **vin rouge** red wine.

Vintage Years for Wines

This chart indicates the best years for wines that age well. In years not included, the wines were not very good or are now too old to drink. A chart like this is based on broad generalizations only, so there will be considerable variations with each wine.

VINTAGE CHAMPAGNE	92	90	89	88	86	85	83	82	81	79	78	76	75
	7◗	9◗	8◗	8◗	7●	9●	7★	9●	8★	8★	7★	7★	9○

ALSACE	94	93	92	91	90	89	88	87	86	85	83	81	76
Grand Cru	5◗	6◗	8◗	6●	9◗	10●	8○	5★	6★	9★	10★	7★	10○
Vendange Tardive, Sélection de Grains Nobles	9◗	5◗	7◗	4●	9◗	9◗	8◗	3★	7★	8●	10●	6★	9★

LOIRE (WHITE)	94	93	92	91	90	89	88	87	86	85	83	76	71
Muscadet	6●	7★	6○	4○									
Savennières	6◗	7◗	6◗	5◗	10◗	9●	8●	6★	7★	9●	9★	9★	
Sweet Anjou, Vouvray	8◗	5◗	5◗	4◗	10◗	10◗	8●	5◗	6★	9●	9★	9★	9★
Central Vineyards (Sancerre, etc.)	7◗	7●	6★	7★	8★	8★	9★	6○					

LOIRE (RED)	94	93	92	91	90	89	88	87	86	85	83
Bourgueil, Chinon, Saumur-Champigny	6◗	6●	5●	4★	9●	8●	8★	5○	6★	9★	8○
Central Vineyards (Sancerre, etc.)	6◗	6◗	5●	4★	8★	8★	7★	4○	6○	8★	7○

BORDEAUX (WHITE)	94	93	92	91	90	89	88	87	86	85	83	82	81
Dry Graves, Pessac-Léognan	7◗	5●	5●	5★	9★	8★	9★	7★	6○	7○			
Sauternes	8◗	4◗	3●	3●	10◗	9◗	9◗	3★	9◗	6●	9●	5★	6★

BORDEAUX (RED)	94	93	92	91	90	89	88	87	86	85	83	82	81
Northern Haut-Médoc (incl. St.-Estèphe, Pauillac, St.-Julien)	8◗	5◗	5◗	6◗	9◗	9◗	8◗	6★	8◗	8●	7★	9●	7★
Southern Haut-Médoc (incl. Margaux)	7◗	5◗	5●	6●	9◗	8◗	7●	5★	8●	8★	9●	8●	7★
Listrac, Moulis	6◗	5◗	4◗	6◗	9◗	8●	7●	5★	8●	8★	7★	8★	7○
Graves, Pessac-Léognan	7◗	6◗	5◗	6◗	8◗	8◗	8◗	5★	8●	8●	9●	8★	8★
St.-Emilion, Pomerol	8◗	7◗	5◗	3●	10◗	9◗	8●	6★	8●	9★	8★	8★	7★

KEY

0 = worst   10 = best   These numerals represent an overall rating for each year, based on a score out of ten.

◗ = Needs more time   ● = Ready but will improve
★ = At its peak   ○ = Fading or tired

BURGUNDY (WHITE)	94	93	92	91	90	89	88	87	86	85	83	79	78
Chablis	6▶	6▶	6▶	6●	9●	8★	8★	6○	8★	8★	8★	5○	9★
Côte de Beaune	7▶	6▶	9▶	6●	8●	9●	8★	6★	8★	9●	6★	7★	8★
Côte Chalonnaise	6▶	6●	8●	6●	8★	9★	7●	6○	8★	8★	7★	7○	8○
Pouilly-Fuissé, Mâconnais	7▶	7●	8●	8★	7★	8★	8●	6○	8○	8○	8○	6○	8○

BURGUNDY (RED)	94	93	92	91	90	89	88	87	86	85	83	82	78
Côte de Nuits	5▶	7▶	8▶	6▶	10▶	8●	8▶	7★	6★	9●	7★	6★	8★
Côte de Beaune	5▶	7▶	7●	7▶	10▶	8●	8●	7★	5★	9★	7★	6★	8★
Côte Chalonnaise	5▶	7▶	7●	7●	9●	8★	8★	6★	5○	8★	7○		

RHONE (WHITE)	94	93	92	91	90	89	88	87	86	85	83
Condrieu	8●	6★	7★	9★	8★	9○					
Hermitage	7●	6●	7●	9▶	9●	8●	9★	8★	7★	9★	9★
Crozes-Hermitage, St.-Joseph	8●	6●	7●	9★	8★	8★	8★	8★	7○	9○	8○
Southern (esp. Châteauneuf-du-Pape)	7●	6●	8★	7★	8★	8★	8★	7○	8○		

RHONE (RED)	94	93	92	91	90	89	88	87	86	85	83	81	78
Côte-Rôtie	6▶	6▶	6▶	8▶	7▶	8▶	9▶	7★	6★	10●	9●	5○	10●
Hermitage	6▶	6▶	6▶	7▶	10▶	9▶	9▶	7★	6●	9●	10●	4○	10●
Crozes-Hermitage	6▶	6▶	6●	7●	9▶	7●	8●	5○	5★	9★	8★	4○	10★
Cornas	7▶	6●	6▶	7▶	9▶	8▶	8▶	6★	6★	8★	8★	5★	10●
St.-Joseph	6▶	6▶	6●	7●	9●	8★	8★	6○	6★	9★	9★	5○	10★
Southern (esp. Châteauneuf-du-Pape)	7▶	6▶	7●	4●	9●	10●	9●	4○	5○	8★	7★	8★	10★

USEFUL ADDRESSES

FRENCH GOVERNMENT TOURIST OFFICES

In France
127, Ave. des Champs Elysées
75001 Paris
tel: (1) 49 52 53 54
fax: (1) 49 52 53 00

In the United States
16th Floor
444 Madison Avenue
New York, NY 10020
tel: (212) 838 7800
fax: (212) 838 7855

In Canada
Suite 700
30 St. Patrick Street
Toronto, Ontario M5T 3A3
tel: (416) 593 4723
fax: (416) 979 7587

SOPEXA (Society for the Promotion of Sales of Food and Agricultural Products)
In France
43–45, Rue de Naples
75008 Paris
tel: (1) 42 94 40 65
fax: (1) 42 94 40 71

In the United States
Suite 1601
215 Park Avenue South
New York, NY 10003
tel: (212) 477 9800
fax: (212) 473 4315

In Canada
Suite 406
207 Queen's Quay West
P.O. Box 55
Toronto, Ontario M5J 1A7
tel: (416) 203 0417
fax: (416) 203 0372

Food & Wine Combinations

Agneau rôti (roast lamb) Classic Cabernet Sauvignon red wine from Bordeaux's Médoc, especially Pauillac; warm, spicy red from Les Baux-de-Provence.

Anchoïade Full, dry rosé from Tavel, Lirac, or Coteaux d'Aix-en-Provence.

Boeuf bourguignon Mature Pinot Noir Burgundy from Nuits St.-Georges, Pommard, or Gevrey-Chambertin; medium-weight red from Mâcon-Villages; *cru* Beaujolais.

Bouillabaisse Forceful dry white such as Cassis from Provence; assertive, dry rosé such as Bandol, Côtes de Provence, or Tavel.

Camembert, brie, and **other pâte fleurie cheeses** Fruity young red such as Beaujolais or other Gamay based example; young, light Côtes du Rhône; *demi-sec* white such as Vouvray or Montlouis from Loire Valley.

Cantal, laguiole, tomme de Savoie, and **other hard mountain cheeses** Medium-weight Cabernet Sauvignon based wine from Bordeaux; medium-weight red Côtes du Rhône.

Cassoulet Warm, spicy, medium-weight red from Languedoc or the Southwest such as Madiran, Cahors.

Cepes and **other wild mushrooms** Warm, fleshy red such as Merlot based St.-Emilion or Pomerol; rustic country red such as Madiran or Cahors; Cabernet based Bordeaux from Graves or Médoc.

Charcuterie, sliced cold meats, and **sausages** Fruity, slightly acidic young red such as Beaujolais or young Côtes du Rhône, slightly chilled; medium-weight country red from Bergerac or Cahors.

Choucroute garnie Full-bodied, aromatic dry white such as Tokay-Pinot Gris or Pinot Gris; lighter, aromatic dry white such as Sylvaner or Pinot Blanc d'Alsace.

Comté, beaufort, and **other gruyère-type cheeses** Medium-weight, aged red from Jura; unoaked Chardonnay from Savoie; Vin Jaune from Jura.

Coq au riesling or **other chicken stews in cream sauce** Aromatic, dry white such as Riesling d'Alsace; medium dry white such as Vouvray from the Loire Valley; Champagne.

Coq au vin Pinot Noir based red from Burgundy's Côte de Beaune or Côte de Nuits; medium-weight *cru* Beaujolais from Morgon or Moulin-à-Vent; country red such as Pécharmant or Cahors from Southwest.

Crêpes and **galettes de sarrasin savory pancakes** Muscadet *sur lie*.

Daube de boeuf à la provençale and **other beef in wine stews** Rich, spicy, southern red such as Châteauneuf-du-Pape or Gigondas; mature, tannic red such as Bandol; warm, spicy reds from Les Baux-de-Provence.

Entrecôte or **other char-grilled steak** Elegant, medium-weight red from Bordeaux; spicy, warm red from southern Côtes du Rhône.

Escargots (snails) in garlic butter Crisp, unoaked white such as Bourgogne Aligoté; assertive dry white such as Pinot Blanc d'Alsace or Sylvaner d'Alsace.

Foie gras de canard or **d'oie** Dessert wine such as Sauternes or Barsac; medium-sweet from Southwest such as Jurançon *moelleux;* great late-harvested Gewürztraminer from Alsace.

Fondue savoyarde Zesty white from Savoie such as Apremont or Chardonnay.

Fromages de brebis (ewe's milk cheeses) Hard, tannic red such as Madiran or Irouléguy from the Southwest; full-bodied southern Côtes du Rhône; warm, spicy red from Côtes de Provence and Les Baux-de-Provence.

Fromages de chèvre (goat's milk cheeses) Fresh, young cheeses go with fruity, low in tannin reds such as Beaujolais or light Vin de Pays d'Oc; aged, hard cheeses should be partnered with pungent but elegant Sauvignon based whites such Sancerre or Pouilly Fumé.

Fruits de mer Light, crisp, lemony dry white such as Gros Plant du Pays

Nantais, Vin de Pays Charentais, or Muscadet *sur lie;* medium-weight unoaked Chardonnay from Chablis.

Gougères Fruity, chilled goblet of Beaujolais; young Côtes du Rhône.

Grillade aux sarments Classic Bordeaux red from St.-Emilion, Pomerol, or Médoc; Cabernet based wines from Bergerac, Côtes de Duras, Côtes du Marmandais, Buzet.

Homard grillé (grilled lobster) Rich, concentrated, oak fermented white Burgundy from Puligny-Montrachet or Pouilly-Fuissé.

Huîtres (oysters) Crisp, light, lemony dry white such as Gros Plant du Pays Nantais or Muscadet *sur lie;* forceful dry white such as Bordeaux Blanc or Entre-Deux-Mers; steely, unoaked Chardonnay such as Chablis; crisp, dry white from Languedoc such as Picpoul de Pinet.

Livarot, maroilles, munster, epoisses, and **other rind-washed cheeses** Classic Pinot Noir red such as village examples from Burgundy's Côte de Nuits; big, spicy, warm red from southern Côtes du Rhône such as Châteauneuf-du-Pape or Gigondas; full-bodied aromatic white such as Tokay-Pinot Gris from Alsace.

Magret de canard grillé au feu de bois Medium-weight country red from the Southwest such as Pécharmant, Cahors, Buzet; elegant, medium-weight classed growth from Médoc.

Moules à la marinière Dry, lemony white such as Muscadet *sur lie;* unoaked Chardonnay.

Pâté Lightly sweet white wine such as Monbazillac from the Dordogne, Coteaux du Layon from Loire Valley, or Loupiac or Ste.-Croix-du-Mont from Bordeaux; aromatic, spicy white from Alsace such as Tokay-Pinot Gris or Gewürztraminer; low tannin red such as Beaujolais or young Côtes du Rhône.

Porc aux pruneaux Medium dry to medium sweet classic from the Loire Valley such as Vouvray or Montlouis.

Porc rôti (roast pork) Medium-dry, slightly honeyed Chenin Blanc based white such as Vouvray or Montlouis; aromatic, dry, full-bodied white such as Tokay-Pinot Gris from Alsace; low tannin, medium-weight red from Côtes du Rhône.

Quiche lorraine Fruity, dry white such as Sylvaner or Edelzwicker from Alsace; unoaked dry white such as Sauvignon de Touraine.

Roquefort, bleu d'Auvergne, and **other blue cheeses** Dessert wine such as Sauternes or Barsac; fortified *vin doux naturel* such as Muscat de Rivesaltes or Beaumes-de-Venise; fortified, old, aged *vin doux naturel* such as Banyuls *rancio.*

Salade niçoise Dry rosé such as Côtes de Provence of Coteaux d'Aix-en-Provence.

Saumon au beurre blanc Aromatic, pungent Sauvignon based white from the Loire Valley's Touraine; sparkling Saumur or Crémant de Loire; light, low tannin Cabernet Franc red such as Chinon or Bourgueil; not quite dry Cabernet d'Anjou rosé.

Sole meunière Unoaked, dry Chardonnay from Chablis or Mâcon Villages; dry, characterful Chenin Blanc based white from Savennières.

Soupe à l'oignon Fruity, young, quaffable red such as Beaujolais or young Côtes du Rhône; aromatic, pungent Sauvignon based white such as Sauvignon de Touraine or Sancerre.

Soupe de poissons Assertive, dry rosé from Provence, including Côtes de Provence, Tavel, and Lirac; fresh, dry white such as Muscadet *sur lie.*

Tarte aux pommes Dessert wine such as Sauternes or Barsac; light, honeyed sweet Loire such as Coteaux du Layon; *vendange tardive* late-harvested dessert wine from Alsace.

Thon rouge (bluefin tuna) Medium-weight red from Southwest such as Madiran or Cahors; full-bodied white such as Corbières or white Châteauneuf-du-Pape.

Bibliography

Bienvenue à la Ferme (Paris: Chambres d'Agriculture, annual)

Christian, Glynn, *Edible France* (London: Ebury Press, 1986)

Crewe, Quentin, *Foods from France* (London: Ebury Press, 1993)

Davidson, Alan, *Mediterranean Seafood* (London: Penguin Books, 1981); *North Atlantic Seafood* (New York: HarperCollins, 1989)

Delpal, Jacques Louis, *France: A Phaidon Cultural Guide* (Englewood Cliffs: Prentice-Hall Inc., 1985)

de Meurville, Elisabeth and Creignou, Michel, *Le Guide des Gourmands* (Paris: Edition 1, 1991)

Eyewitness Travel Guide Paris (New York: DK Inc., 1994)

Feifer, Maxine, *Everyman's France* (London: J. M. Dent & Sons Ltd., 1982)

French Country Welcome (Paris: Fédération Nationale des Gîtes de France, annual)

Girard, Sylvie and de Meurville, Elisabeth, *L'Atlas de la France Gourmande* (Paris: Editions Jean-Pierre de Monza, 1990)

Grigson, Jane, *Charcuterie and French Pork Cookery* (London: Penguin Books, 1981)

Guide des Hôtels-Restaurants Logis de France (Paris: Fédération Nationale des Logis de France, annual)

Guide des Relais Routiers (Paris: Guide des Relais Routiers, annual)

Guide Hachette des Vins (Paris: Hachette, annual)

Harris, John, *Easy Living in France* (London: Arrow Books, 1982)

Lichine, Alexis, *Wines and Vineyards of France* (London: Macmillan Publishers Ltd., 1982)

Michelin Green Tourist Guides: Châteaux of the Loire; Dordogne; French Riviera; Provence; Normandy; Brittany; *Flanders, Artois, Picardie* (Clermont-Ferrand: Michelin et Cie.)

Michelin Red Guide: France (Clermont-Ferrand: Michelin et Cie., annual)

Millau, Christian, ed., *Guide France* (Paris: Gault-Millau, annual)

Millon, Marc and Kim, *The Wine and Food of Europe: An Illustrated Guide* (Exeter: Webb & Bower, 1982); *The Wine Roads of Europe* (New York: Simon & Schuster, 1984); *The Wine Roads of France* (London: HarperCollins, 1993); *Le Shuttle Small Hotels & Restaurants in Northern France and Belgium* (London: Pavilion, 1994); *Le Shuttle Shopping for Food & Drink in Northern France and Belgium* (London: Pavilion, 1994)

Petrini, Carlo, ed., *Slow Food Guide to the Wines of the World* (Bra: Slow Food Editore, 1993)

Pitiot, Sylvain and Servant, Jean-Charles, *The Wines of Burgundy* (Paris: Presses Universitaires de France, 1994)

Sharman, Fay, *The Taste of France* (London: Macmillan Reference Books, 1982)

Sigal, Jane, *Normandy Gastronomique* (New York: Abbeville, 1993)

Spurrier, Steven, *French Country Wines* (London: Willow Books, 1984)

The Best of France (Los Angeles: Gault Millau, 1994)

The Best of Paris (Los Angeles: Gault Millau, 1994)

Vandyke Price, Pamela, *Guide to the Wines of Bordeaux* (London: Pitman Publishing Ltd., 1977)

Wells, Patricia, *The Food Lover's Guide to Paris* (New York: Workman, 1993); *The Food Lover's Guide to France* (New York: Workman, 1987)

Willan, Anne, *French Regional Cooking* (New York: William Morrow and Co. Inc., 1981)

Index

ACKNOWLEDGMENTS

Author's acknowledgments:
It would not have been possible to
write and take photographs for this
book without the considerable
assistance of many people.
In France, we owe an enormous debt
to the many people who welcomed us
into their lives, taught and showed us
so much, and were so generous with
sharing foods, wines, and good times.
    Putting this volume together has
been an immense practical task, and I
would particularly like to acknowledge
our editor Shirin Patel who has been
so efficient, thorough, and sensitive;
and our book designer Joanna Pocock,
who has done such a magnificent job
in making the book look so good.
John Bradbury kept our office ticking
over while we were on the road, and
assisted us in practical tasks too

numerous to recount here. I would
also like to thank our agents, Rivers
Scott and Gloria Ferris, for their
considerable support.
    Finally, we would like to thank
Pauline Redford and Jane Gibson,
who accompanied us during our
lengthy research travels in France, and
helped us to look after our young
children Guy and Bella.

Publisher's acknowledgments:
Websters International Publishers
would like to thank the following for
their assistance:
Keith Banbury; Lorna Bateson;
Andrew Carton-Kelly; Anne Crane;
Jonathan Harley; Tim Lewis; David
Lucas; Caroline Manyon; Kim
Parsons; Valérie Pocock; Phillip
Williamson; Martha Worthington.